Grand National,
Producers Releasing Corporation,
and Screen Guild/Lippert

ALSO BY TED OKUDA
AND FROM MCFARLAND

*The Monogram Checklist: The Films of Monogram
Pictures Corporation, 1931–1952* (1987; paperback 1999)

*The Columbia Comedy Shorts: Two-Reel
Hollywood Film Comedies, 1933–1958* (1986; paperback 1998)

Grand National, Producers Releasing Corporation, and Screen Guild/Lippert

Complete Filmographies with Studio Histories

TED OKUDA

McFarland & Company, Inc., Publishers
Jefferson, North Carolina, and London

The present work is a reprint of the library bound edition of Grand National, Producers Releasing Corporation, and Screen Guild/Lippert: Complete Filmographies with Studio Histories, *first published in 1989 by McFarland.*

LIBRARY OF CONGRESS CATALOGUING-IN-PUBLICATION DATA

Okuda, Ted, 1953–
 Grand National, Producers Releasing Corporation, and Screen Guild/Lippert : complete filmographies with studio histories / Ted Okuda.
   p.   cm.
 Includes bibliographical references and index.

 ISBN 978-0-7864-6713-6
 softcover : acid free paper ∞

 1. B films—United States—History and criticism.
 2. Motion picture studios—United States—History.
 3. Grand National Pictures—History. 4. Producers Releasing Corporation (Hollywood, Los Angeles, Calif.)—History. 5. Screen Guild Productions—History.
 6. Lippert Pictures, Inc.—History. I. Title.
 PN1993.5.U6037 2012
 791.43′75′0973   89-42743

BRITISH LIBRARY CATALOGUING DATA ARE AVAILABLE

© 1989 Ted Okuda. All rights reserved

No part of this book may be reproduced or transmitted in any form or by any means, electronic or mechanical, including photocopying or recording, or by any information storage and retrieval system, without permission in writing from the publisher.

On the cover: Harry Langdon and Marian Marsh in *House of Errors* (1942 Producers Releasing Corporation); background image © 2012 Shutterstock

Manufactured in the United States of America

McFarland & Company, Inc., Publishers
 Box 611, Jefferson, North Carolina 28640
  www.mcfarlandpub.com

For Edward Bernds

Acknowledgments

My sincere thanks to the following people for their help with this project: John Aben, Dick Andersen, Bob Andrews, John Cavallo, Tony Crnkovich, Ron Downey, Erwin Dumbrille, the late Carol Epstein, Alex Gordon, Mike Hawks, Roy Kinnard, Scott MacGillivray, Rob McKay, Ann McKee, Maureen Miller, Cody Morgan, James Neibaur, the late Nell O'Day, Gregory and Mary Revak, Robert J. Robinson, Victor Rothstein, Sam Rubin, Joe Savage, Ralph Schiller, Susan, Marcia, and Dorothy Schmidt, Veto Stasiunaitis, Maurice Terenzio, Edward Watz, Tom White, and the staff of the Margaret Herrick Library of the Academy of Motion Picture Arts and Sciences.

Table of Contents

Acknowledgments   ix
Preface   xiii

Grand National Pictures   1
   Corporate History   2
   Feature Films   3
Producers Releasing Corporation   31
   Corporate History   32
   Feature Films   33
   Short Subjects   122
   Special Featurettes   122
Screen Guild/Lippert Pictures   123
   Corporate History   124
   Feature Films   124
   Short Subjects   183

Bibliography   185
Name Index   187
Film Title Index   231

Preface

Throughout the 1930s, '40s and '50s, several independent film production companies (referred to as "poverty row" studios) turned out hundreds of "B" movies—low-budget feature films that were specifically designed to play the bottom half of double bills (higher budgeted films—"A" pictures—usually played the top half of these bills). This volume focuses on the output of three of these independents: Grand National Pictures, Producers Releasing Corporation, and Screen Guild/Lippert Pictures.

This book is not intended to be an in-depth examination of B movies or definitive histories of the production companies profiled. Rather, this should be looked upon as a handy reference guide to the output of these operations.

As was the case doing research for my previous B movie volume, *The Monogram Checklist: The Films of Monogram Pictures Corporation, 1931–1952*, the greatest obstacle in gathering information was the contradictory data found in the industry trade journals, supposedly the "official" sources for such material; it was not uncommon to find multiple running times and release dates for a single title. Given this situation, I have attempted to furnish the most accurate data possible from these records.

Grand National Pictures

Grand National's logo was a modernistic clock tower; with a sweep of the clock hands, the company name would appear. Unfortunately, the actual film that followed was not nearly as impressive. Generally speaking, the quality of Grand National product fell within a limited range: at best, the films were pleasant yet unremarkable; at worst, they were excruciatingly dull.

Grand National's basic failure was that they tried to cater to two kinds of audiences—those seeking action and thrills and those looking for prestige pictures—and never really satisfied either group. A number of Grand Nationals were hampered by a heavy dependence on dialogue scenes and sound-stage shooting, with leaden, claustrophobic results. Productions like *Devil on Horseback* (1936) and *We're in the Legion Now* (1937) had the added novelty of having been filmed in "Hirlicolor" (as it was called by producer George A. Hirliman; it was actually the Cinecolor process), but the content of the films differed little from other GN fare.

The company received a tremendous shot in the arm when it secured the services of James Cagney. Although the resulting films (*Great Guy, Something to Sing About*) had some good things in them, a star of Cagney's stature clearly deserved better vehicles. It was inevitable that the Cagney–Grand National alliance would come to an end; when it did, GN was never able to recover from the loss.

Cagney had been their strongest drawing card; without him, their roster consisted of once-popular players—Reginald Denny, Esther Ralston, Conrad Nagel, Richard Barthelmess, Stuart Erwin—whose careers were on the decline. A notable exception, however, was cowboy star Tex Ritter, whom GN had introduced to the screen.

Grand National's existence was brief; growing financial problems were the cause of the firm's demise. Had they survived, Grand National may have, in time, been able to gauge their potential market a little better, and continue along the lines of Monogram and Republic by turning out reliable (if undistinguished) "bread-and-butter" fare for the masses.

Corporate History

Grand National Pictures was formed in the spring of 1936 by Edward L. Alperson, a former film exchange manager; Alperson served as president, Carl M. Leserman as vice president and general sales manager, W. C. Bright as secretary-treasurer, and Edward Finney in charge of advertising and publicity. After establishing offices in New York and Hollywood, the firm eventually acquired the Educational Pictures Studio, which had once been a leader in the comedy shorts market.

George A. Hirliman, B. F. Zeidman, Zion Myers, Max and Arthur Alexander, and Douglas MacLean were among the producers responsible for the Grand National releases (imports of British pictures helped to pad out the schedule). Advertising chief Edward Finney produced a series of westerns starring Tex Ritter, a Finney discovery.

Grand National's greatest coup came when Alperson signed James Cagney. Cagney had walked out on Warner Bros. after a contract dispute and Alperson seized the opportunity to sign the major box office star. *Great Guy* (1937), the first Cagney Grand National, did good business, although it was decidedly inferior to the actor's Warners efforts.

Just when it looked as though the newly-formed company was going to succeed where other independents had failed, Alperson made a major error in selecting the next property for Cagney. Although he had purchased the rights to Rowland Brown's story "Angels with Dirty Faces" for $25,000 (some sources claim $30,000), Alperson decided on the musical-comedy titled *Something to Sing About* as the next Cagney vehicle. The resulting film went way over budget (the total cost was around $900,000) and met with lukewarm critical response and public apathy. Cagney then returned to Warners, having been offered a better contract by the studio. (Without Cagney, Grand National dropped plans to film "Angels with Dirty Faces"; the rights reverted back to Rowland Brown, who then sold the story to Warners).

Grand National never recovered from the *Something to Sing About* error. Financial troubles eventually engulfed the company; in February 1939 Alperson announced his resignation.

Short subjects producer Earle W. Hammons, who had originally built the Educational Studios, attempted to revitalize Grand National, but these plans were abandoned when he failed to secure financial aid (Hammons was refused a loan from the U. S. government's Reconstruction Finance Corporation). With insurmountable debts leveled against the firm, Grand National liquidated in 1940. Films that were slated for release through GN were eventually released by others (*Isle of Destiny* was released by RKO, *Half a Sinner* by Columbia, *Miracle on Main Street* by Columbia; the Tex Ritter and *Renfrew of the Royal Mounted* series, starring James Newill, both went to Monogram Pictures), and the studio later became the property of PRC (Producers Releasing Corporation).

The Feature Films of Grand National Pictures (1936–1939)

This listing does not include the films released through Grand National Distributing Corporation, a New York–based company that handled the distribution of First Division and, in some territories, Alliance, Diversion, Normandy, Colony, Associated Talking, Monogram, Liberty, Chesterfield and Invincible Pictures product. Titles handled by Grand National Distributing include the following 1936 releases: *August Week-End* (Chesterfield), *Bridge of Sighs* (Invincible), *Feud of the West* (Diversion), *The Idaho Kid* (Colony), *Little Red School House* (Chesterfield), Ring Around the Moon (Chesterfield), *Stormy Trails* (Colony), *Tango* (Invincible), *Three of a Kind* (Invincible) and *Too Much Beef* (Colony). Grand National Distributing also released a series of short subjects: "Musical Moods" (in Technicolor), "Newslaughs," and "6 Thrilling Journeys."

Also omitted are titles that were announced for release but never materialized (either they were working titles or projects that were dropped prior to production). These titles include *La Vie Parisienne, Romance on the Rio, Song of the Andes, Empire of the West, At Your Age, Wonder World, Full Speed Ahead, Love Runs Into Money, Death Takes a Cruise, Never Mind the Guard, Painter in the Sky* and *Honolulu Honeymoon.*

Research has uncovered a questionable Grand National film. A comedy-drama titled *Lady Takes a Chance* (working title: *Everything Happens to Ann*) was announced in the trade journals; it was an Arcadia Production to be released by Grand National, directed by Al Christie from a screenplay by Frederick Jackson and a story by Dalton Trumbo. It was to tell the tale of a young woman, traveling abroad, who becomes involved with three gangsters; the cast was to have included Heather Angel, John King, Constance Collier, Clem Bevans, Henry Brandon, Tom Dugan, Emma Dunn, Walter Catlett, Robert Elliott, Wilbur Mack, Fred Kohler, Sr., Antonia Oland, Joe Devlin and Fern Emmett. However, no confirmation can be found as to whether this film was released—or even made.

1936

1. **In His Steps** (drama) Directed by Karl Brown. Produced by B. F. Zeidman. Screenplay by Karl Brown. Additional dialogue by Hinton Smith. Suggested by the novel by Charles M. Sheldon.

Cast: Eric Linden, Cecilia Parker, Henry Kolker, Charles Richman,

Eric Linden and Cecilia Parker in *In His Steps* (1936), Grand National's first release.

Olive Tell, Harry Beresford, Roger Imhof, Clara Blandick, Robert Warwick, Warner Richmond, Donald Kirke, Stanley Andrews.

Two wealthy young elopers (Eric Linden, Cecilia Parker), by their devotion to each other and to the life they have chosen tilling the soil, dispel parental objection to their marriage.

Running time: 79 minutes. Release date: October 4, 1936.

Also known as *Sins of the Children*.

2. Spy of Napoleon (drama) Directed by Maurice Elvey. Produced by Julius Hagen. Screenplay by Fred V. Merrick and Harold Simpson. From the novel by Baroness Orczy.

Cast: Richard Barthelmess, Dolly Haas, Frank Vosper, Francis L. Sullivan, Joyce Bland, C. Denier Warren, Henry Oscar, Marjorie Mars, Brian Buschell, Lyn Harding, Wilfrid Caithness, George Merritt, Stafford Hilliard.

During the Franco-Prussian War, Gerald de Lanoy (Richard Barthelmess) poses as the illegitimate son of Emperor Louis Napoleon III (Frank Vosper) in order to uncover an assassination plot.

Running time: 98 minutes. Release date: October 10, 1936.

Produced and released in Great Britain by J.H. Productions (Wardour); released in the U.S. by Grand National.

Del Campo, Lili Damita and Fred Keating in *Devil on Horseback* (1936).

3. Devil on Horseback (musical) Directed by Crane Wilbur. Produced by George A. Hirliman. Story and screenplay by Crane Wilbur. In Hirlicolor (Cinecolor).

Cast: Lili Damita, Del Campo, Fred Keating, Jean Chatburn, Tiffany Thayer.

A dashing gaucho (Del Campo) and a millionaire's son (Fred Keating) vie for the affections of a tempestuous movie actress (Lili Damita).

Running time: 71 minutes. Release date: October 11, 1936.

4. The White Legion (drama) Directed by Karl Brown. Produced by B. F. Ziedman. Story by Karl Brown.

Cast: Ian Keith, Tala Birell, Ferdinand Gottschalk, Rollo Lloyd, Lionel Pape, Teru Shimada, Suzanne Kaaren, Ferdinand Munier, Nigel de Brulier, Nina Campana, Warner Richmond, Harry Allen, Don Barclay, Snub Pollard, Robert Warwick, Edward Peil, Jason Robards (Sr.).

During the days of the United States' construction of the Panama Canal, a heroic doctor (Ian Keith) leads the fight against yellow fever.

Running time: 81 minutes. Release date: October 25, 1936.

5. Yellow Cargo (drama) Directed by Crane Wilbur. Produced by George A. Hirliman. Story and screenplay by Crane Wilbur.

Cast: Conrad Nagel, Eleanor Hunt, Vince Barnett, Jack LaRue, Claudia Dell, Henry Strange, John Ivan, Vance Carroll.

An undercover agent (Conrad Nagel), working for the Immigration Service, and a G-woman (Eleanor Hunt), posing as a newspaper reporter, smash an operation which is smuggling Chinese aliens into Los Angeles harbor.

Running time: 63 minutes. Release date: November 8, 1936 (released earlier in the year by Pacific Pictures).

6. Song of the Gringo (western) Directed by John P. McCarthy. Produced by Edward Finney. Screenplay by John P. McCarthy, Robert Emmett (Tansey) and Al Jennings. Story by John P. McCarthy and Robert Emmett (Tansey).

Cast: Tex Ritter, Joan Woodbury, Fuzzy Knight, Monte Blue, Richard Adams, Warner Richmond, Martin Garralaga, Al Jennings, William Desmond, Glenn Strange, Budd Buster, Murdock McQuarrie, Ethan Laidlaw, Charles "Slim" Whitaker, Edward Cassidy, Earl Dwire, Jack Kirk, Bob Burns, Forrest Taylor, Robert Fiske, and White Flash the horse.

Tex pretends to participate in a mine raid in order to get evidence against a bandit gang.

Running time: 62 minutes. Release date: November 22, 1936.

7. Captain Calamity (adventure) Directed by John Reinhardt. Produced by George A. Hirliman. Screenplay by Crane Wilbur. Original story by Gordon Young. A Regal Production. In Hirlicolor (Cinecolor).

Cast: George Houston, Marian Nixon, Vince Barnett, Juan Torena, Movita, Crane Wilbur, George Lewis, Roy D'Arcy, Margaret Irving, Barry Norton, Louis Natheaux, Lloyd Ingraham.

Captain Calamity (George Houston), a South Seas skipper, pretends to have found a Spanish pirate treasure—and the result is that every crook in the islands attempts to kill him for the fortune.

Running time: 66 minutes. Release date: November 29, 1936 (originally released by Regal as *Captain Hurricane*).

8. Headin' for the Rio Grande (western) Directed by Robert N. Bradbury. Produced by Edward Finney. Screenplay by Robert Emmett (Tansey). Story of Lindsley Parsons.

Cast: Tex Ritter, Eleanor Stewart, Syd Saylor, Snub Pollard, Warner Richmond, Charles King, Earl Dwire, Forrest Taylor, William Desmond, Charles K. French, Budd Buster, Bud Osborne, Tex Palmer, Jack C. Smith, Sherry Tansey, James Mason, Bill Woods, and White Flash the horse.

Tex and his pal Chile (Syd Saylor) set out to break up a protectionist gang operating along the Rio Grande.
Running time: 61 minutes. Release date: December 20, 1936.

1937

9. Great Guy (drama) Directed by John G. Blystone. Produced by Douglas MacLean. Screenplay by Henry McCarthy, Henry Johnson, James Edward Grant and Harry Ruskin. Additional dialogue by Horace McCoy. Based on the "Johnny Cave Stories" by James Edward Grant.

Cast: James Cagney, Mae Clarke, James Burke, Edward Brophy, Henry Kolker, Bernadene Hayes, Edward J. McNamara, Robert Glecker, Joe Sawyer, Ed Gargan, Matty Fain, Mary Gordon, Wallis Clark, Douglas Wood, Jeffrey Sayre, Eddy Chandler, Henry Roquemore, Murdock McQuarrie, Kate Price, Frank O'Connor, Arthur Hoyt, Jack Pennick, Lynton Brent, John Dilson, Bud Geary, Dennis O'Keefe, Robert Lowery, Bobby Barber, Gertrude Green, Ethelreda Leopold, Bruce Mitchell, James Ford, Frank Mills, Ben Hendricks, Jr., Kernan Cripps, Bill O'Brien, Lester Dorr, Harry Tenbrook, Lee Shumway, Gertrude Astor, Vera Steadman, Mildred Harris, Bert Kalmar, Jr., Walter D. Clarke, Jr.

Johnny Cave (James Cagney), chief deputy of the Bureau of Weights and Measures, battles a gang of crooks who are employing various short-weight tactics to defraud consumers.

Running Time: 73 minutes. Release date: January 2, 1937. (This is the "official" date listed in the *Motion Picture Almanac*; some sources claim the film was released in December 1936.)

Released in Great Britain as *Pluck of the Irish*.

10. We're in the Legion Now (adventure-comedy) Directed by Crane Wilbur. Produced by George A. Hirliman. Screenplay by Roger Whateley. Additional dialogue by Crane Wilbur. From the story "The Rest Cure" by J. D. Newson. In Hirlicolor (Cinecolor). (Some credits say "Magnacolor.")

Cast: Reginald Denny, Esther Ralston, Eleanor Hunt, Vince Barnett, Claudia Dell, Robert Frazer, Rudolph Amendt, Merrill McCormack, Frank Hoyt, Manuel Pelufo, Charles Moyer, Lou Hicks.

Seeking refuge from rival gangsters in Europe, a pair of American gangsters (Reginald Denny, Vince Barnett) enlist in the Foreign Legion.

Running time: 70 minutes. Release date: January 16, 1937. (Some sources give the running time as 55 minutes. Originally released by Regal in 1936 as *Rest Cure*.)

Mae Clarke and James Cagney in *Great Guy* (1937).

11. **Scotland Yard Commands** (drama) Directed by James Flood. Produced by Basil Dean. From the novel by Nevil Shute.

Cast: Clive Brook, Victoria Hopper, Nora Swinburne, Malcolm Keen, Cecil Ramage, Charles Farrell, Lawrence Hanray, Frederick Peisley, Ethel Coleridge, Warburton Gamble, Dennis Wyndham.

A Scotland Yard secret service agent (Clive Brook) tries to halt the activities of a gang of gun smugglers.

Running time: 61 minutes. Release date: January 23, 1937.

Produced and released in Great Britain in 1936 as *The Lonely Road*; released in the U. S. by Grand National.

12. **Arizona Days** (western) Directed by Jack English. Produced by Edward Finney. Screenplay by Sherman Lowe. Story by Lindsley Parsons.

Cast: Tex Ritter, Eleanor Stewart, Syd Saylor, Ethelind Terry, William Faversham, Forrest Taylor, Snub Pollard, Glenn Strange, Horace Murphy,

Yakima Canutt, Rita Cansino (Hayworth) and Tex Ritter are pictured on this lobby card for *Trouble in Texas* (1937).

Earl Dwire, Budd Buster, William Desmond, Edward Cassidy, Salty Holmes, Tommy Bupp, Tex Palmer, White Flash the horse.

To help a traveling show out of a financial crisis, Tex goes to work as a tax collector.

Running time: 52 minutes. Release date: January 30, 1937.

13. **Romance and Riches** (comedy) Produced and directed by Alfred Zeisler. Screenplay by John L. Balderston. From the story "The Amazing Guest of Mr. Ernest Bliss" by Edward Phillips Oppenheim. A Garret-Klement Production.

Cast: Cary Grant, Mary Brian, Peter Cawthorne, Henry Kendall, Leon M. Lion, John Turnbull, Arthur Hardy, Iris Ashley, Garry Marsh, Andrea Malandrinos, Alfred Wellesley, Marie Wright, Buena Bent, Charles Farrell, Quinton MacPherson, Hal Gordon.

A rich young idler (Cary Grant) wagers that he can rise in business without using his money or influence to get ahead.

Running time: 59 minutes (some sources say 70 minutes). Release date: February 27, 1937.

Produced and released in Great Britain by Empire Films as *The Amazing Quest of Ernest Bliss* (1936); originally released in the U. S. by United

Artists in 1936 as *The Amazing Adventure*; released in the U. S. in 1937 by Grand National.

14. Trouble in Texas (western) Directed by Robert N. Bradbury. Produced by Edward Finney. Screenplay by Robert Emmett (Tansey).

Cast: Tex Ritter, Rita Cansino (Hayworth), Earl Dwire, Yakima Canutt, Dick Palmer, Hal Price, Fred Parker, Horace Murphy, Charles King, Tom Cooper, Milburn Morante, Jack C. Smith, Shorty Miller, George Morrell, Rudy Sooter, Chick Hannon, Oral Zumalt, Bob Crosby, Foxy Callahan, Harry Knight, Tex Sherman, Glenn Strange, the Texas Tornadoes, White Flash the horse.

Tex clashes with crooks who are employing unorthodox tactics to win rodeo contests.

Running time: 53 minutes. Release date: March 6, 1937.

15. Navy Spy (drama) Directed by Crane Wilbur. Produced by George A. Hirliman. Screenplay by Crane Wilbur. A Condor Production.

Cast: Conrad Nagel, Eleanor Hunt, Judith Allen, Jack Doyle, Phil Dunham, Don Barclay, Howard Lang, Crauford Kent.

A G-man (Conrad Nagel) tangles with spies who are after a secret poison gas formula.

Running time: 58 minutes. Release date: March 13, 1937.

16. 23½ Hours Leave (comedy) Directed by John G. Blystone. Produced by Douglas MacLean. Screenplay by Harry Ruskin and Henry McCarthy. Based on the *Saturday Evening Post* story by Mary Roberts Rinehart.

Cast: James Ellison, Terry Walker, Morgan Hill, Arthur Lake, Paul Harvey, Wally Maher, Andy Andrews, Murray Alper, Pat Gleason, John Kelly, Russell Hicks, Ward Bond.

Through a fluke, a rookie soldier (James Ellison) manages to capture a couple of spies.

Running time: 72 minutes. Release date: March 21, 1937.

17. Girl Loves Boy (drama) Directed by Duncan Mansfield. Produced by B. F. Zeidman. Screenplay by Duncan Mansfield and Carroll Graham. Story by Karl Brown and Hinton Smith.

Cast: Eric Linden, Cecilia Parker, Roger Imhof, Dorothy Peterson, Pedro de Cordoba, Bernadene Hayes, Otto Hoffman, Patsy O'Connor, Rollo Lloyd, Buster Phelps, John T. Murray, Spencer Charters, Sherwood Bailey, Edwin Mordant, Jameson Thomas.

The town squire's playboy son (Eric Linden) falls in love with a poor widow's daughter (Cecilia Parker).

Running time: 77 minutes. Release date: March 27, 1937.

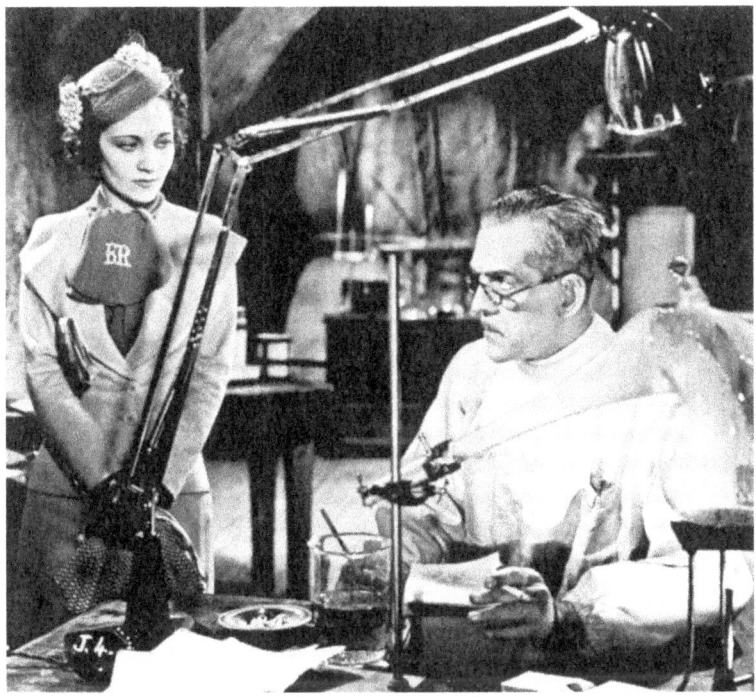

Joan Wyndham and Boris Karloff in *Juggernaut* (1937), a British production released in the U. S. by Grand National.

18. Hittin' the Trail (western) Directed by Robert N. Bradbury. Produced by Edward Finney. Screenplay by Robert Emmett (Tansey).

Cast: Tex Ritter, Jerry Bergh, Tommy Bupp, Earl Dwire, Jack Smith, Snub Pollard, Archie Ricks, Heber Snow (Hank Worden), Charles King, Edward Cassidy, Ray Whitley and His Range Ramblers (the Phelps Brothers, Ken Card), the Texas Tornadoes, White Flash the horse.

Tex clashes with a gang of horse thieves.

Running time: 58 minutes. Release date: April 3, 1937.

19. The Gold Racket (action-drama) Directed by Louis Gasnier. Produced by George A. Hirliman. Screenplay by David Levy and Griffin Jay. Story by Howard Higgin.

Cast: Conrad Nagel, Eleanor Hunt, Fuzzy Knight, Frank Milan, Charles Delaney, Karl Hackett, Warner Richmond, Albert J. Smith, Edward LeSaint, William L. Thorne, Paul Weigel, Fred Malatesta.

Two federal agents (Conrad Nagel, Eleanor Hunt) are assigned to catch smugglers flying gold into the U. S. from Mexico.

Running time: 66 minutes. Release date: April 10, 1937.

20. The Man in the Mirror (comedy) Directed by Maurice Elvey. Produced by Julius Hagen. Scenario by Hugh Mills. From the novel by William Garrett. Adaptation and dialogue by F. McGrew Willis.

Cast: Edward Everett Horton, Genevieve Tobin, Ursula Jeans, Garry Marsh, Aubrey Mather, Alistair Sim, Renee Gadd, Viola Compton, Stafford Hilliard, Felix Aylmer.

A meek little man (Edward Everett Horton) is confronted by his confident, aggressive "mirror image," an image which takes control of his life, accomplishing all the enterprising things this spineless personality has failed to tackle.

Running time: 71 minutes. (Some sources list the running time of the British release as 85 minutes.) Release date: April 24, 1937.

Produced and released in Great Britain by Twickenham Films in 1936; released in the U. S. in 1937 by Grand National.

21. Juggernaut (mystery-drama) Directed by Henry Edwards. Produced by Julius Hagen. Screenplay by Cyril Campion and H. Fowler Mear. From the novel by Alice Campbell.

Cast: Boris Karloff, Arthur Margetson, Joan Wyndham, Mona Goya, Anthony Ireland, Morton Selten, Nina Boucicault, Gibb McLaughlin, J. H. Roberts, Victor Rietti.

A medical specialist (Boris Karloff), on the verge of discovering a cure for paralysis, resorts to murder in an effort to get funds to continue his experiments.

Running time: 64 minutes. (Some sources list the running time of the British release as 73 minutes.) Release date: April 30, 1937.

Produced and released in Great Britain by Twickenham Films in 1936; released in the U. S. by Grand National. Reissued as *The Demon Doctor*. Remade as *The Temptress* (Ambassador Films, 1949).

22. Killers of the Sea (adventure-documentary) Produced and directed by Ray Friedgen. Screenplay by Adrian Johnson. Story by Frederick H. Wagner. Additional dialogue by John P. Medbury.

Cast: Captain Wallace Caswell, Jr., "Spot" Hayes, Bruce Stillwell, Steve Beadon, Hubert Dykes, "Evolution" Henderson, Bryant Lee, Julius Randy. *Narrated by* Lowell Thomas.

Captain Wallace Caswell, Jr., self-appointed protector of all gamefish in the Gulf of Mexico, is seen in hand-to-fin, knife-to-tooth battles with sharks, devil fish and other marine monsters.

Running time: 49 minutes. Release date: May 8, 1937.

23. Two Who Dared (drama) Produced and directed by Eugene Frenke. Screenplay by W. Chetham Strede. Story by Fedor Alzep.

Cast: Anna Sten, Henry Wilcoxon, John Garrick, Viola Keats, Guy Middleton, Romilly Lunge, Francis L. Sullivan, Esme Percy, Peter Gawthorne, Frank Atkinson, Minnie Rayner, Pat Noonan.

A carefree Russian officer (Henry Wilcoxon) falls in love with his child's nurse (Anna Sten).

Running time: 73 minutes. Release date: May 8, 1937.

Produced and released in Great Britain as *A Woman Alone* (1936); released in the U. S. by Grand National.

24. Forever Yours (musical-drama) Directed by Stanley Irving. Produced by Alexander Korda. Story and screenplay by Hugh Gray and Arthur Wimperis. (Korda, who usually had his product distributed in the U. S. through United Artists, released this film through Grand National on the understanding that his name would not figure in any way in the advertising or billing.)

Cast: Benjamino Gigli, Joan Gardner, Hugh Wakefield, Allan Jeayes, Charles Carson, Ivan Brandt, Jeanne Stuart, Hay Petrie, Richard Gofe.

A young English secretary (Joan Gardner) journeys to America, where she falls in love with a noted opera singer (Benjamino Gigli).

Running time: 70 minutes. (Some sources list the running time for British release prints as 78 minutes.) Release date: May 15, 1937.

Produced in Great Britain.

25. Sing, Cowboy, Sing (western) Directed by Robert N. Bradbury. Produced by Edward Finney. Screenplay by Robert Emmett (Tansey).

Cast: Tex Ritter, Louise Stanley, Al St. John, Karl Hackett, Charles King, Robert McKenzie, Chester Conklin, Budd Buster, Heber Snow (Hank Worden), Chick Hannon, Horace Murphy, Snub Pollard, Tex Palmer, Jack C. Smith, Oscar Gahan, Herman Hack.

Tex and his friend Biff (Al St. John) protect a young woman (Louise Stanley) from hoodlums trying to take over her covered wagon freight-carrying franchise.

Running time: 59 minutes. Release date: May 22, 1937.

26. Sweetheart of the Navy (drama) Directed by Duncan Mansfield. Produced by B. F. Zeidman. Screenplay by Carroll Graham. Story by Garrett Graham and Jay Strauss.

Cast: Eric Linden, Cecilia Parker, Roger Imhof, Bernadene Hayes, Jason Robards (Sr.), Cully Richards, Etta McDaniel, Don Barclay.

A sailor (Eric Linden) is coaxed into staging a fight in order to help a pretty singer (Cecilia Parker) out of financial difficulty.

Running time: 61 minutes. Release date: June 8, 1937.

14   Grand National Pictures

Lobby card for *Trailing Trouble* (1937).

27. **Bank Alarm** (action-drama) Directed by Louis J. Gasnier. Produced by George A. Hirliman. Screenplay by David S. Levy and Griffin Jay. Original story by Cynthia and Laurence Meade.

Cast: Conrad Nagel, Eleanor Hunt, Vince Barnett, Frank Milan, Wilma Francis, William L. Thorne, Wheeler Oakman, Charles Delaney, Phil Dunham, Sid D'Albrook, Pat Gleason, Wilson Benge, Henry Roquemore.

Two Department of Justice agents (Conrad Nagel, Eleanor Hunt) pursue a gang of bankrobbers who leave a trail of counterfeit bills and murder victims.

Running time: 61 minutes. Release date: June 25, 1937.

28. **Riders of the Rockies** (western) Directed by Robert N. Bradbury. Produced by Edward Finney. Screenplay by Robert Emmett (Tansey). Story by Lindsley Parsons.

Cast: Tex Ritter, Louise Stanley, Charles King, Snub Pollard, Yakima Canutt, Earl Dwire, Horace Murphy, Martin Garralaga, Jack Rockwell, Paul Lopez, Heber Snow (Hank Worden), Tex Palmer, Clyde McClary, the Texas Tornadoes, White Flash the horse.

An Arizona Ranger (Tex Ritter), suspected of conspiring with rustlers, escapes from prison and sets out to prove his innocence.

Running time: 56 minutes. Release date: July 2, 1937.

Feature Films 1937

29. Boots of Destiny (western) Directed by Arthur Rosson. Produced by M. H. Hoffman. Screenplay by Arthur Rosson. Story by E. Morton Hough.

Cast: Ken Maynard, Claudia Dell, Vince Barnett, Edward Cassidy, Walter Patterson, Martin Garralaga, George Morrell, Fred Cordova, Sid D'Albrook, Carl Mathews, Wally West, Tarzan the horse.

Ken Maynard and his pal Acey Deucy (Vince Barnett) go to the aid of a ranch owner (Claudia Dell) whose foreman (Edward Cassidy) is trying to seize control of her property.

Running time: 56 minutes. Release date: July 16, 1937.

30. Hideout in the Alps (drama) Directed by Bernard Vorhaus. Produced by Julius Hagen. Screenplay by L. DuGarde Peach and Michael Hankinson. Additional dialogue by Paul Harvey Fox and Arthur Macrae. Adapted from a play by Neil Grant.

Cast: Ronald Squire, Jane Baxter, Arthur Macrae, Anthony Bushnell, Athole Stewart, Katie Johnson, Margaret Rutherford, Davina Craig, Austin Trevor, Felix Aylmer, Hal Gordon.

A forger, who has just been released from prison, takes the blame when his young nephew becomes involved with a gang of counterfeiters.

Running time: 75 minutes. Release date: July 23, 1937.

Working title: *Rendezvous in the Alps*.

Produced and released in Great Britain by Twickenham Films as *Dusty Ermine* (1936).

31. Mystery of the Hooded Horseman (western) Directed by Ray Taylor. Produced by Edward Finney. Story and screenplay by Edmond Kelso.

Cast: Tex Ritter, Iris Meredith, Horace Murphy, Charles King, Earl Dwire, Forrest Taylor, Joseph Girard, Lafe McKee, Heber Snow (Hank Worden), Oscar Gahan, Jack C. Smith, Chick Hannon, Tex Palmer, Lynton Brent, Ray Whitley and His Range Busters (the Phelps Brothers, Ken Card), White Flash the horse.

Tex Martin (Tex Ritter) is after the hooded horseman who is out to strip Martin's niece (Iris Meredith) of her heritage, the Four Square Mine.

Running time: 60 minutes. Release date: August 6, 1937.

32. Trailing Trouble (western) Directed by Arthur Rosson. Produced by M. H. Hoffman. Screenplay by Philip Graham White.

Cast: Ken Maynard, Lona Andre, Vince Barnett, Roger Williams, Grace Woods, Fred Burns, Phil Dunham, Edward Cassidy, Horace B. Carpenter, Marin Sais, Tex Palmer, Tarzan the horse.

Mistaken for a notorious gunslinger, Friendly Fielding (Ken Maynard) helps a young woman (Lona Andre) save her ranch.

Running time: 57 minutes. Release date: August 27, 1937.

16   Grand National Pictures

Carol Hughes, Lightning, and James Newill in *Renfrew of the Royal Mounted* (1937).

33. Small Town Boy (comedy) Directed by Glenn Tryon. Produced by Zion Myers. Screenplay by Glenn Tryon. From the story "The Thousand Dollar Bill" by Manuel Komroff.

Cast: Stuart Erwin, Joyce Compton, Erville Alderson, Dorothy Appleby, Jed Prouty, Clara Blandick, James Blakely, Clarence Wilson, Paul Hurst, Edward Woller, Eddie Kane, George Chandler, Victor Potel.

A small-town lad (Stuart Erwin) finds a $1000 bill; this monetary windfall gives him the confidence to become a demon go-getter.

Running time: 63 minutes. Release date: September 24, 1937.

Working title: *The Thousand Dollar Bill.*

34. Renfrew of the Royal Mounted (adventure) Produced and directed by Al Herman. Screenplay by Charles Logue. From the books and radio program by Laurie York Erskine.

Cast: James Newill, Carol Hughes, William Royle, Herbert Corthell, Kenneth Harlan, Dickie Jones, Chief Thunder Cloud, William Austin, Donald Reed, Bob Terry, William Gould, David Barclay (Dave O'Brien), Lightning the dog, Vera Ross, Harry Tyler, Richard Tucker, Mildred Rogers, Frank Moulan, Josef Swickard, Arthur Kay, Horace Murphy, Bert Roach, Allan Rogers, Max Davidson, Caritz Crawford.

Evelyn Daw and James Cagney in *Something to Sing About* (1937).

Renfrew of the Royal Canadian Mounties (James Newill) trails a gang of counterfeiters.
Running time: 57 minutes. Release date: September 29, 1937.

35. The Girl Said No (musical-comedy) Produced and directed by Andrew L. Stone. Screenplay by Betty Laidlaw and Robert Lively. Original story by Andrew L. Stone.
Cast: Robert Armstrong, Irene Hervey, Paula Stone, Edward Brophy, Vivian Hart, William Danforth, Holmes Herbert, Gwili Andre.
A race track tout (Robert Armstrong), seeking revenge on a taxi dancer (Irene Hervey) who gave him a trimming, convinces her that she has the makings of a musical comedy star; she falls for the trick and finances the promotion of a new show.
Running time: 76 minutes. Release date: October 15, 1937.

36. The Shadow Strikes (mystery) Directed by Lynn Shores. Produced by Max and Arthur Alexander. Screenplay by Al Martin. From the "Shadow" stories by Maxwell Grant (Walter B. Gibson). Adapted by Martin and Rex Taylor.
Cast: Rod LaRocque, Lynn Anders, James Blakely, John St. Polis,

Walter McGrail, Bill Kellogg, Cy Kendall, Kenneth Harlan, Norman Ainsley, Wilson Benge, John Carnavale.

Amateur sleuth Lamont Cranston (Rod LaRocque), alias "The Shadow," attempts to solve the mystery behind two strange slayings.

Running time: 61 minutes. Release date: October 29, 1937.

Working title: *The Shadow*.

Also known as *Womantrap*.

37. Love Takes Flight (drama) Directed by Conrad Nagel. Produced by George A. Hirliman. Screenplay by Lionel O. and Mervin Houser. Original story by Ann Morrison Chapin. A Condor Production.

Cast: Bruce Cabot, Beatrice Roberts, John Sheehan, Astrid Allwyn, Elliot Fisher, Gordon ("Wild Bill") Elliott, Edwin Maxwell, Harry Tyler, William Moore, Grady Sutton, Arthur Hoyt, William L. Thorne, Brooks Benedict, Henry Roquemore.

A swell-headed commercial pilot (Bruce Cabot) jilts his air-hostess sweetheart (Beatrice Roberts) to become a film star.

Running time: 71 minutes. Release date: November 5, 1937.

38. Something to Sing About (musical) Directed by Victor Schertzinger. Produced by Zion Myers. Screenplay by Austin Parker. Original story by Victor Schertzinger. A Victor Schertzinger Production.

Cast: James Cagney, Evelyn Daw, William Frawley, Mona Barrie, Gene Lockhart, James Newill, Harry Barris, Cully Richards, Candy Candido, William Davidson, Richard Tucker, Mavek Windheim, Johnny Arthur, Dwight Frye, Philip Ahn.

An orchestra leader (James Cagney) from New York becomes a movie star and suffers the inconveniences that result from studio publicity.

Running time: 93 minutes. Release date: November 19, 1937.

Reissued in 1947 by Screencraft Pictures in an 82 minute version titled *Battling Hoofer*.

39. Hats Off (musical) Produced and directed by Boris Petroff. Story by Sam Fuller and Edmund Joseph. Additional dialogue by Lawrence Thiele.

Cast: Mae Clarke, John Payne, Helen Lynd, Luis Alberni, Skeets Gallagher, Franklin Pangborn, Robert Middlemass, George Irving, Clarence Wilson, Val and Ernie Stanton, the Radio Rogues (Jimmy Hollywood, Eddie Bartell, Henry Taylor).

A romance develops between two rival press agents (Mae Clarke, John Payne).

Running time: 66 minutes. Release date: December 6, 1937.

40. Wallaby Jim of the Islands (adventure) Directed by Charles Lamont. Produced by Bud Barsky. Screenplay by Bennett Cohen and Houston Branch. Story by Albert Richard Wetjen.

Cast: George Houston, Ruth Coleman, Douglas Walton, William von Brincken, Mamo Clark, Colin Campbell, Syd Saylor, Juan Torena, Nick Thompson, Warner Richmond, Wilson Benge.

Wallaby Jim (George Houston), skipper of a pearl fishing brig, roams the waters of the South Seas.

Running time: 61 minutes. Release date: December 17, 1937.

1938

41. Here's Flash Casey (mystery) Directed by Lynn Shores. Produced by Max and Arthur Alexander. Screenplay by John Krafft. Story by George Harmon Cox.

Cast: Eric Linden, Boots Mallory, Cully Richards, Holmes Herbert, Joseph Crehan, Howard Lang, Victor Adams, Harry Harvey, Suzanne Kaaren, Matty Kemp, Dorothy Vaughn, Maynard Holmes.

Having snapped a prize-winning photo while still in school, a young man (Eric Linden) gives himself two years after graduation to own the world's largest news photo agency.

Running time: 58 minutes. Release date: January 7, 1938.

42. Tex Rides with the Boy Scouts (western) Directed by Ray Taylor. Produced by Edward Finney. Screenplay by Edmond Kelso. Story by Edmond Kelso and Lindsley Parsons.

Cast: Tex Ritter, Marjorie Reynolds, Snub Pollard, Horace Murphy, Edward Cassidy, Charles King, Tommy Bupp, Karl Hackett, Tim Davis, Philip Ahn, Lynton Brent, Heber Snow (Hank Worden), Forrest Taylor, White Flash the horse.

The Boy Scouts help Tex pursue a gang of train robbers who got away with a gold bullion shipment.

Running time: 57 minutes. Release date: January 21, 1938.

43. Swing It, Sailor (comedy) Directed by Raymond Cannon. Produced by David Diamond. Original story and screenplay by Clarence Marks and David Diamond.

Cast: Wallace Ford, Isabel Jewell, Ray Mayer, Mary Treen, Cully Richards, Rex Lease, Tom Kennedy, Alexander Leftwich, Max Hoffman, Jr.

Two gobs (Wallace Ford, Ray Mayer) vie for the affections of a pretty blonde (Isabel Jewell).

Running time: 57 minutes. Release date: February 4, 1938.

Working title: *He Wanted to Marry*.

44. **Mr. Boggs Steps Out** (comedy) Directed by Gordon Wiles. Produced by Ben Pivar. Screenplay by Richard English. From the *Saturday Evening Post* story "Face the Facts" by Clarence Budington Kelland.

Cast: Stuart Erwin, Helen Chandler, Harry Tyler, Milburn Stone, Nora Cecil, Wilson Benge, Walter Byron, Spencer Charters, Betty Mack, Toby Wing.

A country yokel (Stuart Erwin) purchases a run-down barrel factory.

Running time: 68 minutes. Release date: February 18, 1938.

Working titles: *Mr. Boggs Buys a Barrel* and *Face the Facts*.

45. **Frontier Town** (western) Directed by Ray Taylor. Produced by Edward Finney. Screenplay by Edmond Kelso.

Cast: Tex Ritter, Ann Evers, Snub Pollard, Charles King, Horace Murphy, Karl Hackett, Lynton Brent, Edward Cassidy, Forrest Taylor, Jack C. Smith, Don Marion, Babe Lawrence, Hank Worden, John Elliott, Jimmy LeFieur's Saddle Pals, White Flash the horse.

Tex Lansing (Tex Ritter) enters a rodeo contest in an effort to obtain some badly needed funds.

Running time: 60 minutes. Release date: March 4, 1938.

46. **Damaged Goods** (drama) Directed by Phil Goldstone. Produced by Phil Goldstone and Irving Starr. Screenplay by Joseph Hoffman. Adapted by Upton Sinclair from the play by Eugene Brieux. A Condor Production.

Cast: Pedro de Cordoba, Phyllis Barry, Douglas Walton, Arlene Duncan, Ferdinand Munier, Esther Dale, Clarence Wilson, Wheeler Oakman, Frank Melton, Gretchen Thomas.

A married man (Douglas Walton) contracts syphilis and infects his wife and unborn child.

Running time: 56 minutes. Release date: March 15, 1938.

A remake of a 1914 film of the same title.

47. **He Loved an Actress** (musical-comedy) Directed by Melville Brown. Produced by William Rowland. Screenplay by John Meehan, Jr. Story by John F. Harding.

Cast: Lupe Velez, Ben Lyon, Wallace Ford, Jean Colin, Harry Langdon, Mary Cole, Cyril Raymond, Ronald Ward, Arthur Finn, Philip Pearman, Andrea Malandrinos, Olive Sloane, Peggy Novak, John Stobart, Ronald Hill, Albert Whelan, Alan Shires.

A couple of bankrupt film producers (Ben Lyon, Wallace Ford) seek financing from a Mexican heiress (Lupe Velez) who is really a poor actress.

Running time: 68 minutes. (Some sources list the running time for British release prints as 78 minutes.) Release date: March 25, 1938.

Produced in England by Biltmore Pictures; released in Great Britain in 1937 as *Stardust*, and later it was retitled *Mad About Money*. Distributed in the U. S. by Grand National as *He Loved an Actress*.

48. Spirit of Youth (drama) Directed by Harry Fraser. Produced by Lew Golder. Original screenplay by Arthur Hoerl. Presented by Globe Pictures Corporation.

Cast: Joe Louis, Clarence Muse, Edna Mae Harris, Mae Turner, Mantan Moreland, Cleo Desmond, Clarence Brooks, Anthony Scott, Janette O'Dell.

Aspiring boxer Joe Thomas (Joe Louis) rises to fame and fortune as a result of his success in the fight arena.

Running time: 66 minutes. Release date: April 1, 1938.

49. Zamboanga (documentary) Directed by Eduardo de Castro. Produced by Tait and Harris.

A documentary on the beautiful city of Zamboanga in the Philippines.

Running time: 64 minutes. Release date: April 15, 1938.

Produced by Filippine Film Productions, Inc.; released in the U. S. by Grand National.

50. International Crime (mystery) Directed by Charles Lamont. Produced by Max and Arthur Alexander. Screenplay by Jack Natteford. Additional dialogue by John Krafft. From the "Shadow" stories by Maxwell Grant (Walter B. Gibson).

Cast: Rod LaRocque, Astrid Allwyn, Thomas Jackson, Oscar O'Shea, William von Brincken, William Pawley, Walter Bonn, William Moore, Lou Hearn, Tennen Holtz, John St. Polis, Lloyd Whitlock, Jack Baxley.

Lamont Cranston (Rod LaRocque), alias "The Shadow," matches wits with an international spy ring.

Running time: 60 minutes. Release date: April 22, 1938.

51. Whirlwind Horseman (western) Directed by Bob Hill. Produced by Max and Arthur Alexander. Screenplay by George Plympton.

Cast: Ken Maynard, Joan Barclay, Bill Griffith, Joe Girard, Kenny Dix, Roger Williams, Dave O'Brien, Walter Shumway, Budd Buster, Lew Meehan, Glenn Strange, Tarzan the horse.

Maynard thwarts a bandit gang trying to seize control of some oil-rich property.

Running time: 58 minutes. Release date: April 29, 1938.

52. Six-Shootin' Sheriff (western) Directed by Harry Fraser. Produced by Max and Arthur Alexander. Story by Weston Edwards (Harry Fraser).

Cast: Ken Maynard, Marjorie Reynolds, Lafe McKee, Harry Harvey,

Jane Keckely, Walter Long, Bob Terry, Tom London, Warner Richmond, Dick Alexander, Ben Corbett, Earl Dwire, Glenn Strange, Roger Williams, Bud Osborne, Edward Peil, Milburn Morante, Carl Mathews, Herb Holcombe, Tarzan the horse.

An outlaw (Ken Maynard) redeems himself and turns sheriff to make up for his lawless past.

Running time: 59 minutes. Release date: May 20, 1938.

53. Life Returns (drama) Directed by Eugene Frenke. Produced by Lou Ostrow. Screenplay by Arthur T. Horman and John F. Goodrich. Original story by Eugene Frenke and James Hogan (based on Dr. Robert E. Cornish's May 22, 1934, experiment restoring life to a dog).

Cast: Onslow Stevens, George Breakston, Lois Wilson, Valerie Hobson, Stanley Fields, Frank Reicher, Richard Carle, Dean Benton, Lois January, Richard Quine, Maidel Turner, George McQuarrie, Otis Harlan, Dr. Robert E. Cornish.

A doctor (Onslow Stevens) conducts experiments in bringing asphyxiation victims back to life. (This film uses actual footage of Dr. Cornish's experiment.)

Running time: 63 minutes. Release date: June 10, 1938 (originally released January 1935 by Universal Pictures, producers of the picture).

54. Held for Ransom (mystery) Directed by Clarence Bricker. Story and screenplay by Barry Barringer.

Cast: Blanche Mehaffey, Grant Withers, Bruce Warren, Jack Mulhall, Kenneth Harlan, Harry Harvey, Edward Foster, Walter McGrail, George Moore, Robert McKenzie, Richard Lancaster, John McCallum, Joseph Girard.

FBI agent Betty Mason (Blanche Mehaffey) pursues the kidnappers of a wealthy businessman.

Running time: 59 minutes. Release date: June 17, 1938.

55. I Married a Spy (drama) Directed by Edmond T. Greville. Produced by Hugh Perceval. Screenplay by Basil Mason. From the novel by Paul de Saint-Colombe.

Cast: Brigitte Horney, Neil Hamilton, Gyles Isham, Ivor Barnard, Charles Carson, Raymond Lovell, Frederick Lloyd, Ben Field, Hay Petrie, Leslie Perrins.

A German girl (Birgitte Horney), in love with a French lieutenant (Neil Hamilton), is forced to spy for France.

Running time: 59 minutes. (Some sources list the running time for British release prints as 80 minutes.) Release date: July 1, 1938.

Produced in Great Britain by IFP-Phoenix and released by ABFD

(Associated British Film Distributors) as *Secret Lives* in 1937; released in the U. S. by Grand National.

56. Rollin' Plains (western) Directed by Al Herman. Produced by Edward Finney. Screenplay by Lindsley Parsons and Edmond Kelso. Story by Jacques and Ciela Jacquard.

Cast: Tex Ritter, Hobart Bosworth, Harriet Bennett, Horace Murphy, Snub Pollard, Edward Cassidy, Karl Hackett, Charles King, Ernie Adams, Lynton Brent, Horace B. Carpenter, Hank Worden, Augie Gomez, Oscar Gahan, Rudy Sooter, Carl Mathews, George Morrell, the Beverly Hillbillies, White Flash the horse.

A drifter (Tex Ritter) tries to settle a conflict between cattlemen and sheepmen.

Running time: 57 minutes. Release date: July 8, 1938.

Uses footage from *Sing, Cowboy, Sing* (Grand National, 1937).

57. The High Command (drama) Directed by Thorold Dickinson. Produced by Gordon Wong Wellesley. Screenplay by Katharine Strueby, Walter Meade and Val Valentine. From the novel "The General Goes Too Far" by Lewis Robinson.

Cast: Lionel Atwill, Lucie Mannheim, Steve Geray, James Mason, Allan Jeayes, Wally Patch, Kathleen Gibson, Henry Hewitt, Leslie Perrins, Michael Lambart.

A British officer (Lionel Atwill) traps a blackmailer's murderer to save his daughter from scandal.

Running time: 59 minutes. (Some sources list the running time for the British release prints as 90 minutes.) Release date: July 15, 1938.

Produced in Great Britain by Fanfare Productions and released by ABFD (Associated British Film Distributors) in 1937; released in the U. S. by Grand National.

58. Renfrew on the Great White Trail (adventure) Produced and directed by Al Herman. From the books and radio program by Laurie York Erskine.

Cast: James Newill, Terry Walker, Robert Frazer, Dick Alexander, Richard Tucker, Robert Terry, Eddie Gribbon, Walter McGrail, Philo McCullough, Charles King, Juan Duval, Carl Mathews, Silver King the dog.

Renfrew of the Royal Canadian Mounted (James Newill) must track down and arrest the father of the girl he loves for an unproven crime.

Running time: 58 minutes. Release date: July 22, 1938.

Also known as *On the Great White Trail*.

59. Utah Trail (western) Directed by Al Herman. Produced by Edward Finney. Screenplay by Edmond Kelso. Story by Edmond Kelso and Lindsley Parsons (from an original idea by Tex Ritter).

Cast: Tex Ritter, Horace Murphy, Snub Pollard, Adele Pearce (Pamela Blake), Karl Hackett, Charles King, Edward Cassidy, Dave O'Brien, Bud Osborne, Lynton Brent, Sherry Tansey, George Morrell, Horace B. Carpenter, Ray Jones, Oscar Gahan, Herman Hack, Chick Hannon, Rudy Sooter, White Flash the horse.

Tex pursues a gang of cattle rustlers who have escaped on a train that has seemed to disappear.

Running time: 56 minutes. Release date: August 12, 1938.

60. Frontier Scout (western) Directed by Samuel Newfield. Produced by Franklyn Warner and Maurice Conn. Story and screenplay by Frances Guihan. A Fine Arts Picture.

Cast: George Houston, Al St. John, Beth Marion, Guy (Alden) Chase, Dave O'Brien, Jack Ingram, Charles "Slim" Whitaker, Kenne Duncan, Carl Mathews, Kit Guard, Bob Woodward, Jack C. Smith, Walter Byron, Budd Buster, Mantan Moreland, Dorothy Fay, Minerva Urecal, Frank LaRue, Roger Williams, Joseph Girard.

Wild Bill Hickok (George Houston) clashes with cattle rustlers.

Running time: 61 minutes. Release date: September 16, 1938.

61. Shadows Over Shanghai (adventure) Directed by Charles Lamont. Produced by Franklyn Warner. Screenplay by Joseph Hoffman. Story by Richard B. Sale. A Fine Arts Picture.

Cast: James Dunn, Ralph Morgan, Linda Gray, Robert Barrat, Paul Sutton, Edward Woods, Edwin Mordant, Chester Gan, Victor Wong, Edward Keane, Billy Bevan, William Haade, Richard Loo, Victor Sen Yung.

In the midst of the Sino-Japanese War, a newspaper photographer (James Dunn) and a school teacher (Linda Gray) encounter Japanese, Chinese and Russian agents when they try to get a valuable jade amulet out of China and back to San Francisco.

Running time: 65 minutes. Release date: October 14, 1938.

62. Titans of the Deep (documentary) Produced and directed by Otis Barton. Story by Lowell Thomas.

Cast: Dr. William Beebe, Otis Barton, Joan Igou, Gloria Hollister, Jocelyn Crane, John Tee Van.

A documentary on undersea life off the Bermuda coast.

Running time: 47 minutes (also offered to exhibitors in a 38 minute "short version"). Release date: October 28, 1938.

Feature Films 1938

Sally Rand in *The Sunset Murder Case* (1938).

63. Cipher Bureau (action-drama) Directed by Charles Lamont. Produced by Franklyn Warner. Screenplay by Arthur Hoerl and Monroe Shaff. A Fine Arts Picture.

Cast: Leon Ames, Charlotte Wynters, Joan Woodbury, Don Dillaway, Tenen Holtz, Gustav von Seyffertitz, Walter Bohn, Si Wills, Peter Lynn, Jason Robards (Sr.), Joe Romantini.

Major Phillip Waring (Leon Ames), head of the cipher bureau — a government agency in charge of decoding intercepted messages between foreign governments — and his secretary, Helen Lane (Charlotte Wynters), thwart the machinations of a spy ring.

Running time: 70 minutes. Release date: November 4, 1938.

Sequel: *Panama Patrol* (Grand National, 1939).

64. The Sunset Murder Case (mystery) Directed by Louis J. Gasnier. Produced by George A. Hirliman. Screenplay by Arthur Hoerl and Paul Franklin. From the original story "Murder on Sunset Boulevard" by Harold Joyce.

Cast: Sally Rand, Reed Hadley, Henry King and His Orchestra, Sugar Kane.

A dancer (Sally Rand) sets out to avenge the murder of her father by tracking down the killer.

Running time: 57 minutes. Release date: November 11, 1938. Also known as *The Sunset Strip Case*.

65. King of the Sierras (western) Directed by Samuel Diege. Produced by George A. Hirliman. Screenplay by W. Scott Darling. Based on a story by Frank Gay. A Condor Production.

Cast: Hobart Bosworth, Harry Harvey, Jr., Frank Campeau, Harry Harvey, Sr., Jack Lindell; horses: Sheik and Rex.

Uncle Hank (Hobart Bosworth) tells his young nephew Tom (Harry Harvey, Jr.) about a white horse named Whitey (Sheik) and a black stallion, El Diablo (Rex).

Running time: 53 minutes. Release date: 1938 (exact date unknown).

1939

66. The Long Shot (drama) Directed by Charles Lamont. Produced by Franklyn Warner. Screenplay by Ewart Adamson. Original story by Harry Beresford and George Callahan. A Fine Arts Picture.

Cast: Marsha Hunt, Gordon Jones, C. Henry Gordon, George Meeker, Harry Davenport, George E. Stone, Dorothy Fay, Frank Darien, Tom Kennedy, Earle Hodgins, Emerson Tracy, Gay Seabrook, Lee Phelps, Ben Burt, James Robinson, Denmore Chief, Joe Hernandez, James Keefe.

A young couple (Marsha Hunt, Gordon Jones) train a thoroughbred for the Santa Anita Handicap and encounter crooked gamblers who are trying to fix the big race.

Running time: 69 minutes. Release date: January 6, 1939.

67. Water Rustlers (western) Directed by Samuel Diege. Produced by Don Lieberman. Original screenplay by Arthur Hoerl. A Coronado Picture.

Cast: Dorothy Page, David O'Brien, Vince Barnett, Ethan Allen, Leonard Trainer, Merrill McCormick, Stanley Price, Warner Richmond, Lloyd Ingraham.

Shirley Martin (Dorothy Page), a rancher, and Bob Lawson (David O'Brien), her foreman, battle a land owner (Stanley Price) who is attempting to drive ranchers off their land by damming up the only creek in the area.

Running time: 54 minutes. Release date: January 6, 1939.

68. Trigger Pals (western) Directed by Samuel Newfield. Produced by Phil Krasne. Screenplay by George Plympton. Story by George Plympton and Ted Richmond. A Cinemart Picture.

Cast: Arthur Jarrett, Lee Powell, Al "Fuzzy" St. John, Dorothy Fay,

Dorothy Page and Milton Frome in *Ride 'Em, Cowgirl* (1939).

Charles King, Frank LaRue, Stanley Blystone, Ted Adams, Earl Douglas, Nina Guilbert, Ethan Allen, Ernie Adams.

Ranch foreman Lucky Morgan (Arthur Jarrett) and his pals Stormy (Lee Powell) and Fuzzy (Al St. John) clash with a corrupt land trader (Ted Adams) who heads a gang of cattle rustlers.

Running time: 55 minutes. Release date: January 13, 1939.

69. Ride 'Em, Cowgirl (western) Directed by Samuel Diege. Produced by George A. Hirliman and Arthur Dreifuss. Story and screenplay by Arthur Hoerl. A Coronado Picture.

Cast: Dorothy Page, Milton Frome, Vince Barnett, Lynn Mayberry, Joseph Girard, Frank Ellis, Harrington Reynolds, Merrill McCormick, Fred Berhle, Pat Henning, Edward Gordon, Fred Cordova, Lester Dorr, Walter Patterson, Snowey the horse.

After a gambler (Harrington Reynolds) frames her father (Joseph Girard) for a theft, Helen Rickson (Dorothy Page) confesses to the crime; facing a jail term, she escapes and sets out to expose the real culprit.

Running time: 52 minutes. Release date: January 20, 1939.

70. Six-Gun Rhythm (western) Produced and directed by Samuel Newfield. Story and screenplay by Fred Myton. An Arcadia Picture.

Cast: Tex Fletcher, Joan Barclay, Ralph Peters, Reed Howes, Malcolm "Bud" McTaggart, Ted Adams, Walter Shumway, Slim Hacker, Carl Mathews, Art Davis, Robert Frazer, Jack McHugh, Sherry Tansey, Kit Guard, Art Felix, Joe Pazen, Jack O'Shea, Cliff Parkinson, Frank Ellis, Wade Walker, Adrian Hughes.

After his father's death, a professional football player (Tex Fletcher) moves to Texas where he encounters a gang of cattle rustlers.

Running time: 55 minutes. Release date: February 17, 1939.

71. The Mind of Mr. Reeder (mystery) Produced and directed by Jack Raymond. Screenplay by Bryan Wallace, Marjorie Gaffney and Michael Hogan. From a story by Edgar Wallace.

Cast: Will Fyffe, Kay Walsh, George Curzon, Chili Bouchier, John Warwick, Leslie Waring, Romilly Lunge, Bettey Astell, Derek Gost, Ronald Shiner, Wally Patch, George Hayes, Dorothy Dewhurst.

J. G. Reeder (Will Fyffe), an elderly eccentric employed by the Director of Public Prosecutions, sets out to expose a counterfeiting ring.

Running time: 77 minutes. Release date: March 11, 1939.

Produced in Great Britain; released in the U. S. in 1939 by Grand National; released in 1940 by Monogram Pictures as *The Mysterious Mr. Reeder*.

72. Panama Patrol (action-drama) Directed by Charles Lamont. Produced by Franklyn Warner. Original screenplay by Arthur Hoerl. Based on characters created by Arthur Hoerl and Monroe Sheff. A Fine Arts Picture.

Cast: Leon Ames, Charlotte Wynters, Adrienne Ames, Weldon Heyburn, Abner Biberman, Sidney Miller, John Smart, Donald Barry, Hugh McArthur, William von Brincken, Frank Darien, Paul McVey.

Cipher bureau agents Phillip Waring (Leon Ames) and Helen Lane (Charlotte Wynters) encounter an Oriental spy ring stealing Panama Canal secrets.

Running time: 69 minutes. Release date: May 20, 1939.

A sequel to *Cipher Bureau* (Grand National, 1938).

73. Exile Express (drama) Directed by Otis Garrett. Produced by Eugene Frenke. Screenplay by Edwin Justus Mayer and Ethel LaBlanche. A United Players Production.

Cast: Anna Sten, Alan Marshal, Jerome Cowan, Jed Prouty, Walter Catlett, Stanley Fields, Leonid Kinsky, Irving Pichel, Harry Davenport, Addison Richards, Feodor Chaliapin, Jr., Spencer Charters, Byron Foulger, Etienne Girardot, Don Brodie, Henry Roquemore, Maude Eburne, Vince Barnett, Charles Richman.

Implicated in a murder and deported as an undesirable alien, a young woman (Anna Sten) is used as an innocent dupe in a plot to obtain a secret poison gas formula.
Running time: 71 minutes. Release date: May 27, 1939.

74. The Singing Cowgirl (western) Directed by Samuel Diege. Produced by George A. Hirliman. Screenplay by Arthur Hoerl. A Coronado Picture.

Cast: Dorothy Page, David O'Brien, Vince Barnett, Warner Richmond, Dorothy Short, Edward Peil, Dix Davis, Stanley Price, Paul Barrett, Lloyd Ingraham, Ethan Allen, Ed Gordon, Merrill McCormick.

A cowgirl (Dorothy Page) clashes with a rustler (Warner Richmond) and a crooked lawyer (Stanley Price) who are trying to seize control of some valuable ranch property.
Running time: 59 minutes. Release date: June 1939.

Although *The Singing Cowgirl* was the last "official" Grand National release, the company later distributed the following films:

75. I Killed the Count (mystery) Directed by Fred Zelnik. Produced by I. Goldsmith. Screenplay by Laurence Huntington. From the play by Alec Coppel.

Cast: Syd Walker, Ben Lyon, Terence de Marney, Barbara Blair, Athole Stewart, Antoinette Cellier, Leslie Perrins, Dave Burns, Kathleen Harrison, Gus McNaughton, Ronald Shiner, Aubrey Mallalieu, Robert Adair.

Inspector Davidson (Syd Walker) of Scotland Yard is called in when four people confess to have murdered Count Mattoni (Leslie Perrins), each of them with a plausible motive.
Running time: 89 minutes. Release date: September 2, 1939.

A Grafton Production, produced in Great Britain; released in 1940 by Monogram Pictures as *Who Is Guilty?*

76. Discoveries (musical) Directed by Redd Davis. Screenplay by Redd Davis, Cyril Campion and Anatole de Grunwald. Based on the Carroll Levis radio series.

Cast: Carroll Levis, Afrique, Issy Bonn, Julien Vedey, Bertha Belmore, Ronald Shiner, Doris Hare, Kathleen Harrison, Zoe Wynn, Barbara Everest, Shayle Gardner, Cyril Levis, Three Ginx, Dump and Tony, George Meaton, Radio Rascals, Pearl Venters, Archie Galbraith, Glyn Davies, Tony Vaughan, David Delmonte.

Rival manufacturers vie to sponsor Carroll Levis' radio talent show.
Running time: 68 minutes. Release date: September 15, 1939.
Produced and released in Great Britain by Vogue.

77. **Children of the Wild** (drama)
    Cast: Joan Valerie, James Bush.
    Other credits and plot synopsis unavailable.
    Running time: 57 minutes. Release date: October 14, 1939.

78. **Sons of the Sea** (drama) Directed by Maurice Elvey. Produced by K. C. Alexander. Screenplay by Maurice Elvey, Gerald Elliott and William Woolf. In Dufaycolor.
    Cast: Leslie Banks, Kay Walsh, Mackenzie Ward, Cecil Parker, Simon Lack, Ellen Pollock, Peter Shaw, Nigel Stock, Kynaston Reeves.
    A naval commander's son unwittingly aids an enemy spy.
    Running time: 83 minutes. Release date: December 23, 1939.
    Produced and released in Great Britain by British Consolidated.

Producers Releasing Corporation

For many film enthusiasts and historians, Producers Releasing Corporation, or PRC, represents the nadir of independent film operations. Some of the harsher detractors have remarked that the company's initials should have stood for "Pretty Rotten Crap." Their product always had a slapdash look to it, and was considered cheap even by poverty row standards. But as undeniably shoddy as their output was, PRC did manage to produce a few noteworthy efforts in spite of themselves, ranging from some interesting entries—*When the Lights Go On Again* (1944), *The Town Went Wild* (1944), *Strange Illusion* (1945), *The Enchanted Forest* (1945), *The Mask of Diijon* (1946)—to two minor classics, *Bluebeard* (1944) and *Detour* (1945).

The PRC films, the majority of which were westerns and melodramas, were churned out at an alarming rate under the guidance of several veteran directors, including William Beaudine, Jean Yarbrough, Joseph H. Lewis, Frank Wisbar, William K. Howard, Phil Rosen, Arthur Dreifuss, Spencer Gordon Bennet, William Nigh, Christy Cabanne, Wallace Fox, Lew Landers and Bernard B. Ray.

Edgar G. Ulmer, the most acclaimed of the company's house directors, was responsible for *The Wife of Monte Cristo* (1946) and the aforementioned *Bluebeard* and *Detour*, which are quite remarkable given PRC's limited budgets and shooting schedules.

But the most prolific director at PRC—indeed, the most prolific director in Hollywood—was Sam Newfield. Newfield, with his brother, producer Sigmund Neufeld, was able to turn out feature films at a rate unsurpassed by anyone before or since; in his 25-year career, Newfield directed more than 140 films. Newfield was so prolific that he directed pictures under the pseudonyms Sherman Scott and Peter Stewart to disguise the fact that one man was responsible for so much of the studio's product. As to be expected, much of Newfield's work is simply commercial dreck: *The Mad Monster* (1942), *I Accuse My Parents* (1944), *White Pongo* (1945) and *Queen of Burlesque* (1946), just to name a few.

A surprising number of distinguished actors appeared in PRC films (some whose careers were at a low ebb, others did so in between major studio assignments), including Erich von Stroheim (*The Mask of Diijon*), Bela Lugosi (*The Devil Bat*), Harry Langdon (*Misbehaving Husbands, House of Errors*), Elissa Landi (*Corregidor*), Richard Arlen (*Accomplice*), Edmund Lowe (*The Enchanted Forest*), Lee Tracy (*The Payoff*), Glenda Farrell (*A Night for Crime*), Anna May Wong (*Bombs Over Burma, Lady from Chungking*) and Buster Crabbe (*Jungle Man, Queen of Broadway, Nabonga, The Contender*, the Billy the Kid series).

Corporate History

PRC began as Producers Distributing Corporation, founded in the spring of 1939 by Ben Judell. (This was the name of the distribution unit; the film company was incorporated as Producers Pictures and initial releases carried this label.) Rather than sell off films on a states' rights (market by market) basis, Judell, a distributor-turned-producer, formed his own distribution system of franchises. Judell placed ads in exhibitor trade publications, promising to produce a series of low-budget features (mostly westerns) aimed at the small independent theater markets. Sigmund Neufeld, a veteran "quickie" producer, was made executive producer.

But after producing seven pictures, Judell had overextended himself to the point where PDC was facing bankruptcy. In April 1940 Sigmund Neufeld formed his own production company; thus Producers Distributing Corporation became Producers Releasing Corporation. Harry Rathner, who was in sales at PDC, became the president of PRC.

The new company struggled along for a few months until December 1940, at which time it was completely absorbed by the Pathe Corporation (although it would still retain the PRC title). O. Henry Briggs was appointed president of the reorganized company. Leon Fromkess, formerly Monogram Pictures' treasurer, was made general sales manager in charge of production; George Batcheller, who had previously headed Chesterfield Pictures, was made production supervisor.

In June 1942 Leon Fromkess was made production supervisor, replacing Batcheller who had resigned to join the armed forces. O. Henry Briggs resigned as president in early 1944, reportedly because of differences with the Youngs, a family of international financiers who controlled the Pathe Corporation. In July 1944 Leon Fromkess was chosen to take Briggs' place, but by September 1945 Fromkess announced his resignation, also citing differences with the Youngs and making it known that he was leaving at their request. Kenneth Young, board chairman, was then elected president.

In 1947 PRC was absorbed by the Eagle Lion Corporation, which was owned by British filmmaker J. Arthur Rank, who wanted to form an international distribution company. Later, Eagle Lion merged with United Artists.

The Feature Films of Producers Pictures Corporation (1939), Producers Distributing Corporation (1939-1940) and Producers Releasing Corporation (1940-1948)

This listing does not include the PRC productions *Hitler's Hangman* and *Strange Music*. *Hitler's Hangman* (directed by Douglas Sirk, produced by Seymour Nebenzal, and starring John Carradine, Alan Curtis and Patricia Morison) was sold to Metro-Goldwyn-Mayer; they released the picture in 1943 under the title *Hitler's Madman*. *Strange Music* (directed by Arthur Ripley, starring Francis Lederer, Sigrid Gurie and J. Edward Bromberg) was sold to United Artists, and the film was released in 1944 as *A Voice in the Wind*.

Also omitted are the Edward Small productions originally released through United Artists that were reissued by PRC; among the titles: *Kit Carson*, *The Last of the Mohicans*, *The Corsican Brothers* and *South of Pago Pago*.

Producers Pictures Corporation

1939

79. Hitler, Beast of Berlin (drama) Directed by Sherman Scott (Samuel Newfield). Produced by Ben Judell. Original story ("Goose Step") by Shepard Traube.

Cast: Roland Drew, Steffi Duna, Greta Granstedt, Bodil Rosing, Allan (Alan) Ladd, Vernon Dent, Hans Joby, Lucien Prival, John Ellis, George Rosener, Hans Von Twardowski, Willie Kaufman, Frederick Giermann, Clem Wilenchick, Henry von Zynda, John Voight, Hans Schumm, John Peters, Hans Von Morhart, Walter Stahl.

The story of a heroic underground group banded in opposition to Nazism.

Running time: 84 minutes. Release date: October 15, 1939.
Also known as *Beasts of Berlin* and *Goose Step*.
Reissued as *Hell's Devils*.

80. Torture Ship (drama) Directed by Victor Halperin. Produced by Ben Judell. Screenplay by George Wallace Sayre and Harvey Huntley. Suggested by the story "A Thousand Deaths" by Jack London.

Cast: Lyle Talbot, Jacqueline Wells (Julie Bishop), Sheila Bromley, Irving Pichel, Wheeler Oakman, Russell Hopton, Anthony Averill, Skelton Knaggs, Adia Kuznetzof, Stanley Blystone, Leander DeCordova, Julian Madison, Eddie Holden.

A scientist (Irving Pichel) takes a group of criminals to sea, planning to conduct experiments that may cure their criminal minds.
Running time: 62 minutes. Release date: October 28, 1939.

Producers Distributing Corporation

1939

81. Buried Alive (mystery) Directed by Victor Halperin. Produced by Ben Judell. Screenplay by George Bricker. Original story by William A. Ullman, Jr.

Cast: Beverly Roberts, Robert Wilcox, George Pembroke, Ted Osborne, Paul McVey, Alden Chase, Don Rowan, Peter Lynn, Norman Budd, Clem Wilenchick, Bob McKenzie, Wheeler Oakman, Robert Fiske, Joe Coits, Edward Earle, James H. McNamara.

A prison trustee (Robert Wilcox) is sentenced to die after he is framed for the murder of a prison guard.

Running time: 62 minutes. Release date: November 11, 1939.

82. The Invisible Killer (mystery) Directed by Sherman Scott (Samuel Newfield). Produced by Ben Judell. Screenplay by Joseph O'Donnell. From the novel "Murder for Millions" by Carter Wayne.

Cast: Grace Bradley, Roland Drew, William Newell, Alex Callam, Jeanne Kelly, Sidney Grayler, Boyd Irwin, David Oliver, Harry Worth, Ernie Adams.

A reporter (Grace Bradley) and her reporter boyfriend (Roland Drew) investigate three murders which were committed in the same mysterious manner.

Running time: 63 minutes. Release date: November 18, 1939.

Working title: *Wanted for Murder*.

Top: Frederick Giermann, Roland Drew, Allan (Alan) Ladd and an unidentified player in *Hitler, Beast of Berlin* (1939), Producers Distributing Corporation's first release (although PDC's first production was *Torture Ship*). The film met with censorship problems; some state censor boards refused to approve the picture because of the reference to Hitler in the title, while others turned it down because it had not been granted a Production Seal by the Motion Picture Association. After softening the title to *Beasts of Berlin*, it was finally approved as *Goose Step*. The film also marked an early screen appearance by Alan Ladd, then an obscure supporting player. After Ladd's subsequent stardom, the picture was reissued as *Hell's Devils*, with Ladd misleadingly given star billing. Bottom: Sheila Bromley, Lyle Talbot and Irving Pichel in *Torture Ship* (1939).

83. Mercy Plane (mystery) Directed by Richard Harlan. Produced by Ben Judell. Original screenplay by William Lively.

Cast: James Dunn, Frances Gifford, Matty Fain, William Pawley, Harry Harvey, Forbes Murray, Edwin Miller, Duke York.

A pilot (James Dunn) exposes a criminal ring which is stealing airplanes and selling them to foreign powers.

Running time: 72 minutes. Release date: December 4, 1939. Released in Great Britain as *Wonder Plane*.

1940

84. The Sagebrush Family Trails West (western) Directed by Peter Stewart (Sam Newfield). Produced by Sigmund Neufeld. Story and screenplay by William Lively.

Cast: Bobby Clark ("13-year-old World's Champion Junior Cowboy"), Earle Hodgins, Nina Guilbert, Joyce Bryant, Minerva Urecal, Archie Hall, Kenne Duncan, Forrest Taylor, Carl Mathews, Wally West, Byron Vance, Augie Gomez.

A young lad (Bobby Clark) tries to clear his father (Earle Hodgins) who has been falsely accused of thievery.

Running time: 60 minutes. Release date: January 14, 1940.

85. Texas Renegades (western) Directed by Peter Stewart (Sam Newfield). Produced by Sigmund Neufeld. Original screenplay by Joseph O'Donnell.

Cast: Tim McCoy, Nora Lane, Harry Harvey, Kenne Duncan, Lee Prather, Earl Gunn, Hal Price, Joe McGuinn, Raphael Bennett, Edward Cassidy.

A lawman (Tim McCoy) poses as an outlaw so he can infiltrate a gang terrorizing a western town.

Running time: 59 minutes. Release date: January 17, 1940.

Working title: *Swift Justice*.

Producers Releasing Corporation

1940

86. I Take This Oath (drama) Directed by Sherman Scott (Sam Newfield). Produced by Sigmund Neufeld. Screenplay by George Bricker. Story by William A. Ullman, Jr.

Cast: Gordon Jones, Joyce Compton, Craig Reynolds, J. Farrell Mac-Donald, Robert Homans, Guy Usher, Mary Gordon, Sam Flint, Brooks Benedict, Veda Ann Borg, Edward Peil, Sr., Budd Buster, Arthur Hoyt.

A rookie cop (Gordon Jones) sets out to avenge the murder of his police inspector father (Robert Homans) who was killed by the leader of a policy racket gang.

Running time: 67 minutes. Release date: May 20, 1940.
Working title: *Sons of the Finest*.

87. Frontier Crusader (western) Directed by Peter Stewart (Sam Newfield). Produced by Sigmund Neufeld. Screenplay by William Lively. Original story by Arthur Durlam.

Cast: Tim McCoy, Dorothy Short, Forrest Taylor, Ted Adams, John Merton, Lou Fulton, Karl Hackett, Hal Price, Kenne Duncan, Frank LaRue, George Chesebro, Frank Ellis, Carl Mathews, Reed Howes, Herman Hack, Sherry Tansey, Lane Bradford, Ray Henderson.

A freelance agent of law and order (Tim McCoy) pursues a gang of payroll thieves.

Running time: 62 minutes. Release date: June 1, 1940.

88. Hold That Woman! (comedy) Directed by Sherman Scott (Samuel Newfield). Produced by Sigmund Neufeld. Screenplay by George Bricker. Original story by Raymond L. Schrock and William Pierce.

Cast: James Dunn, Frances Gifford, George Douglas, Rita LeRoy, Martin Spellman, Eddie Fetherstone, Guy Usher, Paul Bryar, Edwin Miller, John Dilson, Dave O'Brien, Anna Lisa, Marie Rice, William Hall, Frank Meredith, Art Myers, William Newell, Jack Roper.

A skip tracer (James Dunn) finds a cache of stolen jewels hidden in a radio he has just repossessed.

Running time: 67 minutes. Release date: July 15, 1940.

89. Billy the Kid Outlawed (western) Directed by Peter Stewart (Sam Newfield). Produced by Sigmund Neufeld. Original screenplay by Oliver Drake.

Cast: Bob Steele, Al "Fuzzy" St. John, Louise Currie, Carleton Young, John Merton, Joe McGuinn, Ted Adams, Walter McGrail, Hal Price, Kenne Duncan, Reed Howes, George Chesebro, Steve Clark, Budd Buster.

Wrongfully accused of being an outlaw, Billy the Kid (Bob Steele) tries to clear himself by capturing a real bandit.

Running time: 52 minutes. Release date: July 20, 1940.

90. Gun Code (western) Directed by Peter Stewart (Sam Newfield). Produced by Sigmund Neufeld. Original screenplay by Joseph O'Donnell.

Lobby card for *The Sagebrush Family Trails West* (1940). The film was intended to be the first in a series of Sagebrush Family adventures, but plans were cancelled due to the poor reception of this initial entry.

Cast: Tim McCoy, Inna Gest (Ina Guest), Lou Fulton, Dave O'Brien, Alden (Stephen) Chase, Carleton Young, Ted Adams, Robert Winkler, George Chesebro, Jack Richardson, John Elliott, Carl Mathews.

A federal agent (Tim McCoy) goes after mobsters who are forcing merchants to pay protection money.

Running time: 54 minutes. Release date: August 3, 1940.

91. Marked Men (mystery) Directed by Sherman Scott (Samuel Newfield). Produced by Sigmund Neufeld. Screenplay by George Bricker. Original story by Harold Greene.

Cast: Warren Hull, Isabel Jewell, John Dilson, Paul Bryar, Charles Williams, Lyle Clement, Budd Buster, Al St. John, Eddie Fetherstone, Ted Erwin, Art Miles, Wolf the dog.

Wrongfully imprisoned for a crime he did not commit, a man (Warren Hull) tries to obtain a confession from the real crook.

Running time: 66 minutes. Release date: August 28, 1940.

92. Arizona Gangbusters (western) Directed by Peter Stewart (Sam Newfield). Produced by Sigmund Neufeld. Original screenplay by Joseph O'Donnell.

Bela Lugosi and friends in *The Devil Bat* (1940).

Cast: Tim McCoy, Pauline Haddon, Lou Fulton, Forrest Taylor, Julian Rivero, Arno Frey, Kenne Duncan, Jack Rutherford, Elizabeth LaMal, Otto Reichow, Lita Cortez, Carl Mathews, Ben Corbett, Frank Ellis, Curley Dresden.

A cowboy (Tim McCoy) thwarts the evil schemes of Nazi spies who have settled in Arizona.

Running time: 57 minutes. Release date: September 16, 1940.

93. Billy the Kid in Texas (western) Directed by Peter Stewart (Sam Newfield). Produced by Sigmund Neufeld. Original screenplay by Joseph O'Donnell.

Cast: Bob Steele, Al "Fuzzy" St. John, Terry Walker, Carleton Young, Charles King, John Merton, Frank LaRue, Charles "Slim" Whitaker, Curley Dresden, Tex Palmer, Chick Hannon, Merrill McCormack, Denver Dixon (Victor Adamson), Bob Woodward, Sherry Tansey, Herman Hack, Pasquel Perry.

Billy the Kid (Bob Steele) becomes sheriff and battles a gang of outlaws, one of whom is his brother.

Running time: 52 minutes. Release date: September 30, 1940.

94. Riders of Black Mountain (western) Directed by Peter Stewart (Sam Newfield). Produced by Sigmund Neufeld. Original screenplay by Joseph O'Donnell.

Cast: Tim McCoy, Pauline Haddon, Edward Peil, Sr., Frank LaRue, Rex Lease, Ralph Peters, Ted Adams, Julian Rivero, Jack Rutherford, George Chesebro, Dirk Thane, Carl Mathews.

A U. S. Marshal (Tim McCoy) poses as a gambler in order to investigate a series of stagecoach holdups.

Running time: 57 minutes. Release date: November 11, 1940.

95. The Devil Bat (horror) Directed by Jean Yarbrough (misspelled as Yarborough in credits). Produced by Jack Gallagher. Screenplay by John Thomas Neville. Story by Jack Bricker.

Cast: Bela Lugosi, Suzanne Kaaren, Dave O'Brien, Guy Usher, Yolande Mallott, Donald Kerr, Edward Mortimer, Gene O'Donnell, Alan Baldwin, John Ellis, Arthur Q. Bryan, Hal Price, John Davidson, Billy Griffith, Wally Rairdon.

Scientist Dr. Paul Carruthers (Bela Lugosi) breeds giant killer bats that attack the wearers of a specially prepared shaving lotion.

Running time: 68 minutes. Release date: December 12, 1940.

Also known as *Killer Bats*.

Sequel: *Devil Bat's Daughter* (PRC, 1946).

Remade as *The Flying Serpent* (PRC, 1946).

96. Misbehaving Husbands (comedy) Directed by William Beaudine. Produced by Ben Judell. Screenplay by Vernon Smith and Claire Parrish. Original story by Cea Sabin.

Cast: Harry Langdon, Betty Blythe, Ralph Byrd, Esther Muir, Gayne Whitman, Florence Wright, Luana Walters, Frank Jacquet, Charlotte Treadway, Byron Barr (Gig Young), Frank Hagney, Hennie Brown, Billy Mitchell, Mary McLaren, Gertrude Astor.

On their twentieth wedding anniversary, a wife (Betty Blythe) suspects her husband (Harry Langdon) of infidelity when it is reported that he was seen with another woman; unbeknownst to wifey, the "other woman" is actually a department store mannequin.

Running time: 65 minutes. Release date: December 20, 1940.

Also known as *Dummy Trouble*.

97. Billy the Kid's Gun Justice (western) Directed by Peter Stewart (Samuel Newfield). Produced by Sigmund Neufeld. Original screenplay by Oliver Drake.

Cast: Bob Steele, Al "Fuzzy" St. John, Louise Currie, Carleton Young, Charles King, Rex Lease, Kenne Duncan, Forrest Taylor, Ted Adams,

Al Ferguson, Karl Hackett, Edward Peil, Sr., Julian Rivero, Blanca Vischer.
Running time: 57 minutes. Release date: December 27, 1940.

1941

98. The Lone Rider Rides On (western) Directed by Sam Newfield. Produced by Sigmund Neufeld. Original screenplay by Joseph O'Donnell.

Cast: George Houston, Al "Fuzzy" St. John, Hillary Brooke, Lee Powell, Buddy Roosevelt, Al Bridge, Frank Hagney, Tom London, Karl Hackett, Forrest Taylor, Frank Ellis, Curley Dresden, Isabel LaMal, Harry Harvey, Jr., Don Forrest, Bob Kortman, Wally West, Steve Clark.

After twenty years, the Lone Rider (George Houston) returns home to track down the killers of his parents and brother.

Running time: 61 minutes. Release date: January 10, 1941.

99. Caught in the Act (comedy) Directed by Jean Yarbrough. Produced by Ted H. Richmond. Screenplay by Al Martin. Original story by Robert Cosgriff.

Cast: Henry Armetta, Iris Meredith, Robert Baldwin, Charles Miller, Inez Palange, Dick Terry, Joey Ray, Maxine Leslie, William Newell.

A construction foreman-turned-salesman (Henry Armetta) innocently becomes involved with a mob of building racketeers who practice a "shakedown" racket on construction companies.

Running time: 62 minutes. Release date: January 17, 1941.

Working title: *You Betcha My Life*.

100. Billy the Kid's Range War (western) Directed by Peter Stewart (Sam Newfield). Produced by Sigmund Neufeld. Original screenplay by William Lively.

Cast: Bob Steele, Al "Fuzzy" St. John, Joan Barclay, Rex Lease, Carleton Young, Milton Kibbee, Karl Hackett, Ted Adams, Julian Rivero, John Ince, Buddy Roosevelt, Ralph Peters, Alden Chase, Howard Masters, Charles King, George Chesebro, Steve Clark, Tex Palmer.

Billy the Kid (Bob Steele), wrongfully blamed for a series of murders, tries to thwart a plot to prevent the construction on a new stagecoach road.

Running time: 57 minutes. Release date: January 24, 1941.

101. Secret Evidence (mystery) Directed by William Nigh. Produced by E. B. Derr. Screenplay by Brenda Cline. Original story by Edward Bennett.

Cast: Marjorie Reynolds, Charles Quigley, Ward McTaggart, Kenneth Harlan, Donald Curtis, Howard Masters, Bob White, Kitty McHugh, Budd Buster, Charles Phipps, Dorothy Vaughn, Boyd Irwin.

Lobby card for *The Lone Rider Crosses the Rio* (1941), the second in a series of Lone Rider westerns (the character was a blatant imitation of the Lone Ranger).

A district attorney (Charles Quigley) puts an innocent man on trial in order to entrap the real killer.

Running time: 63 minutes. Release date: January 31, 1941.

102. The Lone Rider Crosses the Rio (western) Directed by Samuel Newfield. Produced by Sigmund Newfeld. Original screenplay by William Lively.

Cast: George Houston, Al "Fuzzy" St. John, Raquell Verria, Charles King, Alden Chase, Julian Rivero, Thornton Edwards, Howard Masters, Frank Ellis, Phillip Turich, Jan Wilsey (Buffalo Bill, Jr.), Frank Hagney.

While in old Mexico, the Lone Rider (George Houston) and Fuzzy (Al St. John) try to help a romance between two young lovers.

Running time: 63 minutes. Release date: February 28, 1941.

103. Outlaws of the Rio Grande (western) Directed by Peter Stewart (Sam Newfield). Produced by Sigmund Neufeld. Original screenplay by George H. Plympton.

Cast: Tim McCoy, Virginia Carpenter, Charles King, Ralph Peters, Karl Hackett, Rex Lease, Phillip Turich, Frank Ellis, Kenne Duncan, Thornton Edwards, Joe Dominguez, George Chesebro, Sherry Tansey.

Feature Films 1941   43

A border marshal (Tim McCoy) is out to bag a gang of counterfeiters, unmask their leader, and avenge the death of a friend.
Running time: 63 minutes. Release date: March 7, 1941.

104. Federal Fugitives (mystery-drama) Directed by William Beaudine. Produced by John T. Neville. Story and screenplay by Martin Mooney.

Cast: Neil Hamilton, Doris Day (not the same Doris Day who would later star in a series of musicals and sex farces), Victor Varconi, Charles Wilson, Emmett Vogan, Gerald Oliver Smith, Jack Mulhall, Lyle Latell, George Carlton, Frank Shannon, Betty Blythe, Frank Moran.

A secret service officer (Neil Hamilton), assigned to probe the deaths of three fellow officers, poses as a partner of an airplane manufacturer (Emmett Vogan) in order to investigate two men (Victor Varconi, Charles Wilson) who are anxious to take over the plant.
Running time: 66 minutes. Release date: March 29, 1941.

105. Billy the Kid's Fighting Pals (western) Directed by Sherman Scott (Sam Newfield). Produced by Sigmund Neufeld. Original screenplay by George H. Plympton.

Cast: Bob Steele, Al "Fuzzy" St. John, Phyllis Adair, Carleton Young, Charles King, Curley Dresden, Edward Peil, Sr., Hal Price, George Chesebro, Forrest Taylor, Budd Buster, Julian Rivero, Wally West, Ray Henderson, Art Dillard.

Billy the Kid (Bob Steele) and his pals (Al St. John, Carleton Young) arrive in Paradise, a town which is being victimized by a local banker.
Running time: 62 minutes. Release date: April 18, 1941.
Working titles: *Billy the Kid Trails West* and *Trigger Pals*.

106. South of Panama (action-drama) Directed by Jean Yarbrough. Produced by Ted H. Richmond. Story and screenplay by Ben Roberts and Sidney Sheldon.

Cast: Roger Pryor, Virginia Vale, Lionel Royce, Lucien Prival, Duncan Renaldo, Lester Dorr, Jack Ingram, Hugh Beaumont, Warren Jackson, Sam McDaniel.

Enemy agents mistake an innocent bystander (Roger Pryor) for a government chemist.
Running time: 68 minutes. Release date: May 2, 1941.

107. Emergency Landing (action-drama) Directed by William Beaudine. Produced by Jed Buell. Story and screenplay by Martin Mooney.

Cast: Forrest Tucker, Carol Hughes, Evelyn Brent, Emmett Vogan, William Halligan, Joaquin Edwards, George Sherwood, I. Stanford Jolley, Stanley Price, Jack Lescoulie, Paul Scott.

Foreign agents sabotage a robot-controlled airplane developed by a test pilot (Forrest Taylor) and a weather bureau observer (Emmett Vogan).
Running time: 79 minutes. Release date: May 9, 1941.

108. The Lone Rider in Ghost Town (western) Directed by Sam Newfield. Produced by Sigmund Neufeld. Original screenplay by William Lively.

Cast: George Houston, Al "Fuzzy" St. John, Alaine Brandes, Budd Buster, Frank Hagney, Alden (Stephen) Chase, Reed Howes, Charles King, George Chesebro, Edward Peil, Sr., Archie Hall, Jan Wilsey (Buffalo Bill, Jr.), Karl Hackett, Don Forrest, Frank Ellis, Curley Dresden, Steve Clark, Byron Vance, Jack Ingram, Augie Gomez, Lane Bradford.

Tom Cameron (George Houston), the Lone Rider, helps rid a frontier town of crooked racketeers who jump the claims of local gold prospectors.
Running time: 64 minutes. Release date: May 16, 1941.

109. Paper Bullets (drama) Directed by Phil Rosen. Produced by Maurice and Frank Kozinsky (King Brothers). Story and screenplay by Martin Mooney. A K-B Production.

Cast: Joan Woodbury, John Archer, Linda Ware, Jack LaRue, Vince Barnett, Gavin Gordon, Philip Trent, William Halligan, Allan (Alan) Ladd, George Pembroke, Selmer Jackson, Kenneth Harlan, Bryant Washburn, Alden (Stephen) Chase, Robert Strange, Alex Callam.

A woman (Joan Woodbury) aids an undercover agent (John Archer) to obtain evidence against a mobster (Jack LaRue).
Running time: 72 minutes. Release date: June 13, 1941.
Also known as *Crime, Inc.* and *Gangs, Inc.*

110. Criminals Within (drama) Directed by Joseph H. Lewis. Produced by E. B. Derr. Screenplay by Edward Bennett. Original story by Arthur Hoerl.

Cast: Eric Linden, Ann Doran, Constance Worth, Donald Curtis, Weldon Heyburn, Ben Alexander, Dudley Dickerson, Bernice Pilot, Ray Erlenborn, I. Stanford Jolley, Emmett Vogan, Robert Frazer, Boyd Irwin, William Ruhl.

An army private (Eric Linden) tries to clear himself when he's accused of stealing a list containing the names of five scientists working on an explosive formula.
Running time: 70 minutes. Release date: June 27, 1941.

111. Double Cross (drama) Directed by Albert Kelley. Produced by John G. Bachmann. Screenplay by Milton Raison and Ron Ferguson. Original story by John A. Albert.

Cast: Kane Richmond, Pauline Moore, Wynne Gibson, John Miljan, Richard Beach, Mary Gordon, Robert Homans, William Halligan, Frank

Jack LaRue, John Archer and Joan Woodbury in *Paper Bullets* (1941). In the supporting cast was a young actor named Allan (Alan) Ladd; because of his subsequent stardom, *Paper Bullets* was reissued as *Gangs, Inc.*, with Ladd given star billing.

Moran, Charles "Heine" Conklin, Daisy Ford, Edward Keane, Walter Shumway, Ted Wray, Jimmie Fox, Harry Harvey.

A police officer (Kane Richmond) tries to clear the name of a friend (Richard Beach) who was wrongfully accused of murdering a fellow officer.

Running time: 61 minutes. Release date: June 27, 1941.

Also known as *Motorcycle Squad*.

112. Desperate Cargo (drama) Directed by William Beaudine. Produced by John T. Coyle. Screenplay by Morgan Cox and John T. Coyle. Based on the story "Loot Below" by Eustace L. Adams.

Cast: Ralph Byrd, Carol Hughes, Julie Duncan, Jack Mulhall, I. Stanford Jolley, Kenneth Harlan, Richard Clarke, Johnstone White, Paul Bryar, Don Forrest, Loretta Russell, Thornton Edwards.

A purser (Ralph Byrd) and a showgirl (Carol Hughes) become involved with a band of airplane hi-jackers.

Running time: 69 minutes. Release date: July 4, 1941.

113. Billy the Kid in Santa Fe (western) Directed by Sherman Scott (Sam Newfield). Produced by Sigmund Neufeld. Original screenplay by Joseph O'Donnell.

Cast: Bob Steele, Al "Fuzzy" St. John, Rex Lease, Marin Sais, Dennis Moore, Karl Hackett, Charles King, Frank Ellis, Dave O'Brien, Kenne Duncan, Hal Price, Curley Dresden.

Billy the Kid (Bob Steele), framed on a murder charge, escapes from jail and heads for Santa Fe, where he tries to get a confession from the real killer.

Running time: 66 minutes. Release date: July 11, 1941.

114. The Texas Marshal (western) Directed by Peter Stewart (Sam Newfield). Produced by Sigmund Neufeld. Original screenplay by William Lively.

Cast: Tim McCoy, Art Davis and His Rhythm Riders, Kay Leslie, Karl Hackett, Edward Peil, Sr., Charles King, Budd Buster, John Elliott, Dave O'Brien, Wilson Edwards, Byron Vance, Frank Ellis.

A Texas Marshal (Tim McCoy) clashes with a phony "league of patriots," which is a front for a gold mine–grabbing gang.

Running time: 58 minutes. Release date: July 13, 1941.

115. Gambling Daughters (drama) Directed by Max Nosseck. Produced by Ted H. Richmond. Screenplay by Joel Kay and Arnold Phillips. Original story by Sidney Sheldon and Ben Roberts.

Cast: Cecilia Parker, Roger Pryor, Robert Baldwin, Gale Storm, Sig Arno, Janet Shaw, Charles Miller, Eddie Foster, Alfred Hall, Judy Kilgore, Gertrude Messinger, Marvelle Andre, Roberta Smith.

Two students (Gale Storm, Janet Shaw) enrolled in an exclusive girls school become embroiled in the blackmailing schemes of a mysterious gambler (Roger Pryor).

Running time: 67 minutes. Release date: August 1, 1941.

116. The Lone Rider in Frontier Fury (western) Directed by Sam Newfield. Produced by Sigmund Neufeld. Original screenplay by Fred Myton.

Cast: George Houston, Al "Fuzzy" St. John, Hillary Brooke, Karl Hackett, Ted Adams, Archie Hall, Budd Buster, Virginia Card, Edward Peil, Sr., John Elliott, Tom London, Frank Ellis, Dan White, Horace B. Carpenter, Tex Cooper, Tex Palmer, Curley Dresden, Wally West, Herman Hack.

When the owner of the JB Ranch is shot by a mysterious stranger, Tom Cameron (George Houston), the Lone Rider, is wrongfully accused of the murder.

Running time: 62 minutes. Release date: August 8, 1941.

117. The Lone Rider Ambushed (western) Directed by Sam Newfield. Produced by Sigmund Neufeld. Original screenplay by Oliver Drake.

Cast: George Houston, Al "Fuzzy" St. John, Maxine Leslie, Frank Hagney, Jack Ingram, Hal Price, Ted Adams, George Chesebro, Ralph Peters, Steve Clark, Carl Mathews, Charles King.

The Lone Rider (George Houston), posing as a jailed crook who is his lookalike, helps to prove the innocence of a bank teller accused of robbery.

Running time: 67 minutes. Release date: August 29, 1941.

118. Reg'lar Fellers (comedy) Produced and directed by Arthur Dreifuss. Screenplay by Arthur Hoerl, Arthur Dreifuss and William C. Kent. Story by Arthur Hoerl. Based on the comic strip by Gene Byrnes.

Cast: Billy Lee, Carl "Alfalfa" Switzer, Buddy Boles, Janet Dempsey, Jerry Wilson, Malcolm Hutton, Danna Callahan, Sarah Padden, Roscoe Ates, Maren Mayo, Sharon Lynne, Netta Packer, Jack C. Smith, Marguerite De LaMotte, Pat O'Malley, Ann Ruth Hughes, Don Stowell, Lew Luana, Daisy Ford, Herb Vigran, Billy Lee's Band with the Meglin Glee Club.

The "Reg'lar Fellers" (Billy Lee, Carl Switzer, Buddy Boles, Janet Dempsey, Jerry Wilson, Malcolm Hutton) thwart the plans of two crooks (Don Stowell, Lew Luana) out to bilk a wealthy eccentric (Sarah Padden).

Running time: 65 minutes. Release date: September 5, 1941.

119. Dangerous Lady (mystery-comedy) Produced and directed by Bernard B. Ray. Screenplay by Jack Natteford. Story by Leslie T. White. Additional dialogue by Sidney Sheldon.

Cast: Neil Hamilton, June Storey, Douglas Fowley, John Holland, Emmett Vogan, Evelyn Brent, Greta Granstedt, Carl Stockdale, Jack Mulhall, Kenneth Harlan, John Ince, Terry Walker, James Aubrey, Ward McTaggart.

A private detective (Neil Hamilton) and his attorney wife (June Storey) help prove the innocence of a woman (Evelyn Brent) falsely accused of murder.

Running time: 67 minutes. Release date: September 12, 1941.

120. Billy the Kid Wanted (western) Directed by Sherman Scott (Sam Newfield). Produced by Sigmund Neufeld. Original screenplay by Fred Myton.

Cast: Buster Crabbe, Al "Fuzzy" St. John, Dave O'Brien, Glenn Strange, Choti Sherwood, Charles King, Charles "Slim" Whitaker, Howard Masters, Joe Newfield, Budd Buster, Frank Ellis, Curley Dresden, Wally West.

After being framed for a crime they didn't commit, Billy the Kid (Buster Crabbe) and his pals (Al St. John, Dave O'Brien) hide out with friendly ranchers.

Running time: 64 minutes. Release date: October 4, 1941.

121. Jungle Man (adventure) Directed by Harry Fraser. Produced by Ted H. Richmond. Original story and screenplay by Rita Douglas.

Cast: Buster Crabbe, Sheila Darcey, Charles Middleton, Vince Barnett, Weldon Heyburn, Robert Carson, Paul Scott, Hal Price, Floyd Shakleforth.

A German U-Boat sinks a ship carrying a serum used to cure jungle fever; when his sweetheart (Sheila Darcey) is stricken ill, a doctor (Buster Crabbe) makes plans to dive and retrieve the medication.

Running time: 63 minutes. Release date: October 10, 1941.

122. Hard Guy (drama) Directed by Elmer Clifton. Produced by George M. Merrick and Max Alexander. Original story and screenplay by Oliver Drake.

Cast: Jack LaRue, Mary Healy, Kane Richmond, Iris Adrian, Gayle Millott, Jack Mulhall, Howard Banks, Ben Taggart, Montague Shaw, Inna Gest (Ina Guest), Arthur Gardner.

A gangster (Jack LaRue) operates a marriage racket out of his nightclub. After a showgirl is killed, her sister (Mary Healy) and a detective (Kane Richmond) set out to bring the mobster to justice.

Running time: 68 minutes. Release date: October 17, 1941.

Released in Great Britain as *Professional Bride*.

123. Mr. Celebrity (comedy-drama) Directed by William Beaudine. Produced by Martin Mooney. Original story and screenplay by Martin Mooney.

Cast: Robert "Buzzy" Henry, James Seay, Doris Day (not the same Doris Day who would later star in a series of musicals and sex farces), William Halligan, Gavin Gordon, Johnny Berkes, Jack Baxley, Larry Gray, John E. Ince, Frank Hagney, Jack Richardson, Alfred Hall, Francis X. Bushman, Clara Kimball Young, Jim Jeffries.

An orphaned boy (Robert "Buzzy" Henry) fights to stay under the custody of his veterinarian uncle (James Seay) who is training a winning racehorse.

Running time: 66 minutes. Release date: November 1, 1941.

124. The Lone Rider Fights Back (western) Directed by Sam Newfield. Produced by Sigmund Neufeld. Original screenplay by Joseph O'Donnell.

Cast: George Houston, Al "Fuzzy" St. John, Dorothy Short, Dennis Moore, Frank Hagney, Charles King, Frank Ellis, Hal Price, Jack O'Shea, Merrill McCormack.

Tom Cameron (George Houston), alias The Lone Rider, and Fuzzy (Al St. John) arrive at the ranch of Uncle Joe Hawkes, only to find their old friend murdered. Cameron then joins a gang of outlaws, hoping to obtain enough evidence against the killer.

Running time: 64 minutes. Release date: November 7, 1941.

125. The Miracle Kid (drama) Directed by William Beaudine. Produced by John T. Coyle. Story and screenplay by Gerald D. Adams, Henry Sucher and John T. Coyle. From an idea by Harry Sucher.

Cast: Tom Neal, Carol Hughes, Vicki Lester, Betty Blythe, Ben Taggart, Alex Callam, Thornton Edwards, Joe Grey, Paul Bryar, Pat Glesch, Billy McGown, John Ince, Gene O'Donnell, Warren Jackson, Larry McGrath, Sam Lufkin.

Against the wishes of his fiancee (Carol Hughes), a professional boxer (Tom Neal) signs a contract to fight as "Kid Hex."

Running time: 69 minutes. Release date: November 14, 1941.

126. Swamp Woman (drama) Directed by Elmer Clifton. Produced by George M. Merrick and Max Alexander. Screenplay by Arthur G. Durlam. Original story by Fred McConnell.

Cast: Ann Corio, Jack LaRue, Mary Hull, Ian MacDonald, Richard Deane, Jay Novello, Lois Austin, Earl Gunn, Guy Wilkerson, Jimmy Aubrey, Carlin Sturdevant.

Honky-tonk dancer Annabelle Tollington (Ann Corio) returns to the swamplands to resume her romance with Peter Oliver (Jack LaRue), only to learn he is intent on marrying another woman (Mary Hull).

Running time: 68 minutes. Release date: December 5, 1941.

Also known as *Swamp Lady*.

127. Billy the Kid's Roundup (western) Directed by Sherman Scott (Sam Neufield). Produced by Sigmund Neufeld. Original screenplay by Fred Myton.

Cast: Buster Crabbe, Al "Fuzzy" St. John, Carleton Young, Joan Barclay, Glenn Strange, Charles King, Charles "Slim" Whitaker, John Elliott, Dennis Moore, Kenne Duncan, Curley Dresden, Dick Cramer, Wally West, Tex Palmer, Tex Cooper, Horace B. Carpenter, Jim Mason.

Billy the Kid (Buster Crabbe) and his pals (Al St. John, Carleton Young) combat a gang of outlaws responsible for kidnapping a newspaper editor's daughter (Joan Barclay).

Running time: 58 minutes. Release date: December 12, 1941.

128. Law of the Timber (adventure) Produced and directed by Bernard B. Ray. Screenplay by Jack Natteford. Adapted from the story "The Speck on the Wall" by James Oliver Curwood.

Cast: Marjorie Reynolds, Monte Blue, J. Farrell MacDonald, Hal Brazeal, Earle Ebe, Sven-Hugo Borg, George Humbert, Milburn Morante, Betty Zoadman, Eddie Phillips, Zero the dog.

After her father is killed in a forest fire, a young woman (Marjorie Reynolds) takes charge of his lumber company.

Running time: 63 minutes. Release date: December 19, 1941.

129. The Blonde Comet (action-drama) Directed by William Beaudine. Produced by Ted H. Richmond. Screenplay by Martin Mooney. Original story by Philip Juergens and Robin Daniels.

Cast: Virginia Vale, Robert Kent, Barney Oldfield, Vince Barnett, William Halligan, Joey Ray, Rod Knight, Diana Hughes.

After establishing a reputation in Europe, a racing automobilist (Virginia Vale) journeys to America where she meets another racer (Robert Kent) and a state of rivalry is created.

Running time: 67 minutes. Release date: December 26, 1941.

1942

130. Texas Man Hunt (western) Directed by Peter Stewart (Sam Newfield). Produced by Sigmund Neufeld. Original screenplay by William Lively.

Cast: Bill "Cowboy Rambler" Boyd, Art Davis, Lee Powell, Julie Duncan, Frank Hagney, Karl Hackett, Dennis Moore, Arno Frey, Frank Ellis, Eddie Phillips, Kenne Duncan.

The Frontier Marshals (Bill "Cowboy Rambler" Boyd, Art Davis, Lee Powell) lock horns with a rancher (Frank Hagney), a banker (Karl Hackett) and an enemy agent (Arno Frey), ringleaders of a gang of saboteurs.

Running time: 60 minutes. Release date: January 2, 1942.

131. The Lone Rider and the Bandit (western) Directed by Sam Newfield. Produced by Sigmund Neufeld. Screenplay by Steve Braxton (Sam Robins).

Cast: George Houston, Al "Fuzzy" St. John, Dennis Moore, Vicki Lester, Glenn Strange, Jack Ingram, Carl Sepulveda, Milt Kibbee, Lloyd "Arkansas Slim" Andrews, Eddie Dean, Charles "Slim" Whitaker, Hal Price, Kenne Duncan, Curley Dresden.

Tom Cameron (George Houston), the Lone Rider, poses as an infamous outlaw in order to learn the identity of the real bandit.

Running time: 54 minutes. Release date: January 16, 1942.

132. Duke of the Navy (adventure) Directed by William Beaudine. Produced by John T. Coyle. Story and screenplay by Gerald D. Adams, William Beaudine and John T. Coyle.

Cast: Ralph Byrd, Veda Ann Borg, Stubby Kruger, Herbert Corthell, Margaret Armstrong, Val Stanton, Paul Bryar, Sammy Cohen, Red Knight, Lester Towne, William Beaudine, Jr., Zack Williams.

On furlough, Breezy Duke (Ralph Byrd) and his sidekick Cookie (Stubby Kruger) are offered the use of the "Duke suite" at an expensive hotel because of their identical names. A phony adventurer, thinking the boys are rich, offers to cut them in on some hidden treasure for two

thousand dollars, so the gobs borrow the money from their shipmates and head for San Torga Island, where the fortune is supposed to be located.
Running time: 65 minutes. Release date: January 23, 1942.

133. Today I Hang (mystery) Directed by George M. Merrick and Oliver Drake. Produced by Max Alexander and Alfred Stern. Original story and screenplay by Oliver Drake.
Cast: Walter Woolf King, Mona Barrie, William Farnum, Harry Woods, James Craven, Michael Raffetto, Sam Bernard, Robert Fiske, Paul Scardon.
A jewelry salesman (Walter Woolf King) is framed for murder; with the help of the victim's widow (Mona Barrie) he tries to clear himself.
Running time: 63 minutes. Release date: January 30, 1942.

134. Broadway Big Shot (action-comedy) Directed by William Beaudine. Produced by Jed Buell. Original story and screenplay by Martin Mooney.
Cast: Ralph Byrd, Virginia Vale, William Halligan, Dick Rich, Herbert Rawlinson, Cecile Weston, Tom Herbert, Stubby Kruger, Frank Hagney, Jack Buckley, Harry Deep, Jack Roper, Al Goldsmith, John Ince, Alfred Hall, James Aubrey, Dick Cramer, Jack Cheatham, Jack Perrin.
A reporter (Ralph Byrd) has himself imprisoned so he can gain evidence from a convict who took the rap for a racketeer's crimes.
Running time: 59 minutes. Release date: February 6, 1942.

135. Raiders of the West (western) Directed by Peter Stewart (Sam Newfield). Produced by Sigmund Neufeld. Original screenplay by Oliver Drake.
Cast: Bill "Cowboy Rambler" Boyd, Art Davis, Lee Powell, Virginia Carroll, Rex Lease, Charles King, Glenn Strange, Charles "Slim" Whitaker, Milt Kibbee, Lynton Brent, John Elliott, Eddie Dean, Curley Dresden, William Desmond, Dale Sherwood, Kenne Duncan, Bill Cody, Jr., Reed Howes, Hal Price, Fred "Snowflake" Toones, Carl Sepulveda, Frank Ellis, John (Bob) Cason.
The Frontier Marshals (Bill "Cowboy Rambler" Boyd, Art Davis, Lee Powell) pose as horse traders in an attempt to get information about a mysterious counterfeiting ring.
Running time: 60 minutes. Release date: February 20, 1942.

136. Billy the Kid Trapped (western) Directed by Sherman Scott (Sam Newfield). Produced by Sigmund Neufeld. Original screenplay by Oliver Drake.
Cast: Buster Crabbe, Al "Fuzzy" St. John, Bud McTaggart, Anne Jeffreys, Glenn Strange, Walter McGrail, Ted Adams, Jack Ingram, Milton

Kibbee, Eddie Phillips, Budd Buster, Jack Kinney, Jimmy Aubrey, Wally West, Bert Dillard, Kenne Duncan, George Chesebro, Carl Mathews, Dick Cramer, Ray Henderson, Curley Dresden, Augie Gomez, Horace B. Carpenter, Herman Hack, James Mason, Hank Bell, Oscar Gahan.

A bandit, posing as Billy the Kid, commits a crime; the real Billy (Buster Crabbe) then tries to bring him to justice.

Running time: 59 minutes. Release date: February 27, 1942.

137. Too Many Women (comedy) Produced and directed by Bernard B. Ray. Story and screenplay by Eddie M. Davis.

Cast: Neil Hamilton, June Lang, Joyce Compton, Barbara Read, Matt McHugh, Marlo Dwyer, Fred Sherman, Kate McKenna, Maurice Cass, Bertram Marburgh, George Davis, Dora Clement, Harry Holman, Tom Herbert, Pat Gleason, Leonard St. Leo, Frank Hagney, Patsy Moran, Marjorie Haynes, Adele Smith, Adele Kerr, Harry Johnson, Charles Hutchinson.

When word gets out that he's wealthy, a man (Neil Hamilton) finds himself pursued by marriage-minded females.

Running time: 67 minutes. Release date: February 27, 1942.

Working title: *Girl Trouble.*

138. Girls Town (drama) Directed by Victor Halperin. Produced by Lou Brock and Jack Schwarz. Screenplay by Gene Kerr and Victor McLeod.

Cast: Edith Fellows, June Storey, Kenneth Howell, Anna Q. Nilsson, Warren Hymer, Alice White, Vince Barnett, Paul Dubov, Peggy Ryan, Bernice Kay, Helen McCloud, Charlie Williams.

Two sisters — one a beauty contest winner (June Storey), the other an "ugly duckling" type (Edith Fellows) — journey to Hollywood, with hopes of becoming movie stars.

Running time: 69 minutes. Release date: March 6, 1942.

139. Rodeo Rhythm (western) Directed by Fred Neumeyer. Produced by Leo J. McCarthy. Screenplay by Gene Tuttle and Eugene Allen. Original story by Leo J. McCarthy.

Cast: Fred Scott, Patricia Redpath, The Ray Knapp Rough Riders, Lori Bridge, Pat Dunn, Jack Cooper, John Frank, Doc Hartley, London Laird, Raylene Smith, Vernon Brown, Donna Lee Meinke, Gloria Morse.

Orphans perform in a rodeo show in order to raise funds to pay the mortgage on their home.

Running time: 72 minutes. Release date: March 13, 1942.

140. The Lone Rider in Cheyenne (western) Directed by Sam Newfield. Produced by Sigmund Neufeld. Original screenplay by Oliver Drake and Elizabeth Beecher.

Edith Fellows, June Storey and Kenneth Howell in *Girls Town* (1942).

Cast: George Houston, Al "Fuzzy" St. John, Dennis Moore, Ella Neal, Roy Barcroft, Kenne Duncan, Lynton Brent, Milt Kibbee, Jack Holmes, Karl Hackett, Jack Ingram, George Chesebro.

The Lone Rider (George Houston) runs afoul with stagecoach bandits and helps to clear an innocent man (Dennis Moore) of a murder charge.

Running time: 59 minutes. Release date: March 20, 1942.

141. Dawn Express (mystery) Directed by Albert Herman. Produced by George M. Merrick and Max Alexander. Original story and screenplay by Arthur St. Claire.

Cast: Michael Whalen, Anne Nagel, Constance Worth, William Bakewell, Hans Von Twardowski, Jack Mulhall, George Pembroke, Kenneth Harlan, Robert Fraser, Hans Von Morhart, Michael Vallin, Maurice Costello.

A scientist (Michael Whalen) responsible for developing a gasoline substitute is suspected of being a member of a Nazi spy ring.

Running time: 66 minutes. Release date: March 27, 1942.

Also known as *The Nazi Spy Ring*.

142. The Strangler (mystery) Directed by Harold Huth. Produced by Walter C. Mycroft. Screenplay by J. Lee Thompson and Lesley Storm. From the novel by Gordon Beckles.

Cast: Judy Campbell, Sebastian Shaw, Niall MacGinnis, Henry

Harry Langdon and Marian Marsh in *House of Errors* (1942).

Edwards, George Pughe, Martita Hunt, George Hayes, Cameron Hall, Edana Romney, Bunty Payne, Charles Victor, Frederick Piper, June Corda.

A reporter (Judy Campbell) and a novelist (Sebastian Shaw) try to uncover the identity of a mysterious killer who uses silk stockings to strangle young women.

Running time: 79 minutes. Release date: April 3, 1942.

A British National Picture, produced and released in Great Britain as *East of Piccadilly*; released in the U. S. by PRC.

143. House of Errors (comedy) Directed by Bernard B. Ray. Produced by George R. Batcheller and Bernard B. Ray. Screenplay by Ewart Adamson and Eddie M. Davis. Story by Harry Langdon.

Cast: Harry Langdon, Charles Rogers, Marian Marsh, Ray Walker, John Holland, Betty Blythe, Vernon Dent.

Two messenger boys (Harry Langdon, Charles Rogers), aspiring to be reporters, pass themselves off as servants in order to gain entry to a scientist's home and learn about his invention—a new type of machine gun.

Running time: 67 minutes. Release date: April 10, 1942.

Working title: *Gun Shy*.

144. Rolling Down the Great Divide (western) Directed by Peter Stewart (Sam Newfield). Produced by Sigmund Neufeld. Original screenplay by George Milton (George Wallace Sayre and Milton Raison).

Cast: Bill "Cowboy Rambler" Boyd, Art Davis, Lee Powell, Wanda

Glenn Strange carries off a young victim in *The Mad Monster* (1942), PRC's answer to *The Wolf Man* (Universal, 1941).

McKay, Glenn Strange, Karl Hackett, J. Merrill Holmes, Ted Adams, Jack Ingram, John Elliott, George Chesebro, Horace B. Carpenter, Jack Roper, Curley Dresden, Dennis Moore, Tex Palmer.

The Frontier Marshals (Bill Boyd, Art Davis, Lee Powell) hunt cattle rustlers who make their plans via a secret mobile shortwave station.

Running time: 59 minutes. Release date: April 24, 1942.

145. Billy the Kid's Smoking Guns (western) Directed by Sherman Scott (Sam Newfield). Produced by Sigmund Neufeld. Original screenplay by George Milton (George Wallace Sayre and Milton Raison).

Cast: Buster Crabbe, Al "Fuzzy" St. John, Dave O'Brien, Joan Barclay, John Merton, Milton Kibbee, Ted Adams, Frank Ellis, Karl Hackett, Budd Buster, Joel Newfield, Charles "Slim" Whitaker, Bert Dillard.

Billy the Kid (Buster Crabbe) and his cohorts (Al St. John, Dave O'Brien) battle a gang of outlaws who resort to underhanded business tactics and even murder in order to force ranchers off their property.

Running time: 58 minutes. Release date: May 1, 1942.

Released in Great Britain as *Smoking Guns*.

146. Inside the Law (comedy-drama) Directed by Hamilton MacFadden. Produced by Dixon R. Harwin. Original screenplay by Jack Natteford.

Cast: Wallace Ford, Frank Sully, Harry Holman, Luana Walters,

Lafayette McKee, Barton Hepburn, Danny Duncan, Earle Hodgins, Rose Plummer.

A gang of crooks gain control of a small-town bank and plan to flee with the loot, but have a change of heart.

Running time: 62 minutes. Release date: May 8, 1942.

147. The Panther's Claw (mystery) Directed by William Beaudine. Produced by Lester Cutler. Screenplay by Martin Mooney. Original story by Anthony Abbott.

Cast: Sidney Blackmer, Rick Vallin, Byron Foulger, Herbert Rawlinson, Gerta Rogan, Lynn Starr, Barry Bernard, John Ince, Martin Ashe, Joaquin Edwards, Walter James, William Costello, Billy Mitchell, Florence O'Brien.

Police Commissioner Thatcher Colt (Sidney Blackmer) tries to prove the innocence of a man (Byron Foulger) suspected of murdering the star of an opera troupe.

Running time: 75 minutes. Release date: May 8, 1942.

148. The Mad Monster (horror) Directed by Sam Newfield. Produced by Sigmund Neufeld. Original screenplay by Fred Myton.

Cast: George Zucco, Johnny Downs, Anne Nagel, Glenn Strange, Robert Strange, Mae Busch, Sarah Padden, Henry Hall, Edward Cassidy, Eddie Holden, John Elliott, Charles "Slim" Whitaker, Gil Patric, Gordon DeMain, Reginald Barlow.

A scientist (George Zucco), conducting experiments involving wolf blood, transforms a slow-witted handyman (Glenn Strange) into a beast and uses him to exact revenge on his enemies.

Running time: 72 minutes. Release date: May 15, 1942.

149. Men of San Quentin (drama) Directed by William Beaudine. Produced by Martin Mooney and Max King. Screenplay by Ernest Booth. Original story by Martin Mooney.

Cast: J. Anthony Hughes, Eleanor Stewart, Dick Curtis, Charles Middleton, Jeffrey Sayre, George Breakston, Art Mills, Michael Mark, John Ince, Joe Whitehead, Skins Miller, Jack Shay, Jack Cheatham, Drew Demarest, Nancy Evans.

A progressive guard (J. Anthony Hughes) tries to change the conditions in a corrupt prison.

Running time: 78 minutes. Release date: May 22, 1942.

150. Gallant Lady (drama) Directed by William Beaudine. Produced by Lester Cutler. Screenplay by Arthur St. Claire. Original story by Octavius Roy Cohen.

Cast: Rose Hobart, Sidney Blackmer, Claire Rochelle, Lynn Starr,

Vince Barnett, Jack Baxley, Crane Whitney, John Ince, Frank Brownley, Richard Clarke, Spec O'Donnell, Inez Call, Pat McKee, Ruby Dandridge, Henry Hastings.

Convicted for a mercy killing, a doctor (Rose Hobart) seeks refuge at the home of a country medico (Sidney Blackmer).

Running time: 63 minutes. Release date: May 24, 1942.

Also known as *Prison Girls*.

151. Bombs Over Burma (adventure-mystery) Directed by Joseph H. Lewis. Produced by Alfred Stern and Arthur Alexander. Original screenplay by Milton Raison and Joseph H. Lewis.

Cast: Anna May Wong, Noel Madison, Leslie Denison, Nedrick Young, Dan Seymour, Frank Lackteen, Judith Gibson, Dennis Moore, Connie Leon, Hayward Soo Hoo, Richard Loo, Paul Fung.

A Chinese teacher (Anna May Wong) is assigned the task of learning the identity of the spy who is leaking information about the Burma Road convoys to the Japanese.

Running time: 62 minutes. Release date: June 5, 1942.

152. Texas Justice (western) Directed by Sam Newfield. Produced by Sigmund Neufeld. Original screenplay by Steve Braxton (Sam Robins).

Cast: George Houston, Al "Fuzzy" St. John, Dennis Moore, Wanda McKay, Claire Rochelle, Archie Hall, Charles "Slim" Whitaker, Edward Peil, Sr., Karl Hackett, Julian Rivero, Curley Dresden, Dirk Thane, Horace B. Carpenter, Steve Clark, Frank Ellis, Merrill McCormack, Ray Jones.

Running time: 58 minutes. Release date: June 5, 1942.

Also known as *The Lone Rider in Texas Justice*.

153. They Raid by Night (action-drama) Directed by Spencer Gordon Bennet. Produced by Dixon R. Harwin. Screenplay by Jack Natteford.

Cast: Lyle Talbot, June Duprez, Victor Varconi, George Neise, Charles Rogers, Paul Baratoff, Leslie Denison, Crane Whitney, Sven Hugo Borg, Eric Wilton, Pierce Lyden, John Beck, William Kellogg, Robert C. Fisher, Sigfrid Tor, Brian O'Hara.

Two commandos (Lyle Talbot, Victor Varconi) are sent to Norway to liberate an imprisoned general (Paul Baratoff).

Running time: 72 minutes. Release date: July 3, 1942.

Subtitled: *A Story of the Commandos*.

154. Tumbleweed Trail (western) Directed by Peter Stewart (Sam Newfield). Produced by Sigmund Neufeld. Screenplay by Fred Myton.

Cast: Bill "Cowboy Rambler" Boyd, Art Davis, Lee Powell, Marjorie Manners, Jack Rockwell, Charles King, Karl Hackett, George Chesebro,

Buster Crabbe romances burlesque queen Ann Corio in *Jungle Siren* (1942).

Frank Hagney, Reed Howes, Curley Dresden, George Morrell, Jack Montgomery, Art Dillard, Steve Clark, Dan White, Augie Gomez.

Running time: 57 minutes. Release date: July 10, 1942.

155. Prisoner of Japan (action-drama) Directed by Arthur Ripley. Produced by Seymour Nebenzal. Screenplay by Robert Chapin and Arthur Ripley. Story by Edgar G. Ulmer.

Cast: Alan Baxter, Gertrude Michael, Ernest Dorian, Corinna Mura, Dwight Frye, Tommy Seidel, Bill Boya, Ray Bennett, Dave O'Brien, Ann Staunton, Beal Wong, Gilbert Frye, Kent Thurber.

An astronomical researcher (Alan Baxter), stationed on a Pacific island, is captured by Japanese troops. His base is turned into an enemy outpost.

Running time: 64 minutes. Release date: July 22, 1942.

156. A Yank in Lybia (adventure) Directed by Albert Herman. Produced by George M. Merrick. Original story and screenplay by Arthur St. Claire and Sherman Lowe.

Cast: Walter Woolf King, Joan Woodbury, H. B. Warner, Duncan Renaldo, Parkyarkarkus (Harry Einstein), George Lewis, William Vaughn, Howard Banks, Amarillo Morris.

An American correspondent (Walter Woolf King) becomes embroiled in a Nazi plot to incite Lybian tribes to attack a British garrison.

Running time: 67 minutes. Release date: July 31, 1942.

157. Law and Order (western) Directed by Sherman Scott (Sam Newfield). Produced by Sigmund Neufeld. Original screenplay by Sam Robins.

Cast: Buster Crabbe, Al "Fuzzy" St. John, Dave "Tex" O'Brien, Sarah Padden, Wanda McKay, Charles King, Hal Price, John Merton, Kenne Duncan, Ted Adams, Budd Buster, Kermit Maynard.

Billy the Kid (Buster Crabbe) impersonates a deceased army officer in order to save the dead man's aunt (Sarah Padden) from an ill-fated marriage.

Running time: 56 minutes. Release date: August 21, 1942.

Also known as *Billy the Kid in Law and Order*.

Released in Great Britain as *Double Alibi*.

158. Jungle Siren (adventure) Directed by Sam Newfield. Produced by Sigmund Neufeld. Screenplay by George Wallace Sayre and Sam Robins. Original story by George Wallace Sayre and Milton Raison.

Cast: Ann Corio, Buster Crabbe, Evelyn Wahl, Milton Kibbee, Paul Bryar, Arno Frey, Jess Brooks, Manart Kippen, James Adamson.

Nazi forces in Africa attempt to incite the natives to rebel against white residents; a young woman (Ann Corio) raised in the jungle and a conscientious American (Buster Crabbe) try to stop them.

Running time: 68 minutes. Release date: August 21, 1942.

159. Prairie Pals (western) Directed by Peter Stewart (Sam Newfield). Produced by Sigmund Neufeld. Original screenplay by Patricia Harper.

Cast: Bill "Cowboy Rambler" Boyd, Art Davis, Lee Powell, Charles King, Esther Estrella, John Merton, J. Merrill Holmes, Kermit Maynard, I. Stanford Jolley, Karl Hackett, Bob Burns, Al St. John, Al Taylor, Art Dillard, Curley Dresden, Frank McCarroll, Bill Patton, Carl Mathews, Frank Ellis, Jack Kinney, Morgan Flowers.

The Frontier Marshals (Bill "Cowboy Rambler" Boyd, Art Davis, Lee Powell) go to the rescue of a kidnapped research scientist.

Running time: 60 minutes. Release date: September 4, 1942.

160. Baby Face Morgan (comedy-drama) Directed by Arthur Dreifuss. Produced by Jack Schwarz. Screenplay by Edward Dein and Jack Rubin. Story by Oscar Brodney and Jack Rubin.

Cast: Richard Cromwell, Mary Carlisle, Robert Armstrong, Chick Chandler, Warren Hymer, Charles Judels, Vince Barnett, Ralf Harolde, Teddy Peterson, Hal Dawson, Pierce Lyden, Sam Bernard, Kenny Chryst.

Because his father was a notorious gangster, a young man (Richard Cromwell) is forced to pose as a tough racketeer.

Running time: 63 minutes. Release date: September 15, 1942.

161. Border Roundup (western) Directed by Sam Newfield. Produced by Sigmund Neufeld. Original screenplay by Stephen Worth.

Cast: George Houston, Al "Fuzzy" St. John, Dennis Moore, Patricia Knox, Charles King, I. Stanford Jolley, Edward Peil, Sr., Jimmy Aubrey, John Elliott, Dale Sherwood, Nick Thompson, Frank Ellis, Curley Dresden, Lynton Brent.

The Lone Rider (George Houston) and his pals (Al St. John, Dennis Moore) clash with crooks who are after a gold mine.

Running time: 60 minutes. Release date: September 18, 1942.

Also known as *The Lone Rider in Border Roundup*.

162. **Tomorrow We Live** (drama) Directed by Edgar G. Ulmer. Produced by Seymour Nebenzal. Story and screenplay by Bert Lytton. An Atlantic Pictures Production.

Cast: Jean Parker, Ricardo Cortez, Emmett Lynn, William Marshall, Roseanne Stevens, Ray Miller, Frank Hagney, Rex Lease, Jack Ingram, Barbara Slater, Jane Hale.

An innocent young woman (Jean Parker) falls into the clutches of a psychopathic gangster (Ricardo Cortez).

Running time: 64 minutes. Release date: September 29, 1942.

163. **Along the Sundown Trail** (western) Directed by Peter Stewart (Sam Newfield). Produced by Sigmund Neufeld. Screenplay by Arthur St. Claire.

Cast: Bill "Cowboy Rambler" Boyd, Art Davis, Lee Powell, Julie Duncan, Kermit Maynard, Charles King, Howard Masters, Karl Hackett, John Merton, Jack Ingram, Ted Adams, Herman Hack, Frank Ellis, Jack Holmes, Reed Howes, Al St. John, Augie Gomez, Art Dillard, Al Taylor, Tex Palmer, Curley Dresden, Steve Clark, Hal Price, Jimmy Aubrey, Roy Bucko, Buck Bucko.

The Frontier Marshals (Bill "Cowboy Rambler" Boyd, Art Davis, Lee Powell) go after a crooked superintendent who is stealing valuable ore from a tungsten mine.

Running time: 60 minutes. Release date: October 1, 1942.

164. **Sheriff of Sage Valley** (western) Directed by Sherman Scott (Sam Newfield). Produced by Sigmund Neufeld. Original screenplay by Milton Raison and George Wallace Sayre.

Cast: Buster Crabbe, Al "Fuzzy" St. John, Dave "Tex" O'Brien, Maxine Leslie, Charles King, John Merton, Kermit Maynard, Hal Price, Curley Dresden, Jack Kirk, Lynton Brent.

After the sheriff of Sage Valley is murdered, Billy the Kid (Buster Crabbe) takes his place and cleans up the town.

Running time: 56 minutes. Release date: October 2, 1942.

Also known as *Billy the Kid, Sheriff of Sage Valley*.

Feature Films 1942

165. City of Silent Men (drama) Directed by William Nigh. Produced by Darwin R. Harwin. Screenplay by Joseph Hoffman. Original story by Robert E. Kent and Joseph Hoffman.

Cast: Frank Albertson, June Lang, Jan Wiley, Dick Curtis, Richard Clarke, William Gould, Emmett Lynn, Pat Gleason, Barton Hepburn, Frank Jacquet, Frank Ferguson, Richard Bailey, Jack Baxley, William Kellogg, Charles Jordan.

The mayor of a small town helps ex-convicts establish a canning factory that will hire other ex-cons and help them lead a straight life.

Running time: 64 minutes. Release date: October 12, 1942.

166. Secrets of a Co-Ed (mystery-drama) Directed by Joseph H. Lewis. Produced by Alfred Stern and Arthur Alexander. Original screenplay by George Wallace Sayre.

Cast: Otto Kruger, Tina Thayer, Rick Vallin, Russell Hoyt, Marcia Mae Jones, Geraldine Spreckles, Diana Del Rio, Herbert Vigran, Patricia Knox, Claire Rochelle, Addison Richards, Isabel LaMal.

To the dismay of her defense attorney father (Otto Kruger), a college student (Tina Thayer) becomes romantically involved with a slimy gangster (Rick Vallin) who is the secret boss of a mob of gamblers.

Running time: 67 minutes. Release date: October 26, 1942.

Released in Great Britain as *Silent Witness*.

167. The Yanks Are Coming (musical-comedy) Directed by Alexis Thurn-Taxis. Produced by Lester Cutler. Screenplay by Arthur St. Claire and Sherman Lowe. Original story by Tony Stern, Lee Pollack and Edward E. Kaye.

Cast: Henry King and his orchestra, Mary Healy, Dave O'Brien, Little Jackie Heller, "Slapsic" Maxie Rosenbloom, William Roberts, Parkyarkarkus (Harry Einstein), Dorothy Dare, Lynn Starr, Jane Novak, Charles Purcell, Forrest Taylor, Lew Pollack.

Two young lovers (Mary Healy, Dave O'Brien) who work for Henry King's Band are separated when he enlists in the army.

Running time: 65 minutes. Release date: November 9, 1942.

168. The Mysterious Rider (western) Directed by Sherman Scott (Sam Newfield). Produced by Sigmund Neufeld. Original screenplay by Steve Braxton (Sam Robins).

Cast: Buster Crabbe, Al "Fuzzy" St. John, Caroline Burke, John Merton, Jack Ingram, Charles "Slim" Whitaker, Kermit Maynard, Ted Adams, Guy Wilkerson, Edwin Brien, Frank Ellis.

Billy the Kid (Buster Crabbe) prevents two young people from being swindled out of their gold mine inheritance.

Running time: 56 minutes. Release date: November 20, 1942.
Also known as *Billy the Kid in the Mysterious Rider*.
A 40-minute version was reissued in 1947 under the title *Panhandle Trail*.

169. Miss V from Moscow (suspense-drama) Directed by Albert Herman. Produced by George M. Merrick. Original story and screenplay by Arthur St. Claire and Sherman Lowe. An M & H Production.

Cast: Lola Lane, Noel Madison, Howard Banks, Paul Weigel, John Vosper, Anna Demetria, William Vaughn, Juan De LaCruz, Kathryn Sheldon, Victor Kendall, Richard Kipling.

A Soviet agent (Lola Lane) in occupied Paris masquerades as a dead German spy and comes to the aid of a downed Allied flyer (Howard Banks).

Running time: 71 minutes. Release date: November 23, 1942.
Also known as *Intrigue in Paris*.

170. Outlaws of Boulder Pass (western) Directed by Sam Newfield. Produced by Sigmund Neufeld. Original screenplay by Steve Braxton (Sam Robins).

Cast: George Houston, Al "Fuzzy" St. John, Dennis "Smokey" Moore, Marjorie Manners, Charles King, I. Stanford Jolley, Karl Hackett, Ted Adams, Kenne Duncan, Frank Ellis, Steve Clark, Jimmy Aubrey, Budd Buster.

The Lone Rider (George Houston) and his pals (Al St. John, Dennis Moore) try to get the goods on a gang charging illegal cattle tolls.

Running time: 60 minutes. Release date: November 28, 1942.
Also known as *The Lone Rider in Outlaws of Boulder Pass*.

171. Boss of Big Town (mystery-drama) Directed by Arthur Dreifuss. Produced by Jack Schwarz. Screenplay by Edward Dein. Original story by Arthur Hoerl.

Cast: John Litel, Florence Rice, H. B. Warner, Jean Brooks, John Miljan, David Bacon, Mary Gordon, Frank Ferguson, John Maxwell, Paul Dubov, Lloyd Ingraham, Patricia Prest.

A city market official (John Litel) battles a gang trying to seize control of a food distribution market.

Running time: 64 minutes. Release date: December 7, 1942.

172. Overland Stagecoach (western) Directed by Sam Newfield. Produced by Sigmund Neufeld. Original screenplay by Steve Braxton (Sam Robins).

Cast: Bob Livingston, Al "Fuzzy" St. John, Dennis "Smokey" Moore, Julie Duncan, Glenn Strange, Charles King, Art Mix, Budd Buster, Ted Adams, Julian Rivero, John Elliott, Tex Cooper.

The Lone Rider (Bob Livingston) and his pals (Al St. John, Dennis Moore) go after a crooked partner in a stagecoach line who is sabotaging the railroad's efforts to expand.
Running time: 58 minutes. Release date: December 11, 1942.
Also known as *The Lone Rider in Overland Stagecoach*.

173. **Lady from Chungking** (action-drama) Directed by William Nigh. Produced by Alfred Stern and Arthur Alexander. Screenplay by Sam Robins. Original story by Milton Raison and Sam Robins.
Cast: Anna May Wong, Harold Huber, Mae Clarke, Rick Vallin, Paul Bryar, Ted Hecht, Louis Donath, James Leong, Archie Got, Walter Soo Hoo.
A Chinese patriot (Anna May Wong), the daughter of a wealthy family, secretly heads a band of guerillas fighting the Japanese troops.
Running time: 66 minutes. Release date: December 21, 1942.

174. **The Rangers Take Over** (western) Directed by Albert Herman. Produced by Alfred Stern and Arthur Alexander. Original story and screenplay by Elmer Clifton.
Cast: Dave "Tex" O'Brien, James Newill, Guy Wilkerson, Iris Meredith, Forrest Taylor, I. Stanford Jolley, Charles King, Carl Mathews, Harry Harvey, Lynton Brent, Bud Osborne, Cal Shrum and the Rhythm Rangers.
A Texas Ranger (Dave "Tex" O'Brien) infiltrates a band of rustlers.
Running time: 60 minutes. Release date: December 25, 1942.

1943

175. **Man of Courage** (drama) Directed by Alexis Thurn-Taxis. Produced by Lester Cutler. Screenplay by Arthur St. Claire, Barton MacLane and John Vlahos. Original story by Barton MacLane, Herman Ruby and Lew Pollack.
Cast: Barton MacLane, Charlotte Wynters, Lyle Talbot, Dorothy Burgess, Forrest Taylor, John Ince, Jane Novak, Patsy Nash, Erskine Johnson, Claire Grey, Steve Clark, Billy Gray, Frank Yaconelli.
A governor (Barton MacLane) becomes romantically involved with a suspected murderess (Charlotte Wynters).
Running time: 67 minutes. Release date: January 4, 1943.

176. **The Payoff** (mystery) Directed by Arthur Dreifuss. Produced by Jack Schwarz. Screenplay by Edward Dein. Original story by Arthur Hohl.

Cast: Lee Tracy, Tom Brown, Tina Thayer, Evelyn Brent, Jack LaRue, Ian Keith, Robert Middlemass, John Maxwell, John Sheehan, Harry Bradley, Forrest Taylor, Pat Costello.

A star reporter (Lee Tracy) investigates the murder of a special prosecutor who was preparing evidence against a racketeer (Jack LaRue).

Running time: 74 minutes. Release date: January 21, 1943.

177. The Kid Rides Again (western) Directed by Sherman Scott (Sam Newfield). Produced by Sigmund Neufeld. Original screenplay by Fred Myton.

Cast: Buster Crabbe, Al "Fuzzy" St. John, Iris Meredith, Glenn Strange, Charles King, I. Stanford Jolley, Edward Peil, Sr., Ted Adams, Charles "Slim" Whitaker, Snub Pollard, Karl Hackett, Kenne Duncan, Curley Dresden, John Merton.

Billy the Kid (Buster Crabbe) is falsely accused of committing a train robbery and sets out to find the real holdup man.

Running time: 57 minutes. Release date: January 27, 1943.

Also known as *Billy the Kid Rides Again*.

178. Dead Men Walk (horror) Directed by Sam Newfield. Produced by Sigmund Neufeld. Original screenplay by Fred Myton.

Cast: George Zucco, Mary Carlisle, Nedrick Young, Dwight Frye, Fern Emmett, Robert Strange, Hal Price, Sam Flint.

A doctor (George Zucco) murders his twin brother (also played by Zucco); when the latter returns as a vampire, it is the doctor who is blamed for the resulting deaths.

Running time: 63 minutes. Release date: February 10, 1943.

179. Wild Horse Rustlers (western) Directed by Sam Newfield. Produced by Sigmund Neufeld. Original screenplay by Steve Braxton (Sam Robins).

Cast: Bob Livingston, Al "Fuzzy" St. John, Linda Johnson, Lane Chandler, Stanley Price, Frank Ellis, Karl Hackett, Jimmy Aubrey, Kansas Moehring, Silver Harr.

The Lone Rider (Bob Livingston) thwarts a Nazi plot to sabotage an army horse procurement program.

Running time: 58 minutes. Release date: February 12, 1943.

Also known as *The Lone Rider in Wild Horse Rustlers*.

180. A Night for Crime (mystery) Directed by Alex Thurn-Taxis. Produced by Lester Cutler. Screenplay by Arthur St. Claire and Sherman Lowe. Original story by Jimmy Starr.

Cast: Glenda Farrell, Lyle Talbot, Lina Basquette, Donald Kirk, Ralph Sanford, Forrest Taylor, Rick Vallin, Lynn Starr, Edna Harris, Marjorie

Echoing his role in the horror classic *Frankenstein* (Universal, 1931), Dwight Frye played an evil hunchback in *Dead Men Walk* (1943).

Manners, Joseph DeVillard, Niels Bogge, Ruby Dandridge, Florence O'Brien, Robert Frazer, Jimmy Starr, Erskine Johnson, Edwin Schallert, Harry Crocker.

A female reporter (Glenda Farrell) investigates the murder of a movie extra (Marjorie Manners) and the disappearance of a film star (Lina Basquette) in the middle of a picture's production.

Running time: 78 minutes. Release date: February 18, 1943.

181. Bad Men of Thunder Gap (western) Directed by Al Herman. Produced by Alfred Stern and Arthur Alexander. Original story and screenplay by Elmer Clifton.

Cast: Dave "Tex" O'Brien, Jim Newill, Guy Wilkerson, Janet Shaw, Jack Ingram, Charles King, Tom London, Michael Vallon, Lucille Vance, I. Stanford Jolley, Bud Osborne, Jimmy Aubrey, Artie Ortego, Cal Shrum and His Rhythm Rangers (Robert Hoag, Don Weston, Rusty Cline, Art Wenzel).

The Texas Rangers (Dave O'Brien, Jim Newill) ride into town as part of a medicine show to investigate the plight of miners whose supply wagons are being held up.

Running time: 57 minutes. Release date: March 5, 1943.

A 40-minute version was reissued in 1947 under the title *Thundergap Outlaws*.

182. Queen of Broadway (drama) Directed by Sam Newfield. Produced by Bert Sternbach. Screenplay by Rusty McCullough and George Wallace Sayre. Original story by George Wallace Sayre.

Cast: Rochelle Hudson, Buster Crabbe, Paul Bryar, Donald Mayo, Emmett Lynn, Vince Barnett, Jack Mulhall, Isabel LaMal, Blanche Rose, Henry Hall, John Dilson, Milton Kibbee, Fred "Snowflake" Toones.

A gambler (Rochelle Hudson) tries to adopt a young orphan (Donald Mayo).

Running time: 62 minutes. Release date: March 8, 1943.

183. Behind Prison Walls (comedy) Directed by Steve Sekely. Produced by Arthur Ripley. Screenplay by Van Norcross. Original story by W. A. Ullman, Jr.

Cast: Alan Baxter, Gertrude Michael, Tully Marshall, Edwin Maxwell, Jacqueline Dalya, Matt Willis, Olga Sabin, Richard Kipling, Isabelle Winters, Lane Chandler, Paul Everton, George Guhl, Regina Wallace.

A business tycoon (Tully Marshall) and his son (Alan Baxter) are sent to prison, where they continue to outwit scheming rivals who are attempting to take over the father's business.

Running time: 64 minutes. Release date: March 22, 1943.

184. Corregidor (drama) Directed by William Nigh. Produced by Dixon R. Harwin and Edward Finney. Original story and screenplay by Doris Malloy and Edgar G. Ulmer. An Atlantis Pictures Production.

Cast: Otto Kruger, Elissa Landi, Donald Woods, Frank Jenks, Rick Vallin, Wanda McKay, Ian Keith, Ruby Dandridge, Eddie Hall, Charles Jordan, Ted Hecht, Frank Hagney, Frank Jacquet, Jack Rutherford, I. Stanford Jolley, John Grant, Jimmy Vilan, Gordon Hayes, Forrest Taylor.

Three doctors (Otto Kruger, Elissa Landi, Donald Woods) witness the heroic stand by U. S. forces against the Japanese at Corregidor.

Running time: 74 minutes. Release date: March 29, 1943.

185. Fugitive of the Plains (western) Directed by Sam Newfield. Produced by Sigmund Neufeld. Original screenplay by George Wallace Sayre.

Cast: Buster Crabbe, Al "Fuzzy" St. John, Maxine Leslie, Kermit Maynard, Jack Ingram, Karl Hackett, Hal Price, Budd Buster, Artie Ortego, Carl Sepulveda.

A female outlaw (Maxine Leslie) and her gang falsely implicate Billy the Kid (Buster Crabbe) for their crimes.

Running time: 57 minutes. Release date: April 1, 1943.
Also known as *Billy the Kid in Fugitive of the Plains.*
A 40-minute version was reissued in 1947 under the title *Raiders of Red Rock.*

186. My Son, the Hero (comedy) Directed by Edgar G. Ulmer. Produced by Leon Fromkess. Original screenplay by Doris Malloy and Edgar G. Ulmer. An Atlantis Pictures Production.

Cast: Patsy Kelly, Roscoe Karns, Joan Blair, Carol Hughes, Maxie Rosenbloom, Luis Alberni, Joseph Allen, Jr., Lois Collier, Jennie LeGon, Nick Stewart, Hal Price, Al St. John, Isabel LaMal, Elvira Curcy, Maxine Leslie.

A broken-down fight manager (Roscoe Karns) puts on a false front of affluence to try to impress his son (Joseph Allen, Jr.), a heroic war correspondent.

Running time: 68 minutes. Release date: April 5, 1943.

187. The Ghost and the Guest (comedy) Directed by William Nigh. Produced by Arthur Alexander and Alfred Stern. Screenplay by Morey Amsterdam. Original story by Milt Gross.

Cast: James Dunn, Florence Rice, Mabel Todd, Sam McDaniel, Robert Dudley, Eddy Chandler, Jim Toney, Robert Bice, Renee Carson, Anthony Warde, Anthony Caruso, Eddie Foster.

Newlyweds (James Dunn, Florence Rice) honeymooning in an eerie country house encounter gangsters searching for hidden diamonds.

Running time: 61 minutes. Release date: April 19, 1943.

188. Terror House (mystery) Directed by Leslie Arliss. Produced by John Argyle. Screenplay by John Argyle and Leslie Arliss. From the novel by Alan Kennington.

Cast: James Mason, Joyce Howard, Mary Clare, Tucker McGuire, John Fernald, Wilfrid Lawson, Dorothy Black, Amy Daley.

During a terrific thunderstorm, two schoolteachers (Joyce Howard, Tucker McGuire) hiking in the Yorkshire Moors are forced to take shelter in the home of a shellshocked musician (James Mason).

Running time: 79 minutes. Release date: April 19, 1943.

Produced and released in Great Britain by Associated British Pathe as *The Night Has Eyes* (1942); released in the U. S. by PRC.

189. Death Rides the Plains (western) Directed by Sam Newfield. Produced by Sigmund Neufeld. Screenplay by Joseph O'Donnell. Original story by Patricia Harper.

Cast: Bob Livingston, Al "Fuzzy" St. John, Nica Doret, Ray Bennett,

I. Stanford Jolley, George Chesebro, John Elliott, Kermit Maynard, Charles "Slim" Whitaker, Karl Hackett, Frank Ellis, Ted Mapes, Dan White, Jimmy Aubrey.

The Lone Rider (Bob Livingston) goes after a gang of outlaws who are killing off prospective land buyers.

Running time: 56 minutes. Release date: May 7, 1946.

Also known as *The Lone Rider in Death Rides the Plains*.

190. West of Texas (western) Directed by Oliver Drake. Produced by Alfred Stern and Arthur Alexander. Original screenplay by Oliver Drake.

Cast: Dave "Tex" O'Brien, Jim Newill, Guy Wilkerson, Frances Gladwin, Madilyn Hare, Robert Barron, Tom London, Jack Rockwell, Jack Ingraham, Art Fowler, Roy Butler.

The Texas Rangers (Dave O'Brien, Jim Newill) go to Mexico to set up a ranger outfit that will protect ranchers from land-grabbing railroad surveyors.

Running time: 54 minutes. Release date: May 10, 1943.

A 40-minute version was reissued in 1947 under the title *Shootin' Irons*.

191. Western Cyclone (western) Directed by Sam Newfield. Produced by Sigmund Neufeld. Original screenplay by Patricia Harper.

Cast: Buster Crabbe, Al "Fuzzy" St. John, Marjorie Manners, Karl Hackett, Milton Kibbee, Glenn Strange, Charles King, Hal Price, Kermit Maynard, Frank Ellis, Frank McCarroll, Artie Ortego, Herman Hack, Al Haskell.

When a young woman (Marjorie Manners) is kidnapped, Billy the Kid (Buster Crabbe) is wrongfully accused of the crime.

Running time: 56 minutes. Release date: May 14, 1943.

Also known as *Billy the Kid in Western Cyclone*.

A 40-minute version was reissued in 1947 under the title *Frontier Fighters*.

192. Girls in Chains (drama) Directed by Edgar G. Ulmer. Produced by Peter R. Van Duinen. Screenplay by Albert Beich. Story by Edgar G. Ulmer.

Cast: Arline Judge, Roger Clark, Robin Raymond, Barbara Pepper, Dorothy Burgess, Clancy Cooper, Allan Bryon, Patricia Knox, Sid Melton, Russell Gage, Emmett Lynn, Richard Clarke, Betty Blythe, Peggy Stewart, Beverly Boyd, Bob Hill, Henry Hall, Crane Whitney, Francis Ford, Mrs. Gardener Crane.

A teacher (Arline Judge) valiantly tries to correct the conditions in a corrupt reform school.

Running time: 71 minutes. Release date: May 17, 1943.

193. The Black Raven (mystery) Directed by Sam Newfield. Produced by Sigmund Neufeld. Original screenplay by Fred Myton.

Cast: George Zucco, Wanda McKay, Robert Randall (Bob Livingston), Noel Madison, Byron Foulger, Charles Middleton, Glenn Strange, Robert Middlemass, I. Stanford Jolley.

Caught in a storm, a young couple (Wanda McKay, Robert Randall) are among the various people stranded at a mysterious roadside inn called "The Black Raven."

Running time: 64 minutes. Release date: May 31, 1943.

194. Border Buckeroos (western) Directed by Oliver Drake. Produced by Alfred Stern and Arthur Alexander. Original screenplay by Oliver Drake.

Cast: Dave "Tex" O'Brien, Jim Newill, Guy Wilkerson, Christine McIntyre, Eleanor Counts, Charles King, Jack Ingram, Ethan Laidlaw, Michael Vallon, Kenne Duncan, Reed Howes, Kermit Maynard, Bud Osborne.

Texas Rangers Tex Wyatt (Dave O'Brien) and Jim Steele (Jim Newill) pose as a gunman and a ranch heir, respectively, in order to keep a valuable ranch and mine from falling into the hands of a gang who murdered the former owner.

Running time: 59 minutes. Release date: June 15, 1943.

195. Wolves of the Range (western) Directed by Sam Newfield. Produced by Sigmund Neufeld. Original story and screenplay by Joseph O'Donnell.

Cast: Bob Livingston, Al "Fuzzy" St. John, Frances Gladwin, I. Stanford Jolley, Karl Hackett, Edward Cassidy, Jack Ingram, Kenne Duncan, Budd Buster, Robert Hill, Charles "Slim" Whitaker, Jack Holmes, Roy Bucko.

The Lone Rider (Bob Livingston) and Fuzzy (Al St. John) go to the aid of ranchers when the head of the Cattleman's Association starts a reign of terror to drive them off their properties so he can put through an irrigation project.

Running time: 69 minutes. Release date: June 21, 1943.

196. Follies Girl (musical) Produced and directed by William Rowland. Screenplay by Marcy Klauber and Charles Robinson. Story by Marcy Klauber and Art Jarrett. Additional dialogue by Pat. C. Flick and Lew Hearn.

Cast: Wendy Barrie, Doris Nolan, Gordon Oliver, Anne Barrett, Arthur Pierson, J. C. Nugent, Cora Witherspoon, William Harrigan, Jay Brennan, Lew Hearn, Cliff Hall, Marion McGuire, Pat C. Flick, Anthony Blair, Jerri Blanchard, Serjei Radamsky, G. Swayne Gordon, Ray Heatherton and his band, Johnny Long and his band, Bobby Byrne and his band,

Ernie Holst and his band, Claire and Arene, The Charles Weidman Dancers, The Song Spinners, The Heat Waves, Lazare and Castellanos, Fritzi Scheff, Hal Thompson.

A young soldier (Gordon Oliver) mistakenly believes that his father (J. C. Nugent), a railroad magnate who owns a costume company, is having an affair with a burlesque queen (Wendy Barrie).

Running time: 72 minutes. Release date: June 26, 1943.

197. Submarine Base (drama) Directed by Albert Kelley. Produced by Jack Schwarz. Original screenplay by Arthur St. Claire and George Merrick.

Cast: John Litel, Alan Baxter, Fifi D'Orsay, Eric Blore, Iris Adrian, George Metaxa, Luis Alberni, Jacqueline Dalya, George Lee, Rafael Storm, Anna Demetria, Lucien Prival.

Off the coast of Brazil, a New York racketeer (John Litel) sabotages several Nazi submarines.

Running time: 65 minutes. Release date: July 20, 1943.

198. Fighting Valley (western) Directed by Oliver Drake. Produced by Alfred Stern and Arthur Alexander. Original screenplay by Oliver Drake.

Cast: Dave "Tex" O'Brien, Jim Newill, Guy Wilkerson, Patti McCarthy, John Merton, Robert Bice, Stanley Price, Mary McLaren, John Elliott, Charles King, Dan White, Carl Mathews, Curley Dresden, Jimmy Aubrey, Jess Cavin.

The Texas Rangers (Dave O'Brien, Jim Newill) try to find out who's been hijacking the ore from a smelting mine.

Running time: 58 minutes. Release date: August 8, 1943.

199. Isle of Forgotten Sins (adventure-drama) Directed by Edgar G. Ulmer. Produced by Peter R. Van Duinen. Screenplay by Raymond L. Schrock. Original story by Edgar G. Ulmer.

Cast: John Carradine, Gale Sondergaard, Sidney Toler, Frank Fenton, Rita Quigley, Veda Ann Borg, Rick Vallin, Tala Birell, Patti McCarthy, Marian Colby, William Edmonds, Betty Amann.

Two pearl divers (John Carradine, Frank Fenton) plot to retrieve a shipment of $3,000,000 in gold aboard a sunken vessel.

Running time: 86 minutes. Release date: August 15, 1943.

Also known as *Monsoon*.

200. Cattle Stampede (western) Directed by Sam Newfield. Produced by Sigmund Neufeld. Original story and screenplay by Joseph O'Donnell.

Cast: Buster Crabbe, Al "Fuzzy" St. John, Frances Gladwin, Charles King, Edward Cassidy, Hansel Warner, Ray Bennett, Frank Ellis, Steve Clark, Roy Brent, John Elliott, Budd Buster, Hank Bell, Tex Cooper, Ted Adams, Frank McCarroll, Ray Jones, Rose Plummer, George Morrell.

Billy the Kid (Buster Crabbe) and Fuzzy Q. Jones (Al St. John) help a group of Oklahoma ranchers in their fight against cattle rustlers.
Running time: 58 minutes. Release date: August 16, 1943.
Also known as *Billy the Kid in Cattle Stampede*.

201. Danger! Women at Work (comedy) Directed by Sam Newfield. Produced by Jack Schwarz. Screenplay by Martin Mooney. Story by Gertrude Walker and Edgar G. Ulmer.

Cast: Patsy Kelly, Mary Brian, Isabel Jewell, Wanda McKay, Betty Compson, Cobina Wright, Jr., Allan Byron, Warren Hymer, Vince Barnett, Michael Kirk, Charles King, Jack Ingram.

A woman (Patsy Kelly) inherits a trucking firm; she and her friends (Mary Brian, Isabel Jewell) decide to take over the business.
Running time: 59 minutes. Release date: August 23, 1943.

202. The Renegade (western) Directed by Sam Newfield. Produced by Sigmund Neufeld. Screenplay by Joseph O'Donnell. Original story by George Milton (George Wallace Sayre and Milton Raison).

Cast: Buster Crabbe, Al "Fuzzy" St. John, Lois Ransom, Karl Hackett, Ray Bennett, Frank Hagney, Jack Rockwell, Tom London, George Chesebro, Jimmy Aubrey, Carl Sepulveda, Dan White, Wally West.

Billy the Kid (Buster Crabbe) and Fuzzy (Al St. John) smash a land-grabbing operation designed to wreck the local bank as well as obtain possession of property.
Running time: 58 minutes. Release date: August 25, 1943.
Also known as *Billy the Kid in the Renegade*.
A 40-minute version was reissued in 1947 under the title *Code of the Plains*.

203. Law of the Saddle (western) Directed by Melville DeLay. Produced by Sigmund Neufeld. Original story and screenplay by Fred Myton.

Cast: Bob Livingston, Al "Fuzzy" St. John, Betty Miles, Lane Chandler, John Elliott, Reed Howes, Frank Ellis, Curley Dresden, Al Ferguson, Frank Hagney, Jimmy Aubrey.

The Lone Rider (Bob Livingston) is called in to get the goods on a crooked sheriff (Lane Chandler) who moves from town to town with a gang of highwaymen.
Running time: 59 minutes. Release date: August 28, 1943.
Also known as *The Lone Rider in Law of the Saddle*.

204. Blazing Frontier (western) Directed by Sam Newfield. Produced by Sigmund Neufeld. Original story and screenplay by Patricia Harper.

Cast: Buster Crabbe, Al "Fuzzy" St. John, Marjorie Manners, Milton

Kibbee, I. Stanford Jolley, Kermit Maynard, Frank Hagney, George Chesebro, Frank Ellis, Hank Bell, Jimmy Aubrey.

Billy the Kid (Buster Crabbe) steps in when a feud develops between settlers and the land agents for a railroad company.

Running time: 59 minutes. Release date: September 4, 1943.

Also known as *Billy the Kid in Blazing Frontier*.

205. Trail of Terror (western) Directed by Oliver Drake. Produced by Alfred Stern and Arthur Alexander. Original screenplay by Oliver Drake.

Cast: Dave "Tex" O'Brien, Jim Newill, Guy Wilkerson, Patricia Knox, Jack Ingram, I. Stanford Jolley, Budd Buster, Kenne Duncan, Frank Ellis, Robert Hill, Dan White, Jimmy Aubrey, Rose Plummer, Tom Smith, Artie Ortego.

The death of his outlaw twin brother provides a Texas Ranger (Dave O'Brien) with an opportunity to infiltrate a gang of stagecoach robbers.

Running time: 63 minutes. Release date: September 7, 1943.

206. Tiger Fangs (adventure) Directed by Sam Newfield. Produced by Arthur Schwarz. Original screenplay by Arthur St. Claire.

Cast: Frank Buck, June Duprez, Duncan Renaldo, Howard Banks, J. Farrell MacDonald, Arno Frey, Dan Seymour, J. Alex Havier, Pedro Regas.

Frank Buck battles Nazi saboteurs who are invading the Asian rubber industry.

Running time: 59 minutes. Release date: September 10, 1943.

207. Raiders of Red Gap (western) Directed by Sam Newfield. Produced by Sigmund Neufeld. Original story and screenplay by Joseph O'Donnell.

Cast: Bob Livingston, Al "Fuzzy" St. John, Myrna Dell, Edward Cassidy, Charles King, Charles "Slim" Whitaker, Kermit Maynard, Roy Brent, Frank Ellis, George Chesebro, Bud Osborne, Jimmy Aubrey, Merrill McCormack, George Morrell, Wally West, Reed Howes.

A would-be cattle baron trying to gain control of all grazing land in Arizona mistakes Rocky Cameron (Bob Livingston), alias The Lone Rider, and Fuzzy (Al St. John) for hired killers.

Running time: 57 minutes. Release date: September 30, 1943.

208. The Girl from Monterey (comedy) Directed by Wallace Fox. Produced by Jack Schwarz. Screenplay by Arthur Hoerl. Original story by George Green and Robert Gordon.

Cast: Armida, Edgar Kennedy, Jack LaRue, Veda Ann Borg, Terry Frost, Anthony Caruso, Charles Williams, Jay Silverheels, Wheeler Oakman, Bryant Washburn, Renee White, Alphonse Martel, Guy Zanett.

A cabaret singer (Armida) manages the career of her brother (Anthony Caruso), an aspiring prizefighter.
Running time: 61 minutes. Release date: October 4, 1943.

209. The Underdog (adventure-drama) Directed by William Nigh. Produced by Max Alexander. Screenplay by Ben Lithman. Original story by Lawrence E. Taylor and Malvin Wald.

Cast: Barton MacLane, Bobby Larson, Jan Wiley, Charlotte Wynters, Conrad Binyon, Kenneth Harlan, Elizabeth Valentine, George Anderson, Jack Kennedy, Hobo the dog.

A young boy (Bobby Larson) attempts to enlist his pet dog in the service, but the canine is rejected; later, they manage to thwart a gang of saboteurs.

Running time: 65 minutes. Release date: October 10, 1943.

210. Return of the Rangers (western) Directed by Elmer Clifton. Produced by Arthur Alexander. Original screenplay by Elmer Clifton.

Cast: Dave "Tex" O'Brien, Jim Newill, Guy Wilkerson, Nell O'Day, Glenn Strange, Emmett Lynn, Robert Barron, Henry Hall, Harry Harvey, I. Stanford Jolley, Richard Alexander, Charles King.

The Texas Rangers (Dave O'Brien, Jim Newill) go undercover to investigate the activities of a gang of cattle rustlers.

Running time: 60 minutes. Release date: October 26, 1943.

211. Devil Riders (western) Directed by Sam Newfield. Produced by Sigmund Neufeld. Original story and screenplay by Joseph O'Donnell.

Cast: Buster Crabbe, Al "Fuzzy" St. John, Patti McCarthy, Charles King, John Merton, Kermit Maynard, Frank LaRue, Jack Ingram, George Chesebro, Edward Cassidy, Al Ferguson, Frank Ellis, Bert Dillard, Bud Osborne, Artie Ortego, Herman Hack, Roy Bucko, Buck Bucko.

Billy Carson (Buster Crabbe) opposes a gang robbing the pony express in order to keep a stagecoach line running.

Running time: 58 minutes. Release date: November 5, 1943.

212. Boss of Rawhide (western) Directed by Elmer Clifton. Produced by Alfred Stern. Original screenplay by Elmer Clifton.

Cast: Dave "Tex" O'Brien, Jim Newill, Guy Wilkerson, Nell O'Day, Edward Cassidy, Jack Ingram, Charles King, Billy Bletcher, George Chesebro, Robert Hill, Dan White, Lucille Vance, Bob Kortman.

The Texas Rangers (Dave O'Brien, Jim Newill) track down the mastermind behind a gang that is murdering ranchers and buying up their property from the widows.

Running time: 57 minutes. Release date: November 20, 1943.

Jim Newill and Nell O'Day in *Return of the Rangers* (1943).

213. Harvest Melody (musical-comedy) Directed by Sam Newfield. Produced by Walter J. Colmes. Screenplay by Allan Gale. Original story by Martin Mooney and Ande Lamb.

Cast: Rosemary Lane, Johnny Downs, Sheldon Leonard, Charlotte Wynters, Luis Alberni, Claire Rochelle, Syd Saylor, Marjorie Manners, Sunny Fox, Henry Hall, Billy Wilson, Frances Gladwin, The Radio Rogues (Jimmy Hollywood, Eddie Bartell, Syd Chalton), The Vigilantes, Eddie LeBaron and his orchestra.

As a publicity stunt, a movie star (Rosemary Lane) moves to a farm to harvest crops for the war effort.

Running time: 71 minutes. Release date: November 22, 1943.

214. Suspected Person (mystery) Directed by Lawrence Huntington. Produced by Warwick Ward. Story and screenplay by Lawrence Huntington.

Cast: Clifford Evans, Patricia Roc, David Farrar, Anne Firth, Robert Beatty, Eric Clavering, Leslie Perrins, Eliot Makeham, John Salew, Billy Hartnell.

When his two accomplices are arrested, a crook (Clifford Evans) hides their stolen loot; after the pair is acquitted, they go looking for their elusive crony.

Tina Thayer, Dickie Moore and Gerra Young in *Jive Junction* (1943).

Running time: 78 minutes. Release date: November 29, 1943.
An Associated British Pathe Production released in the U.S. by PRC.

215. Jive Junction (musical) Directed by Edgar G. Ulmer. Produced by Leon Fromkess. Screenplay by Irving Wallace, Walter Doniger and Malvin Wald. Story by Malvin Wald and Walter Doniger.

Cast: Dickie Moore, Tina Thayer, Gerra Young, Johnny Michaels, Jack Wagner, Beverley Boyd, Bill Halligan, Johnny Duncan, John Clark, Frederick Feher, Bess Flowers, Jan Wiley, Venise Grove, Myrna Dell, Tom Quinn, Carol Ashley, Bob McKenzie, Harry Strange, Joe Oakie, Betty Alden, Jack George, Odessa Laurin.

A high school student (Dickie Moore) organizes an all-girl swing band and turns an old barn into "Jive Junction," a nightclub canteen for servicemen.

Running time: 62 minutes. Release date: December 16, 1943.

1944

216. Gunsmoke Mesa (western) Directed by Harry Fraser. Produced by Arthur Alexander. Original screenplay by Elmer Clifton.

Cast: Dave "Tex" O'Brien, Jim Newill, Guy Wilkerson, Patti McCarthy, Jack Ingram, Kermit Maynard, Robert Barron, Richard Alexander, Roy Brent, Michael Vallon, Jack Rockwell.

The Texas Rangers (Dave O'Brien, Jim Newill) set out after the villainous Henry Black (Jack Ingram) who is trying to gain control of the Gold Star mine.

Running time: 59 minutes. Release date: January 3, 1944.

217. Career Girl (musical) Directed by Wallace Fox. Produced by Jack Schwarz. Screenplay by Sam Neuman. Original story by Dave Silverstein and Stanley Rauh.

Cast: Frances Langford, Edward Norris, Iris Adrian, Craig Wood, Linda Brent, Alec Craig, Ariel Heath, Lorraine Krueger, Renee White, Gladys Blake, Charles Judels, Charles Williams.

An aspiring actress (Frances Langford) journeys to New York to pursue a show business career.

Running time: 69 minutes. Release date: January 11, 1944.

218. Nabonga (adventure) Directed by Sam Newfield. Produced by Sigmund Neufeld. Original story and screenplay by Fred Myton.

Cast: Buster Crabbe, Julie London, Barton MacLane, Fifi D'Orsay, Bryant Washburn, Herbert Rawlinson, Jackie Newfield, Prince Modupe.

A jungle explorer (Buster Crabbe) discovers a "white witch" — a young woman (Julie London) who was raised by gorillas.

Running time: 73 minutes. Release date: January 25, 1944.

Also known as *Gorilla* and *The Girl and the Gorilla*.

Released in Great Britain as *The Jungle Woman*.

219. Outlaw's Roundup (western) Directed by Harry Fraser. Produced by Alfred Stern and Arthur Alexander. Original screenplay by Elmer Clifton.

Cast: Dave "Tex" O'Brien, Jim Newill, Guy Wilkerson, Helen Chapman, Jack Ingram, I. Stanford Jolley, Charles King, Reed Howes, Bud Osborne, Frank Ellis, Budd Buster, Frank McCarroll, Jimmy Aubrey.

A Texas Ranger (Dave O'Brien) poses as a mysterious bandit leader in order to flush out a gang of cutthroats hiding in Devil's Gulch.

Running time: 55 minutes. Release date: February 10, 1944.

220. Men on Her Mind (drama) Directed by Wallace W. Fox. Produced by Alfred Stern. Original screenplay by Raymond L. Schrock.

Cast: Mary Beth Hughes, Edward Norris, Ted North, Alan Edwards, Kay Linaker, Luis Alberni, Lane Chandler, Lyle Latell, Claire McDowell, Claire Rochelle, Eva Hamill, Isabel LaMal.

Feature Films 1944

An ambitious singer (Mary Beth Hughes) refuses to let love and marriage interfere with her career.
Running time: 67 minutes. Release date: February 12, 1944.

221. Frontier Outlaws (western) Directed by Sam Newfield. Produced by Sigmund Neufeld. Original story and screenplay by Joseph O'Donnell.
Cast: Buster Crabbe, Al "Fuzzy" St. John, Frances Gladwin, Marin Sais, Charles King, Jack Ingram, Kermit Maynard, Edward Cassidy, Emmett Lynn, Budd Buster, Frank Ellis.
Billy Carson (Buster Crabbe) traps a gang of Wolf Valley outlaws by posing as a Mexican who's interested in buying stolen cattle.
Running time: 56 minutes. Release date: March 4, 1944.

222. Lady in the Death House (mystery-drama) Directed by Steve Sekely. Produced by Jack Schwarz. Screenplay by Harry O. Hoyt. Based on the story "Meet the Executioner" by Frederick C. Davis.
Cast: Jean Parker, Lionel Atwill, Douglas Fowley, Marcia Mae Jones, Robert Middlemass, Joe Devlin, Cy Kendall, John Maxwell, George Irving, Forrest Taylor.
An innocent woman (Jean Parker) winds up on death row when she's convicted for a murder she didn't commit.
Running time: 64 minutes. Release date: March 15, 1944.
Working titles: *Her Last Mile* and *The Executioner*.

223. Thundering Gun Slingers (western) Directed by Sam Newfield. Produced by Sigmund Neufeld. Original story and screenplay by Fred Myton.
Cast: Buster Crabbe, Al "Fuzzy" St. John, Frances Gladwin, George Chesebro, Karl Hackett, Charles King, Jack Ingram, Kermit Maynard, Budd Buster.
Billy Carson (Buster Crabbe) clashes with an outlaw leader who is framing innocent ranchers on rustling charges so he can buy up their property.
Running time: 59 minutes. Release date: March 25, 1944.

224. The Amazing Mr. Forrest (comedy) Directed by Thornton Freeland. Produced by Walter C. Mycroft and Jack Buchanan. Story and screenplay by Ralph Spence.
Cast: Jack Buchanan, Syd Walker, Edward Everett Horton, Googie Withers, Otto Kruger, Jack LaRue, Walter Rilla, David Burns, Charles Carson, Leslie Perrins, Ronald Shiner, Robb Wilson, Edward Lexy.
A British insurance investigator (Jack Buchanan) poses as an American gangster so he can gather evidence against a notorious jewel thief.
Running time: 71 minutes. Release date: March 29, 1944.

Jungle girl Julie London calms a wild gorilla as Buster Crabbe cowers in the background in *Nabonga* (1944).

An Associated British Pathe Production, released in Great Britain as *The Gang's All Here* (1939); released in the U. S. by PRC.

225. Guns of the Law (western) Directed by Elmer Clifton. Produced by Arthur Alexander. Story and screenplay by Elmer Clifton.
Cast: Dave "Tex" O'Brien, Jim Newill, Guy Wilkerson, Jack Ingram, Robert Kortman, Robert Barron, Frank McCarroll, Budd Buster, Bud Osborne.
The Texas Rangers (Dave O'Brien, Jim Newill) thwart a gang of outlaws trying to run a family off their land.
Running time: 55 minutes. Release date: March 31, 1944.

226. The Monster Maker (horror) Directed by Sam Newfield. Produced by Sigmund Neufeld. Screenplay by Pierre Gendron. Story by Lawrence Williams (and Nell O'Day, uncredited).
Cast: J. Carrol Naish, Ralph Morgan, Wanda McKay, Terry Frost, Tala Birell, Glenn Strange, Alexander Pollard, Sam Flint.
A mad doctor (J. Carrol Naish) injects a concert pianist (Ralph Morgan) with an experimental serum, resulting in acromegaly, a disease which horribly deforms his face and body.
Running time: 62 minutes. Release date: April 15, 1944.

227. Shake Hands with Murder (mystery) Directed by Albert Herman. Produced by Donald C. McKean and Albert Herman. Screenplay by John T. Neville. Original story by Martin Mooney.

Cast: Iris Adrian, Frank Jenks, Douglas Fowley, Jack Raymond, Claire Rochelle, Herbert Rawlinson, I. Stanford Jolley, Juan De LaCruz, Forrest Taylor, George Kirby, Gene Stutenroth (Roth), Anitra Sparrow, Buck Harrington.

A bail-bond broker (Iris Adrian) and her partner (Frank Jenks) help an accused embezzler (Douglas Fowley) prove his innocence.

Running time: 62 minutes. Release date: April 22, 1944.

228. The Pinto Bandit (western) Directed by Elmer Clifton. Produced by Alfred Stern. Original screenplay by Elmer Clifton.

Cast: Dave "Tex" O'Brien, Jim Newill, Guy Wilkerson, James Martin, Mady Lawrence, Jack Ingram, Edward Cassidy, Budd Buster, Karl Hackett, Robert Kortman, Charles King.

The Texas Rangers (Dave O'Brien, Jim Newill) set out to learn the identity of a masked rider who is trying to stop a mail line run between two cities.

Running time: 56 minutes. Release date: April 27, 1944.

229. Men of the Sea (drama) Directed by Norman Walker. Produced by James B. Sloan. Screenplay by Manning Haynes, Lydia Hayward and Harold Simpson. Based on a poem by Louise Haskin.

Cast: Wilfrid Lawson, Mary Jerrold, William Freshman, Kathleen O'Regan, Hubert Harlen, Charles Rolfe.

A seafaring Cornish family decide to settle down and become farmers; later, when war breaks out, the father and son join the navy.

Running time: 48 minutes. Release date: April 30, 1944.

Produced in Great Britain by G. H. W. Productions as *The Man at the Gate* (1940); released in the U. S. by PRC.

230. Valley of Vengeance (western) Directed by Sam Newfield. Produced by Sigmund Neufeld. Original story and screenplay by Joseph O'Donnell.

Cast: Buster Crabbe, Al "Fuzzy" St. John, Evelyn Finley, Glenn Strange, Donald Mayo, Charles King, John Merton, Lynton Brent, Jack Ingram, Bud Osborne, Nora Bush, Steve Clark, David Polonsky, Budd Buster.

Billy Carson (Buster Crabbe) and Fuzzy (Al St. John) round up an outlaw gang which, 20 years earlier, had killed their families.

Running time: 56 minutes. Release date: May 5, 1944.

231. The Contender (drama) Directed by Sam Newfield. Produced by Bert Sternbach. Screenplay by George Wallace Sayre, Jay Doten and Raymond L. Schrock. Original story by George Wallace Sayre and Jay Doten.

Cast: Buster Crabbe, Arline Judge, Julie Gibson, Donald Mayo, Charles D. Brown, Glenn Strange, Milton Kibbee, Roland Drew, Sam Flint, Duke York, Joel Newfield, George Turner.

A truck driver (Buster Crabbe) becomes a professional boxer in order to earn enough money to keep his son (Donald Mayo) in an expensive military academy.

Running time: 66 minutes. Release date: May 10, 1944.

232. Spook Town (western) Directed by Elmer Clifton. Produced by Arthur Alexander. Original screenplay by Elmer Clifton.

Cast: Dave "Tex" O'Brien, Jim Newill, Guy Wilkerson, Mady Lawrence, Dick Curtis, Harry Harvey, Edward Cassidy, Charles King, Robert Barron, Richard Alexander, John (Bob) Cason.

The Texas Rangers (Dave O'Brien, Jim Newill) go after a trading post operator who stole the money entrusted to them by local ranchers.

Running time: 59 minutes. Release date: June 3, 1944.

233. Waterfront (mystery-drama) Directed by Steve Sekely. Produced by Arthur Alexander. Screenplay by Martin Mooney and Irwin R. Franklin. Story by Martin Mooney.

Cast: John Carradine, J. Carrol Naish, Maris Wrixon, Terry Frost, Olga Fabian, Edwin Maxwell, John Bleifer, Marten Lamont, Claire Rochelle, Billy Nelson.

On the San Francisco waterfront, an optometrist (John Carradine), who is really a Nazi spy, attempts to retrieve a stolen Nazi codebook.

Running time: 68 minutes. Release date: June 10, 1944.

234. The Drifter (western) Directed by Sam Newfield. Produced by Sigmund Neufeld. Original screenplay by Patricia Harper.

Cast: Buster Crabbe, Al "Fuzzy" St. John, Carol Parker, Kermit Maynard, Jack Ingram, Roy Brent, George Chesebro, Ray Bennett, Jimmy Aubrey, Charles "Slim" Whitaker.

Billy Carson (Buster Crabbe) impersonates a lookalike sharpshooter who has been using a carnival as a front for his robberies.

Running time: 62 minutes. Release date: June 14, 1944.

235. Fuzzy Settles Down (western) Directed by Sam Newfield. Produced by Sigmund Neufeld. Original story and screenplay by Louise Rousseau.

Cast: Buster Crabbe, Al "Fuzzy" St. John, Patti McCarthy, Charles King, John Merton, Frank McCarroll, Hal Price, John Elliott, Edward Cassidy, Robert Hill, Ted Mapes, Tex Palmer.

Fuzzy Q. Jones (Al St. John) decides to settle down and buys a newspaper office. When a large sum of money is stolen, he is accused of the theft; Billy Carson (Buster Crabbe) comes to his defense.

Running time: 60 minutes. Release date: July 25, 1944.

236. Brand of the Devil (western) Directed by Harry Fraser. Produced by Arthur Alexander. Original screenplay by Elmer Clifton.

Cast: Dave "Tex" O'Brien, Jim Newill, Guy Wilkerson, Ellen Hall, Charles King, I. Stanford Jolley, Reed Howes, Budd Buster, Karl Hackett, Kermit Maynard, Edward Cassidy.

The Texas Rangers (Dave O'Brien, Jim Newill) pursue an outlaw gang known as the "Brand of the Devil."

Running time: 57 minutes. Release date: July 30, 1944.

237. Minstrel Man (musical-drama) Directed by Joseph H. Lewis. Produced by Leon Fromkess. Screenplay by Irwin R. Franklin and Pierre Gendron. Original story by Martin Mooney and Raymond L. Schrock.

Cast: Benny Fields, Gladys George, Alan Dinehart, Roscoe Karns, Judy Clark, Gloria Petroff, Molly Lamont, Jerome Cowan, John Raitt, Eddie Kane, Lee "Lasses" White.

Grief-stricken after the death of his wife (Molly Lamont), a minstrel man (Benny Fields) leaves his baby daughter with actor friends (Gladys George, Roscoe Karns) and goes off to Europe for five years; when he returns, the couple refuses to give the girl up.

Running time: 69 minutes. Release date: August 1, 1944.

Academy Award Nominations: Best Music Scoring of a Musical Picture (Leo Erdody and Ferde Grofe); Best Song: "Remember Me to Carolina" (music by Harry Revel, lyrics by Paul Webster).

238. Seven Doors to Death (mystery) Directed by Elmer Clifton. Produced by Alfred Stern. Screenplay by Elmer Clifton. Original story by Helen Kiely.

Cast: Chick Chandler, June Clyde, George Meeker, Michael Raffetto, Gregory Gaye, Rebel Randall, Milton Wallace, Edgar Dearing, Casey MacGregor.

A man (Chick Chandler) and a woman (June Clyde) are both suspected of committing a double murder and gem burglary, so they work together to clear themselves.

Running time: 64 minutes. Release date: August 5, 1944.

239. Delinquent Daughters (drama) Directed by Albert Herman. Produced by Donald C. McKean and Albert Herman. Original screenplay by Arthur St. Claire.

Guy Wilkerson, Dave "Tex" O'Brien and Jim Newill in *Brand of the Devil* (1944), an entry in the Texas Rangers series.

Cast: June Carlson, Fifi D'Orsay, Teala Loring, Julie Gibson, Johnny Duncan, Mary Bovard, Parker Gee, Jon Dawson, Margia Dean, Frank McGlynn, Sr., Joe Devlin, Warren Mills, John Christian, Jimmy Zaner.

A cafe proprietor (Jon Dawson) exploits three teenagers after they are involved in a hit-and-run auto accident.

Running time: 72 minutes. Release date: August 10, 1944.

240. **Dixie Jamboree** (musical) Directed by Christy Cabanne. Produced by Jack Schwarz. Screenplay by Sam Neuman. Story by Lawrence E. Taylor.

Cast: Frances Langford, Guy Kibbee, Eddie Quillan, Charles Butterworth, Fifi D'Orsay, Lyle Talbot, Frank Jenks, Almira Sessions, Louise Beavers, Ben Carter and his choir, Joe Devlin, Edward Shattuck, Ethel Shattuck, Anthony Warde, Angel Cruz.

Hiding aboard a Mississippi showboat, two crooks (Lyle Talbot, Frank Jenks) uncover a cargo of whiskey and try to think of a way to sell it.

Running time: 72 minutes. Release date: August 15, 1944.

241. **Machine Gun Mama** (adventure-comedy) Directed by Harold Young. Produced by Jack Schwarz. Original screenplay by Sam Neuman.

Cast: Armida, Wallace Ford, El Brendel, Jack LaRue, Luis Alberni, Anthony Warde, Julian Rivero, Ariel Heath, Eumonio Blanco.

A drifter (Wallace Ford) falls in love with a carnival owner's daughter (Armida).

Running time: 67 minutes. Release date: August 18, 1944.

Working title: *Mexican Fiesta*.

Also known as *Tropical Fury*.

242. Castle of Crimes (mystery) Directed by Harold French. Produced by Walter C. Mycroft. Screenplay by Doreen Montgomery. Adapted from the novel "The House of the Arrow" by A. E. W. Mason.

Cast: Diana Churchill, Keneth Kent, Belle Chrystall, Peter Murray-Hill, Clifford Evans, Catherine Lacey, James Harcourt, Aubrey Dexter, Louise Hampton, Ivor Barnard.

Police inspector Hanuad (Keneth Kent) investigates the murder of a wealthy spinster (Louise Hampton) who was killed by a rare type of poison.

Running time: 66 minutes. Release date: August 25, 1944.

An Associated British Pathe Production released in Great Britain as *The House of the Arrow* (1940); released in the U. S. by PRC.

243. Rustlers' Hideout (western) Directed by Sam Newfield. Produced by Sigmund Neufeld. Original story and screenplay by Joseph O'Donnell.

Cast: Buster Crabbe, Al "Fuzzy" St. John, Patti McCarthy, Charles King, John Merton, Terry Frost, Hal Price, Edward Cassidy, Lane Chandler, Al Ferguson, Frank McCarroll, Bud Osborne.

Billy Carson (Buster Crabbe) and Fuzzy (Al St. John) clash with cattle rustlers who have made raids on their herd.

Running time: 60 minutes. Release date: September 2, 1944.

244. Swing Hostess (musical) Directed by Sam Newfield. Produced by Sigmund Neufeld. Original story and screenplay by Louise Rousseau and Gail Davenport.

Cast: Martha Tilton, Iris Adrian, Charles Collins, Cliff Nazarro, Phil Van Zandt, Emmett Lynn, Betty Brodel, Earle Bruce, Harry Holman.

An aspiring singer (Martha Tilton) gets a job as switchboard operator at a jukebox company.

Running time: 76 minutes. Release date: September 8, 1944.

245. Gangsters of the Frontier (western) Directed by Elmer Clifton. Produced by Arthur Alexander. Original screenplay by Elmer Clifton.

Cast: Tex Ritter, Dave O'Brien, Guy Wilkerson, Patti McCarthy, Betty Miles, Harry Harvey, I. Stanford Jolley, Marshall Reed, Charles King, Clarke Stevens.

The Texas Rangers (Tex Ritter, Dave O'Brien) go after jailbirds who have taken over the town of Red Rock.
Running time: 56 minutes. Release date: September 21, 1944.

246. When the Lights Go On Again (drama) Directed by William K. Howard. Produced by Leon Fromkess. Screenplay by Milton Lazarus. Original story by Frank Craven.

Cast: Jimmy Lydon, Barbara Belden, George Cleveland, Dorothy Peterson, Regis Toomey, Grant Mitchell, Lucien Littlefield, Luis Alberni, Harry Shannon, Warren Mills, Williard Jielson, Jac Turrell, Bill Nelson, Larry Thompson, Myrtle Ferguson, Emmett Lynn, Jill Browning, Roberta Carlin, Guy Blake, Al Stewart, Elmo Lincoln, Joseph Crehan, James Hope.

A war veteran (Jimmy Lydon) suffering from amnesia returns home to his wife (Barbara Belden) and his family.
Running time: 76 minutes. Release date: October 23, 1944.

247. Wild Horse Phantom (western) Directed by Sam Newfield. Produced by Sigmund Neufeld. Original story and screenplay by George Milton (George Wallace Sayre and Milton Raison).

Cast: Buster Crabbe, Al "Fuzzy" St. John, Elaine Morey, Kermit Maynard, Hal Price, Budd Buster, Frank Ellis, Robert Meredith, Frank McCarroll, Bob Cason, John Elliott.

Billy Carson (Buster Crabbe) steps in when the bank is robbed after local ranchers deposit their mortgage payments.
Running time: 56 minutes. Release date: October 28, 1944.

248. I'm from Arkansas (comedy) Directed by Lew Landers. Produced by E. H. Kleinert and Irving Vershel. Screenplay by Marcy Klauber and Joseph Carole. Original story by Marcy Klauber.

Cast: Slim Summerville, El Brendel, Iris Adrian, Bruce Bennett, Al "Fuzzy" St. John, Maude Eburne, Cliff Nazarro, Walter Baldwin, Flo Bert, Carolina Cotton, Donny Jackson, Paul Newlan, Harry Harvey, Arthur Ryan, John Hamilton, Douglas Wood, Jimmy Wakely, The Pied Pipers, The Sunshine Girls, The Milo Twins.

In Pitchfork, Arkansas, a sow owned by a farmer (Slim Summerville) gives birth to eighteen piglets; when the news leaks out, several people try to cash in on the publicity.
Running time: 68 minutes. Release date: October 31, 1944.

249. I Accuse My Parents (drama) Directed by Sam Newfield. Produced by Max Alexander. Screenplay by Harry Fraser. Story by Arthur Caesar.

Cast: Mary Beth Hughes, Robert Lowell, John Miljan, George Meeker, Vivienne Osborne, George Lloyd, Patricia Knox, Florence Johnson, Edward Earle, Richard Bartell.

Feature Films 1944

Poster for *Bluebeard* (1944), one of PRC's best efforts.

Traumatized by an unhappy home life, a young man (Robert Lowell) turns to a nightclub singer (Mary Beth Hughes) for understanding and compassion. To earn money to indulge her champagne tastes, he goes to work for a racketeer.

Running time: 68 minutes. Release date: November 4, 1944.

250. Dead or Alive (western) Directed by Elmer Clifton. Produced by Arthur Alexander. Original screenplay by Harry Fraser.

Cast: Tex Ritter, Dave O'Brien, Guy Wilkerson, Marjorie Clements, Rebel Randall, Ray Bennett, Charles King, Budd Buster, Henry Hall, Ted Mapes, Bud Osborne, Reed Howes.

The Texas Rangers (Tex Ritter, Dave O'Brien) pose as tough gunslingers in order to infiltrate a gang of outlaws who have been terrorizing the town of DeLano.

Running time: 56 minutes. Release date: November 9, 1944.

251. Bluebeard (drama) Directed by Edgar G. Ulmer. Produced by Leon Fromkess. Screenplay by Pierre Gendron. Original story by Arnold Phillips and Werner H. Furst.

Cast: John Carradine, Jean Parker, Nils Asther, Ludwig Stossell, George Pembroke, Teala Loring, Sonia Sorel, Henry Kolker, Emmett Lynn, Iris Adrian, Patti McCarthy, Carrive Deven, Anne Sterling.

A young woman (Jean Parker) becomes romantically involved with a Parisian puppeteer (John Carradine); later she suspects that he may be "Bluebeard," the notorious murderer.

Running time: 73 minutes. Release date: November 11, 1944.

252. The Great Mike (comedy-drama) Directed by Wallace W. Fox. Produced by Leon Fromkess. Screenplay by Raymond L. Schrock. Original story by Martin Mooney.

Cast: Stuart Erwin, Robert "Buzzy" Henry, Carl "Alfalfa" Switzer, Marion Martin, Pierre Watkin, Lane Chandler, Gwen Kenyon, Edythe Elliott, Bob Meredith, Edward Cassidy, William Halligan, Leon Tyler, Charles King, Eddie Rocco.

A young boy (Robert "Buzzy" Henry) and a trainer (Stuart Erwin) enter a milkwagon horse in a championship race.

Running time: 73 minutes. Release date: November 15, 1944.

253. Rogues' Gallery (mystery) Directed by Albert Herman. Produced by Donald C. McKean and Albert Herman. Original screenplay by John T. Neville.

Cast: Frank Jenks, Robin Raymond, H. B. Warner, Ray Walker, Davidson Clark, Bob Homans, Frank McGlynn, Pat Gleason, Edward Keane, Earl Dewey, Milton Kibbee.

While trying to obtain information about a trick listening device, a reporter (Robin Raymond) and a newspaper photographer (Frank Jenks) stumble their way into a murder case.

Running time: 60 minutes. Release date: December 6, 1944.

254. Oath of Vengeance (western) Directed by Sam Newfield. Produced by Sigmund Neufeld. Original story and screenplay by Fred Myton.

Cast: Buster Crabbe, Al "Fuzzy" St. John, Mady Lawrence, Karl Hackett, Marin Sais, Jack Ingram, Charles King, Kermit Maynard, Frank Ellis, Budd Buster, Jimmy Aubrey.

Billy Carson (Buster Crabbe) and Fuzzy (Al St. John) come to the aid of an innocent man accused of murder.

Running time: 57 minutes. Release date: December 9, 1944.

255. The Town Went Wild (comedy) Directed by Ralph Murphy. Written and produced by Bernard R. Roth, Clarence Greene and Russell Rouse.

Cast: Freddie Bartholomew, James Lydon, Edward Everett Horton, Tom Tully, Frederick Burton, Jill Browning, Minna Gombell, Maude Eburne, Charles Halton, Ruth Lee, Roberta Smith, Forrest Taylor, Jimmy Conlin, Monty Collins, Olin Howland, Charles Middleton, Emmett Lynn, Dorothy Vaughn.

Two young men (Freddie Bartholomew, James Lydon), whose respective fathers have been feuding for years, discover that their birth records may have been switched, meaning that they may have been raised by the wrong set of parents.
Running time: 79 minutes. Release date: December 15, 1944.

256. The Whispering Skull (western) Directed by Elmer Clifton. Produced by Arthur Alexander. Original screenplay by Harry Fraser.
Cast: Tex Ritter, Dave O'Brien, Guy Wilkerson, Denny Burke, I. Stanford Jolley, Henry Hall, Edward Cassidy, George Morrell, Robert Kortman, Wen Wright.
The Texas Rangers (Tex Ritter, Dave O'Brien) are after "The Whispering Skull," a mysterious night rider who murdered the sheriff.
Running time: 56 minutes. Release date: December 20, 1944.

1945

257. His Brother's Ghost (western) Directed by Sam Newfield. Produced by Sigmund Neufeld. Original story and screenplay by George Plympton.
Cast: Buster Crabbe, Al "Fuzzy" St. John, Charles King, Roy Brent, Frank McCarroll, Richard Alexander, Bud Osborne, Bob Cason, Karl Hackett, Archie Hall, George Morrell.
After Andy (Al St. John) is murdered, his twin brother Fuzzy (also played by St. John) masquerades as his sibling, making the killers think that they're being haunted by a ghost.
Running time: 54 minutes. Release date: February 3, 1945.

258. The Kid Sister (comedy-drama) Directed by Sam Newfield. Produced by Sigmund Neufeld. Original story and screenplay by Fred Myton.
Cast: Roger Pryor, Judy Clark, Frank Jenks, Constance Worth, Tom Dugan, Minerva Urecal, Ruth Robinson, Richard Byron, Peggy Wynne.
Unable to wed until her older sister (Constance Worth) gets married first, a young woman (Judy Clark) studies psychology and takes matters into her own hands.
Running time: 66 minutes. Release date: February 6, 1945.

259. Marked for Murder (western) Directed by Elmer Clifton. Produced by Arthur Alexander. Original screenplay by Elmer Clifton.
Cast: Tex Ritter, Dave O'Brien, Guy Wilkerson, Marilyn McConnell, Henry Hall, Edward Cassidy, Charles King, Jack Ingram, Robert Kortman, Wen Wright, The Milos Twins, Kermit Maynard.

Buster Crabbe and Al "Fuzzy" St. John in *His Brother's Ghost* (1945), an entry in the Billy Carson series, which was formerly the Billy the Kid series. In these films, Billy the Kid was on the side of law and order, in spite of bearing the same name as the legendary badman. In 1941 Crabbe took over the role from Bob Steele, who starred in the first six entries; by 1943 the character's name was changed to Billy Carson, although the content of the pictures remained the same. The likability of Crabbe and St. John, both fine performers, helped to make this PRC's most popular western series.

The Texas Rangers (Tex Ritter, Dave O'Brien) try to settle a feud between the cattlemen and the sheepmen.

Running time: 58 minutes. Release date: February 8, 1945.

260. The Spell of Amy Nugent (drama) Directed by John Harlow. Produced by R. Murray Leslie. Screenplay by Miles Malleson. Adapted from the novel "The Necromancers" by Robert Benson.

Cast: Derek Farr, Vera Lindsay, Frederick Leister, Hay Petrie, Felix Aylmer, Diana King, W.G. Fay, Gibb McLaughlin, Marian Spencer, Hannen Swaffer, Enid Hewitt, Joyce Redman, Cameron Hall, Irene Handl, Stafford Hilliard.

A young woman (Vera Lindsay) falls in love with a man (Derek Farr) who is under the spell of the spirit of his dead sweetheart (Diana King).

Running time: 63 minutes. Release date: February 10, 1945.

A Pyramid Amalgamated Production, produced and released in Great Britain as *Spellbound*; released in the U. S. by PRC.

Feature Films 1945

261. Fog Island (mystery) Directed by Terry Morse. Produced by Leon Fromkess. Screenplay by Pierre Gendron. Based on the play "Angel Island" by Bernadine Angus.

Cast: Lionel Atwill, Jerome Cowan, George Zucco, Veda Ann Borg, Sharon Douglas, Ian Keith, Jacqueline DeWit, George Lloyd, John Whitney.

Trying to find out which one of his associates was responsible for his wife's death, a man (Lionel Atwill) invites them to his fog-shrouded island, on the promise of searching for buried treasure.

Running time: 72 minutes. Release date: February 15, 1945.

262. I Ring Doorbells (mystery) Directed by Frank R. Strayer. Produced by Martin Mooney. Screenplay by Dick Irving Hyland. Based on the book by Russell Birdwell. Adapted by Dick Irving Hyland and Raymond L. Schrock.

Cast: Anne Gwynne, Robert Shayne, Roscoe Karns, Pierre Watkin, Harry Shannon, John Eldredge, Harry Tyler, Doris Caron, Jan Wiley, Joel McGinnis, Charles Wilson, Hank Patterson, Eugene Stutenroth (Gene Roth), Roy Darmour.

A newshawk (Robert Shayne), returning to his old reporting job after failing as a playwright, and a photographer (Roscoe Karns) try to get the goods on a gold-digging blonde (Jan Wiley) out to snare a millionaire's son; when the girl is found dead, the reporter and the lensman come under suspicion.

Running time: 67 minutes. Release date: February 25, 1945.

263. The Man Who Walked Alone (comedy) Directed by Christy Cabanne. Produced by Leon Fromkess. Screenplay by Robert Lee Johnson. Story by Christy Cabanne.

Cast: David O'Brien, Kay Aldridge, Walter Catlett, Guinn "Big Boy" Williams, Isabel Randolph, Ruth Lee, Smith Ballew, Nancy June Robinson, Chester Clute, Vivian Oakland, Tom Dugan, Jack Mulhall, Vicki Saunders, Robert Hartnell, Charles Williams, Dick Elliott, William B. Davidson, Jack Raymond, Dick Raymond.

A rich woman (Kay Aldridge) hires a hitchhiking soldier (David O'Brien) as her chauffeur; the two eventually fall in love.

Running time: 64 minutes. Release date: March 15, 1945.

Academy Award Nomination: Best Music Scoring of a Dramatic or Comedy Picture (Karl Hajos).

264. Strange Illusion (mystery-drama) Directed by Edgar G. Ulmer. Produced by Leon Fromkess. Screenplay by Adele Comandini. Story by Fritz Rotter.

Cast: James Lydon, Sally Eilers, Warren William, Regis Toomey, Charles Arnt, George H. Reed, Jayne Hazard, Jimmy Clark, Mary McLeod, Pierre Watkin, John Hamilton, Sonia Sorel, Vic Potel.

A young man (James Lydon) believes his father was murdered by the man (Warren William) who is now courting his mother (Sally Eilers).

Running time: 86 minutes. Release date: March 31, 1945.

Also known as *Out of the Night*.

265. Crime, Inc. (mystery-drama) Directed by Lew Landers. Produced by Martin Mooney. Screenplay by Raymond L. Schrock. From the book by Martin Mooney.

Cast: Leo Carrillo, Tom Neal, Martha Tilton, Lionel Atwill, Grant Mitchell, Sheldon Leonard, Harry Shannon, Danny Morton, Don Beddoe, Virginia Vale, George Meeker, Red Rodgers, Ed Cromley, Jack Gordon, Monk Friedman.

A crime reporter (Tom Neal) tries to expose a gang of racketeers and winds up falling in love with the sister (Martha Tilton) of one of the mobsters.

Running time: 76 minutes. Release date: April 15, 1945.

266. Shadows of Death (western) Directed by Sam Newfield. Produced by Sigmund Neufeld. Original story and screenplay by Fred Myton.

Cast: Buster Crabbe, Al "Fuzzy" St. John, Donna Dax, Charles King, Karl Hackett, Edward Peil, Sr., Bob Cason, Frank Ellis, Frank McCarroll.

Billy Carson (Buster Crabbe) thwarts a murderous gang trying to buy up all the land that will be the route of a new railroad line.

Running time: 60 minutes. Release date: April 19, 1945.

Working title: *Barber of Red Gap*.

267. Hollywood and Vine (comedy) Directed by Alexis Thurn-Taxis. Produced by Leon Fromkess. Screenplay by Edith Watkins and Charles Williams. Original story by Edith Watkins, Charles Williams and Robert Wilmot.

Cast: James Ellison, Wanda McKay, June Clyde, Ralph Morgan, Leon Belasco, William (Billy) Benedict, Franklin Pangborn, Emmett Lynn, Vera Lewis, Karin Lang, Robert Greig, Charles Williams, Ray Whitley, Dewey Robinson, Lillian Bronson, John Elliott, Jack Raymond, Hal Taggart, Cy Ring, Grandin Rhodes, Donald Kerr, Charles Jordan, Lou Crocker.

A successful writer (James Ellison) does research for a new screenplay by obtaining a job in a Hollywood drugstore.

Running time: 58 minutes. Release date: April 25, 1945.

Released in Great Britain as *Daisy Goes to Hollywood*.

268. **The Phantom of 42nd Street** (mystery) Directed by Albert Herman. Produced by Martin Mooney and Albert Herman. Screenplay by Milton Raison. Based on the novel by Jack Harvey and Milton Raison.

Cast: Dave O'Brien, Kay Aldridge, Alan Mowbray, Frank Jenks, Edythe Elliott, Jack Mulhall, Vera Marshe, Stanley Price, John Crawford, Cyril Delevante, Paul Power.

A theater critic (Dave O'Brien) investigates the death of an actor who was killed during the performance of a play.

Running time: 58 minutes. Release date: May 2, 1945.

269. **Enemy of the Law** (western) Directed by Harry Fraser. Produced by Arthur Alexander. Original screenplay by Harry Fraser.

Cast: Tex Ritter, Dave O'Brien, Guy Wilkerson, Kay Hughes, Jack Ingram, Charles King, Frank Ellis, Henry Hall, Kermit Maynard, Karl Hackett, Edward Cassidy, Ben Corbett.

The Texas Rangers (Tex Ritter, Dave O'Brien) pursue a gang of terrorists.

Running time: 59 minutes. Release date: May 7, 1945.

270. **The Lady Confesses** (mystery) Directed by Sam Newfield. Produced by Alfred Stern. Screenplay by Helen Martin. Original story by Irwin R. Franklin.

Cast: Mary Beth Hughes, Hugh Beaumont, Edmund MacDonald, Claudia Drake, Emmett Vogan, Dewey Robinson, Barbara Slater, Carol Andrews, Edward Howard, Ruth Brande, Jack George, Jerome Root.

A woman (Mary Beth Hughes) turns sleuth when her fiance (Hugh Beaumont) is accused of murdering his ex-wife (Barbara Slater).

Running time: 64 minutes. Release date: May 16, 1945.

271. **The Missing Corpse** (mystery-comedy) Directed by Albert Herman. Produced by Martin Mooney and Albert Herman. Screenplay by Raymond L. Schrock. Original story by Harry O. Hoyt.

Cast: J. Edward Bromberg, Frank Jenks, Eric Sinclair, Lorell Sheldon, Charles Coleman, Eddy Waller, Ben Welden, Isabel Randolph, Paul Guilfoyle, John Shay, Michael Branden, Elayne Adams, Mary Arden, Charles Jordan, Anne O'Neal, Jean Ransome, Ken Terrell, Isabel Withers.

Rival newspaper publishers, one of whom is a racketeer using his paper for blackmailing purposes, are involved in a feud. The blackmailer (Paul Guilfoyle) is killed, and his body is found in a car belonging to the other publisher (J. Edward Bromberg).

Running time: 62 minutes. Release date: June 1, 1945.

Working title: *Stranger in the Family.*

272. Gangster's Den (western) Directed by Sam Newfield. Produced by Sigmund Neufeld. Screenplay by George H. Plympton.

Cast: Buster Crabbe, Al "Fuzzy" St. John, Sidney Logan, Charles King, Emmett Lynn, Kermit Maynard, Edward Cassidy, I. Stanford Jolley, George Chesebro, Karl Hackett, Michael Owen, Bob Cason, Wally West.

Fuzzy Q. Jones (Al St. John) takes proceeds from the mine he operates in partnership with Billy Carson (Buster Crabbe) and buys a saloon.

Running time: 55 minutes. Release date: June 14, 1945.

273. The Silver Fleet (drama) Directed by Vernon Sewell and Gordon Wellesley. Produced by Michael Powell, Emeric Pressburger and Ralph Richardson. Story and screenplay by Vernon Sewell and Gordon Wellesley.

Cast: Ralph Richardson, Googie Withers, Esmond Knight, Beresford Egan, Frederick Burtwell, Kathleen Byron, Willem Akkerman, Dorothy Gordon, Charles Victor, John Longden, Joss Ambler, Margaret Emden, Ivor Barnard, Valentine Dyall.

A Dutch patriot (Ralph Richardson) pretends to be working in collaboration with the Nazis.

Running time: 81 minutes. Release date: July 1, 1945.

An Archers-GFD Production, produced and released in Great Britain in 1943.

274. Three in the Saddle (western) Directed by Harry Fraser. Produced by Arthur Alexander. Original screenplay by Elmer Clifton.

Cast: Tex Ritter, Dave O'Brien, Guy Wilkerson, Lorraine Miller, Charles King, Ed Howard, Edward Cassidy, Bud Osborne, Frank Ellis.

The Texas Rangers (Tex Ritter, Dave O'Brien) come to the aid of a young woman (Lorraine Miller) who is being forced off her property by a land grabber.

Running time: 61 minutes. Release date: July 26, 1945.

275. Stagecoach Outlaws (western) Directed by Sam Newfield. Produced by Sigmund Neufeld. Original story and screenplay by Fred Myton.

Cast: Buster Crabbe, Al "Fuzzy" St. John, Frances Gladwin, Edward Cassidy, Kermit Maynard, I. Stanford Jolley, Steve Clark, Robert Kortman, Bob Cason, George Chesebro, Hank Bell.

Billy Carson (Buster Crabbe) infiltrates a gang of desperadoes plotting to steal a stagecoach line.

Running time: 55 minutes. Release date: August 17, 1945.

276. Frontier Fugitives (western) Directed by Harry Fraser. Produced by Arthur Alexander. Original screenplay by Elmer Clifton.

Cast: Tex Ritter, Dave O'Brien, Guy Wilkerson, Lorraine Miller, I.

Stanford Jolley, Frank Ellis, Jack Ingram, Jack Hendricks, Charles King, Karl Hackett, Budd Buster.

The Texas Rangers (Tex Ritter, Dave O'Brien) investigate the death of a fur trapper who was murdered by white men disguised as Indians.

Running time: 53 minutes. Release date: September 1, 1945.

277. Arson Squad (mystery) Directed by Lew Landers. Produced by Arthur Alexander. Original screenplay by Arthur St. Claire.

Cast: Frank Albertson, Robert Armstrong, Grace Gillern, Byron Foulger, Chester Clute, Arthur Loft, Jerry Jerome, Stewart Garner, Edward Cassidy, Casey MacGregor.

An insurance investigator (Frank Albertson) and the chief of the police arson squad (Robert Armstrong) try to solve a case of arson that resulted in murder.

Running time: 64 minutes. Release date: September 11, 1945.

278. Dangerous Intruder (mystery) Directed by Vernon Keays. Produced by Martin Mooney. Screenplay by Philip MacDonald. Original story by Philip MacDonald and F. Ruth Howard.

Cast: Charles Arnt, Veda Ann Borg, Richard Powers, Fay Helm, John Rogers, Jo Anne Marlowe, Helena P. Evans, Robert Smith, George Sorel, Forrest Taylor, Eddie Rocco.

While hitchhiking across the country, an actress (Veda Ann Borg) is struck by a car; the driver (Charles Arnt) takes her to his home to recuperate. Later, when the man's wife is found murdered, the actress sets out to solve the crime.

Running time: 65 minutes. Release date: September 21, 1945.

279. Apology for Murder (mystery) Directed by Sam Newfield. Produced by Sigmund Neufeld. Original story and screenplay by Fred Myton.

Cast: Hugh Beaumont, Ann Savage, Russell Hicks, Charles D. Brown, Pierre Watkin, Eva Novak, Norman Willis, Archie Hall, Elizabeth Valentine, Budd Buster, Henry Hall, Wheaton Chambers, George Sherwood.

A woman (Ann Savage) and her lover (Hugh Beaumont), a newspaper reporter, murder her husband (Russell Hicks) then frame an innocent man for the crime.

Running time: 66 minutes. Release date: September 27, 1945.

280. Why Girls Leave Home (drama) Directed by William Berke. Produced by Sam Sax. Screenplay by Fanya Foss Lawrence and Bradford Ropes. Original story by Fanya Foss Lawrence.

Cast: Lola Lane, Sheldon Leonard, Pamela Blake, Elisha Cook, Jr., Paul Guilfoyle, Claudia Drake, Constance Worth, Thomas Jackson, Walter

Baldwin, Fred Kohler, Evelynne Eaton, Virginia Bris, Peggy Lou Bianco, Robert Emmett Keane.

A singer (Pamela Blake) and a newspaper reporter (Sheldon Leonard) expose a nightclub that is being used as a front for an illegal gambling racket.

Running time: 69 minutes. Release date: October 9, 1945.

Academy Award Nominations: Best Music Scoring of a Musical Picture (Walter Greene); Best Song: "The Cat and the Canary" (music by Jay Livingston, lyrics by Ray Evans).

281. **Border Badmen** (western) Directed by Sam Newfield. Produced by Sigmund Neufeld. Original story and screenplay by George Milton (George Wallace Sayre and Milton Raison).

Cast: Buster Crabbe, Al "Fuzzy" St. John, Lorraine Miller, Bob Kortman, Budd Buster, Charles King, Ray Bennett, Archie Hall, Marilyn Gladstone, Marin Sais, Bud Osborne.

Fuzzy Q. Jones (Al St. John) learns that his millionaire cousin has recently died; when he and Billy Carson (Buster Crabbe) go to collect the inheritance, they learn that a gang of swindlers have taken possession of the late cousin's land and property.

Running time: 59 minutes. Release date: October 10, 1945.

282. **Flaming Bullets** (western) Directed by Harry Fraser. Produced by Arthur Alexander. Screenplay by Harry Fraser.

Cast: Tex Ritter, Dave O'Brien, Guy Wilkerson, Patricia Knox, Charles King, I. Stanford Jolley, Bob Duncan, Bud Osborne, Kermit Maynard, Dick Alexander, Dan White.

The Texas Rangers (Tex Ritter, Dave O'Brien) are out to capture an outlaw gang that helps convicts escape from jail, then murders them and collects the reward.

Running time: 55 minutes. Release date: October 15, 1945.

283. **Fighting Bill Carson** (western) Directed by Sam Newfield. Produced by Sigmund Neufeld. Original story and screenplay by Louise Rousseau.

Cast: Buster Crabbe, Al "Fuzzy" St. John, Lorraine Miller, Kay Hughes, I. Stanford Jolley, Kermit Maynard, Bob Cason, Budd Buster, Bud Osborne, Charles King.

Billy Carson (Buster Crabbe) and Fuzzy Q. Jones (Al St. John) learn that the woman they saved from stagecoach robbers is actually a member of the outlaw gang.

Running time: 51 minutes. Release date: October 31, 1945.

Jennifer Holt, Eddie Dean and Sarah Padden in *Song of Old Wyoming* (1945).

284. White Pongo (adventure) Directed by Sam Newfield. Produced by Sigmund Neufeld. Original story and screenplay by Raymond L. Schrock.

Cast: Richard Fraser, Maris Wrixon, Lionel Royce, Al Eben, Michael Dyne, Gordon Richards, George Lloyd, Egon Brecher, Jack Collins, Milton Kibbee, Larry Steers, Joel Fluellen.

An undercover policeman (Richard Fraser) suspects a jungle guide of murder and joins a safari in an effort to gather evidence against him. During their trek through the Belgian Congo, the expedition encounters a white gorilla thought to be the missing link.

Running time: 73 minutes. Release date: November 2, 1945.

Working title: *Congo Pongo*.

285. Shadow of Terror (mystery) Directed by Lew Landers. Produced by Jack Grant. Screenplay by Arthur St. Claire. Original story by Sheldon Leonard.

Cast: Richard Fraser, Grace Gillern, Cy Kendall, Emmett Lynn, Kenneth MacDonald, Eddie Acuff, Sam Flint.

A research scientist (Richard Fraser), working on a new explosive, is attacked and thrown from a moving train; as a result, he comes down with amnesia. A rancher (Grace Gillern) tries to nurse him back to health.

Running time: 64 minutes. Release date: November 5, 1945.

Working title: *Checkmate*.

286. Prairie Rustlers (western) Directed by Sam Newfield. Produced by Sigmund Neufeld. Original story and screenplay by Fred Myton.

Cast: Buster Crabbe, Al "Fuzzy" St. John, Evelyn Finley, Karl Hackett, I. Stanford Jolley, Bud Osborne, Kermit Maynard, Marin Sais, Herman Hack, George Morrell, Tex Cooper, Dorothy Vernon.

Billy Carson (Buster Crabbe) is blamed for a murder committed by his lookalike cousin (also played by Crabbe).

Running time: 56 minutes. Release date: November 7, 1945.

287. Song of Old Wyoming (western) Produced and directed by Robert Emmett (Tansey). Original screenplay by Frances Kavanaugh. In Cinecolor.

Cast: Eddie Dean, Jennifer Holt, Sarah Padden, Al "Lash" LaRue, Emmett Lynn, Ray Elder, Ian Keith, John Carpenter, Robert Barron, Horace Murphy, Pete Natchenaro, Rocky Camron, Bill Lovett, Richard Cramer, Steve Clark.

A ranch hand (Eddie Dean) helps his boss (Sarah Padden) drive a gang of spoilers out of Wyoming and make the territory part of the Union.

Running time: 65 minutes. Release date: November 12, 1945.

Working title: *In Old Wyoming*.

288. The Navajo Kid (western) Directed by Harry Fraser. Produced by Arthur Alexander. Original screenplay by Harry Fraser.

Cast: Bob Steele, Syd Saylor, Caren Marsh, Edward Cassidy, Bud Osborne, Henry Hall, Stanley Blystone, Edward Howard, Charles King, Budd Buster, Gertrude Glorie, Rex Rossi, Bert Dillard.

An adopted Indian (Bob Steele) tracks down the killers of his foster father.

Running time: 59 minutes. Release date: November 21, 1945.

289. Club Havana (mystery) Directed by Edgar G. Ulmer. Produced by Leon Fromkess. Screenplay by Raymond L. Schrock. Original story by Fred S. Jackson.

Cast: Tom Neal, Margaret Lindsay, Don Douglas, Isabelita (Lita Baron), Dorothy Morris, Ernest Truex, Renie Riano, Gertrude Michael, Carlos Molina (and His Music of the Americas), Marc Lawrence, Paul Cavanaugh, Pedro de Cordoba, Eric Sinclair, Sonia Sorel, Iris and Pierre.

A murder occurs at Club Havana, a popular nightclub, where six couples—unacquainted with each other—have gone to spend the evening.

Running time: 62 minutes. Release date: November 23, 1945.

290. Detour (drama) Directed by Edgar G. Ulmer. Produced by Leon Fromkess. Screenplay by Martin Goldsmith (and Martin Mooney, uncredited). From a novel by Martin Goldsmith.

Ann Savage and Tom Neal in *Detour* (1945), a cheaply-made but effective melodrama which is now considered a cult classic (it has been called the greatest B movie ever made). Perhaps PRC's best-known film, *Detour* features an outstanding performance by Savage, who never had a better movie role.

Cast: Tom Neal, Ann Savage, Claudia Drake, Edmund MacDonald, Tim Ryan, Esther Howard, Roger Clark.

A down-and-out musician (Tom Neal) unwittingly becomes involved with a cruel and domineering hitchhiker (Ann Savage).

Running time: 69 minutes. Release date: November 30, 1945.

291. The Enchanted Forest (fantasy) Directed by Lew Landers. Produced by Jack Schwarz. Screenplay by Robert Lee Johnson, John Leber and Lou Brock. Original story by John Leber. Adaptation by Sam Neuman and Lou Brock. In Cinecolor.

Cast: Edmund Lowe, Brenda Joyce, Billy Severn, Harry Davenport, John Litel, Clancy Cooper, Jim the crow.

While lost in the forest, a young boy (Billy Severn) is befriended by an old hermit (Harry Davenport) who lives in a hollow redwood tree.

Running time: 70 minutes. Release date: December 8, 1945.

292. How Doooo You Do? (comedy) Directed by Ralph Murphy. Produced by Harry Sauber. Screenplay by Harry Sauber and Joseph Carole. Original story by Harry Sauber.

Cast: Bert Gordon, Harry Von Zell, Cheryl Walker, Frank Albertson, Ella Mae Morse, Claire Windsor, Keye Luke, Fred Kelsey, James Burke, Thomas Jackson, Sidney Marion, Leslie Denison, Charles Middleton, Matt McHugh, Eddie Kane, Francis Pierlot.

While vacationing in Desert Springs, two radio comics—"The Mad Russian" (Bert Gordon) and Harry Von Zell—become entangled in a murder mystery.

Running time: 80 minutes. Release date: December 24, 1945.

1946

293. Strangler of the Swamp (horror) Directed by Frank Wisbar. Produced by Leon Fromkess. Screenplay by Frank Wisbar. Original story by Frank Wisbar and Leo McCarthy.

Cast: Rosemary LaPlanche, Robert Barrat, Blake Edwards, Busie Laird, Charles Middleton, Effie Parnell, Nolan Leary, Frank Conlan, Theresa Lyon, Virginia Farmer.

Years after a man (Charles Middleton) is lynched, his spirit returns to the swamp to murder the descendants of the mob who killed him.

Running time: 60 minutes. Release date: January 1, 1946.

294. Lightning Raiders (western) Directed by Sam Newfield. Produced by Sigmund Neufeld. Original story and screenplay by Elmer Clifton.

Cast: Buster Crabbe, Al "Fuzzy" St. John, Mady Lawrence, Roy Brent, Steve Darnell, I. Stanford Jolley, Karl Hackett, Marin Sais, John (Bob) Cason, Al Ferguson.

Billy Carson (Buster Crabbe) investigates a series of bank robberies engineered by the bank president.

Running time: 61 minutes. Release date: January 7, 1946.

295. Danny Boy (drama) Directed by Terry Morse. Produced by Leon Fromkess. Screenplay by Raymond L. Schrock. Original story by Taylor Caven.

Cast: Robert "Buzzy" Henry, Ralph Lewis, Sybil Merritt, Helen Brown, Eve March, Bobby Valentine, Charles Bates, Larry Dixon, Richard Kipling, James Metcalf, Pat Gleason, Eric Younger, Myron Wilton, Tay Dunn, Joseph Granby, Walter Soderling, Michael McGuire, Ace the dog.

Top: Cheryl Walker, Claire Windsor, Harry Von Zell, Bert Gordon and Charles Middleton in *How Doooo You Do?* (1945). Bottom: Brenda Joyce and Billy Severn are captivated by the antics of Jim the crow in *The Enchanted Forest* (1945), a charming film that was one of PRC's biggest critical and financial successes.

Bob Steele and Lorraine Miller in *Ambush Trail* (1946).

Danny Boy, a war dog, is kidnapped and mistreated; he later manages to escape and return to his young master (Robert "Buzzy" Henry).

Running time: 64 minutes. Release date: January 8, 1946.

296. Six Gun Man (western) Directed by Harry Fraser. Produced by Arthur Alexander. Original screenplay by Harry Fraser.

Cast: Bob Steele, Syd Saylor, Jean Carlin, Bud Osborne, Brooke Temple, I. Stanford Jolley, Budd Buster, Roy Brent, Jimmie Martin, Stanley Blystone, Steve Clark, Dorothy Whitmore, Ray Jones.

A U. S. Marshal (Bob Steele) goes after a gang of cattle rustlers terrorizing a small town.

Running time: 57 minutes. Release date: February 1, 1946.

Working title: *Six Gun for Hire*.

297. Ambush Trail (western) Directed Harry Fraser. Produced by Arthur Alexander. Original screenplay by Elmer Clifton.

Cast: Bob Steele, Syd Saylor, Lorraine Miller, I. Stanford Jolley, Charles King, Bob Cason, Budd Buster, Kermit Maynard, Frank Ellis, Edward Cassidy.

A stranger in town (Bob Steele) clashes with a power-hungry villain (I. Stanford Jolley) trying to ruin the local ranchers.

Running time: 59 minutes. Release date: February 17, 1946.

298. The Flying Serpent (horror) Directed by Sherman Scott (Sam Newfield). Produced by Sigmund Neufeld. Original story and screenplay by John Thomas Neville.

Cast: George Zucco, Ralph Lewis, Hope Kramer, Eddie Acuff, Wheaton Chambers, James Metcalf, Henry Hall, Milton Kibbee, Budd Buster, Terry Frost.

An archaeologist (George Zucco) discovers an Aztec treasure in New Mexico and uses a winged reptile to guard it.

Running time: 59 minutes. Release date: February 20, 1946.

A remake of *The Devil Bat* (PRC, 1940).

299. The Mask of Diijon (drama) Directed by Lew Landers. Produced by Max Alexander and Alfred Stern. Screenplay by Arthur St. Claire and Griffin Jay. Original story by Arthur St. Claire.

Cast: Erich von Stroheim, Jeanne Bates, William Wright, Edward Van Sloan, Denise Vernac, Mauritz Hugo, Robert Malcolm, Hope Landin, Simen Ruskin, Roy Darmour, Antonio Filauri, George Chandler.

A magician (Erich von Stroheim), who is a master in the art of hypnotism, believes his young wife (Jeanne Bates) has been unfaithful and plots revenge.

Running time: 74 minutes. Release date: March 7, 1946.

300. Romance of the West (western) Produced and directed by Robert Emmett (Tansey). Original screenplay by Frances Kavanaugh. In Cinecolor.

Cast: Eddie Dean, Joan Barton, Emmett Lynn, Robert McKenzie, Forrest Taylor, Jerry Jerome, Stanley Price, Chief Thunder Cloud, Don Kay Reynolds, Rocky Cameron, Lee Roberts, Lottie Harrison, Don Williams, Jack Richardson, Matty Roubert, Forbes Murray, Jack O'Shea, Tex Cooper, Grace Christy, Jerry Riggio.

A government agent (Eddie Dean) tries to stop a band of outlaws who are inciting trouble between the Indians and white settlers in an effort to obtain valuable silver land.

Running time: 58 minutes. Release date: March 20, 1946.

301. Gentlemen with Guns (western) Directed by Sam Newfield. Produced by Sigmund Neufeld. Original story and screenplay by Fred Myton.

Cast: Buster Crabbe, Al "Fuzzy" St. John, Patricia Knox, Steve Darrell, George Chesebro, Karl Hackett, Budd Buster, Frank Ellis, George Morrell.

Fuzzy (Al St. John) is framed on a murder charge after he refuses to sell valuable water rights; Billy Carson (Buster Crabbe) steps in to prove his old friend's innocence.

Running time: 52 minutes. Release date: March 27, 1946.

Feature Films 1946

The title monstrosity in *The Flying Serpent* (1946).

302. Murder Is My Business (mystery) Directed by Sam Newfield. Produced by Sigmund Neufeld. Screenplay by Fred Myton. Based on the novel "The Uncomplaining Corpse" by Brett Halliday (Davis Dresser).

Cast: Hugh Beaumont, Cheryl Walker, Lyle Talbot, George Meeker, Pierre Watkin, Richard Keene, Ralph Dunn, David Reed, Carol Andrews, Julia McMillan, Helene Keigh, Parker Garvie, Virginia Christine, Donald Kerr.

Detective Michael Shayne (Hugh Beaumont) investigates the death of a woman who hired him to protect her from blackmail.

Running time: 63 minutes. Release date: April 10, 1946.

303. Thunder Town (western) Directed by Harry Fraser. Produced by Arthur Alexander. Original screenplay by James Oliver.

Cast: Bob Steele, Syd Saylor, Ellen Hall, Bud Geary, Charles King, Edward Howard, Steve Clark, Bud Osborne, Jimmy Aubrey, Pascale Perry.

An ex-convict (Bob Steele), determined to prove that he was framed for a robbery, sets out to gather evidence against the real crooks.

Running time: 57 minutes. Release date: April 12, 1946.

A poster of *The Mask of Diijon* (1946) starring Erich von Stroheim, one of the most distinguished talents ever to grace a PRC production. Note: Denise Vernac's name is misspelled "Vernae" on this advertisement.

304. Devil Bat's Daughter (horror) Produced and directed by Frank Wisbar. Screenplay by Griffin Jay. Story by Frank Wisbar and Ernst Jaeger.

Cast: Rosemary LaPlanche, John James, Molly Lamont, Edward Cassidy, Michael Hale, Nolan Leary, Monica Mars, Eddie Kane.

Fearing that her late father, a scientist, was a vampire, a young woman (Rosemary LaPlanche) is hypnotized into believing that she's committed a murder.

Running time: 66 minutes. Release date: April 15, 1946.

A sequel to (and uses stock footage from) *The Devil Bat* (PRC, 1940).

305. The Caravan Trail (western) Produced and directed by Robert Emmett (Tansey). Original screenplay by Frances Kavanaugh. Story by Robert Emmett Tansey (uncredited). In Cinecolor.

Cast: Eddie Dean, Emmett Lynn, Al "Lash" LaRue, Jean Carlin, Robert Malcolm, Terry Frost, Jack O'Shea, Charles King, Robert Barron, Forrest Taylor, Bob Duncan, George Chesebro, Bud Osborne, Lee Roberts, Wylie Grant, Lee Bennett, Lloyd Ingraham.

A wagon train master (Eddie Dean) becomes the sheriff of a new territory and sets out to prevent land grabbers from stealing property away from the homesteaders.

Running time: 57 minutes. Release date: April 20, 1946.

306. The Wife of Monte Cristo (action-drama) Directed by Edgar G. Ulmer. Produced by Leon Fromkess. Screenplay by Dorcas Cochran. From the character created by Alexander Dumas. Adapted by Franz Rosewald and Edgar G. Ulmer.

Cast: John Loder, Lenore Aubert, Charles Dingle, Fritz Kortner, Eduardo Ciannelli, Martin Kosleck, Fritz Feld, Eva Gabor, Virginia Christine, Clancy Cooper, Colin Campbell.

After the Count of Monte Cristo (Martin Kosleck) goes into hiding, his wife (Lenore Aubert) assumes his disguise and carries on his heroic deeds.

Running time: 80 minutes. Release date: April 23, 1946.

307. Terrors on Horseback (western) Directed by Sam Newfield. Produced by Sigmund Neufeld. Original story and screenplay by George Milton (George Wallace Sayre and Milton Raison).

Cast: Buster Crabbe, Al "Fuzzy" St. John, Patti McCarthy, I. Stanford Jolley, Henry Hall, Kermit Maynard, Karl Hackett, Marin Sais, Budd Buster, Steve Darrell, Steve Clark, Bud Osborne, Al Ferguson, George Chesebro, Frank Ellis, Jack Kirk, Lane Bradford.

After his niece is killed in a stagecoach robbery, Billy Carson (Buster Crabbe) vows to track down the murderers and bring them to justice.

Running time: 55 minutes. Release date: May 1, 1946.

John James carries an unconscious Rosemary LaPlanche who plays the title role in *Devil Bat's Daughter* (1946).

308. Ghost of Hidden Vallen (western) Directed by Sam Newfield. Produced by Sigmund Neufeld. Original story and screenplay by Ellen Coyle.

Cast: Buster Crabbe, Al "Fuzzy" St. John, Jean Carlin, John Meredith, Charles King, Jimmy Aubrey, George Morrell, Bert Dillard, Karl Hackett, Silver Harr, John (Bob) Cason, Zon Murray, Cecil Trenton.

Billy Carson (Buster Crabbe) and Fuzzy (Al St. John) help a young couple (Jean Carlin, John Meredith) fight a gang of rustlers who are using their land to conceal stolen cattle.

Running time: 56 minutes. Release date: June 5, 1946.

309. Avalanche (adventure-mystery) Directed by Irving Allen. Produced by Pat di Cicco. Story and screenplay by Andrew Holt.

Cast: Bruce Cabot, Helen Mowery, Roscoe Karns, Veda Ann Borg, Regina Wallace, Phil Van Zandt, John Good, Eddie Parks, Wilton Graff, Harry Hays Morgan, Eddie Hyans, Eddy Waller, Syd Saylor, Joe the raven.

Treasury agents (Bruce Cabot, Roscoe Karns) go to a mountain winter resort to track down a wealthy businessman on tax evasion charges. A series of snowslides trap the guests in the lodge, where several murders occur.

Running time: 70 minutes. Release date: June 20, 1946.

310. Colorado Serenade (western) Produced and directed by Robert Emmett Tansey. Original screenplay by Frances Kavanaugh. In Cinecolor.

Cast: Eddie Dean, Roscoe Ates, Mary Kenyon, Warner Richmond, David Sharpe, Forrest Taylor, Dennis Moore, Abigail Adams, Lee Bennett, Bob Duncan, Robert McKenzie, Charles King, Bud Osborne.

Two cowboys (Eddie Dean, Roscoe Ates) fight a group of gangsters who have taken control of a small western town.

Running time: 68 minutes. Release date: June 30, 1946.

311. Larceny in Her Heart (mystery) Directed by Sam Newfield. Produced by Sigmund Neufeld. Screenplay by Raymond L. Schrock. Based on a story by Brett Halliday (Davis Dresser).

Cast: Hugh Beaumont, Cheryl Walker, Ralph Dunn, Paul Bryar, Charles Wilson, Douglas Fowley, Gordon Richards, Charles Quigley, Julia McMillan, Marie Harmon, Lee Bennett, Henry Hall, Milton Kibbee.

Detective Michael Shayne (Hugh Beaumont) is hired to locate a civic leader's missing stepdaughter (Marie Harmon).

Running time: 68 minutes. Release date: July 10, 1946.

312. Prairie Badmen (western) Directed by Sam Newfield. Produced by Sigmund Neufeld. Original story and screenplay by Fred Myton.

Cast: Buster Crabbe, Al "Fuzzy" St. John, Patricia Knox, Charles King, Edward Cassidy, Kermit Maynard, John (Bob) Cason, Steve Clark, Frank Ellis, Budd Buster.

Billy Carson (Buster Crabbe) and Fuzzy (Al St. John) meet a medicine show proprietor (Edward Cassidy) who has discovered hidden gold, and they attempt to return it to the rightful owner.

Running time: 55 minutes. Release date: July 17, 1946.

313. Queen of Burlesque (musical-mystery) Directed by Sam Newfield. Produced by Arthur Alexander and Alfred Stern. Original screenplay by David Lang. Additional dialogue by Arthur St. Claire.

Cast: Evelyn Ankers, Carleton Young, Marion Martin, Rose LaRose, Alice Fleming, Craig Reynolds, Jacqueline Dalya, Murray Leonard, Emory Parnell, Nolan Leary, Gordon Clark, Red Marshall, David Frisco, Charles King.

A burlesque queen (Evelyn Ankers) is suspected of murdering a rival stripper (Rose LaRose).

Running time: 70 minutes. Release date: July 24, 1946.

Working title: *Ladies of the Chorus*.

314. Down Missouri Way (musical) Produced and directed by Josef Berne. Original screenplay by Sam Neuman.

Cast: Martha O'Driscoll, John Carradine, Eddie Dean, William Wright, Roscoe Ates, Renee Godfrey, Mabel Todd, Eddie Craven, Chester Clute, Paul Scardon, Earl Hodgins.

A lady professor (Martha O'Driscoll) returns to her Missouri home and gets involved with a motion picture unit doing location filming.

Running time: 73 minutes. Release date: August 15, 1946.

Working title: *Missouri Hayride*.

315. Secrets of a Sorority Girl (drama) Directed by Frank Wisbar. Produced by Max Alexander and Alfred Stern. Screenplay by George Wallace Sayre and Arthur St. Claire. Original story by George Wallace Sayre.

Cast: Mary Ware, Rick Vallin, Addison Richards, Frank Ferguson, Anthony Warde, Ray Walker, Marie Harmon, Caren Marsh, Mary Kenyon, Marilyn Johnson, Rosemond James, Mauritz Hugo, Emmett Vogan, Bill Murphy, Pierre Watkin.

A district attorney's daughter (Mary Ware) becomes romantically involved with a mobster (Rick Vallin).

Running time: 58 minutes. Release date: August 15, 1946.

316. Overland Riders (western) Directed by Sam Newfield. Produced by Sigmund Neufeld. Original story and screenplay by Ellen Coyle.

Cast: Buster Crabbe, Al "Fuzzy" St. John, Patti McCarthy, Charles "Slim" Whitaker, Bud Osborne, Jack O'Shea, Frank Ellis, Al Ferguson, John (Bob) Cason, George Chesebro, Lane Bradford, Wally West.

Billy Carson (Buster Crabbe) and Fuzzy (Al St. John) set out to recover mortgage money stolen in a stagecoach holdup.

Running time: 55 minutes. Release date: August 21, 1946.

317. Blonde for a Day (mystery) Directed by Sam Newfield. Produced by Sigmund Neufeld. Screenplay by Fred Myton. From the original story "Michael Shayne, Detective" by Brett Halliday (Davis Dresser).

Cast: Hugh Beaumont, Kathryn Adams, Cy Kendal, Marjorie Hoshelle, Richard Fraser, Paul Bryar, Mauritz Hugo, Charles Wilson, Sonia Sorel, Frank Ferguson, Claire Rochelle.

After a reporter writes a series of scathing attacks against the police force, an attempt is made on her life; detective Michael Shayne (Hugh Beaumont) steps in to solve the case.

Running time: 68 minutes. Release date: August 29, 1946.

318. Strange Holiday (drama) Directed by Arch Oboler. Produced by A. W. Hackel, Edward Finney and Max King. Screenplay by Arch Oboler, Charles McAvoy, Priscilla Lyon and David Bradford.

Cast: Claude Rains, Martin Kosleck, Milton Kibbee, Gloria Holden,

Claude Rains (center) in *Strange Holiday* (1946).

Barbara Bates, Helen Mack, Griff Barnett, Bobbie Stebbins, Walter White, Jr., Tommy Cook, Ed Max, Paul Dubov, Paul Hilton, Wallie Maher, Priscilla Lyon, David Bradford, Charles McAvoy.

An American businessman (Claude Rains) returns home from a vacation to discover that the United States government has been taken over by the Nazis.

Running time: 61 minutes. Release date: September 2, 1946. (*Strange Holiday* was made in 1942 [some sources claim 1940] for General Motors to boost the morale of their employees. General Motors shelved the picture; Arch Oboler then sold it to Metro-Goldwyn-Mayer, where the picture received the same treatment until Oboler and Claude Rains bought it back and released it through the independent Elite Pictures Corporation. The film received limited theatrical engagements in 1945 [it played New York in October of that year]; it was finally picked up by PRC in 1946.)

319. Outlaw of the Plains (western) Directed by Sam Newfield. Produced by Sigmund Neufeld. Screenplay by Elmer Clifton.

Cast: Buster Crabbe, Al "Fuzzy" St. John, Patti McCarthy, Charles King, Karl Hackett, Jack O'Shea, Bud Osborne, Roy Brent, Charles "Slim" Whitaker, John (Bob) Cason.

Fuzzy (Al St. John) mistakenly believes that there's gold to be found on a worthless strip of land and gets a number of townsfolk to invest in it; Billy Carson (Buster Crabbe) steps in and straightens things out.
Running time: 56 minutes. Release date: September 22, 1946.

320. **Her Sister's Secret** (drama) Directed by Edgar G. Ulmer. Produced by Henry Brash. Screenplay by Anne Green. Based on the novel "Dark Angel" by Gina Kaus.
Cast: Nancy Coleman, Margaret Lindsay, Phillip Reed, Felix Bressart, Regis Toomey, Henry Stephenson, Fritz Feld, Winston Severn, George Meeker, Helene Hugh, Frances Williams, Rudolph Anders.
A young woman (Nancy Coleman) discovers she's pregnant after having a brief affair with a soldier (Phillip Reed); her married sister (Margaret Lindsay), who is childless, adopts the baby.
Running time: 86 minutes. Release date: September 23, 1946.

321. **Accomplice** (mystery) Directed by Walter J. Colmes. Produced by John K. Teaford. Screenplay by Irving Elman and Frank Gruber. From the novel "Simon Lash, Detective" by Frank Gruber.
Cast: Richard Arlen, Veda Ann Borg, Tom Dugan, Michael Branden, Marjorie Manners, Edward Earle, Francis Ford, Herbert Rawlinson, Earle Hodgins, Sherry Hall.
An old flame (Veda Ann Borg) hires detective Simon Lash (Richard Arlen) to find her missing husband (Edward Earle).
Running time: 68 minutes. Release date: September 29, 1946.

322. **The Brute Man** (horror) Directed by Jean Yarbrough. Produced by Ben Pivar. Screenplay by George Bricker and M. Coates Webster. Original story by Dwight V. Babcock.
Cast: Tom Neal, Rondo Hatton, Jane Adams, Jan Wiley, Peter Whitney, Donald MacBride.
Disfigured by acid in a college chemistry lab, a paranoic killer (Rondo Hatton) seeks vengeance upon his former classmates (Tom Neal, Jan Wiley) whom he believes responsible for his plight.
Running time: 58 minutes. Release date: October 1, 1946. (*The Brute Man* was made by Universal Pictures and sold to PRC for distribution. Explanations vary as to why Universal chose to let go of the picture; some sources claim that Universal lost interest in the property after the death of its star, Rondo Hatton (who died on February 2, 1946). Others have stated that the film failed to come up to Universal standards (whatever *they* were) and was peddled off to PRC because of it. But the most logical reason is that Universal had merged with the independent International Pictures (forming Universal-International) and adopted a heavy schedule of prestige

pictures, which meant an end to much of their "B" product. In line with this new policy, *The Brute Man* was turned over to PRC.

323. Driftin' River (western) Produced and directed by Robert Emmett Tansey. Original screenplay by Frances Kavanaugh.

Cast: Eddie Dean, Roscoe Ates, Shirley Patterson, Lee Bennett, William Fawcett, Dennis Moore, Bob Callahan, Lottie Harrison, Forrest Taylor, Don Murphy, Lee Roberts, Wiley Grant, Marion Carney, The Sunshine Boys (M.H. Richman, J.O. Smith, A.L. Smith, Edward F. Wallace), Flash the horse.

Two special investigators (Eddie Dean, Roscoe Ates) pursue outlaws who have stolen army horses.

Running time: 59 minutes. Release date: October 1, 1946.

324. Gas House Kids (comedy) Directed by Sam Newfield. Produced by Sigmund Neufeld. Screenplay by Raymond L. Schrock and George and Elsie Bricker. Story by George and Elsie Bricker.

Cast: Robert Lowery, Teala Loring, Billy Halop, Carl "Alfalfa" Switzer, Rex Downing, Hope Landin, Paul Bryar, David Reed, Rocco Lanza, Ralph Dunn, Nanette Vallon, Charles Wilson.

The Gas House Kids (Billy Halop, Carl Switzer, Rex Downing, David Reed, Rocco Lanza) help out a war veteran (Robert Lowery) who lacks the money to purchase a chicken ranch he wants.

Running time: 68 minutes. Release date: October 28, 1946.

Working title: *East Side Rascals*.

325. Tumbleweed Trail (western) Produced and directed by Robert Emmett Tansey. Original screenplay by Frances Kavanaugh.

Cast: Eddie Dean, Roscoe Ates, Shirley Patterson, Bob Duncan, Johnny McGovern, Ted Adams, Jack O'Shea, Kermit Maynard, William Fawcett, Carl Mathews, Matty Roubert, Lee Roberts, Frank Ellis, The Sunshine Boys (M. H. Richman, J. O. Smith, A. L. Smith, Edward F. Wallace), Flash the horse.

An undercover agent (Eddie Dean) saves a young woman (Shirley Patterson) from cattle rustlers trying to seize control of her property.

Running time: 57 minutes. Release date: October 28, 1946.

326. Don Ricardo Returns (adventure) Directed by Terry O. Morse. Produced by James S. Burkett. Screenplay by Jack DeWitt and Renault Duncan (Duncan Renaldo). Original story by Johnston McCully.

Cast: Fred Colby, Isabelita (Lita Baron), Martin Garralaga, Paul Newton, Claire DuBrey, David Leonard, Anthony Warde, Michael Visaroff.

Don Ricardo (Fred Colby) journeys to California to collect his

inheritance; once there, he learns he has been declared dead by his crooked cousin. Disguising himself as a peon, Don Ricardo then sets out to gather evidence against his greedy relative.
Running time: 63 minutes. Release date: November 5, 1946.

327. Stars Over Texas (western) Produced and directed by Robert Emmett Tansey. Original screenplay by Frances Kavanaugh.
Cast: Eddie Dean, Roscoe Ates, Shirley Patterson, Lee Bennett, Lee Roberts, Kermit Maynard, Jack O'Shea, Hal Smith, Matty Roubert, Carl Mathews, William Fawcett, The Sunshine Boys (M. H. Richman, J. O. Smith, A. L. Smith, Edward F. Wallace), Flash the horse.
The Cattleman's Association sends a special investigator (Eddie Dean) to track down gang of murderous cattle rustlers.
Running time: 57 minutes. Release date: November 18, 1946.

328. Lady Chaser (mystery) Directed by Sam Newfield. Produced by Sigmund Neufeld. Screenplay by Fred Myton. Original story by R. T. Fleming-Roberts.
Cast: Ann Savage, Robert Lowery, Inez Cooper, Frank Ferguson, William Haade, Ralph Dunn, Paul Bryar, Charles Williams, Garry Owen, Marie Martino.
While in a department store, a young lady (Inez Cooper) is given an aspirin by a total stranger (Ann Savage). Her uncle takes the pill and dies of poisoning; accused of murder, she tries to trace the identity of the mysterious woman.
Running time: 58 minutes. Release date: November 25, 1946.

329. Wild West (western) Produced and directed by Robert Emmett Tansey. Original screenplay by Frances Kavanaugh. In Cinecolor.
Cast: Eddie Dean, Roscoe Ates, Al "Lash" LaRue, Robert "Buzzy" Henry, Sarah Padden, Louise Currie, Jean Carlin, Lee Bennett, Terry Frost, Warner Richmond, Bob Allen, Chief Yowlachie, Bob Duncan, Frank Pharr, Matty Roubert, John Bridges, Al Ferguson, Bud Osborne, Lee Roberts, Flash the horse.
Three U. S. Rangers (Eddie Dean, Roscoe Ates, Al "Lash" LaRue) prevent a band of outlaws from interfering with the completion of a telegraph line.
Running time: 73 minutes. Release date: December 1, 1946.
Working title: *Melody Roundup*.
This film was reissued by Eagle Lion as *Prairie Outlaws* (1948); *that* version was in black and white and had been edited down to 58 minutes, with a few new scenes of Eddie Dean and Roscoe Ates added.

1947

330. Lighthouse (drama) Directed by Frank Wisbar. Produced by Franklin Gilbert. Screenplay by Robert B. Churchill. Original story and adaptation by Don Martin.

Cast: Don Castle, June Lang, John Litel, Marion Martin, Charles Wagenheim.

Angered by her lover, a lighthouse keeper, a young woman (June Lang) marries his partner to spite him.

Running time: 62 minutes. Release date: January 10, 1947.

331. Born to Speed (drama) Directed by Edward L. Cahn. Produced by Marvin D. Stahl. Screenplay by Crane Wilbur, W. Scott Darling and Robert B. Churchill. From an unpublished story "Hell on Wheels" by Robert B. Churchill.

Cast: Johnny Sands, Terry Austin, Geraldine Wall, Frank Orth, Don Castle, Joe Haworth.

Against the wishes of loved ones, a young man (Johnny Sands) pursues a career as a race car driver.

Running time: 61 minutes. Release date: January 12, 1947.

332. Wild Country (western) Directed by Ray Taylor. Produced by Jerry Thomas. Original screenplay by Arthur E. Orloff.

Cast: Eddie Dean, Roscoe Ates, Peggy Wynne, Douglas Fowley, I. Stanford Jolley, Steve Clark, Henry Hall, Lee Roberts, Forrest Matthews, William Fawcett, Charles Jordan, Richard Cramer, Gus Taute, The Sunshine Boys (M. H. Richman, J. O. Smith, A. L. Smith, Edward F. Wallace), Flash the horse.

Two federal marshals (Eddie Dean, Roscoe Ates) pursue an escaped convict (I. Stanford Jolley) who has killed the sheriff responsible for sending him to prison.

Running time: 55 minutes. Release date: January 17, 1947.

333. The Return of Rin Tin Tin (adventure) Directed by Max Nosseck. Produced by William Stephens. Screenplay by Jack DeWitt. Based on an original idea by William Stephens. In Vitacolor.

Cast: Rin Tin Tin III, Donald Woods, Bobby Blake, Claudia Drake, Gaylord (Steve) Pendleton, Earl Hodgins.

A European boy (Bobby Blake), orphaned by the war, has lost all faith in humanity; brought to America by a mission priest (Donald Woods), his confidence and faith are gradually restored through his association with Rin Tin Tin.

Feature Films 1947

Darryl Hickman and Noreen Nash in *The Devil on Wheels* (1947).

Running time: 68 minutes. Release date: February 20, 1947. (Rescheduled for November 1, 1947, by Eagle Lion.)

334. Law of the Lash (western) Directed by Ray Taylor. Produced by Jerry Thomas. Original screenplay by William L. Nolte.

Cast: Lash LaRue, Al "Fuzzy" St. John, Mary Scott, Lee Roberts, Jack O'Shea, Charles King, John Elliott, Carl Mathews, Matty Roubert, Charles "Slim" Whitaker, Ted French, Richard Cramer, Brad Slavin.

The Cheyenne Kid (Lash LaRue) tracks down a stagecoach robber via three rings that were taken in a holdup.

Running time: 53 minutes. Release date: February 28, 1947.

335. The Devil on Wheels (drama) Directed by Crane Wilbur. Produced by Ben Stoloff. Original story and screenplay by Crane Wilbur. Based on an idea by Tony Sargent.

Cast: Noreen Nash, Darryl Hickman, Jan Ford (Terry Moore), James Cardwell, Damian O'Flynn, Lenita Love, Ann Burr, Robert Arthur, Sue England, William Forrest.

An irresponsible youth (Darryl Hickman) drives his hopped-up car at illegal speeds; his carelessness results in a hit-and-run accident.

Running time: 67 minutes. Release date: March 2, 1947.

336. Range Beyond the Blue (western) Directed by Ray Taylor. Produced by Jerry Thomas. Original screenplay by Patricia Harper.

Cast: Eddie Dean, Roscoe Ates, Helen Mowery, Ted Adams, Bob Duncan, Bill Hammond, George Turner, Ted French, Brad Slavin, Steve Clark, The Sunshine Boys (M. H. Richman, J. O. Smith, A. L. Smith, Edward F. Wallace), Flash the horse.

Undercover investigators Eddie Dean and Soapy (Roscoe Ates) help a stagecoach line owner (Helen Mowery) battle a gang of bandits who have been stealing gold shipments.

Running time: 53 minutes. Release date: March 17, 1947.

337. Philo Vance's Secret Mission (mystery) Directed by Reginald LeBorg. Produced by Howard Welsch. Screenplay by Lawrence Edmund Taylor. Based on the character by S. S. Van Dine (Willard Huntington Wright).

Cast: Alan Curtis, Sheila Ryan, Tala Birell, Frank Jenks, James Bell, Frank Fenton, Paul Maxey, Kenneth Farrell, Toni Todd, David Leonard.

Philo Vance (Alan Curtis) investigates the murder of a wealthy pulp magazine publisher who had hired him to solve the mystery behind a former partner's death.

Running time: 58 minutes. Release date: March 20, 1947. (Originally released on this date, then rescheduled for August 30, 1947, by Eagle Lion.)

338. Untamed Fury (action-drama) Produced and directed by Ewing Scott. Screenplay by Taylor Caven and Paul Gerard Smith. From the story "Gator Bait" by Ewing Scott. A Danches Brothers Production.

Cast: Gaylord (Steve) Pendleton, Leigh Whipper, Arthur Murphy, Mikel Conrad, Mary Conwell, Jack Rutherford, Charles Keane, Rodman Bruce, Paul Savage, E. G. Marshall, Norman MacKay.

A state engineer (Gaylord Pendleton) tries to convince residents of Florida's Okefenokee Swamp to permit the construction of schools and roads.

Running time: 61 minutes. Release date: March 22, 1947.

339. Three on a Ticket (mystery) Directed by Sam Newfield. Produced by Sigmund Neufeld. Screenplay by Fred Myton. Based on a story and characters created by Brett Halliday (Davis Dresser).

Cast: Hugh Beaumont, Cheryl Walker, Douglas Fowley, Louise Currie, Brooks Benedict, Paul Bryar, Ralph Dunn, Gavin Gordon, Charles Quigley, Noel Cravat, Charles King.

With his only clue being a baggage claim check found in a dead man's hand, Michael Shayne (Hugh Beaumont) tracks down a gang of thieves.

Running time: 64 minutes. Release date: April 5, 1947.

340. Philo Vance's Gamble (mystery) Directed by Basil Wrangell. Produced by Howard Welsch. Screenplay by Eugene Conrad and Arthur St.

Claire. Original story by Lawrence Edmund Taylor. Based on the character created by S. S. Van Dine (Willard Huntington Wright).

Cast: Alan Curtis, Terry Austin, Frank Jenks, Tala Birell, Gavin Gordon, Cliff Clark, Toni Todd, James Burke, Francis Pierlot, Joseph Crehan, Garnett Marks, Grady Sutton, Charles Mitchell, Joane Frank, Dan Seymour.

In this mystery concerning the disappearance of an emerald that has been smuggled into the country, Philo Vance (Alan Curtis) investigates two murders and becomes involved with a jewel smuggling operation.

Running time: 62 minutes. Release date: April 12, 1947.

341. West to Glory (western) Directed by Ray Taylor. Produced by Jerry Thomas. Original screenplay by Elmer Clifton and Robert B. Churchill.

Cast: Eddie Dean, Roscoe Ates, Delores Castle, Gregg Barton, Jimmie Martin, Zon Murray, Casey MacGregor, Billy Hammond, Ted French, Carl Mathews, Alex Montoya, Harry Vejar, The Sunshine Boys (M. H. Richman, J. O. Smith, A. L. Smith, Edward F. Wallace).

Eddie Dean and Soapy (Roscoe Ates) unmask a gang of crooks plotting to steal a valuable necklace from a Mexican rancher.

Running time: 56 minutes. Release date: April 12, 1947.

342. The Big Fix (drama) Directed by James Flood. Produced by Marvin D. Stahl. Screenplay by George Bricker and Aubrey Wisberg. Original story by Sonia Chernus and George Rose. Adaptation by Joel Malone.

Cast: James Brown, Noreen Nash, Sheila Ryan, Regis Toomey, Tom Noonan, John Shelton, Charles McGraw, Charles Mitchell, John Morgan, Nana Bryant, Howard Nebley.

A college basketball player (James Brown) discovers that a police lieutenant (Regis Toomey) is actually the head of a gambling ring attempting to win money by bribing players to throw some important games.

Running time: 63 minutes. Release date: April 19, 1947.

343. Code of the Plains (western).
An edited reissue of *The Renegade* (PRC, 1943).
Running time: 40 minutes. Release date: April 26, 1947.

344. Frontier Fighters (western).
An edited reissue of *Western Cyclone* (PRC, 1943).
Running time: 40 minutes. Release date: April 26, 1947.

345. Panhandle Trail (western).
An edited reissue of *The Mysterious Rider* (PRC, 1942).
Running time: 40 minutes. Release date: April 26, 1947.

346. Raiders of Red Rock (western).
An edited reissue of *Fugitive of the Plains* (PRC, 1943).
Running time: 40 minutes. Release date: April 26, 1947.

347. Shootin' Irons (western).
An edited reissue of *West of Texas* (PRC, 1943).
Running time: 40 minutes. Release date: April 26, 1947.

348. Thundergap Outlaws (western).
An edited reissue of *Bad Men of Thunder Gap* (PRC, 1943).
Running time: 40 minutes. Release date: April 26, 1947.

Although the following feature films were released by Eagle Lion, they were still advertised and distributed as PRC product.

1947

349. Border Feud (western) Directed by Ray Taylor. Produced by Jerry Thomas. Screenplay by Patricia Harper. Story by Joseph O'Donnell.
Cast: Lash LaRue, Al "Fuzzy" St. John, Gloria Marlen, Bob Duncan, Brad Slavin, Ian Keith, Kenneth Farrell, Casey MacGregor, Mikel Conrad, Edward Cassidy, Bud Osborne, Frank Ellis, Dick Cramer.
The Cheyenne Kid (Lash LaRue) infiltrates an outlaw gang responsible for a feud between two mine owners (Brad Slavin, Kenneth Farrell).
Running time: 55 minutes. Release date: May 10, 1947.

350. Too Many Winners (mystery) Directed by William Beaudine. Produced by John Sutherland. Screenplay by John Sutherland. From a story and characters created by Brett Halliday (Davis Dresser). Adaptation by Fred Myton and W. Scott Darling.
Cast: Hugh Beaumont, Trudy Marshall, Ralph Dunn, Claire Carleton, Charles Mitchell, John Hamilton, Grandon Rhodes, Ben Welden, Byron Foulger, Jean Andren, George Meader, Frank Hagney, Maurice B. Mozelle.
Detective Michael Shayne (Hugh Beaumont) investigates the murder of a woman who had information concerning counterfeit racetrack tickets.
Running time: 60 minutes. Release date: May 24, 1947.

351. Killer at Large (mystery) Directed by William Beaudine. Produced by Buck Gottlieb. Screenplay by Fenton Earnshaw and Tom Blackburn.
Cast: Robert Lowery, Annabel Shaw, Leonard Penn, Ann Staunton, Charles Evans, Frank Ferguson, Dick Rich, George Lynn, Eddie Parks, Stanley Blystone, Charles King, Howard Mitchell, Jack Cheatham, Hazel Kerner, Hildegard Ackerman, Brooks Benedict, Phil Arnold.

A former newspaper reporter (Robert Lowery) clashes with the corrupt administration of veterans housing.
Running time: 61 minutes. Release date: May 31, 1947.

352. Stepchild (drama) Directed by James Flood. Produced by Jerry Briskin. Screenplay by Karen DeWolf. Original story by Jules Levine.

Cast: Brenda Joyce, Donald Woods, Terry Austin, Gregory Marshall, Tommy Ivo, James Millican, Griff Barnett, Selmer Jackson, Ruth Robinson.

When a woman (Brenda Joyce) ignores her family for the sake of her career, her husband (Donald Woods) divorces her and is awarded custody of their children (Gregory Marshall, Tommy Ivo). When he remarries, the youngsters are mistreated by their stepmother (Terry Austin).
Running time: 70 minutes. Release date: June 7, 1947.

353. Philo Vance Returns (mystery) Directed by William Beaudine. Produced by Howard Welsch. Original screenplay by Robert E. Kent. Based on the character created by S. S. Van Dine (Willard Huntington Wright).

Cast: William Wright, Terry Austin, Leon Belasco, Iris Adrian, Clara Blandick, Ramsay Ames, Damian O'Flynn, Frank Wilcox, Ann Staunton, Tim Murdock, Mary Scott.

Philo Vance (William Wright) investigates the murder of a rich playboy; the man's numerous ex-wives and former fiancees are among the suspects.
Running time: 64 minutes. Release date: June 14, 1947.

354. Heartaches (mystery) Directed by Basil Wrangell. Produced by Marvin D. Stahl. Screenplay by George Bricker. Original story by Monty F. Collins and Julian I. Peyser. A Ben Stoloff Production.

Cast: Sheila Ryan, Edward Norris, Ken Farrell, Chill Wills, James Seay, Frank Orth, Chili Williams, Charles Mitchell, Al "Lash" LaRue, Phyllis Blanchard, Ann Staunton.

A film crooner (Ken Farrell), whose "voice" is actually supplied by another singer (Chill Wills), begins receiving death threats. When the star's press agent (Frank Orth) is murdered, a reporter (Edward Norris) steps in to investigate.
Running time: 71 minutes. Release date: June 28, 1947.

355. Pioneer Justice (western) Directed by Ray Taylor. Produced by Jerry Thomas. Original screenplay by Adrian Page.

Cast: Lash LaRue, Al "Fuzzy" St. John, Jennifer Holt, William Fawcett, Jack Ingram, Dee Cooper, Lane Bradford, Henry Hall, Steve Drake, Bob Woodard, Terry Frost, Wally West, Charles "Slim" Whitaker.

When three deputies meet mysterious deaths, two trouble-shooters

Tommy Bond (seated) "Alfalfa" Switzer, Rudy Wissler, Bennie Bartlett (seated) and Ray Dolciame in *Gas House Kids Go West* (1947).

(Lash LaRue, Al St. John) are sent to investigate; they uncover a plot by landgrabbers trying to drive honest people from their homeland.
Running time: 56 minutes. Release date: June 28, 1947.

356. Gas House Kids Go West (comedy) Directed by William Beaudine. Produced by Sam Baerwitz. Screenplay by Robert E. Kent, Robert A. MacGowan and Eugene Conrad. Original story by Sam Baerwitz. A Ben Stoloff Production.

Cast: Carl "Alfalfa" Switzer, Bennie Bartlett, Tommy Bond, Rudy Wissler, Ray Dolciame, Vince Barnett, John Sheldon, Chili Williams, Emory Parnell, William Wright, Lela Bliss, Jay Silverheels, Ronn Marvin.

The Gas House Kids (Carl "Alfalfa" Switzer, Bennie Bartlett, Tommy Bond, Rudy Wissler, Ray Dolciame) vacation at a California ranch which is being used as a hideout for stolen cars.
Running time: 62 minutes. Release date: July 12, 1947.

357. Ghost Town Renegades (western) Directed by Ray Taylor. Produced by Jerry Thomas. Original screenplay by Patricia Harper.

Cast: Lash LaRue, Al "Fuzzy" St. John, Jennifer Holt, Jack Ingram, Terry Frost, William Fawcett, Henry Hall, Steve Clark, Lee Roberts, Lane Bradford, Mason Wynn, Dee Cooper.

The Cheyenne Kid (Lash LaRue) and Fuzzy (Al St. John) foil a plot to take over an abandoned mining town from its rightful owners.
Running time: 57 minutes. Release date: July 26, 1947.

358. Gas House Kids in Hollywood (comedy) Directed by Edward L. Cahn. Produced by Sam Baerwitz. Original screenplay by Robert E. Kent.

Cast: Carl "Alfalfa" Switzer, Bennie Bartlett, Tommy Bond, Rudy Wissler, James Burke, Michael Whalen, Douglas Fowley, Jan Bryant.

En route to Hollywood, the Gas House Kids (Carl "Alfalfa" Switzer, Benie Bartlett, Tommy Bond, Rudy Wissler) are invited to spend the night at a scientist's home, where they tangle with gangsters trying to recover some stolen loot.
Running time: 63 minutes. Release date: August 23, 1947.

359. Stage to Mesa City (western) Directed by Ray Taylor. Produced by Jerry Thomas. Screenplay by Joseph F. Poland.

Cast: Lash LaRue, Al "Fuzzy" St. John, Jennifer Holt, George Chesebro, Brad Slavin, Marshall Reed, Terry Frost, Carl Mathews, Bob Woodward, Steve Clark, Frank Ellis, Lee Morgan, Dee Cooper, Wally West, Russell Arms.

The Cheyenne Kid (Lash LaRue) thwarts a plot by outlaws who want to take over the Mesa City stage line because of a lucrative mail contract.
Running time: 52 minutes. Release date: September 13, 1947. (Originally released on this date, then rescheduled for February 15, 1948, by Eagle Lion.)

360. Black Hills (western) Directed by Ray Taylor. Produced by Jerry Thomas. Original screenplay by Joseph F. Poland.

Cast: Eddie Dean, Roscoe Ates, Shirley Patterson, Terry Frost, Steve Drake, Nina Bara, William Fawcett, Lane Bradford, Lee Morgan, George Chesebro, Steve Crane, Bud Osborne, Carl Mathews, The Plainsmen (Earl Murphy, Paul Smith, George Bamby, Charles Morgan), White Cloud the horse.

Eddie Dean and Soapy (Roscoe Ates) pursue a saloonkeeper (Terry Frost) who murdered a rancher (Steve Drake) in order to gain possession of a secret gold mine.
Running time: 60 minutes. Release date: October 10, 1947.

361. Return of the Lash (western) Directed by Ray Taylor. Produced by Jerry Thomas. Screenplay by Joseph O'Donnell.

Cast: Lash LaRue, Al "Fuzzy" St. John, Mary Maynard, Brad Slavin, George Chesebro, George DeNormand, Lee Morgan, Lane Bradford, John Gibson, Dee Cooper, Carl Mathews, Bud Osborne, Charles "Slim" Whitaker, Kermit Maynard, Frank Ellis, Bob Woodward.

The Cheyenne Kid (Lash LaRue) and Fuzzy (Al St. John) raise money for the ranchers by rounding up six outlaws, all of whom have a price on their head. On his way home with the money, Fuzzy falls from his horse and comes down with amnesia.

Running time: 55 minutes. Release date: October 11, 1947.

362. **The Fighting Vigilantes** (western) Directed by Ray Taylor. Produced by Jerry Thomas. Original screenplay by Robert B. Churchill.

Cast: Lash LaRue, Al "Fuzzy" St. John, Jennifer Holt, George Chesebro, Steve Clark, Lee Morgan, Marshall Reed, Carl Mathews, Russell Arms, John Elliott, Felice Richmond.

Lash LaRue and Fuzzy (Al St. John) aid a citizens group known as "The Vigilantes" in their fight against a provision dispenser (George Chesebro) who is trying to create a monopoly on food sales.

Running time: 51 minutes. Release date: November 15, 1947.

363. **Shadow Valley** (western) Directed by Ray Taylor. Produced by Jerry Thomas. Screenplay by Arthur Sherman.

Cast: Eddie Dean, Roscoe Ates, Jennifer Holt, George Chesebro, Eddie Parker, Lee Morgan, Lane Bradford, Carl Mathews, Budd Buster, Forrest Taylor, Andy Parker and the Plainsmen (Earl Murphy, Paul Smith, George Bamby, Charles Morgan), White Cloud the horse.

A U. S. Marshal (Eddie Dean) aids a young woman (Jennifer Holt) in her fight against a crooked attorney (George Chesebro) who's trying to seize control of her ranch.

Running time: 58 minutes. Release date: November 29, 1947.

364. **Cheyenne Takes Over** (western) Directed by Ray Taylor. Produced by Jerry Thomas. Screenplay by Arthur E. Orloff.

Cast: Lash LaRue, Al "Fuzzy" St. John, Nancy Gates, George Chesebro, Lee Morgan, John Merton, Steve Clark, Bob Woodward, Marshall Reed, Budd Buster, Carl Mathews, Dee Cooper, Brad Slavin, Hank Bell.

Cheyenne (Lash LaRue) and Fuzzy (Al St. John) investigate the mysterious murder of the owner of a valuable ranch property.

Running time: 58 minutes. Release date: December 13, 1947.

1948

365. **Check Your Guns** (western) Directed by Ray Taylor. Produced by Jerry Thomas. Screenplay by Joseph O'Donnell.

Cast: Eddie Dean, Roscoe Ates, Nancy Gates, George Chesebro, I. Stanford Jolley, Mikel Conrad, Lane Bradford, Terry Frost, Mason Wynn, Dee Cooper, William Fawcett, Ted Adams, Budd Buster, Wally West,

Edward Cassidy, Andy Parker and the Plainsmen (Earl Murphy, Paul Smith, George Bamby, Charles Morgan), White Cloud the horse.

Eddie Dean becomes the sheriff of Red Gap and protects the citizens from an outlaw leader (I. Stanford Jolley) who's working in league with a corrupt judge (William Fawcett).

Running time: 55 minutes. Release date: January 24, 1948.

366. Tornado Range (western) Directed by Ray Taylor. Produced by Jerry Thomas. Screenplay by William Lively.

Cast: Eddie Dean, Roscoe Ates, Jennifer Holt, George Chesebro, Brad Slavin, Marshall Reed, Terry Frost, Lane Bradford, Russell Arms, Steve Clark, Hank Bell, Jack Hendricks, Ray Jones, Andy Parker and the Plainsmen (Earl Murphy, Paul Smith, George Bamby, Charles Morgan), Copper the horse.

Eddie Dean is assigned by the U. S. Land Office to settle a range war between homesteaders and cattlemen.

Running time: 56 minutes. Release date: February 21, 1948.

367. The Westward Trail (western) Directed by Ray Taylor. Produced by Jerry Thomas. Original screenplay by Robert Alan Miller.

Cast: Eddie Dean, Roscoe Ates, Phyllis Blanchard, Eileen Hardin, Steve Drake, Bob Duncan, Carl Mathews, Lee Morgan, Bob Woodward, Budd Buster, Charles "Slim" Whitaker, Frank Ellis, Andy Parker and the Plainsmen (Earl Murphy, Paul Smith, George Bamby, Charles Morgan), Copper the horse.

Eddie Dean, a representative of the U. S. Marshal, comes to the aid of a young woman (Phyllis Blanchard) who's on the verge of losing her newly-purchased ranch to the local badman (Bob Duncan).

Running time: 56 minutes. Release date: March 13, 1948.

368. The Hawk of Powder River (western) Directed by Ray Taylor. Produced by Jerry Thomas. Screenplay by George Smith.

Cast: Eddie Dean, Roscoe Ates, Jennifer Holt, June Carlson, Terry Frost, Lane Bradford, Eddie Parker, Carl Mathews, Ted French, Steve Clark, Tex Palmer, Charles King, Marshall Reed, Andy Parker and the Plainsmen (Earl Murphy, Paul Smith, George Bamby, Charles Morgan).

Eddie Dean and Soapy (Roscoe Ates) pursue an outlaw gang led by "The Hawk" (Jennifer Holt).

Running time: 54 minutes. Release date: April 10, 1948.

369. Prairie Outlaws (western).

A re-edited, black and white version of *Wild West* (PRC, 1946).

Running time: 58 minutes. Release date: May 12, 1948.

370. The Tioga Kid (western) Directed by Ray Taylor. Produced by Jerry Thomas. Screenplay by Ed Earl Repp.

Cast: Eddie Dean, Roscoe Ates, Jennifer Holt, Dennis Moore, Lee Bennett, William Fawcett, Eddie Parker, Bob Woodward, Louis J. Corbett, Terry Frost, Tex Palmer, Andy Parker and the Plainsmen (Earl Murphy, Paul Smith, George Bamby, Charles Morgan), Flash the horse.

Eddie Dean plays two roles in this one: a Texas Ranger and a notorious outlaw known as "The Tioga Kid," a lone wolf who's trying to muscle in on a gang of horse rustlers victimizing a pretty young ranch owner (Jennifer Holt).

Running time: 54 minutes. Release date: June 17, 1948.

Short Subjects

American History

This series of two-reel (approximately 20 minutes in length) educational shorts was produced by Max and Arthur Alexander for the Academic Film Co., Inc., and released by PRC. All were written and directed by George Arthur Durlam.

371a. "Our Bill of Rights" (Release date: March 1, 1941)
371b. "Our Constitution" (Release date: March 1, 1941)
371c. "Our Declaration of Independence" (Release date: March 1, 1941)
371d. "Our Monroe Doctrine" (Release date: March 1, 1941)
371e. "Our Louisiana Purchase" (Release date: August 1, 1941)
371f. "Our Freedom of the Seas" (Release date: November 1, 1941)

Special Featurettes

372. Man, the Enigma (documentary) Produced by Stacy and Horace Woodward.

An analogy of the social life of man to the animal kingdom.
Running time: 22 minutes. Release date: May 7, 1941.

373. Alive in the Deep (documentary) Produced by Stacy and Horace Woodward.

A documentary on marine life, photographed on the Pribiloff Islands in the Bering Sea, in Florida's Marineland and in the research laboratories of the California Institute of Technology.
Running time: 25 minutes. Release date: May 7, 1941.

Contrary to some reports, PRC never produced a serial.

Screen Guild/Lippert Pictures

With few exceptions, the Lippert films are unremarkable programmers of no real merit.

During its formative years as Screen Guild Productions, the company offered some change-of-pace fare, ranging from "streamliners" (mini-features that ran approximately 45 minutes in length) to productions photographed in the always-blurry Cinecolor process. Most of the Screen Guild releases are, to put it bluntly, unwatchable; a few are notable only for the performers who appeared in them, such as *God's Country* (1946) with Buster Keaton and *Scared to Death* (1947) with Bela Lugosi.

On the whole, the Lippert pictures aren't much of an improvement over their predecessors: *Square Dance Jubilee* (1949), *Everybody's Dancin'* (1950), *Hi-Jacked* (1950), *Holiday Rhythm* (1950), *Stop that Cab* (1951), *Kentucky Jubilee* (1951) and *Varieties on Parade* (1951) are typically lame Lippert offerings.

As Lippert Pictures, the company still made attempts to offer something different. In 1949 Lippert released a handful of features photographed with the Garutso Balanced Lens, which was "a photographic principle which creates a three dimensional effect." But films like *Deputy Marshal, Apache Chief* and *Tough Assignment* were mediocre regardless of the dimension they were viewed in.

In 1951 Hugh Beaumont starred in three one-hour mysteries (*Danger Zone, Roaring City, Pier 23*), each advertised as "an adventure presented in two parts—each a complete story." These films were made with the intention of playing theatrically first, then being split in half for television airings (whether they were actually televised in a half-hour format is not known).

Despite the generally low quality of the Lippert product, some worthwhile entries did emerge. Samuel Fuller's *The Steel Helmet* (1951) is an outstanding war drama, easily Lippert's finest hour. *Superman and the Mole Men* (1951), perhaps Lippert's most famous effort, is a highly enjoyable science fiction–fantasy that marked George Reeves' first appearance as the Man of Steel. *Rocketship X-M* (1950), *F.B.I. Girl* (1952) and *For Men Only* (1952) are also among the better Lippert films, faint praise that it is.

Corporate History

In 1945 Robert L. Lippert, a West Coast theater-chain owner, headed Action Pictures, Inc., an independent production unit that made three low-budget features filmed in Cinecolor. These films eventually saw release through Screen Guild Productions, a new firm in which Lippert served as executive vice president (Joseph Blumenfeld was the president of the organization).

In the spring of 1949 Lippert reorganized Screen Guild, assumed the post of president, and by the summer of that year was releasing films under the company's new name, Lippert Pictures, Incorporated.

Lippert Pictures lasted until the end of 1955; the following year Lippert formed Regal Films, a new organization that had its product released through 20th Century–Fox.

The Feature Films of Screen Guild Productions (1945–1949) and Lippert Pictures, Inc. (1949–1955)

This listing does not cover the feature films originally distributed by other studios that were reissued through Screen Guild and Lippert, among them: *Babes in Toyland* (MGM; reissued as *March of the Wooden Soldiers*), *Midnight* (Universal; reissued as *Call It Murder*), *The People's Enemy* (RKO; reissued as *Racketeers*), *Flirting with Fate* (MGM), *King of the Turf* (United Artists), *Miss Annie Rooney* (United Artists), *Duke of West Point* (United Artists) and twelve Hopalong Cassidy westerns (Paramount).

However, several foreign productions (mostly British) that Lippert distributed in the U. S. (to help pad out their release schedule) have been included.

Screen Guild Productions

1945

374. Wildfire (western) Directed by Robert Tansey. Produced by William B. David. Screenplay by Frances Kavanaugh. Story by W. C. Tuttle. An Action Picture Production. In Cinecolor.

Cast: Bob Steele, Sterling Holloway, John Miljan, William Farnum, Virginia Mapes, Eddie Dean, Sarah Padden, Wee Willie Davis, Rocky Camron, Al Ferguson, Francis Ford, Frank Ellis, Hal Price.

A wild horse, doomed to extermination by ranchers who believe him guilty of luring their stock away to join his herd, is saved by two horsetraders (Bob Steele, Sterling Holloway).
Running time: 57 minutes. Release date: July 18, 1945.
Sequel: *Return of Wildfire* (Screen Guild, 1948).

375. **Northwest Trail** (adventure) Directed by Derwin Abrahams. Produced by William B. David and Max M. King. Screenplay by Harvey Gates and Leslie J. Schwabacher. Based on a story by James Oliver Curwood. An Action Pictures Production. In Cinecolor.

Cast: Bob Steele, Joan Woodbury, John Litel, Raymond Hatton, Madge Bellamy, Ian Keith, George Meeker, Charles Middleton, John Hamilton, Poodles Hanneford, Gracie Hanneford, Bud Osborne, Al Ferguson, Bob Duncan, Josh (John) Carpenter.

A Mountie (Bob Steele) guides a young woman (Joan Woodbury) who is bringing $20,000 through the wilderness to her father.
Running time: 66 minutes. Release date: November 30, 1945.

1946

376. **God's Country** (adventure) Directed by Robert Tansey. Produced by William B. David. Original story and screenplay by Robert Tansey. An Action Pictures Production. In Cinecolor.

Cast: Robert Lowery, Helen Gilbert, William Farnum, Buster Keaton, Stanley Andrews, Trevor Bardette, Si Jenks, Estelle Zarco, Juan Reyes, Al Ferguson, Ace the dog.

A fugitive from justice (Robert Lowery) helps Indians and fur trappers battle a timber baron (Stanley Andrews) trying to seize control of their territory.
Running time: 64 minutes. Release date: April 15, 1946.

377. **Death Valley** (western-drama) Directed by Lew Landers. Produced by William B. David. Original story and screenplay by Doris Schroeder. A Golden Gate Pictures Production. In Natural Color (Cinecolor).

Cast: Nat Pendleton, Helen Gilbert, Robert Lowery, Sterling Holloway, Barbara Reed, Russell Simpson, Paul Hurst, Dick Scott, Stan Price, Bob Benton, Sammy Stein.

A prospector (Nat Pendleton) is overcome by greed, resorting to thievery and murder to obtain gold.
Running time: 72 minutes. Release date: August 15, 1946.

Inez Cooper and Russell Hayden in 'Neath Canadian Skies (1946), a "streamline" feature.

378. Flight to Nowhere (mystery) Directed by William Rowland. Produced by William B. David. Original screenplay by Arthur V. Jones. A Golden Gate Pictures Production.

Cast: Alan Curtis, Evelyn Ankers, Jack Holt, Robert Armstrong, Micheline Cheirel, Jerome Cowan, John Craven, Inez Cooper, Roland Varno, Michael Visaroff, Gordon Richards, Hoot Gibson.

A pilot (Alan Curtis) works with an F. B. I. man (Jack Holt) to try to stop spies who are after the key to the hidden uranium deposits.

Running time: 74 minutes. Release date: October 1, 1946.

379. 'Neath Canadian Skies (adventure) Directed by B. Reeves Eason. Produced by William B. David. Screenplay by Arthur V. Jones. Story by James Oliver Curwood. Original treatment by George H. Plympton. A Golden Gate Pictures Production.

Cast: Russell Hayden, Inez Cooper, Douglas Fowley, Cliff Nazarro, I. Stanford Jolley, Kermit Maynard, Jack Mulhall, Dick Alexander, Pat Hurst, Gil Patrick, Boyd Stockman, Jimmie Martin.

Following the murder of a prospector, a Mountie (Russell Hayden) poses as a wanted criminal in order to nab a gang of claim jumpers.
Running time: 41 minutes. Release date: October 15, 1946.

380. Rolling Home (drama) Produced and directed by William Berke. Screenplay by Edwin V. Westrate. Original story by William Berke.

Cast: Jean Parker, Russell Hayden, Jo Ann Marlowe, Raymond Hatton, Pamela Blake, James Colin, Jonathan Hale, George Tyne, Jimmy Dodd, Robert Dee Henry.

A horse is entered in a race to help a parson (Russell Hayden) raise money to pay off a mortgage.
Running time: 71 minutes. Release date: November 1, 1946.

381. North of the Border (adventure) Directed by B. Reeves Eason. Produced by William B. David. Screenplay by Arthur V. Jones. Story by James Oliver Curwood.

Cast: Russell Hayden, Lyle Talbot, Inez Cooper, Anthony Warde, Guy Beach, Jack Mulhall, I. Stanford Jolley, Dick Alexander, Douglas Fowley, Artie Ortego.

A Mountie (Russell Hayden) searches for a missing fur trapper.
Running time: 42 minutes. Release date: November 15, 1946.
Working title: *Ranson of the Mounted*.

382. My Dog Shep (drama) Directed by Ford Beebe. Produced by William B. David. Screenplay by Gertrude Walker, from her original story "Wolf Pack."

Cast: Tom Neal, Helen Chapman, Craig Reynolds, Lanny Rees, William Farnum, Russell Simpson, J. Farrell MacDonald, Sarah Padden.

A runaway orphan (Lanny Rees), his dog and an old soldier (William Farnum) take to the road, and become involved in a kidnapping plot.
Running time: 60 minutes. Release date: December 1, 1946.
Sequel: *Shep Comes Home* (Screen Guild, 1948).

383. Renegade Girl (western) Produced and directed by William Berke. Original screenplay by Edwin V. Westrate. An Affiliated Production.

Cast: Ann Savage, Alan Curtis, Edward Brophy, Russell Wade, Jack Holt, Claudia Drake, Ray Corrigan, John King, Chief Thunder Cloud, Edmund Cobb, Richard (Dick) Curtis, Nick Thompson, Harry Cording, Ernie Adams, James Martin.

After the Civil War, a Yankee-hating girl (Ann Savage) turns outlaw; she finds herself faced with a dilemma when she falls in love with her captor (Alan Curtis), a Union Army officer.
Running time: 65 minutes. Release date: December 25, 1946.

Screen Guild/Lippert Pictures

Ann Savage and Alan Curtis in *Renegade Girl* (1946).

1947

384. **Queen of the Amazons** (adventure) Produced and directed by Edward Finney. Original story and screenplay by Roger Merton.

Cast: Robert Lowery, Patricia Morison, J. Edward Bromberg, John Miljan, Amira Moustafa, Keith Richards, Bruce Edwards, Wilson Benge, Jack George, Cay Forester, Vida Aldana, Hassam Kayyam.

An expedition, headed by a jungle guide (Robert Lowery) and a young woman (Patricia Morison) searching for a missing explorer, encounters ivory thieves, deadly natives and a white jungle queen (Amira Moustafa).

Running time: 61 minutes. Release date: January 15, 1947.

385. **Bells of San Fernando** (adventure-western) Directed by Terry Morse. Produced by James S. Burkett. Original story and screenplay by Jack DeWitt and Renault Duncan (Duncan Renaldo). A Hillcrest Production.

Cast: Donald Woods, Gloria Warren, Byron Foulger, Anthony Warde, Monte Blue, David Lenard, Frank Cody, Claire DuBrey, Paul Newlan, Gordon Clark, Drew Allan, Luisa Triana, Shirley O'Hara, Gilbert Galvan, Felipe Turich.

An Irish immigrant (Donald Woods) and a senorita (Gloria Warren)

help the people in their new California town fight for their freedom from a ruthless land baron (Anthony Warde).
Running time: 74 minutes. Release date: March 1, 1947.

386. **Shoot to Kill** (mystery) Produced and directed by William Berke. Original screenplay by Edwin V. Westrate.

Cast: Russell Wade, Edmund MacDonald, Susan Walters, Vince Barnett, Douglas Blackley, Nestor Pavia, Charles Trowbridge, Harry Brown, Ted Hecht, Harry Cheshire, Joe Devlin, Eddie Foster, Frank O'Connor, Sammy Stein, Robert Riordan, Gene Rodgers, Stanley Blystone.

An ambitious reporter (Russell Wade) and a secretary (Susan Walters) uncover the shady operations of corrupt politicians.
Running time: 63 minutes. Release date: March 15, 1947.

387. **Buffalo Bill Rides Again** (western) Directed by Bernard B. Ray. Produced by Jack Schwarz. Original story and screenplay by Barney Sarecky and Fran Gilbert.

Cast: Richard Arlen, Jennifer Holt, Lee Shumway, Gil Patrick, Edward Cassidy, Edmund Cobb, Ted Adams, Shooting Star, Charles Stevens, Chief Many Treaties, John Dexter, Holly Bane, Frank McCarroll, Carl Mathews, Clark Stevens, George Sherwood, Fred Graham, Paul Hill, Phil Arnold, Tom Leffingwell, Frank O'Connor, Fred Fox, Dorothy Curtis.

Buffalo Bill (Richard Arlen) is called in when a syndicate tries to scare settlers off their oil-rich land by stirring up trouble with the Indians.
Running time: 70 minutes. Release date: April 19, 1947.

388. **Scared to Death** (mystery-horror) Directed by Christy Cabanne. Produced by William B. David. Original story and screenplay by W. J. Abbott. In Cinecolor. A Golden Gate Pictures Production.

Cast: Bela Lugosi, Douglas Fowley, Joyce Compton, George Zucco, Nat Pendleton, Roland Varno, Molly Lamont, Angelo Rossitto, Gladys Blake, Lee Bennett, Stanley Andrews, Stanley Price.

A grasping woman (Molly Lamont) is found dead, without any mark of physical violence; flashbacks relate how and why.
Running time: 65 minutes. Release date: May 3, 1947.
Working titles: *The Autopsy* and *Accent on Horror*.

389. **Bush Pilot** (adventure-drama) Directed by Sterling Campbell. Produced by Larry Cromien. A Dominion Production.

Cast: Rochelle Hudson, Jack LaRue, Austin Willis, Frank Perry, Joe Carr, Gordon Adam, Michael Lambert, Florence Kennedy.

A Canadian bush pilot (Austin Willis), in love with a school teacher

Bela Lugosi and Angelo Rossitto in *Scared to Death* (1947).

(Rochelle Hudson), encounters trouble when his half-brother (Jack LaRue) muscles in on his territory and his girl.

Running time: 60 minutes. Release date: June 7, 1947.

390. Hollywood Barn Dance (musical) Directed by Bernard B. Ray. Produced by Jack Schwarz. Screenplay by Dorothea Knox Martin. Story by Bernard B. Ray.

Cast: Ernest Tubb, Lori Talbott, Helen Boyce, Earle Hodgins, Frank McGlynn, Phil Arnold, Larry Reed, Red Harron, Anne Kundi, Betty Mudge, Cy Ring, Frank Bristow, Albin Robeling, Dotti Hackett, Pat Combs, Jack Guthrie, Philharmonic Trio.

In an effort to raise funds to rebuild the village church, Ernest Tubb and his troupe head to Hollywood.

Running time: 72 minutes. Release date: June 21, 1947.

391. The Hat Box Mystery (mystery) Directed by Lambert Hillyer. Produced by Carl K. Hittleman. Screenplay by Don Martin and Carl K. Hittleman. Original story by Maury Nunes and Carl K. Hittleman.

Cast: Tom Neal, Pamela Blake, Allen Jenkins, Virginia Sale, Ed Keane, Leonard Penn, William Ruhl, Zon Murray, Olga Andre.

Rochelle Hudson and Jack LaRue in *Bush Pilot* (1947).

When his secretary (Pamela Blake) is held on a murder charge, a private detective (Tom Neal) sets out to solve the mystery, the key clue being a gun concealed in a hatbox.

Running time: 44 minutes. Release date: July 12, 1947.

392. The Case of the Baby Sitter (mystery) Directed by Lambert Hillyer. Produced by Maury Nunes. Screenplay by Carl K. Hittleman and Ande Lamb.

Cast: Tom Neal, Pamela Blake, Allen Jenkins, Virginia Sale, George Meeker, Rebel Randall, Keith Richards, Lona Andre, Crane Whitley, Eddie Kane, Mickey Simpson, Bill Kennedy, Tom Kennedy.

A pair of jewel thieves (George Meeker, Rebel Randall) hire a private detective (Tom Neal) to watch their swag, under the guise of guarding their baby.

Running time: 41 minutes. Release date: July 26, 1947.

393. Killer Dill (comedy) Directed by Lewis D. Collins. Produced by Max M. King. Screenplay by John O'Dea. Original story by Alan Friedman.

Cast: Stuart Erwin, Anne Gwynne, Frank Albertson, Mike Mazurki, Milburn Stone, Dorothy Granger, Anthony Warde, Ben Welden, Will

Orlean, Stanley Ross, Shirley Hunter, Charles Knight, Stanley Andrews, Julie Mitchum.

A timid salesman (Stuart Erwin) is mistaken for a notorious public enemy.

Running time: 71 minutes. Release date: August 2, 1947.

394. Boy! What a Girl! (musical) Directed by Arthur Leonard. Produced by Jack Goldberg. Story by Vincent Valentini.

Cast: Tim Moore, Elwood Smith, Duke Williams, Al Jackson, Sheila Guyse, Betti Mays, Sybil Lewis, Warren Patterson, Slam Stewart, Deek Watson and His Brown Dots, "Big" Sid Catlett and His Band, Ann Cornell and the International Jitterbugs.

Two would-be producers (Elwood Smith, Duke Williams) hire a female impersonator (Tim Moore) to pose as one of their backers during a meeting with a Chicago financier (Al Jackson).

Running time: 70 minutes. Release date: September 20, 1947.

An "all-colored" picture produced by Herald Pictures, Inc., released thru Screen Guild.

395. The Burning Cross (drama) Produced and directed by Walter Colmes. Original screenplay by Aubrey Wisberg. A Somerset Pictures Production.

Cast: Hank Daniels, Virginia Patton, Raymond Bond, Betty Roadman, Dick Rich, Joel Fluellen, Walden Boyle, Alexander Pope, John Fostini, John Doucette, Jack Shutta, Mady Norman, Glen Allen, Matt Willis, Tom Kennedy, Dick Bailey, Ted Stanhope.

A demoralized ex–GI (Hank Daniels) joins the Ku Klux Klan, following their credo of "kicking out the foreigners and making America a place for Americans."

Running time: 78 minutes. Release date: October 11, 1947.

396. Sepia Cinderella (musical) Directed by Arthur Leonard. Produced by Jack Goldberg and Arthur Leonard. Original story and screenplay by Vincent Valentini.

Cast: Billy Daniels, Sheila Guyse, Tondelayo, Rubie Blake, Jack Carter, Dusty Freeman, George Williams, Fred Gordon, Harold Norton, Lora Pierre, Emory Richardson, Gertrude Saunders, Hilda Offley, Percy Verwayen, Al Young, Jimmy Fuller, Deek Watson and His Brown Dots, Leonardo and Zolo, Ray C. Moore, Apus and Estrellita, John Kirby's Band, Walter Fuller's Orchestra.

The struggles of a pair of newlyweds: he's a songwriter (Billy Daniels) and she's a singer (Sheila Guyse); when he strikes it rich with a hit tune, his head is turned by a femme fatale (Tondelayo).

Running time: 70 minutes. Release date: October 18, 1947.

An "all-colored" feature produced by Herald Pictures, Inc., released thru Screen Guild.

397. The Dragnet (mystery) Directed by Leslie Goodwins. Produced by Maurice H. Conn. Screenplay by Barbara Worth and Harry Essex. Original story by Maurice H. Conn.

Cast: Henry Wilcoxon, Mary Brian, Douglass Dumbrille, Virginia Dale, Douglas Blakely, Tom Fadden, Don Harvey, Maxine Seman, Ralph Dunn, Bert Conway, Douglas Evans, Paul Newlan, Allan Nixon.

A Scotland Yard inspector (Henry Wilcoxon) teams with the New York police force to track down the crooks responsible for London jewel robberies.

Running time: 71 minutes. Release date: October 25, 1947.

398. Miracle in Harlem (mystery) Directed by Jack Kemp. Produced by Jack Goldberg. Screenplay by Vincent Valentini. In Sepiatone.

Cast: Sheila Guyse, Stepin Fetchit, Hilda Offley, Creighton Thompson, Kenneth Freeman, William Greaves, Sybil Lewis, Jack Carter, Lawrence Criner, Milton Williams, Monte Hawley, Rubie Blake, Alfred Chester, Savannah Churchill, Juanita Hall Choir, Lavada Carter, Norma Shepherd, Lynn Proctor Trio.

Kindly old Aunt Hattie (Hilda Offley) and her niece (Sheila Guyse) are swindled out of their candy shop by the owner of a chain of candy stores (Lawrence Criner). When he dies of eating poisoned candy, Aunt Hattie is suspected.

Running time: 69 minutes. Release date: November 29, 1947.

An "all-colored" feature produced by Herald Pictures, Inc., released thru Screen Guild.

399. Road to the Big House (drama) Directed by Walter Colmes. Produced by Selwyn Levinson and Walter Colmes. Original screenplay by Aubrey Wisberg. A Somerset Pictures Production.

Cast: John Shelton, Ann Doran, Guinn "Big Boy" Williams, Dick Bailey, Joe Allen, Jr., Rory Mallinson, Eddy Fields, Walden Boyle, Keith Richards, Jack Conrad, Charles Jordan, C. Montague Shaw, John Doucette, Mickey Simpson.

A bank clerk (John Shelton) tired of being poor, steals $200,000 from the vault. He hides the loot before being jailed for the crime, figuring that he'll be able to enjoy the wealth after he gets out of prison.

Running time: 72 minutes. Release date: December 13, 1947.

Working title: *The Park Road*.

400. Where the North Begins (adventure) Directed by Howard Bretherton. Produced by Carl K. Hittleman. Screenplay by Elizabeth (Betty) Burbridge. Original story by Leslie Schwabacher. Based on a story by James Oliver Curwood. A Bali Pictures, Inc. Production.

Cast: Russell Hayden, Jennifer Holt, Tristram Coffin, Denver Pyle, Steve Barclay, Artie Ortego, Keith Richards, Anthony Warde, Frank Hagney, J. W. Cody, (Chief) Willow Bird.

Sgt. David "Lucky" Sanderson (Russell Hayden), a Mountie, comes to the aid of an undercover officer (Steve Bailey) trying to trap a crook (Tristram Coffin) who's selling liquor and guns to the Indians.

Running time: 42 minutes. Release date: December 13, 1947.

401. Trail of the Mounties (adventure) Directed by Howard Bretherton. Produced by Carl K. Hittleman. Screenplay by Elizabeth (Betty) Burbridge. Original story by Carl K. Hittleman and Harold Klein. Based on a story by James Oliver Curwood. A Bali Pictures, Inc. Production.

Cast: Russell Hayden, Jennifer Holt, Emmett Lynn, Terry Frost, Harry Cording, Charles Bedell, Zon Murray, Pedro Regas, Frank Lackteen, Britt Wood, Felice Raymond.

A Mountie (Russell Hayden) searches for murderous fur thieves in the Canadian wilderness and discovers that the leader of the gang is his twin brother (also played by Hayden).

Running time: 42 minutes. Release date: December 20, 1947.

402. The Prairie (western) Directed by Frank Wisbar. Produced by Edward Finney. Screenplay by Arthur St. Claire. Based on the novel by James Fenimore Cooper.

Cast: Lenore Aubert, Alan Baxter, Russ Vincent, Jack Mitchum, Charles Evans, Edna Holland, Chief Thunder Cloud, Fred Colby, Bill Murphy, David Gerber, Don Lynch, George Morrell, Chief Yowlachie, Jay Silverheels, Beth Taylor. Commentary by Frank Hemingway.

The story of a covered-wagon family's trek into the newly-opened Louisiana Purchase territory.

Running time: 80 mintues. Release date: December 27, 1947.

1948

403. Jungle Goddess (adventure) Directed by Lewis D. Collins. Produced by Robert L. Lippert. Screenplay by Joseph Pagano.

Cast: George Reeves, Ralph Byrd, Wanda McKay, Armida, Robert "Smoki" Whitfield, Dolores Castle, Rudy Robles, Linda Johnson, Helena Grant, Fred Colby, Onest Conley, Zach Williams, Jack Carroll.

Two pilots (George Reeves, Ralph Byrd) seek a missing heiress (Wanda McKay) and discover she's the queen of a jungle tribe.
Running time: 61 minutes. Release date: August 13, 1948.

404. The Return of Wildfire (western) Directed by Ray Taylor. Produced by Carl K. Hittleman. Screenplay by Betty Burbridge and Carl K. Hittleman. In Sepiatone.
Cast: Richard Arlen, Patricia Morison, Mary Beth Hughes, James Millican, Reed Hadley, Chris-Pin Martin, Stanley Andrews, Holly Bane, Highland Dale the horse.
A wrangler (Richard Arlen) comes to the aid of two sisters (Patricia Morison, Mary Beth Hughes) who are being swindled out of their property.
Running time: 81 minutes. Release date: August 13, 1948.
Released in Great Britain as *The Black Stallion*.
A sequel to *Wildfire* (Screen Guild, 1945).

405. Dead Man's Gold (western) Directed by Ray Taylor. Produced by Ron Ormond. Screenplay by Moree Herring and Gloria Welsch. Original story by Ron Ormond and Ira Webb. A Western Adventure Production.
Cast: Lash LaRue, Al "Fuzzy" St. John, Peggy Stewart, John (Bob) Cason, Terry Frost, Lane Bradford, Pierce Lyden, Stephen Keys, Cliff Taylor, Britt Wood, Marshall Reed, Bob Woodward.
Lash LaRue and Fuzzy (Al St. John) help a young woman (Peggy Stewart) solve the murder of her uncle, a ranch owner.
Running time: 60 minutes. Release date: September 10, 1948.

406. S. O. S. Submarine (drama) Written and directed by F. DeRobertis. Produced by C. Zanetti.
A semi-documentary dealing with the safety measures surrounding Italy's submarine fleet and the efforts to rescue thirteen men in a sunken sub.
Running time: 69 minutes. Release date: September 17, 1948.
An Italian-made film, English dubbed; released in the U. S. by Screen Guild.

407. Harpoon (action-drama) Directed by Ewing Scott. Produced by the Danches Brothers. Screenplay by Girard Smith and Ewing Scott.
Cast: John Bromfield, Alyce Lewis, James Cardwell, Patricia Garrison, Jack George, Edgar Hinton, Frank Hagney, Holly Bane, Ruth Castle, Grant Means, Sally Davis, James Martin, Willard Jillson, Gary Garrett, Lee Elson, Alex Sharp, Lee Roberts.
In the Alaskan wilderness, two men (John Bromfield, James Cardwell)

Ralph Byrd, Denise Darcel and George Reeves in *Thunder in the Pines* (1948).

engage in a feud that began with their fathers (Edgar Hinton, Frank Hagney).

Running time: 83 minutes. Release date: September 24, 1948.

408. Mark of the Lash (western) Directed by Ray Taylor. Produced by Ron Ormond. Screenplay by Moree Herring and Gloria Welsch. Original story by Ron Ormond and Ira Webb. A Western Adventure Production.

Cast: Lash LaRue, Al "Fuzzy" St. John, Suzi Crandall, Jimmie Martin, John (Bob) Cason, Marshall Reed, Tom London, Lee Roberts, Steve Dunhill, Jack Hendricks, Cliff Taylor, Harry Cody, Britt Wood.

After a saloon owner has taken the law into his own hands following the death of the sheriff, Lash and Fuzzy (Al St. John) attempt to restore law and order in the town of Red Rock.

Running time: 57 minutes. Release date: October 15, 1948.

409. The Mozart Story (biography) Directed by Carl Hartl. Screenplay by Richard Billinger. A Patrician Pictures Production. Additional dialogue and sequences (22 minutes) produced by Abrasha Haimson and directed by Frank Wisbar in Hollywood.

Cast: Hans Holt, Winnie Markus, Irene von Meyendorf, Rene Deltger,

Edward Veddes, Wilton Graff, Carol Forman, Anthony Barr, Walther Jansson, Rosa Alback Rettas, Anita Rosen, Thea Weiss, Curt Juergens, Paul Hoerbiger, John Siebert, Richard Eybner, Eric Nocowitz, Theo Danagger, Fred Imhoff, Carl Bluhm.

A biography of composer Wolfgang Amadeus Mozart (Hans Holt).

Running time: 93 minutes. Release date: November 13, 1948.

An Austrian-made film; songs in German, dialogue English dubbed. Released in the U. S. by Screen Guild.

410. Thunder in the Pines (action-comedy) Directed by Robert Edwards. Produced by William Stephens. Screenplay by Maurice Tombragel. Original story by Jo Pagano. In Sepiatone.

Cast: George Reeves, Ralph Byrd, Greg McClure, Michael Whalen, Denise Darcel, Marion Martin, Lyle Talbot, Vince Barnett, Roscoe Ates, Tom Kennedy, Arno Tanney, Joey Ray.

Two lumberjacks (George Reeves, Ralph Byrd) engage in a logging race to determine who will win the hand of a lovely French girl (Denise Darcel).

Running time: 62 minutes. Release date: November 19, 1948.

411. Shep Comes Home (drama) Directed by Ford Beebe. Produced by Ron Ormond. Original screenplay by Ford Beebe.

Cast: Robert Lowery, Billy Kimbley, Flame the dog, Margia Dean, Martin Garralaga, Sheldon Leonard, Michael Whalen, J. Farrell MacDonald, Lyle Talbot, Frank Jenks, Edna Holland, Matt Willis, Ben Erway.

A runaway orphan (Billy Kimbley) and his pet dog Shep come to the rescue of an innocent man (Martin Garralaga) who has been accused of crimes that have been committed by a local gangster.

Running time: 58 minutes. Release date: December 3, 1948.

A sequel to *My Dog Shep* (Screen Guild, 1946).

412. Frontier Revenge (western) Directed by Ray Taylor. Produced by Ron Ormond. Original screenplay by Ray Taylor.

Cast: Lash LaRue, Al "Fuzzy" St. John, Peggy Stewart, Jim Bannon, Ray Bennett, Sarah Padden, Jimmie Martin, Jack Hendricks, Lee Morgan, Sandy Sanders, Billy Dix, Cliff Taylor, Steve Raines, Bud Osborne, George Chesebro, Kermit Maynard, Jack Evans, Forrest Matthews.

In order to gather evidence against an outlaw (Ray Bennett) and his gang, Lash and Fuzzy (Al St. John) pose as notorious stagecoach robbers.

Running time: 55 minutes. Release date: December 17, 1948.

413. Last of the Wild Horses (western) Directed by Robert L. Lippert. Produced by Carl K. Hittleman. Original screenplay by Jack Harvey. In Sepiatone.

Cast: James Ellison, Mary Beth Hughes, Jane Frazee, Douglass Dumbrille, James Millican, Reed Hadley, Olin Howlin, Grady Sutton, William Haade, Stanley Andrews, Rory Mallinson.

A crooked ranch foreman (Reed Hadley) is responsible for continual raids on a wild horse herd, with other ranchers fearing that the herd will be depleted. When the foreman murders his boss (Douglass Dumbrille), he frames an innocent man (James Ellison) for the crime.

Running time: 84 minutes. Release date: December 27, 1948.

1949

414. Outlaw Country (western) Directed by Ray Taylor. Produced by Ron Ormond. Screenplay by Ron Ormond and Ira Webb. A Western Adventure Production.

Cast: Lash LaRue, Al "Fuzzy" St. John, Nancy Saunders, Dan White, House Peters, Jr., Steve Dunhill, Lee Roberts, Ted Adams, John Merton, Dee Cooper, Jack O'Shea, Sandy Sanders, Bob Duncan.

Lash LaRue has a dual role in this one, playing himself and his twin brother, an outlaw known as "The Frontier Phantom." Lash and Fuzzy (Al St. John) are commissioned to track down a band of counterfeiters.

Running time: 66 minutes. Release date: January 7, 1949.

415. Highway 13 (drama) Directed by William Berke. Produced by William Stephens. Screenplay by Maurice Tombragel. Original story by John Wilste.

Cast: Robert Lowery, Pamela Blake, Clem Bevans, Michael Whalen, Gaylord (Steve) Pendleton, Lyle Talbot, Maris Wrixon, Mary Gordon, Tom Chatterton.

A truck driver (Robert Lowery) uncovers a plot to gain control of a large transport company.

Running time: 58 minutes. Release date: January 21, 1949.

416. I Shot Jesse James (western) Directed by Samuel Fuller. Produced by Robert L. Lippert and Carl K. Hittleman. Screenplay by Samuel Fuller. Story by Homer Croy.

Cast: John Ireland, Preston Foster, Barbara Britton, J. Edward Bromberg, Victor Kilian, Barbara Woodell, Tom Tyler, Reed Hadley, Tommy Noonan, Byron Foulger, Eddie Dunn, Jeni LeGron, Robin Short.

The story of Bob Ford (John Ireland), the outlaw who killed legendary badman Jesse James (Reed Hadley).

Running time: 81 minutes. Release date: February 26, 1949.

Feature Films 1949

Lash LaRue, Al "Fuzzy" St. John and Noel Neill in *Son of a Bad Man* (1949).

417. Rimfire (western) Directed by B. Reeves Eason. Produced by Ron Ormond. Original screenplay by Arthur St. Claire and Frank Wisbar.

Cast: James Millican, Mary Beth Hughes, Henry Hull, Reed Hadley, Fuzzy Knight, Chris-Pin Martin, Glenn Strange, Dick Alexander, George Cleveland, John (Bob) Cason, Ray Bennett, Margia Dean, I.Stanford Jolley, Victor Kilian, Jason Robards (Sr.), Don Harvey, Lee Roberts, Stanley Price.

A hanged gambler seemingly returns from his grave to haunt his executioners.

Running time: 64 minutes. Release date: March 25, 1949.

418. Son of Billy the Kid (western) Directed by Ray Taylor. Produced by Ron Ormond. Screenplay by Ron Ormond and Ira Webb. A Western Adventure Production.

Cast: Lash LaRue, Al "Fuzzy" St. John, Marion Colby, George Baxter, Terry Frost, June Carr, Johnny Jones, House Peters, Jr., Clarke Stevens, Bob Duncan, Cliff Taylor, William Perrott, Felipe Turich, Rosa Turich, Jerry Riggio, Eileen Dixon, Frazer McMinn, I. Stanford Jolley, Bud Osborne.

A U. S. Marshal (Lash LaRue) and a stage driver (Al St. John) pursue an outlaw gang led by the infamous Billy the Kid (George Baxter) and his son (Johnny Jones).

Running time: 65 minutes. Release date: April 2, 1949.

419. Son of a Bad Man (western) Directed by Ray Taylor. Produced by Ron Ormond. Screenplay by Ron Ormond and Ira Webb. A Western Adventure Production.

Cast: Lash LaRue, Al "Fuzzy" St. John, Noel Neill, Michael Whalen, Don Murray, Frank Lackteen, Francis McDonald, Jack Ingram, Steve Raines, Bob Cason, Don Harvey, Edna Holland, William Norton Bailey, Sandy Sanders, Doyle O'Dell.

A U. S. Marshal (Lash LaRue) and his deputy (Al St. John) pursue an outlaw gang headed by a bandit known as "El Sombre" (Michael Whalen), who is the son of an ex-badman.

Running time: 64 minutes. Release date: April 16, 1949.

Lippert Pictures

1949

420. Omoo, Omoo, the Shark God (adventure-drama) Directed by Leon Leonard. Produced by George S. Picker. Screenplay by Leon Leonard and George Green. Based on a novel by Herman Melville.

Cast: Ron Randell, Devera Burton, Pedro de Cordoba, George Meeker, Michael Whalen, Richard Benedict, Trevor Bardette, Lisa Kincaid, Rudy Robles, Jack Raymond.

Accompanied by his daughter (Devera Burton) and a motley crew (Ron Randell, George Meeker, Michael Whalen, Richard Benedict), a captain of a sailing ship returns to an island where some years before he had stolen and hidden huge black pearls from a native shrine, thus making him victim of a taboo which has kept him ill of a strange malady ever since. When he is killed by a crew member, the curse passes onto his daughter.

Running time: 58 minutes. Release date: June 10, 1949.

Also known as *Omoo, Omoo*.

421. Arson - Inc. (mystery-drama) Directed by William Berke. Produced by William Stephens. Screenplay by Maurice Tombragel. Original story by Arthur Caesar.

Cast: Robert Lowery, Anne Gwynne, Edward Brophy, Marcia Mae Jones, Douglas Fowley, Maude Eburne, William Forrest, Gaylord Pendleton, Byron Foulger, Matt McHugh, Lelah Tyler, Emmett Vogan, John Maxwell, Richard David.

A fireman (Robert Lowery) begins a search for gangsters who resort to arson to conceal their thefts.

Running time: 65 minutes. Release date: June 24, 1949.

422. Ringside (drama) Directed by Frank McDonald. Produced by Ron Ormond. Screenplay by Daniel B. Ullman and Ron Ormond. A Donald Barry Production.

Cast: Don Barry, Tom Brown, Sheila Ryan, Margia Dean, Joey Adams, Tony Canzoneri, Mark Plant, Joseph Crehan, Lyle Talbot, William Edmonds.

A concert pianist (Don Barry) turns pugilist to seek revenge against the boxer who blinded his brother (Tom Brown).

Running time: 63 minutes. Release date: July 14, 1949.

423. Sky Liner (mystery) Directed by William Berke. Produced by William Stephens. Screenplay by Maurice Tombragel.

Cast: Richard Travis, Pamela Blake, Rochelle Hudson, Stephen Geray, Gaylord Pendleton, Ralph Peters, Michael Whalen, Greg McClure, Lisa Ferraday, Roy Butler, Jean Clark, David Holt, Dodie Bauer, William Leicester, Ezelle Poule, Herbert Evans, Alice Ritchie, Jean Sorel, Lu Anne Jones, Jack Mulhall, Alan Hersholt, John McGuire, George Meeker, Anna May Slaughter, Bess Flowers.

When a spy is killed on a cross-country flight, a G-man (Richard Travis) aboard tries to solve the murder.

Running time: 60 minutes. Release date: July 29, 1949.

424. Grand Canyon (comedy) Directed by Paul Landres. Produced by Carl K. Hittleman. Screenplay by Jack Harvey and Milton Luban. Story by Carl K. Hittleman.

Cast: Richard Arlen, Mary Beth Hughes, Reed Hadley, James Millican, Olin Howland, Grady Sutton, Joyce Compton, Charles Williams, Margia Dean, Anna May Slaughter, Holly Bane, Zon Murray, Robert L. Lippert.

A mule skinner (Richard Arlen) replaces the lead actor (James Millican) in a western picture during its location filming.

Running time: 65 minutes. Release date: August 12, 1949.

425. Treasure of Monte Cristo (mystery) Directed by William Berke. Produced by Leonard S. Picker. Original story and screenplay by Aubrey Wisberg and Jack Pollexfen.

Cast: Glenn Langan, Adele Jergens, Steve Brodie, Robert (Bobby) Jordan, Michael Whalen, George Davis, Margia Dean, Sidney Melton, Brian O'Hara, Robert Boon, Jeritza Novak, Jimmy O'Neil, Curtis Jarrett, Charles Reagen, Larry Barton, Rube Schaeffer, Don Junior.

A freighter officer (Glenn Langan), a descendant of the Count of Monte Cristo, is wrongfully accused of murder; he later escapes from the authorities and tries to find out why he was framed.

Running time: 79 minutes. Release date: October 14, 1949.

Jon Hall and Frances Langford (husband and wife at the time) in *Deputy Marshal* (1949).

426. The Dalton Gang (western) Written and directed by Ford Beebe. Produced by Ron Ormond. A Donald Barry Production.

Cast: Don Barry, Robert Lowery, James Millican, Greg McClure, Betty (Julie) Adams, Byron Foulger, J. Farrell MacDonald, George Lewis, Ray Bennett, Marshall Reed, Cliff Taylor, Cactus Mack, Lee Roberts, Dick Curtis, Stanley Price.

A marshal (Don Barry) and the local sheriff (James Millican) attempt to break up the notorious Dalton Gang.

Running time: 58 minutes. Release date: October 21, 1949.

Television title: *Outlaw Gang*.

427. Deputy Marshal (western) Directed by William Berke. Produced by William Stephens. Screenplay by William Berke. Based on the novel "Deputy Marshal" by Charles Huckelmann.

Cast: Jon Hall, Frances Langford, Dick Foran, Julie Bishop, Joe Sawyer, Russell Hayden, Clem Bevans, Vince Barnett, Stanley Blystone, Mary Gordon, Kenne Duncan, Roy Butler, Wheaton Chambers, Forrest Taylor, Tom Greenway, Ted Adams.

A deputy marshal (Jon Hall) tries to prevent crooks from taking over valuable Wyoming land.

Feature Films 1949   143

Running time: 72 minutes. Release date: October 28, 1949.

Photographed by Carl Berger with the Garutso Balanced Lens, a photographic principle which creates a three dimensional effect.

428. Apache Chief (western) Directed by Frank McDonald. Produced by Leonard S. Picker. Original screenplay by Associate Producer George D. Green.

Cast: Alan Curtis, Tom Neal, Russell Hayden, Carol Thurston, Fuzzy Knight, Trevor Bardette, Francis McDonald, Ted Hecht, Alan Wells, Roy Gordon, Billy Wilkerson, Roderic Redwing.

A peace-loving Indian (Alan Curtis) opposes his tribe's treatment of settlers.

Running time: 60 minutes. Release date: November 4, 1949.

Photographed with the Garutso Balanced Lens, "A New Optical Principle Which Creates a Three Dimensional Effect."

429. Square Dance Jubilee (musical) Directed by Paul Landres. Produced by Ron Ormond. Screenplay by Ron Ormond and Daniel B. Ullman. Story by William L. Nolte. A Donald Barry Production.

Cast: Don Barry, Mary Beth Hughes, Wally Vernon, Spade Cooley and His Band, Ginny Jackson, Les Anderson, Max Terhune, John Eldredge, Thurston Hall, Chester Clute, Tom Tyler, Tom Kennedy, Britt Wood, Clarke Stevens, Marshall Reed, Lee Roberts, Alex Montoya, Cliff Taylor, Ralph Moody, Hazel Nilson, Snub Pollard, Tex Cooper, Dorothy Vernon, Slim Gault, Hal King, Cowboy Copas, Claude Casey, The Broome Brothers, Buddy McDowell, Smiley and Kitty, Johnny Downs, Herman the Hermit, Dana Gibson, Ray Vaughn, Charles Cirillo, The Tumbleweed Tumblers, Dot Remey, The Elder Lovelies, Les Gotcher (World Champion Square Dance Caller).

While searching for authentic western entertainers to place on a Spade Cooley TV show, two talent scouts (Don Barry, Wally Vernon) thwart cattle rustlers who are victimizing a pretty young rancher (Mary Beth Hughes).

Running time: 79 minutes. Release date: November 11, 1949.

430. Tough Assignment (action-drama) Directed by William Beaudine. Produced by Carl K. Hittleman. Screenplay by Milton Luban. Story by Carl K. Hittleman. A Donald M. Barry Production.

Cast: Don Barry, Marjorie Steele, Steve Brodie, Marc Lawrence, Iris Adrian, Michael Whalen, Ben Welden, Sid Melton, Fred Kohler, Jr., Frank Richards, John (Bob) Cason, Leander de Cordova, Edith Angold, Dewey Robinson, Stanley Andrews, Stanley Price, Gayle Kellogg, Hugh Simpson, Jack Geddes.

A reporter (Don Barry) and his wife (Marjorie Steele) try to gather evidence against a gang of modern-day cattle rustlers.

Running time: 61 minutes. Release date: November 15, 1949.

Photographed with the Garutso Balanced Lens, "A New Optical Principle Which Creates a Three Dimensional Effect."

431. Call of the Forest (western) Directed by John F. Link. Produced by Edward Finney.

Cast: Robert Lowery, Ken Curtis, Martha Sherrill, Chief Thunder Cloud, Charles Hughes, Tom Hanley.

A man captures King, stallion leader of a wild herd, as a present for his little son. The boy and the horse develop a friendship and the youth nurses the animal back to health after he is badly hurt.

Running time: 74 minutes. Release date: November 18, 1949.

432. Red Desert (western) Directed by Ford Beebe. Produced by Ron Ormond. Story and screenplay by Daniel B. Ullman. A Donald M. Barry Production.

Cast: Don Barry, Tom Neal, Jack Holt, Margia Dean, Joseph Crehan, Byron Foulger, John (Bob) Cason, Tom London, Holly Bane, Hank Bell, George Slocum.

A federal agent (Don Barry) sets out to find an outlaw wanted by the government.

Running time: 60 minutes. Release date: December 17, 1949.

1950

433. Hollywood Varieties (musical-comedy) Directed by Paul Landres. Produced by June Carr and Paul Schreibman. No writing credits given. A Spartan Production.

Cast: Robert Alda, Hoosier Hot Shots, Shaw and Lee, 3 Rio Brothers, Glenn Vernon and Eddie Ryan, Britt Wood, Peggy Stewart, Twirl, Whirl and a Girl, DePina Troupe, The Four Dandies, Lois Ray, Hector and His Pals, Johnson Brothers, Sandy and His Seals, Paul Gordon, Dolores Parker, Shavd Sherman, Sammy Wolfe, Charles Cirillo, Aurora Roche, Cliff Taylor, Russell Trent, The Carlyle Dancers (Evilyn Hetzer, Toby Ford, Kay Whyne, Virginia Nolan, Aileen Marlow, Devvy Davenport, Barbara Mohr).

A vaudeville revue hosted by Robert Alda, featuring a variety of dancers, singers, comedians and novelty acts.

Running time: 60 minutes. Release date: January 14, 1950.

434. Radar Secret Service (mystery) Directed by Sam Newfield. Produced by Barney A. Sarecky. Original screenplay by Beryl Sachs.

Cast: John Howard, Adele Jergens, Tom Neal, Myrna Dell, Sid Melton,

A quartet raise their voices in song in *Hollywood Varieties* (1950), billed as "Big Time Vaudeville on the Screen."

Ralph Byrd, Robert Kent, Pierre Watkin, Tristram Coffin, Riley Hill, Robert Carson, Kenne Duncan, Marshall Reed, John McKee, Holly Bane.

Secret service investigators (John Howard, Ralph Byrd) use radar devices to track down stolen atomic energy material.

Running time: 59 minutes. Release date: January 28, 1950.

Working title: *Radar Patrol*.

435. The Baron of Arizona (drama) Directed by Samuel Fuller. Produced by Carl K. Hittleman. Screenplay by Samuel Fuller. A Deputy Corporation Production.

Cast: Vincent Price, Ellen Drew, Beulah Bondi, Vladimir Sokoloff, Reed Hadley, Robert Barrat, Robin Short, Barbara Woodell, Tina Rome, Margia Dean, Edward Keane, Gene Roth, Karen Kester, Joseph Green, Fred Kohler, Jr., Tristram Coffin, Angelo Rossito, I. Stanford Jolley, Terry Frost, Zachary Yaconelli, Adolfo Ornelas, Wheaton Chambers, Robert O'Neil, Stephen Harrison.

Based on fact, the story of how James Addison Reavis (Vincent Price), a U. S. Land Office clerk, set out in 1861 to prove that the Arizona territory

was the possession of one Baroness Sofia Peralta (Ellen Drew) by reason of a Spanish land grant made to her ancestor by King Ferdinand VI of Spain.
Running time: 93 minutes. Release date: March 4, 1950.

436. Western Pacific Agent (drama) Directed by Sam Newfield. Produced by Sigmund Neufeld. Screenplay by Fred Myton. Original story by Milton Raison.

Cast: Kent Taylor, Sheila Ryan, Mickey Knox, Morris Carnovsky, Robert Lowery, Sid Melton, Frank Richards, Dick Elliott, Ted Jacques, Anthony Jochim, Lee Phelps, Carla Martin, Margia Dean, Gloria Gray, Vera Marshe, Jack Geddes, Jason Robards (Sr.).

A detective (Kent Taylor) pursues a vicious criminal (Mickey Knox) wanted for murder and railroad robbery.

Running time: 65 minutes. Release date: March 17, 1950.

437. Hostile Country (western) Directed by Thomas Carr. Produced by Ron Ormond. Screenplay by Ron Ormond and Maurice Tombragel.

Cast: Jimmie "Shamrock" Ellison, Russ "Lucky" Hayden, Raymond Hatton, Fuzzy Knight, Betty (Julie) Adams, Tom Tyler, George Lewis, John (Bob) Cason, Stanley Price, Stephen Carr, Dennis Moore, George Chesebro, Bud Osborne, Jimmie Martin, Judith Webster, Jimmy Van Horn, Cliff Taylor, Jay Jones, I. Stanford Jolley, George Sowards, J. Farrell MacDonald.

Shamrock (Jimmie Ellison) and Lucky (Russell Hayden) go to the aid of a young woman (Betty Adams) fighting a gang trying to push her off her property by blocking off a pass through which she must get her stock to the market by a certain date.

Running time: 60 minutes. Release date: March 24, 1950.

Television title: *Outlaw Fury*.

438. Everybody's Dancin' (musical-comedy) Directed by Will Jason. Produced by Bob Nunes. Screenplay by Dorothy Raison. Original story by Bob Nunes and Spade Cooley. A Nunes-Cooley Production.

Cast: Spade Cooley, Dick Lane, Barbara Woodell, Ginny Jackson, Hal Derwin, James Millican, Lyle Talbot, Michael Whalen, Sid Melton, Tex Cromer, Les Anderson, Fred Kelsey, Dorothy Lloyd, Bobby Hyatt, George Meader, Dan Rense, Eddie Borden, Sons of the Pioneers, Chuy Reyes, The Flying Taylors, The Great Velardi; guest appearances by Roddy McDowall, Adele Jergens, Jimmy "Shamrock" Ellison, Russ "Lucky" Hayden, Virginia MacPherson (of United Press International).

A phony promoter (Dick Lane) enlists the services of country-and-western singer Spade Cooley to help save "Waltzland," a failing ballroom.

Running time: 65 minutes. Release date: March 31, 1950.

Feature Films 1950

Vincent Price in *The Baron of Arizona* (1950).

439. Marshal of Heldorado (western) Directed by Thomas Carr. Produced by Ron Ormond. Screenplay by Ron Ormond and Maurice Tombragel.

Cast: Jimmie "Shamrock" Ellison, Russ "Lucky" Hayden, Raymond Hatton, Fuzzy Knight, Betty (Julie) Adams, Tom Tyler, George Lewis, John (Bob) Cason, Stanley Price, Stephen Carr, Dennis Moore, George Chesebro, Bud Osborne, Jimmie Martin, Cliff Taylor, Ned Roberts, Jack Hendricks, Wally West, James Van Horn, Jack Geddes, Carl Mathews.

Shrmrock (Jimmie Ellison) and Lucky (Russ Hayden) go to the aid of a banker (Raymond Hatton) who is being blackmailed by a gang of outlaws.

Running time: 53 minutes. Release date: April 21, 1950.

Television title: *Blazing Guns*.

440. Crooked River (western) Directed by Thomas Carr. Produced by Ron Ormond. Screenplay by Ron Ormond and Maurice Tombragel.

Cast: Jimmie "Shamrock" Ellison, Russ "Lucky" Hayden, Raymond Hatton, Fuzzy Knight, Betty (Julie) Adams, Tom Tyler, George Lewis, John (Bob) Cason, Stanley Price, Stephen Carr, Dennis Moore, George Chesebro, Bud Osborne, Jimmie Martin, Cliff Taylor, Helen Gibson, Carl Mathews, George Sowards, Scoop Martin, Joe Phillips.

Betty Adams, Russ "Lucky" Hayden, Jimmie "Shamrock" Ellison and Raymond Hatton in *Hostile Country* (1950), one of six "Four Star" westerns (the four stars being Ellison, Hayden, Hatton and Fuzzy Knight). All six entries were shot simultaneously within one month (!), using the same cast members. Betty Adams, the feminine lead in these films, changed her name to Julia (and later, Julie) and appeared in several pictures for Universal, including *Bend of the River* (1952), *The Lawless Breed* (1952) and *The Creature from the Black Lagoon* (1954).

Shamrock (Jimmie Ellison) sets out to capture the gang of outlaws responsible for murdering his parents.

Running time: 55 minutes. Release date: May 5, 1950.

Television title: *The Last Bullet*.

441. Operation Haylift (action-drama) Directed by William Berke. Produced by Joe Sawyer. Original screenplay by Dean Reisner and Joe Sawyer.

Cast: Bill Williams, Ann Rutherford, Tom Brown, Jane Nigh, Joe Sawyer, Richard Travis, Raymond Hatton, James Conlin, Tommy Ivo, M'Liss McClure, Dean Reisner, Joanna Armstrong, Dink Dean.

An account of how the Air Force saved stranded livestock during the 1949 blizzards.

Running time: 74 minutes. Release date: May 5, 1950.

442. Colorado Ranger (western) Directed by Thomas Carr. Produced by Ron Ormond. Screenplay by Ron Ormond and Maurice Tombragel.

Cast: Jimmie "Shamrock" Ellison, Russ "Lucky" Hayden, Raymond Hatton, Fuzzy Knight, Betty (Julie) Adams, Tom Tyler, George Lewis, John (Bob) Cason, Stanley Price, Stephen Carr, Dennis Moore, George Chesebro, Bud Osborne, Jimmie Martin, Gene Roth, I. Stanford Jolley, Joseph Richards.

Shamrock (Jimmy Ellison), aided by Lucky (Russell Hayden) goes after the gang that kidnapped his stepfather.

Running time: 54 minutes. Release date: May 12, 1950.

Television title: *Guns of Justice*.

443. Rocketship X-M (science fiction) Produced and directed by Kurt Neumann. Screenplay by Kurt Neumann.

Cast: Lloyd Bridges, Osa Massen, John Emery, Noah Beery, Jr., Hugh O'Brian, Morris Ankrum, Patrick Ahern, John Dutra, Katherine Marlowe, Sherry Moreland.

A rocketship launched for the moon is blown off-course by a shower of meteorites and lands on Mars instead.

Running time: 78 minutes. Release date: June 2, 1950.

Working title: *Rocketship Expedition Moon*.

A home video cassette version has new special effects shot in 1976 by producer Wade Williams.

444. West of the Brazos (western) Directed by Thomas Carr. Produced by Ron Ormond. Screenplay by Ron Ormond and Maurice Tombragel.

Cast: Jimmie "Shamrock" Ellison, Russ "Lucky" Hayden, Raymond Hatton, Fuzzy Knight, Betty (Julie) Adams, Tom Tyler, George Lewis, John (Bob) Cason, Stanley Price, Stephen Carr, Dennis Moore, George Chesebro, Bud Osborne, Jimmie Martin, Judith Webster, Gene Roth.

Shamrock (Jimmie Ellison) and Lucky (Russ Hayden) try to prevent oil rich land from falling into the hands of crooks.

Running time: 58 minutes. Release date: June 21, 1950.

Television title: *Rangeland Empire*.

445. Motor Patrol (mystery-drama) Directed by Sam Newfield. Produced by Barney A. Sarecky. Screenplay by Maurice Tombragel and Orville Hampton. Original story by Maurice Tombragel.

Cast: Don Castle, Jane Nigh, Bill Henry, Gwen O'Connor, Reed Hadley, Onslow Stevens, Dick Travis, Charles Vidor, Sid Melton, Frank Jenks, Frank Jacquet, Lt. Lou Fuller, Charles Wagenheim, Margia Dean, Joe Greene, Carla Martin, Don Avelier, Irene Martin.

A rookie cop (Don Castle) poses as a racketeer in order to gather evidence against a gang dealing in stolen cars.

Running time: 67 minutes. Release date: June 16, 1950.

Working title: *Highway Patrol*.

446. Fast on the Draw (western) Directed by Thomas Carr. Produced by Ron Ormond. Screenplay by Ron Ormond and Maurice Tombragel.

Cast: Jimmie "Shamrock" Ellison, Russ "Lucky" Hayden, Raymond Hatton, Fuzzy Knight, Betty (Julie) Adams, Tom Tyler, George Lewis, John (Bob) Cason, Stanley Price, Stephen Carr, Dennis Moore, George Chesebro, Bud Osborne, Jimmie Martin, Gene Roth, Helen Gibson, Cliff Taylor, Jimmy Van Horn, Bud Hooker, Ray Jones, I. Stanford Jolley.

A Colorado Ranger (Jimmie Ellison), who has a mental block every time he lifts his gun to shoot someone, poses as a gunman in order to bring a corrupt landowner to justice.

Running time: 55 minutes. Release date: June 30, 1950.

Television title: *Sudden Death*.

447. Hi-Jacked (drama) Directed by Sam Newfield. Produced by Sigmund Neufeld. Screenplay by Fred Myton and Orville Hampton. Original story by Raymond L. Schrock and Fred Myton.

Cast: Jim Davis, Marcia (Mae) Jones, Sid Melton, David Bruce, Paul Cavanaugh, Ralph Sanford, House Peters, Jr., Iris Adrian, George Eldredge, William E. Green, Margia Dean, Kit Guard, Lee Phelps, Myron Healey, Lee Bennett.

When a truck driver (Jim Davis) is accused of hijacking his own rig, he sets out to prove his innocence by catching the real crooks.

Running time: 66 minutes. Release date: July 7, 1950.

448. Gunfire (western) Written, produced and directed by William Berke.

Cast: Don Barry, Robert Lowery, Wally Vernon, Pamela Blake, Claude Stroud, Leonard Penn, Gaylord (Steve) Pendleton, Tommy Farrell, Dean Reisner, Paul Jordan, Steve Conti, Robert Anderson, Gil Fallman, Kathleen Maggnetti, Bill Bailey (William Norton Bailey).

Retired outlaw Frank James (Don Barry) straps on his guns again when a double commits a series of robberies.

Running time: 59 minutes. Release date: August 11, 1950.

449. I Shot Billy the Kid (western) Produced and directed by William Berke. Screenplay by Ford Beebe and Orville Hampton.

Cast: Don Barry, Robert Lowery, Wally Vernon, Tom Neal, Judith Allen, Wendy Lee, Barbara Woodell, Dick Lane, Sid Melton, Archie Twitchell, John Merton, Claude Stroud, Henry Marud, Bill Kennedy.

The story of how sheriff Pat Garrett (Robert Lowery) gunned down outlaw Billy the Kid (Don Barry).

Running time: 57 minutes. Release date: August 25, 1950.

John Ireland and Ann Dvorak in *The Return of Jesse James* (1950)

450. The Return of Jesse James (western) Directed by Arthur Hilton. Produced by Carl K. Hittleman. Screenplay by Jack Natteford. Story by Carl K. Hittleman.

Cast: John Ireland, Ann Dvorak, Henry Hull, Reed Hadley, Hugh O'Brian, Carleton Young, Barbara Woodell, Margia Dean, Sid Melton, Victor Kilian, Byron Foulger, Sam Flint, Robin Short, Paul Maxey.

A bank robber (John Ireland) who resembles Jesse James spreads the myth that the late outlaw is still alive.

Running time: 75 minutes. *Release date*: September 8, 1950.

Working title: *Return of the James Boys*.

451. Train to Tombstone (western) Produced and directed by William Berke. Screenplay by Orville Hampton and Victor West. Original story by Don Barry. A Donald Barry Production.

Cast: Don Barry, Robert Lowery, Wally Vernon, Tom Neal, Judith Allen, Barbara Stanley, Minna Phillips, Nan Leslie, Claude Stroud, Edward Cassidy.

Passengers aboard a train bound for Tombstone face an Indian attack and an attempted baggage car robbery.

Running time: 56 minutes. *Release date*: September 16, 1950.

Screen Guild/Lippert Pictures

Pamela Blake and Robert Lowery in *Border Rangers* (1950).

452. Border Rangers (western) Produced and directed by William Berke. Screenplay by Victor West and William Berke. A Don Barry Production.

Cast: Don Barry, Robert Lowery, Wally Vernon, Pamela Blake, Lyle Talbot, Claude Stroud, Ezelle Poule, Bill Kennedy, Paul Jordan, Alyn Lockwood, John Merton, Tom Monroe, George Keymas, Tom Kennedy, Eric Norden, Bud Osborne.

Posing as a holdup man, a Texas Ranger (Don Barry) joins a bandit gang in order to bring an outlaw (Robert Lowery), who killed the ranger's brother, to justice.

Running time: 57 minutes. Release date: October 6, 1950.

453. Holiday Rhythm (musical-comedy) Directed by Jack Scholl. Produced by Jack Leewood. Original screenplay by Lee Wainer.

Cast: Mary Beth Hughes, David Street, Wally Vernon, Tex Ritter, Donald MacBride, Chuy Reyes and His Mambo Orchestra, Ike Carpenter and His Orchestra, Nappy Lamare and His Dixieland Band, George Arnold and His "Rhythm on Ice" Show, The Cass County Boys, Sid Melton, Tom Noonan and Pete Marshall, Bobby Chang, Regina Day, Glenn Turnbull, Vera Lee, Tom Ladd, Bill Burns and his birds, Bertil Unger, Gustav Unger, Eva Martell, Neva Martell, Gloria Grey, Alan Harris, Moana, Freddie

Letuli, Lynn Davis, Richard Farmer, Jack Reitzen, Manuel Serrano, Ricci Mari, Neila Mavi, The Four Moroccans.

A television producer (David Street) is knocked unconscious and dreams of an around-the-world talent hunt.

Running time: 60 minutes. (A 70-minute version was made available to exhibitors in single-bill areas [Atlanta, Charlotte, Dallas, Memphis, New Orleans and Philadelphia].) Release date: October 13, 1950.

454. Bandit Queen (western) Produced and directed by William Berke. Screenplay by Victor West and Budd Lesser. Story by Victor West.

Cast: Barbara Britton, Willard Parker, Philip Reed, Barton MacLane, Martin Garralaga, John Merton, Jack Ingram, Victor Kilian, Thurston Hall, Anna Demetrio, Paul Martin, Pepe Hern, Lalo Rios, Jack Perrin, Cecile Weston, Carl Pitti, Hugh Hooker, Mike Conrad, Elias Gamboa, Chuck Roberson, Trina Varela, Nancy Laurenz, Minna Phillips, Margia Dean, Felipe Turich, Joe Dominguez, Roy Butler.

A native-born American (Barbara Britton), who is half Spanish, forms a band of Robin Hood–type riders to stop the seizures of Spanish possessions by lawless Californians.

Running time: 68 minutes. Release date: December 22, 1950.

1951

455. Three Desperate Men (western) Directed by Sam Newfield. Produced by Sigmund Neufeld. Story and screenplay by Orville Hampton. A Mayflower Production.

Cast: Preston Foster, Jim Davis, Virginia Grey, Ross Latimer, William Haade, Monte Blue, Sid Melton, Rory Mallinson, John Brown, Margaret Seddon, House Peters, Jr., Anthony Jochim, Joel Newfield, Lee Bennett, Steve Belmont, Carol Henry, Kermit Maynard, Bert Dillard, Gene Randall, Milton Kibbee, William Norton Bailey.

Falsely accused of crimes they didn't commit, the Denton Brothers (Preston Foster, Jim Davis, Ross Latimer) are forced to become outlaws.

Running time: 71 minutes. Release date: January 12, 1951.

456. The Steel Helmet (drama) Written, produced and directed by Samuel Fuller.

Cast: Gene Evans, Robert Hutton, Steve Brodie, James Edwards, Richard Loo, Sid Melton, Richard Monahan, William Chun, Harold Fung, Neyle Morrow, Lynn Stallmaster.

An American infantry patrol in Korea occupies an abandoned Buddhist temple and sets up an observation post, preparing to combat enemy troops.

Running time: 84 minutes. Release date: February 2, 1951.

Screen Guild/Lippert Pictures

Lobby card for *The Steel Helmet* (1951), Lippert's best film. Pictured: James Edwards, William Chun and Gene Evans.

457. Fingerprints Don't Lie (mystery) Directed by Sam Newfield. Produced by Sigmund Neufeld. Screenplay by Orville Hampton. From a story by Rupert Hughes.

Cast: Richard Travis, Sheila Ryan, Sid Melton, Tom Neal, Margia Dean, Lyle Talbot, Michael Whalen, Richard Emory, Rory Mallinson, George Eldredge, Dee Tatum, Karl Davis, Syra Marty, Forbes Murray, Zon Murray, Roy Butler.

A fingerprint expert (Richard Travis) seeks the killer of the town's mayor.

Running time: 55 minutes. *Release date*: February 23, 1951.

458. Mask of the Dragon (mystery) Directed by Sam Newfield. Produced by Sigmund Neufeld. Screenplay by Orville Hampton.

Cast: Richard Travis, Sheila Ryan, Sid Melton, Michael Whalen, Lyle Talbot, Richard Emory, Dee Tatum, Jack Reitzen, Mr. Moto, Karl Davis, John Grant, Curt Barrett's Trailsmen, Eddie Lee, Ray Singer, Carla Martin.

A private eye (Richard Travis) investigates the murder of a friend — a discharged G. I. lieutenant back from Korea — who delivered a jade dragon to a curio dealer.

Running time: 55 minutes. *Release date*: March 10, 1951.

Feature Films 1951

459. Stop That Cab (comedy) Directed by Eugenio de Liguoro. Produced by Abrasha Haimson. Screenplay by Louella MacFarlane and Walter Abbott. A Spartan Production.

Cast: Sid Melton, Iris Adrian, Marjorie Lord, Tom Neal, Greg McClure, Chester Clute, Minerva Urecal, Glenn Denning, Diane Garrett, Mario Siletti, Renato Vanni, Jack Roper.

A Hollywood cab driver (Sid Melton), saddled with a nagging wife (Iris Adrian), tries to cope with the assorted crazies he encounters on the job.

Running time: 60 minutes. Release date: March 30, 1951.

460. Danger Zone (mystery) Produced and directed by William Berke. Screenplay by Julian Harmon. Based upon stories by Louis Morheim and Herbert Margolis. A Spartan Production.

Cast: Hugh Beaumont, Edward Brophy, Richard Travis, Tom Neal, Pamela Blake, Virginia Dale, Ralph Sanford, Paula Drew, Jack Reitzen, Edward Clark, Richard Monahan, Don Garner.

Amateur detective Denny O'Brien (Hugh Beaumont) in two mystery stories: in the first, a saxophone holds the key to solving the death of a musician; in the second, O'Brien is framed on a murder rap.

Running time: 56 minutes. Release date: April 20, 1951.

461. Roaring City (mystery) Produced and directed by William Berke. Screenplay by Julian Harmon and Victor West. Based upon stories by Louis Morheim and Herbert Margolis. A Spartan Production.

Cast: Hugh Beaumont, Edward Brophy, Richard Travis, Joan Valerie, Wanda McKay, Rebel Randall, William Tannen, Greg McClure, Anthony Warde, Abner Biberman, Stanley Price, A. J. Roth, Paul Brooks.

Amateur detective Denny O'Brien (Hugh Beaumont) tangles with a shady boxing promoter and a gangster's girl (Rebel Randall).

Running time: 58 minutes. Release date: May 4, 1951.

462. Pier 23 (mystery) Produced and directed by William Berke. Screenplay by Julian Harmon and Victor West. Based upon stories by Louis Morheim and Herbert Margolis. A Spartan Production.

Cast: Hugh Beaumont, Ann Savage, Edward Brophy, Richard Travis, Margia Dean, Mike Mazurki, David Bruce, Raymond Greenleaf, Eve Miller, Harry Hayden, Joy (Joi) Lansing, Peter Mamakos, Chris Drake, Johnny Indrisano, Bill Varga, Richard Monahan, Charles Wagenheim.

Amateur detective Denny O'Brien (Hugh Beaumont) investigates the death of a professional wrestler and, as a favor to a priest, tracks down an escaped convict.

Running time: 58 minutes. Release date: May 11, 1951.

463. Kentucky Jubilee (musical-comedy) Produced and directed by Ron Ormond. Screenplay by Maurice Tombragel and Ron Ormond.

Cast: Jerry Colonna, Jean Porter, James Ellison, Fritz Feld, Raymond Hatton, Vince Barnett, Chester Clute, Michael Whalen, Archie Twitchell, Russell Hicks, Margie Dean, Si Jenks, Ralph Sanford, Tom Plank, Jack Reitzen, Jack O'Shea, Cliff Taylor, Bob Carney, Charley Williams, Phil Arnold, Marvelle Andre, Johnny Howard, George Sanders (not the Academy Award–winning actor), George Chesebro, Mickey Simpson, The McQuaig Twins, Claude Casey, Les "Carrot Top" Anderson, Fred Kirby, Slim Andrews, The Broome Brothers, Edna and Gracia Dreon, Donna Kaye, Frankie Randall, Chris Randall, Bobby Clark (not the famed comedian), Buck and Chickie Eddy, Y-Knot Twirlers, Glen Story, John Braislin, Peggy McGuiggan.

A second-rate entertainer (Jerry Colonna), a singer (Jean Porter) and a reporter (James Ellison) travel to the small southern town of Hickory to participate in the "Kentucky Jubilee," an annual fundraising festival, and tangle with crooks trying to steal the gate receipts.

Running time: 67 minutes. Release date: May 18, 1951.

464. Little Big Horn (western) Directed by Charles Marquis Warren. Produced by Carl K. Hittleman. Screenplay by Charles Marquis Warren and Harold Shumate.

Cast: Lloyd Bridges, Marie Windsor, John Ireland, Reed Hadley, Jim Davis, Wally Cassell, Hugh O'Brian, Sheb Wooley, King Donovan, Rodd Redwing, Richard Emory, Jack Pickard, Robert Sherwood, Larry Stewart, Richard Paxton, Barbara Woodell, Ted Avery, Anne Warren.

Troops of soldiers ride to warn General Custer of the impending Indian attack.

Running time: 86 minutes. Release date: June 18, 1951.

Released in Great Britain as *The Fighting 7th*.

465. Savage Drums (adventure) Produced and directed by William Berke. Screenplay by Fenton Earnshaw.

Cast: Sabu, Lita Baron, H. B. Warner, Sid Melton, Steven Geray, Bob Easton, Margia Dean, Francis Pierlot, Paul Marion, Ray Kinney, John Mansfield, Edward Clark, Hugh Beaumont.

An island native (Sabu) returns to his homeland to squelch the warfare that has resulted from Communist domination.

Running time: 70 minutes. Release date: June 22, 1951.

466. G. I. Jane (musical-comedy) Directed by Reginald LeBorg. Produced by Murray Lerner. Screenplay by Jan Jeffries. Original story by Murray Lerner. A Murray Production.

Cast: Jean Porter, Tom Neal, Iris Adrian, Jimmie Dodd, Jeanne Mahoney, Jimmie Lloyd, Mara Lynn, Michael Whalen, Robert (Bobby) Watson, Phil Arnold, Jimmie Cross, Alan Ray, Richard Monahan, Jean Coleman, Amie Bates, Jeri Strong, Olive Krushat, Jack Reitzen.

A fast-talking sergeant (Tom Neal) schemes to get WAC officers transferred to his all-male Army base.

Running time: 62 minutes. Release date: July 6, 1951.

467. Yes Sir, Mr. Bones (musical-comedy) Produced and directed by Ron Ormond. Screenplay by Ron Ormond. A Spartan Production.

Cast: Cotton and Chick Watts, Ches Davis, F. E. Miller, Billy Green, Elliott Carpenter, The Hobnobbers, Ellen Sutton, Sally Anglim, Gary Jackson, Phil Arnold, Slim Williams, Emmett Miller, Ned Haverly, Brother Bones, Scatman Crothers, Monette Moore, Jimmy O'Brien, Archie Twitchell, Cliff Taylor, Boyce and Evans, Pete Daily and His Chicagoans, Jester Hairston Singers.

Veteran performers reminisce about the good old days of showboats and minstrel shows.

Running time: 54 minutes. Release date: July 13, 1951.

468. Varieties on Parade (musical-comedy) Produced and directed by Ron Ormond. A Spartan Production.

Cast: Jackie Coogan, Eddie Garr, Tom Neal, Eddie Dean, Iris Adrian, Lyle Talbot, The Bobby Harrison Trio, Jimmie and Mildred Mulcay, Duke and Harry Johnson, Paul Gordon, The Diacoffs, The Russ Sanders Troupe, Al Mardo, Ormond McGill and His East Indian Miracle Show, Armondo and Lita, Boyce, Evans and Betty Jane, The Lee Sisters, Jean Carroll, Harry Rose, Darling Sisters.

A vaudeville revue hosted by Eddie Garr, presenting a variety of singers, dancers, novelty acts and comedy sketches.

Running time: 60 minutes. Release date: July 20, 1951.

469. The Lost Continent (science fiction) Directed by Samuel Newfield. Produced by Sigmund Neufeld. Screenplay by Richard H. Landau. Story by Carroll Young.

Cast: Cesar Romero, Hillary Brooke, John Hoyt, Hugh Beaumont, Chick Chandler, Sid Melton, Whit Bissell, Acquanetta, Murray Alper, William Green.

Major Joe Nolan (Cesar Romero) leads an expedition to an island mountaintop to recover an atomic-powered rocket; once there, the party encounters prehistoric monsters.

Running time: 86 minutes. Release date: August 17, 1951.

158   Screen Guild/Lippert Pictures

Joe Sawyer, William Tracy and Joan Vohs in *As You Were!* (1951).

470. Leave It to the Marines (comedy) Directed by Sam Newfield. Produced by Sigmund Neufeld. Screenplay by Orville Hampton.

Cast: Sid Melton, Mara Lynn, Gregg Martell, Ida Moore, Sam Flint, Doug Evans, Margia Dean, Richard Monahan, William Haade, Jack George, Paul Bryar.

An amiable nitwit (Sid Melton) goes to obtain a marriage license and accidentally winds up enlisting in the Marines.

Running time: 66 minutes. Release date: September 28, 1951.

471. As You Were! (comedy) Directed by Fred L. Guiol. Produced by Hal Roach, Jr. Original story and screenplay by Edward E. Seabrook. A presentation of Spartan Productions and R and L Productions.

Cast: William Tracy, Joe Sawyer, Russell Hicks, John Ridgeley, Sondra Rodgers, Joan Vohs, Margie Liszt, Rolland Morris, Ed Dearing, Roger McGee, Chris Drake, Maris Wrixon, John Parrish, Ruth Lee, Frank Faylen, Harold Goodwin.

An ex-soldier (William Tracy) with a photographic memory re-enlists, to the dismay of his blustery top sergeant (Joe Sawyer).

Running time: 57 minutes. Release date: October 5, 1951.

A follow-up to earlier Tracy-Sawyer comedies produced by Hal Roach, Sr.

Sequel: *Mr. Walkie Talkie* (Lippert, 1952).

472. Highly Dangerous (mystery-drama) Directed by Roy Baker. Produced by Antony Darnborough. Screenplay by Eric Ambler.

Cast: Dane Clark, Margaret Lockwood, Marius Goring, Naunton Wayne, Wilfrid Hyde-White, Eugene Deckers, Olaf Pooley, Gladys Henson, Paul Hardtmuth, Michael Hordern, Eric Pohlmann.

A British entomologist (Margaret Lockwood) and an American reporter (Dane Clark) investigate reports of secret germ-warfare experiments behind the Iron Curtain.

Running time: 81 minutes. Release date: October 12, 1951.
Produced in England.

473. Sky High (comedy) Directed by Samuel Newfield. Produced by Sigmund Neufeld. Screenplay by Orville Hampton. A Spartan Production.

Cast: Sid Melton, Mara Lynn, Sam Flint, Doug Evans, Fritz Feld, Mark Krah, Margia Dean, Paul Bryar, Thayer Roberts.

A bumbling Air Force tailgunner (Sid Melton) is enlisted to aid Military Intelligence by impersonating his lookalike, a notorious saboteur.

Running time: 60 minutes. Release date: October 19, 1951.

474. Unknown World (science fiction) Directed by Terrell (Terry) O. Morse. Produced by Jack Rabin and Irving Block. Screenplay by Millard Kaufman. Story by Jack Rabin and Irving Block.

Cast: Bruce Kellogg, Marilyn Nash, Victor Kilian, Otto Waldis, Jim Bannon, Tom Handley, Dick Cogan, George Baxter.

Dr. Jeremiah Morley (Victor Kilian) designs and builds the "Cyclotram," a huge drill machine intended to bore to the center of the Earth in search of caverns that will provide safe havens from A-bomb contamination.

Running time: 63 minutes. Release date: October 26, 1951.
Working title: *Night Without Stars*.

475. Superman and the Mole Men (adventure-fantasy) Directed by Lee Sholem. Produced by Robert Maxwell and Barney A. Sarecky. Script by Richard Fielding (Robert Maxwell). Based on the character "Superman" created by Jerry Siegel and Joe Schuster.

Cast: George Reeves, Phyllis Coates, Jeff Corey, Walter Reed, J. Farrell MacDonald, Stanley Andrews, Ray Walker, Hal K. Dawson, Frank Reicher, Beverly Washburn, Stephen Carr, Paul Burns, Margia Dean, Byron Foulger, Irene Martin, John Phillips, John Baer, Adrienne Marden, Jack Banbury, Billy Curtis, Jerry Marvin, Tony Barvis.

In the small town of Silsby, mole men (Jack Banbury, Billy Curtis, Jerry Marvin, Tony Barvis) emerge from their subterranean home through the shaft of a newly-drilled oil well. When an angry mob of townspeople,

The All-Time **ACE OF ACTION!**

in his **FIRST** Full-Length Feature **Adventure!**

SUPERMAN AND THE MoleMen

starring George REEVES · Phyllis COATES
Jeff Corey · Walter Reed · J. Farrell MacDonald
Stanley Andrews

Produced by BARNEY SAREKY · Directed by LEE SHOLEM
Original Screenplay by RICHARD FIELDING
Released by LIPPERT PICTURES, Inc.

Feature Films 1951   161

Cesar Romero, Audrey Totter and George Brent in *F.B.I. Girl* (1951).

headed by Luke Benson (Jeff Corey), prepares to lynch the mole men, Superman (George Reeves) intervenes.

Running time: 58 minutes. (The running time is often incorrectly given as 67 minutes.) Release date: November 23, 1951.

476. F.B.I. Girl (mystery-drama) Produced and directed by William Berke. Screenplay by Richard Landau and Dwight Babcock. Based on a story by Rupert Hughes. A JEDGAR Production.

Cast: Cesar Romero, George Brent, Audrey Totter, Tom Drake, Raymond Burr, Raymond Greenleaf, Margia Dean, Don Garner, Alexander Pope, Richard Monahan, Tom Noonan and Pete Marshall, Jan Kayne, Joy (Joi) Lansing, Walter Coy, Byron Foulger, Joel Marston, Marie Blake, Fenton Earnshaw, O. Z. Whitehead.

An F.B.I. clerk (Audrey Totter) is used as bait to flush out a politician (Raymond Greenleaf) trying to cover up his past criminal record.

Running time: 74 minutes. Release date: November 1951.

477. The Great Adventure (drama) Directed by David MacDonald. Produced by Aubrey Baring. Story and screenplay by Robert Westerby.

A poster for *Superman and the Mole Men* (1951) starring George Reeves as Superman and Phyllis Coates as Lois Lane.

Cast: Jack Hawkins, Peter Hammond, Dennis Price, Gregoire Aslan, Charles Paton, Siobhan McKenna, Bernard Lee, Ronald Adam, Martin Boddey, Phillip Ray, Walter Horsbrugh, Cyril Chamberlain.

Four greedy men (Jack Hawkins, Peter Hammond, Dennis Price, Gregoire Aslan) trek through the African jungle in search of a cache of hidden diamonds.

Running time: 75 minutes. Release date: December 7, 1951.

Also known as *Fortune in Diamonds*.

Produced and released in Great Britain as *The Adventurers* (1950); released in the U. S. by Lippert.

478. Tales of Robin Hood (action-adventure) Directed by James Tinling. Produced by Hal Roach, Jr. Story and screenplay by Leroy H. Zehren.

Cast: Robert Clarke, Mary Hatcher, Paul Cavanaugh, Wade Crosby, Whit Bissell, Ben Welden, Robert Bice, Keith Richards, Bruce Lester, Tiny Stowe, Lester Matthews, John Vosper, Norman Bishop, Margia Dean, Lorin Raker, George Slocum, John Doucette.

In 12th-century England, Robin Hood (Robert Clarke), the hero of Sherwood Forest, fights against the Norman rulers.

Running time: 59 minutes. Release date: December 21, 1951.

1952

479. For Men Only (drama) Produced and directed by Paul Henreid. Screenplay by Lou Morheim. Story by Lou Morheim and Herbert Margolis. An H-N Production.

Cast: Paul Henreid, Margaret Field, James Dobson, Kathleen Hughes, Russell Johnson, Vera Miles, Robert Sherman, Douglas Kennedy, Robert Carson, Virginia Mullen, O. Z. Whitehead.

A college professor (Paul Henreid) tries to put a stop to the cruel fraternity hazing occurring on the campus.

Running time: 93 minutes. Release date: January 11, 1952.

Retitled: *The Tall Lie*.

480. Man Bait (drama) Directed by Terence Fisher. Produced by Anthony Hinds. Screenplay by Frederick Knott. Based on a story by James Hadley Chase.

Cast: George Brent, Marguerite Chapman, Diana Dors, Raymond Huntley, Peter Reynolds, Eleanor Summerfield, Meredith Edwards, Harry Fowler.

A bookstore clerk (Diana Dors), egged on by a small-time crook (Peter Reynolds), blackmails her employer (George Brent).

Running time: 78 minutes (84 minutes in Great Britain). Release date: January 25, 1952.

A Hammer Film production for Exclusive Films Ltd.; produced and released in Great Britain as *The Last Page*.

481. Navajo (docu-drama) Written and directed by Norman Foster. Produced by Hall Bartlett.

Cast: Francis Kee Teller, John Mitchell, Mrs. Teller, Billy Draper, Hall Bartlett, Linda and Eloise Teller. Narration spoken by Sammy Ogg.

A Navajo Indian boy (Francis Kee Teller) rebels when he is forced to go to the "white man's school."

Running time: 70 minutes. Release date: February 12, 1952.

482. Stronghold (adventure) Directed by Steve Sekely. Screenplay by Wells Root.

Cast: Veronica Lake, Zachary Scott, Arturo de Cordova, Rita Lacedo, Alfonso Bedoya, Yadiro Jimmez, Fanny Schiller, Gilberto Gonzalez, Carlos Muzquiz, Frederick A. Mack, Roc Galbin, Gustavo Rojo, Irene Ajay, Felipe de Alba.

Mary Stevens (Veronica Lake), the owner of a silver mine located in the Mexican town of Taxco, falls in love with an aristocrat (Arturo de Cordova) who is heading a revolution against Emperor Maximilian.

Running time: 73 minutes. Release date: February 15, 1952.

483. Wings of Danger (drama) Directed by Terence Fisher. Produced by Anthony Hinds. Screenplay by John Gilling. Adapted from the novel "Dead on Course" by Elleston Trevor and Packham Webb.

Cast: Zachary Scott, Robert Beatty, Naomi Chance, Kay Kendall, Colin Tapley, Arthur Lane, Harold Lang, Diane Cilento.

An airline pilot (Zachary Scott) discovers that another flier is mixed up with smugglers.

Running time: 72 minutes. Release date: April 1, 1952.

A Hammer Film Production for Exclusive Films Ltd.; produced in Great Britain; released in the U. S. by Lippert.

484. Valley of the Eagles (adventure) Directed by Terence Young. Produced by Nat A. Bronsten. Screenplay by Terence Young. Story by Paul Tabori and Nat A. Bronsten.

Cast: Jack Warner, John McCallum, Nadia Gray, Anthony Dawson, Mary Laura Wood, Norman MacOwen, Alfred Maurstad, Martin Boddey, Christopher Lee, Ewen Solon, Njama Wiwstrand, Peter Blitz, Sarah Crawford, Molly Warner, Trillot Billquist, Gosta Cederlund, Sten Lindgren, Holger Kax.

Dorothy Hart and George Raft in *Loan Shark* (1952).

After his wife (Mary Laura Wood) and his assistant (Anthony Dawson) steal his new device which converts sound waves into electrical energy, a scientist (John McCallum) follows the pair to the wastes of Lapland.

Running time: 83 minutes (86 minutes in Great Britain). Release date: April 25, 1952.

An Independent Sovereign Film Production, produced and released in Great Britain as *Valley of Eagles* (1951); released in the U. S. by Lippert.

485. Loan Shark (drama) Directed by Seymour Friedman. Produced by Bernard Luber. Screenplay by Martin Rackin and Eugene Ling. Story by Martin Rackin. An Encore Production.

Cast: George Raft, Dorothy Hart, Paul Stewart, John Hoyt, Helen Westcott, Henry Slate, Russell Johnson, Margia Dean, Benny Baker, Larry Dobkin, William Phipps, Charles Meredith, Harlan Warde, Spring Mitchell, Ross Elliott, Robert Bice, Robert Williams, Michael Regan, Virginia Carroll, George Eldredge, William Tannen, Jack Daley.

After his brother-in-law is murdered, an ex-convict (George Raft) agrees to help the management of a factory break up a loan shark gang which has been victimizing employees.

Running time: 79 minutes. Release date: May 23, 1952.

486. Outlaw Women (western) Directed by Sam Newfield. Produced by Ron Ormond. Screenplay by Orville Hampton. A Howco Production. In Cinecolor.

Cast: Marie Windsor, Richard Rober, Allan Nixon, Carla Balenda, Jacqueline Fontaine, Jackie Coogan, Maria Hart, Billy House, Richard Avonde, Leonard Penn, Lyle Talbot, Brad Johnson.

The western town of Las Mujeres ("The Women") is controlled by a saloon owner (Marie Windsor) and her followers until a strong-willed gambler (Richard Rober) is elected U. S. Marshal.

Running time: 75 minutes. Release date: June 2, 1952.

487. A Stolen Face (drama) Directed by Terence Fisher. Produced by Anthony Hinds. Screenplay by Richard Landau and Martin Berkeley.

Cast: Paul Henreid, Lizabeth Scott, Andre Morell, Mary Mackenzie, John Wood, Susan Stephen, Arnold Ridley, Evereley Gregg, Cyril Smith, Janey Burnell, Grace Gavin, Terence O'Reagan, Diane Beaumont, Alexis France, John Bull, Dorothy Bramhall, Ambrosino Philpotts, Richard Wattis, Russell Napier.

Jilted by a concert pianist (Lizabeth Scott), a plastic surgeon (Paul Henreid) makes over the scarred face of a criminal (also played by Scott) to look like his lost love.

Running time: 71 minutes. Release date: June 16, 1952.

A Hammer Film Production for Exclusive Films Ltd.; produced in Great Britain; released in the U. S. by Lippert.

488. Pirate Submarine (documentary-adventure) Directed by Georges Peclet. Produced by H. Vincent Brechignac. Screenplay by Jane-Edith Saintenoy and Georges Peclet. Based on the log of the French submarine "Casabianca" by Commandant L'Herminier.

Cast: Pierre Dudan, Gerard Landry, Jean Vilar, Alain Terrane, Jean Vilmont, Michel Vadet, Johnny Marchand, Paulette Andrieux, Paul Mesnier, Alan Adair.

The exploits of the French submarine "Casabianca" in aiding the liberation of Corscia from its Nazi and Italian occupation forces during World War II.

Running time: 67 minutes. Release date: July 13, 1952.

A French production; this English-dubbed version was released in the U. S. by Lippert.

489. The Jungle (adventure) Produced and directed by William Berke. Script by Carroll Young.

Cast: Rod Cameron, Cesar Romero, Marie Windsor, Sulochana, M. N. Namblar, David Abraham, Ramakrishna, Chitra Devi.

A hunting expedition journeys to an Indian province to check on reports that prehistoric mammoths are terrifying local elephants and causing them to destroy villages.

Running time: 74 minutes. (The Indian release print of *The Jungle* is reported to be at least two and a half hours in length.) Release date: August 1, 1952.

A Voltaire-Modern Theatres Ltd. Production (a U. S.–Indian coproduction shot on location in India); released in the U. S. by Lippert.

490. The Secret People (drama) Directed by Thorold Dickinson. Produced by Sidney Cole. Screenplay by Thorold Dickinson and Wolfgang Wilhelm. Original story by Thorold Dickinson. Additional dialogue by Christianna Brand.

Cast: Valentina Cortesa, Serge Reggiani, Audrey Hepburn, Charles Goldner, Megs Jenkins, Irene Worth, Reginald Tate, Michael Shepley, Athene Seyler, Geoffrey Hibbert, Sidney Tafler, John Ruddock, Michael Allan, John Field, Charlie Dairoli and Paul, Angela Fouldes.

Two refugee sisters (Valentina Cortesa, Audrey Hepburn) visit Paris in 1937, where they become involved in a plot to assassinate a European dictator.

Running time: 87 minutes. Release date: August 29, 1952.

Produced in Great Britain by Ealing Studios Ltd.; released in the U.S. by Lippert.

491. Hellgate (drama) Directed by Charles Marquis Warren. Produced by John C. Champion. Screenplay by Charles Marquis Warren.

Cast: Sterling Hayden, Joan Leslie, Ward Bond, James Arness, Peter Coe, John Pickard, Robert Wilkie, Lyle James, Richard Emory, Richard Paxton, William R. Hamel, Marshall Bradford, Sheb Wooley, Rory Mallinson, Pat Coleman, Timothy Carey, Kyle Anderson, Rodd Redwing, Stanley Price.

An innocent man (Sterling Hayden), sent to Hellgate Prison in New Mexico, earns a pardon by helping during an epidemic.

Running time: 87 minutes. Release date: September 5, 1952.

A reworking of *The Prisoner of Shark Island* (20th Century–Fox, 1936).

492. Scotland Yard Inspector (mystery) Directed by Sam Newfield. Produced by Anthony Hinds. Screenplay by Orville Hampton. Adapted from the B.B.C. serial by Lester Powell.

Cast: Cesar Romero, Lois Maxwell, Bernadette O'Farrell, Geoffrey Keen, Campbell Singer, Mary Mackenzie, Alastair Hunter.

An American newspaper reporter (Cesar Romero) aids a woman (Bernadette O'Farrell) in her search for her brother's killer.

Running time: 73 minutes (82 minutes in Great Britain). Release date: October 31, 1952.

A Hammer Film Production for Exclusive Films Ltd.; produced and released in Great Britain as *Lady in the Fog*; released in the U. S. by Lippert.

493. Tromba, the Tiger Man (drama) Directed by Helmut Weiss. Produced by Georg Richter. Screenplay by Elisabeth Zimmerman and Helmut Weiss.

Cast: Rene Deltgen, Angelika Hauff, Gustav Knuth, Hilde Weissner, Grethe Weiser, Gardy Granass, Adrian Horen.

Tromba (Rene Deltgen), a tiger trainer with a German circus, uses hypnotism to make his jungle cats and his assorted women do his bidding.

Running time: 63 minutes. Release date: November 14, 1952.

Produced and released in Germany as *Tromba*; English-dubbed version released in the U. S. by Lippert.

494. Mr. Walkie Talkie (comedy) Directed by Fred Guiol. Produced by Hal Roach, Jr. Original story and screenplay by Ned Seabrook and C. Carleton Brown. A Rockingham Production.

Cast: William Tracy, Joe Sawyer, Robert Shayne, Alan Hale, Jr., Russell Hicks, Frank Jenks, Margia Dean, Bill Boyett, James B. Leong, John Breed, Wong Artaine, Peter Ortiz, William Ng, Ralph Brooke.

An army sergeant (Joe Sawyer) has himself transferred to the front lines of Korea so he can get away from a motor-mouthed soldier (William Tracy) who has a photographic memory.

Running time: 65 minutes. Release date: November 28, 1952.

A sequel to *As You Were!* (Lippert, 1951).

495. The Gambler and the Lady (drama) Directed by Patrick Jenkins and Sam Newfield. Produced by Anthony Hinds.

Cast: Dane Clark, Kathleen Byron, Naomi Chance, Meredith Edwards, Anthony Forwood, Eric Pohlmann, Julian Somers, Anthony Ireland, Thomas Gallagher, Max Bacon, Mona Washbourne, Jane Griffiths, Richard Shaw, George Pastell, Martin Benson, Eric Boon, Felix Felton, Hal Osmond, Percy Marmont.

When a gambler (Dane Clark) falls in love, he tries to reform and seeks acceptance into English society.

Running time: 71 minutes (74 minutes in Great Britain). Release date: December 26, 1952.

A Hammer Film Production for Exclusive Films Ltd.; produced in Great Britain; released in the U. S. by Lippert.

1953

496. I'll Get You (mystery) Directed by Seymour Friedman. Produced by Bernard Luber. Screenplay by John V. Baines. Additional scenes and dialogue by Nicholas Phipps.

Cast: George Raft, Sally Gray, Clifford Evans, Reginald Tate, Patricia Laffan, Frederick Piper, Roddy Hughes, June Ashley.

An FBI man (George Raft) and a British Intelligence agent (Sally Gray) are on the trail of international kidnappers.

Running time: 79 minutes. Release date: January 16, 1953.

Produced and released in Great Britain as *Escape Route* (1952); released in the U. S. by Lippert.

497. The Tall Texan (western) Directed by Elmo Williams. Produced by T. Frank Woods. Screenplay by Samuel Roeca.

Cast: Lloyd Bridges, Lee J. Cobb, Marie Windsor, Luther Adler, Samuel R. Herrick, Syd Saylor, Dean Train.

A group of people defy Indian warnings and pan for gold on sacred ground.

Running time: 84 minutes. Release date: February 13, 1953.

498. Perils of the Jungle (adventure) Directed by George Blair. Produced by Walter White, Jr. Story and screenplay by Frank Hart Taussig and Robert T. Smith.

Cast: Clyde Beatty, Stanley Farrar, Phyllis Coates, John Doucette, Leonard Mudie, Joel Fluellen, Roy E. Glenn, Olaf Hytten, Tudor Owen, Shelby Bacon.

Famed hunter Clyde Beatty journeys to the African jungle to track Nubian lions.

Running time: 63 minutes. Release date: March 20, 1953.

499. The White Goddess (adventure) Directed by Wallace Fox. Produced by Rudolph Flothow. Screenplay by Sherman L. Lowe and Eric Taylor.

Cast: Jon Hall, Ray Montgomery, M'Liss McClure, Ludwig Stossel, James Fairfax, Joel Fluellen, Darby Jones, Lucian Prival, Robert Williams, Millicent Patrick.

Dr. Tom Reynolds (Jon Hall) journeys to Africa in search of medicinal herbs and encounters a native tribe ruled by a white woman posing as a goddess.

Compiled from episodes of the syndicated series *Ramar of the Jungle*. Released in Great Britain as *Ramar of the Jungle*.

500. Bad Blonde (drama) Directed by Reginald LeBorg. Produced by Anthony Hinds. Screenplay by Guy Elmes and Richard Landau. Based on a novel by Max Catto.

Cast: Barbara Payton, Frederick Valk, John Slater, Sidney James, Tony Wright, Marie Burke, Selma Vaz Dias, Enzo Coticchia.

A scheming blonde (Barbara Payton) seduces a boxer (Tony Wright) into murdering her fight-manager husband (Frederick Valk).

Running time: 80 minutes. Release date: April 10, 1953.

A Hammer Film Production for Exclusive Films Ltd.; produced and released in Great Britain in 1952 under two titles: *The Flanagan Boy* and *This Woman Is Trouble*; released in the U. S. by Lippert.

501. Bachelor in Paris (comedy) Directed by John Guillermin. Screenplay by Alex Mackinnon. A Vandyke Production.

Cast: Dennis Price, Anne Vernon, Mischa Auer, Hermione Baddeley, Joan Kenny, Brian Worth.

An English businessman (Dennis Price) journeys to Paris where he becomes involved with a French cabaret singer (Anne Vernon).

Running time: 83 minutes. Release date: April 17, 1953.

Produced and released in Great Britain as *Song of Paris* (1952).

502. Twilight Women (drama) Directed by Gordon Parry. Screenplay by Anatole de Grunwald. Based on the play "Women of Twilight."

Cast: Freda Jackson, Rene Ray, Lois Maxwell, Joan Dowling, Dore Bryan, Vida Hope, Mary Germaine, Ingeborg Wells, Dorothy Gordon, Clare James, Laurence Harvey, Betty Henderson, Ben Williams, Marguerite Brennan, Cyril Smith, Katherine Page, Edna Morris.

A spinster runs a home for unwed mothers and farms out babies illegally.

Running time: 89 minutes. Release date: May 15, 1953.

Produced and released in Great Britain as *Women of Twilight* (1952); released in the U. S. by Lippert.

Also known as *Another Chance*.

503. The Slasher (drama) Directed by Lewis Gilbert. Screenplay by Lewis Gilbert and Vernon Harris. From the play "Cosh Boy" by Bruce Walker. A Romulus-Daniel Angel British Production.

Cast: James Kenney, Joan Collins, Betty Ann Davies, Robert Ayers, Hermione Baddeley, Hermione Gingold, Nancy Roberts, Ian Whittaker, Stanley Escane, Sean Lynch, John Briggs, Michael McKeag, Edward Evans, Laurence Naismith.

A ruthless young man (James Kenney) heads a gang of juvenile delinquents.

Running time: 75 minutes. Release date: May 29, 1953.

An IFD Production in association with British Lion; produced and released in Great Britain as *Cosh Boy* (1952); released in the U. S by Lippert. Also known as *Tough Guy*.

504. Johnny the Giant Killer (cartoon) Directed by Jean Image and Charles Frank. Written by Paul Collins, Charles Frank and Nesta Macdonald. Based on an idea by Eraine. In Technicolor.

A group of small boys, led by Johnny, go to a giant's castle to slay him, but wind up being captured and reduced to miniature size.

Running time: 70 minutes. Release date: June 5, 1953.

Made in France by Jean Image Films; released in the U. S. by Lippert.

505. Ghost Ship (mystery) Written, produced and directed by Vernon Sewell.

Cast: Dermot Walsh, Hazel Court, Hugh Burden, John Robinson, Joss Ambler, Joan Carol, Hugh Latimer, Mignon O'Doherty, Laidman Browne, Meadows White, Pat McGrath, Josh Ackland, John King Kelly.

A young Canadian couple (Dermot Walsh, Hazel Court) in England buy a "haunted" yacht and are terrorized by ghostly manifestations.

Running time: 69 minutes. Release date: June 12, 1953.

An ABTCON Production, produced and released in Great Britain in 1952; released in the U. S. by Lippert.

506. Eyes of the Jungle (adventure) Directed by Paul Landres. Produced by Rudolph Flothow. Screenplay by Barry Shipman and Sherman L. Lowe.

Cast: Jon Hall, Ray Montgomery, Victor Millan, Edgar Barrier, Frank Fenton, Merrill McCormick, Robert Shayne, Leonard Penn, James Fairfax, M'Liss McClure, Charles Stevens, William Tannen, Alyce Lewis.

Tom Reynolds (Jon Hall), an American doctor attempting to conduct scientific research in the jungles of India, is threatened by a series of encounters with unscrupulous traders and superstitious natives.

Compiled from episodes of the syndicated television series *Ramar of the Jungle*.

Running time: 79 minutes. Release date: July 1, 1953.

Released in Great Britain as *Destination Danger*.

507. The Great Jesse James Raid (western) Directed by Reginald LeBorg. Produced by Robert L. Lippert, Jr. Screenplay by Richard Landau. In Ansco Color.

Cast: Willard Parker, Barbara Payton, Tom Neal, Wallace Ford, James Anderson, Jim Bannon, Richard Cutting, Barbara Woodell, Marin Sais, Earle Hodgins, Tom Walker, Joan Arnold, Helene Hayden, Steve Pendleton, Bob Griffin, Robin Moore, Ed Russell, Rory Mallinson.

Outlaw Jesse James (Willard Parker) forsakes domestic life and joins up with Bob Ford (Jim Bannon) in a plot to steal $300,000 in gold hidden in a mine.

Running time: 73 minutes. Release date: July 17, 1953.

508. Spaceways (science fiction) Directed by Terence Fisher. Produced by Michael Carreras. Script by Paul Tabori and Richard Landau. Adaptation by Paul Tabori.

Cast: Howard Duff, Eva Bartok, Alan Wheatley, Philip Leaver, Cecile Chevreau, Andrew Osborn, Michael Medwin, Anthony Ireland, Hugh Moxey, David Horne, Jean Wenster-Brough, Leo Phillips, Marianne Stone.

An American scientist (Howard Duff), working on a British rocketry project, is suspected of having murdered his wife (Cecile Chevreau) and her lover (Andrew Osborn).

Running time: 76 minutes. Release date: August 7, 1953.

A Hammer Film Production for Exclusive Films Ltd.; produced in Great Britain; released in the U. S. by Lippert.

Uses footage from *Rocketship X-M* (Lippert, 1950).

509. Project Moonbase (science fiction) Directed by Richard Talmadge. Produced by Jack Seaman. Script by Robert A. Heinlein and Jack Seaman. A Galaxy Production.

Cast: Donna Martell, Ross Ford, Larry Johns, Hayden Rorke, Herb Jacobs, Barbara Morrison, Ernestine Barrier, James Craven, John Hedloe, Peter Adams, Robert Karnes, John Straub, Charles Keane, John Tomecko, Robert Paltz.

Colonel Breiters (Donna Martell) heads an expedition to investigate the possibility of setting up an American base on the moon.

Running time: 63 minutes. Release date: September 4, 1953.

510. Norman Conquest (mystery) Directed by Bernard Knowles. Produced by Bertram Ostrer and Albert Fennel. Screenplay by Bertram Ostrer, Albert Fennel and Bernard Knowles. From the novel "Daredevil Conquest" by Berkley Gray (Edwy. Searles Brooks).

Cast: Tom Conway, Eva Bartok, Joy Shelton, Sidney James, Richard Wattis, Carl Jaffe, Frederick Schiller, Robert Adair, Anton Diffring, Ian Fleming, Edwin Richfield, Michael Balfour, Martin Boddey, Terence Alexander.

Norman Conquest (Tom Conway), troubleshooter, captures a smuggling ring.

Running time: 79 minutes. Release date: September 11, 1953.

Produced and released in Great Britain as *Park Plaza 605*; released in the U. S. by Lippert.

Barbara Payton, Tom Neal and Willard Parker in *The Great Jesse James Raid* (1953).

511. Undercover Agent (mystery) Directed by Vernon Sewell. Produced by W. H. Williams. Screenplay by Guy Elmes and Michael LeFerre.

Cast: Dermot Walsh, Hazel Court, Hermione Baddeley, James Vivian, Archie Duncan, Alexander Guage, Frederick Schrecker, Hugh Latimer, Bill Travers, John Penrose, Gwen Bacon, Maxwell Foster, Howard Lang.

An accountant (Dermot Walsh) is asked to deliver a package to a certain address; there he finds a murdered man and discovers that the package contains vital jet secrets.

Running time: 69 minutes. Release date: October 2, 1953.

An ABTCON Pictures Production, produced and released in Great Britain as *Counterspy*; released in the U. S. by Lippert.

512. The Fighting Men (drama) Directed by Camillo Mastrocinque. Produced by Albert Salvatori and Alan Curtis. Screenplay by Lewis E. Cianelli and Gisella Mathess. Story by G. G. Loschiavo and E. Colombo.

Cast: Rossano Brazzi, Claudine Dupuis, Eduardo Cianelli, Charles Vanel, Giovanni Grasso, Natale Cirino, Ignazio Balzamo, Milly Vitale, Carla Calo, Turi Pandolfini.

A man (Rossano Brazzi) returns to Sicily after a fifteen-year absence and becomes the target of Mafia threats.

Running time: 63 minutes. Release date: October 9, 1953.

An Italian production, produced and released in Italy as *Gli Inesorabili* (1950); English-dubbed version released in the U. S. by Lippert.

513. Shadow Man (mystery) Directed by Richard Vernon. Produced by William H. Williams. Screenplay by Richard Vernon. Based on the novel "The Creaking Chair" by Laurence Mynell. A Nat Cohen and Stuart Levy Production.

Cast: Cesar Romero, Kay Kendall, Edward Underdown, Victor Maddern, Simone Silva, Liam Gaffney, Robert Cawdron, John Penrose, Bill Travers, Molly Hamley Clifford, Eileen Way, Paul Hardtmuth.

After his ex-girlfriend (Simone Silva) is murdered, a casino owner (Cesar Romero) sets out to find the killer.

Running time: 77 minutes. Release date: October 16, 1953.

An Anglo Amalgamated Production, produced and released in Great Britain as *Street of Shadows*; released in the U. S. by Lippert.

514. Sins of Jezebel (drama) Directed by Reginald LeBorg. Produced by Sigmund Neufeld. Written by Richard Landau. In Ansco Color.

Cast: Paulette Goddard, George Nader, Eduard Franz, John Hoyt, Ludwig Donath, John Shelton, Joe Besser, Margia Dean, Carmen D'Antonio.

The biblical tale of Jezebel (Paulette Goddard), the evil Phoenician princess who marries the King of Israel and all but destroys his people.

Running time: 74 minutes. Release date: October 23, 1953.

515. The Man from Cairo (drama) Directed by Ray H. Enright. Produced by Bernard Luber. Screenplay by Eugene Ling, Phillip Stevens and Janice Stevens. From a story by Ladislas Fodor.

Cast: George Raft, Gianna Maria Canale, Massimo Serato, Guido Celano, Irene Papas, Alfredo Varelli, Leon Lenoiv, Mino Doro, Angelo Dessy, Leslie Daniels, Richard McNamara, Franco Silva, Henry Vidon.

An American tourist (George Raft) in Algiers becomes involved with fortune hunters searching for lost gold in the African desert.

Running time: 82 minutes. Release date: November 27, 1953.

An Italian production, released in Great Britain as *Crime Squad*; released in the U. S. by Lippert.

516. Terror Street (mystery) Directed by Montgomery Tully. Produced by Anthony Hinds. Story and screenplay by Steve Fisher.

Cast: Dan Duryea, Elsy Albiin, Ann Gudrin, Eric Pohlmann, John Chandos, Kenneth Griffith, Harold Lang, Jane Carr, Michael Golden, Marianne Stone.

Howard Duff in *Spaceways* (1953), a British production released in the U. S. by Lippert Pictures.

Suspected of murdering his wife, a jet pilot (Dan Duryea) tries to track down the real killer.

Running time: 83 minutes (80 minutes in Great Britain). Release date: December 4, 1953.

A Hammer Film Production for Exclusive Films Ltd.; released in Great Britain as *36 Hours*; released in the U. S. by Lippert.

517. The Limping Man (mystery) Directed by Charles DeLatour. Produced by Donald Ginsberg. Screenplay by Ian Stuart and Reginald Long. Story by Anthony Verney.

Cast: Lloyd Bridges, Moira Lister, Alan Wheatley, Leslie Phillips, Helene Cordet, Andre Van Gyseghem, Tom Gill, Bruce Beeby, Rachel Roberts, Lionel Blair, Verne Morgan, Marjory Hume, Robert Harbin, Charles Bottrill.

Returning to London to see his wartime sweetheart (Moira Lister), an American (Lloyd Bridges) tries to solve the murder of a man killed by a limping sniper.

Running time: 76 minutes. Release date: December 11, 1953.

A British production, released in the U. S. by Lippert.

1954

518. White Fire (mystery) Directed by John Gilling. Produced by Robert S. Baker and Monty Berman. Screenplay by Paul Erickson and John Gilling. Story by Paul Erickson.

Cast: Scott Brady, Mary Castle, John Blythe, Colin Tapley, Lloyd Lamble, Julian Somers, Gabrielle Brune, Bollard Berkeley, Ronan O'Casey, Ferdy Mayne, Paul Erickson.

While searching for his missing brother in London, an American sailor (Scott Brady) becomes involved with a diamond smuggling ring.

Running time: 82 minutes. Release date: January 1, 1954.

A Hammer Film Production for Exclusive Films Ltd.; produced in Great Britain; released in the U. S. by Lippert.

519. Hollywood Thrill-Makers (drama) Directed by Bernard Ray. Produced by Maurice Kosloff. Screenplay by Janet Clark. Story by Bernard Ray.

Cast: James Gleason, Bill Terry, Theila (Diana) Darrin, Jean Holcombe, James Macklin, George Wilhelm, Robert Paquin, Janet Clark.

A stunt man (Bill Terry), who gave up his job for his wife's sake, returns to perform a stunt that his friend was killed trying to do.

Running time: 60 minutes. Release date: January 15, 1954.

520. The Black Glove (mystery) Directed by Terence Fisher. Produced by Michael Carreras. Screenplay by Ernest Borneman. From a novel by Ernest Borneman.

Cast: Alex Nicol, Eleanor Summerfield, John Salew, Paul Carpenter, Geoffrey Keen, Ann Hanslip, Fred Johnson, Arthur Lane, Martin Boddey, Paula Byrne.

An American trumpet player (Alex Nicol) turns detective to nab the killer of a British singer.

Running time: 84 minutes. Release date: January 29, 1954.

A Hammer Film Production for Exclusive Films Ltd.; produced and released in Great Britain as *Face the Music*; released in the U. S. by Lippert.

521. Queen of Sheba (drama) Directed by Pietro Francisci. Produced by Mario Francisci. Screenplay by Raoul De Sarro, Nino Novarese, Pietro Francisci and Georgio Grasiosi.

Cast: Leonora Ruffo, Gino Cervi, Gino Leurini, Marina Berti, Franco Silva, Mario Ferrari, Isa Pola, Nita Dover.

Prince Rehoboam (Gino Leurini), the son of Solomon (Gino Cervi) the King of Jerusalem, falls in love with Balkis (Leonora Ruffo) the Queen of Sheba.

Running time: 99 minutes. Release date: February 12, 1954.

An Oro Film production presented by William M. Pizor and Bernard Luber; produced in Italy; English-dubbed version released in the U. S. by Lippert.

522. We Want a Child (drama) Directed by Alice O'Fredericks and Lau Lauritzen. Screenplay by Leck Fisher. Story by Grethe Frische and Ib Freuchen.

Cast: Ib Schonberg, Ruth Breinholm, Jorgen Efenberg, Grethe Thordahl, Maria Garland, Preben Lerdorff-Rye, Jeanne Darville, Betty Helsengreen, Karen Berg, Else Jarlbak, Orlander Dam Willumsen, Berit Erbe.

A drama about a childless married couple.

Running time: 76 minutes. Release date: February 19, 1954.

An Asa Films Production; English-dubbed version released in the U.S. by Lippert.

523. Blackout (mystery) Directed by Terence Fisher. Produced by Michael Carreras. Screenplay by Richard Landau. From the novel "Murder by Proxy" by Helen Nielsen.

Cast: Dane Clark, Belinda Lee, Betty Ann Davies, Eleanor Summerfield, Andrew Osborn, Harold Lang, Jill Melford, Alvis Maben, Michael Golden, Nora Golden, Alfie Bass.

A war veteran (Dane Clark) wakes up after a drunken binge to discover he may have committed murder.

Running time: 87 minutes. Release date: March 19, 1954.

A Hammer Film Production for Exclusive Films Ltd.; produced and released in Great Britain as *Murder by Proxy*; released in the U. S. by Lippert.

524. Fangs of the Wild (drama) Directed by William Claxton. Produced by Robert Lippert, Jr. Screenplay by Orville Hampton. Based on a story idea by William Claxton.

Cast: Charles Chaplin, Jr., Onslow Stevens, Margia Dean, Freddy Ridgeway, Phil Tead, Robert Stevenson, Buck the dog.

A little boy (Freddy Ridgeway) witnesses a murder but can't get anyone to believe him—except the killer (Charles Chaplin, Jr.).

Running time: 71 minutes. Release date: April 2, 1954.

Also known as *Follow the Leader*.

525. Heat Wave (drama) Directed by Ken Hughes. Produced by Anthony Hinds. Screenplay by Ken Hughes. Based on the novel "High Wray" by Ken Hughes.

Cast: Alex Nicol, Hillary Brooke, Sidney James, Susan Stephen, Paul Carpenter, Alan Wheatley, Peter Illing, Gordon McLeod, Joan Hickson, John Sharp, Hugh Dempster, Monti de Lyle.

A novelist (Alex Nicol) covers up for a scheming blonde (Hillary Brooke) who has murdered her rich husband (Sidney James).

Running time: 68 minutes. Release date: April 16, 1954.

A Hammer Film Production for Exclusive Films Ltd.; produced and released in Great Britain as *The House Across the Lake*; released in the U.S. by Lippert.

526. Monster from the Ocean Floor (science fiction) Directed by Wyott Ordung. Produced by Roger Corman. Script by William Danch. A Palo Alto Production.

Cast: Anne Kimball, Stuart Wade, Dick Pinner, Jack Hayes, Wyott Ordung, Inez Palange.

When a young woman (Anne Kimball) fails to convince anyone that she has actually seen a strange sea monster, she sets out to capture the creature herself.

Running time: 64 minutes (51 minutes in Great Britain). Release date: May 21, 1954.

Working title: *It Stalked the Ocean Floor*.

Released in Canada as *Monster Maker*.

527. The Cowboy (documentary) Directed by Elmo Williams. Produced by Elmo Williams and Larry Dobkin. Written by Lorraine Williams. In Eastman Color.

A documentary focusing on the life of the American cowboy, then and now, narrated by Tex Ritter, Bill Conrad, John Dehner and Larry Dobkin.

Running time: 69 minutes. Release date: May 28, 1954.

528. The Big Chase (action-drama) Directed by Arthur D. Hilton. Produced by Robert L. Lippert, Jr. Written by Fred Freiberger.

Cast: Glenn Langan, Adele Jergens, Lon Chaney, Jim Davis, Douglas Kennedy, Jay Lawrence, Jack Daly, Joseph Flynn, Lou Roberson, Phil Arnold, Gil Perkins.

A patrol-car officer (Glenn Langan) pursues a gang of armored car robbers headed by a tough ex-convict (Jim Davis).

Running time: 60 minutes. Release date: June 18, 1954.

529. Paid to Kill (mystery) Directed by Montgomery Tully. Produced by Anthony Hinds. Original screenplay by Paul Tabori.

Cast: Dane Clark, Cecile Chevreau, Paul Carpenter, Thea Gregory, Anthony Forwood, Arthur Young, Howard Marion Crawford.

A desperate businessman (Dane Clark) hires a thug (Paul Carpenter) to kill him so his wife (Thea Gregory) can collect his insurance benefits, but later he frantically tries to alter his plans.

Running time: 70 minutes. Release date: June 25, 1954.

A Hammer Film Production for Exclusive Films Ltd.; produced and released in Great Britain as *Five Days*; released in the U. S. by Lippert.

530. River Beat (drama) Directed by Guy Green. Produced by Victor Hanburg. Screenplay by Rex Rienits.

Cast: Phyllis Kirk, John Bentley, Robert Ayres, Leonard White, Ewan Roberts, Glyn Houston, Charles Lloyd Pack, David Hurst, Margaret Anderson, Michael Balfour, Isabel George.

A radio operator (Phyllis Kirk), working on an American freighter docked in the Thames, is unwittingly being used to smuggle diamonds ashore.

Running time: 73 minutes. Release date: July 16, 1954.

An ABTCON Production, produced in Great Britain; released in the U. S. by Lippert.

531. Terror Ship (mystery) Directed by Vernon Sewell. Produced by W.H. Williams. Screenplay by Julian Ward. Story by Vernon Sewell.

Cast: William Lundigan, Naomi Chance, Vincent Ball, Jean Lodge, Kenneth Henry, Richard Stewart, John Warwick, Beresford Egan, Frank Littlewood, Armand Guinle, Peter Bathurst, Stanley Van Beers.

Adventure and mystery on the high seas aboard a strange craft.

Running time: 72 minutes. Release date: September 3, 1954.

Produced and released in Great Britain as *Dangerous Voyage*; released in the U. S. by Lippert.

532. Silent Raiders (action-drama) Directed by Richard Bartlett. Produced by Earle Lyon. Screenplay by Richard Bartlett.

Cast: Richard Bartlett, Earle Lyon, Jeannette Bordeaux, Earle Hansen, Robert Knapp, Fred Foote, Frank Stanlow, Carl Swanstrom.

During World War II, a seven-man patrol (Richard Bartlett, Earle Lyon, Earle Hansen, Robert Knapp, Fred Foote, Frank Stanlow, Carl Swanstrom) is sent to wipe out a German communications center near the French coast.

Running time: 65 minutes. Release date: September 17, 1954.

533. Thunder Pass (western) Directed by Frank McDonald. Produced by A. Robert Nunes. Screenplay by Tom Hubbard and Fred Eggers. Story by George Van Marter.

Cast: Dane Clark, Dorothy Patrick, Andy Devine, Raymond Burr, John

Carradine, Mary Ellen Kaye, Raymond Hatton, Nestor Paiva, Charles Fredericks, Tom Hubbard.

A Cavalry officer (Dane Clark) tries to lead settlers to safety from Indians on the warpath.

Running time: 76 minutes. Release date: September 20, 1954.

534. The Unholy Four (mystery) Directed by Terence Fisher. Produced by Michael Carreras. Screenplay by Michael Carreras. From the novel "Stranger at Home" by George Sanders.

Cast: Paulette Goddard, William Sylvester, Patrick Holt, Paul Carpenter, Alvys Maben, Russell Napier, Kay Callard, David King Wood, Jeremy Hawk, Pat Owens.

After a three-year absence, an amnesiac (William Sylvester) returns to confront his wife (Paulette Goddard) at her country home, only to discover that he's the prime suspect in a murder investigation.

Running time: 80 minutes. Release date: September 24, 1954.

A Hammer Film Production for Exclusive Films Ltd.; produced and released in Great Britain as *A Stranger Came Home*; released in the U. S. by Lippert.

535. The Deadly Game (mystery) Directed by Daniel Birt. Produced by Michael Carreras and Robert Dunbar. Screenplay by Robert Dunbar and Daniel Birt. Based on the novel "Third Party Risk" by Nicholas Bentley.

Cast: Lloyd Bridges, Simone Silva, Finlay Currie, Maureen Swanson, Ferdy Mayne, Peter Dineley, Roger Delgardo, George Woodbridge, Leslie Wright, Mary Parker, Seymour Green, Toots Pounds, Patrick Westwood.

An American (Lloyd Bridges) vacationing in Spain becomes involved with a smuggling ring.

Running time: 63 minutes (70 minutes in Great Britain). Release date: October 8, 1954.

A Hammer Film Production for Exclusive Films Ltd.; produced and released in Great Britain as *Third Party Risk*; released in the U. S. by Lippert.

Television title: *Big Deadly Game*.

536. The Siege (drama) Directed by Juan De Orduna. Screenplay by Vicente Escrina. Story by Clements Pamplona and A. F. Marrero.

Cast: Aurora Bautista, Fernando Rey, Virgilio Teixeira, Eduardo Fajardo, Manuel Luna, Jesus Tordesillas, Guillermo Marin, Juan Espantaleon, Fernando Fernandez de Cordoba, Fernando Nogueras, Jose Bodalo.

The story of Augustina (Aurora Bautista), the Spanish "Joan of Arc" who fought against Napoleonic forces.

Running time: 63 minutes. Release date: November 26, 1954.

A Cifesa Production, produced in Spain; English-dubbed version released in the U. S. by Lippert.

537. Race for Life (drama) Directed by Terence Fisher. Produced by Mickey Delamar. Screenplay by Richard Landau. From the novel "Last Race" by Jon Manchip White. Filmed for wide screen.

Cast: Richard Conte, Mari Aldon, George Coulouris, Peter Illing, Alec Mango, Meredith Edwards, James Copeland, Edwin Richfield, Richard Marnen, Tim Turner, Jeremy Hawk, Stirling Moss, Reg Parnell, John Cooper, Alan Brown, Geoffrey Taylor, Leslie Marr.

A race car driver (Richard Conte) attempts to make a comeback despite opposition from his wife (Mari Aldon).

Running time: 69 minutes (79 minutes in Great Britain). Release date: December 10, 1954.

A Hammer Film Production for Exclusive Films Ltd.; produced and released in Great Britain as *Mask of Dust*; released in the U. S. by Lippert.

538. The Black Pirates (adventure) Directed by Allen H. Miner. Produced by Robert L. Lippert, Jr. Screenplay by Fred Freiberger and Al C. Ward. A Salvador Films Production. Filmed for wide screen in Ansco Color.

Cast: Anthony Dexter, Martha Roth, Lon Chaney, Robert Clarke, Victor Manuel Mendoza, Alfonso Bedoya, Toni Gerry, Eddy Dutko.

A band of pirates arrive in a small Latin American town where they force the villagers to dig for buried treasure.

Running time: 74 minutes. Release date: December 24, 1954.

1955

539. They Were So Young (drama) Produced and directed by Kurt Neumann. Screenplay by Felix Leutzkendorf and Kurt Neumann. Based on an outline prepared from official documents by Jacques Companeez with the cooperation of Interpol, Paris (International Police). A Corona Films Production. Filmed for wide screen.

Cast: Scott Brady, Raymond Burr, Johanna Matz, Ingrid Stenn.

A German girl (Johanna Matz) journeys to Rio de Janeiro to work as a fashion model and is trapped into working for a criminal ring.

Running time: 80 minutes. Release date: January 7, 1955.

A German production released in the U. S. by Lippert.

Working title: *Adventure in Rio*.

Also known as *They Were So Young and So in Danger*.

Earle Lyon and Lon Chaney in *The Silver Star* (1955).

540. The Silver Star (western) Directed by Richard Bartlett. Produced by Earle Lyon. Original story and screenplay by Richard Bartlett and Ian MacDonald. An L & B Production. Filmed for wide screen.

Cast: Edgar Buchanan, Marie Windsor, Lon Chaney, Earle Lyon, Richard Bartlett, Barton MacLane, Morris Ankrum, Edith Evanson, Michael Whalen, Steve Rowland, Bob Karnes, Earl Hansen, Tim Graham, Bill Anders, Jill Richards, Chris O'Brien, Charles Knapp, the voice of Jimmy Wakely.

A reluctant sheriff (Earle Lyon) is the target of a gunman's vengeance. *Running time*: 73 minutes. Release date: April 8, 1955.

541. Thunder Over Sangoland (adventure) Directed by Sam Newfield. Produced by Rudolph C. Flothow. Screenplay by Sherman L. Lowe.

Cast: Jon Hall, Ray Montgomery, Marjorie Lord, House Peters, Jr., Myron Healey, Nick Stewart, Frank Richards, James Edwards, Louise Franklin, James Fairfax, M'Liss McClure.

Tom Reynolds (Jon Hall), an American doctor in Africa, helps a missionary and his sister (Marjorie Lord) quell a native uprising that was provoked by two fortune hunters trying to drive white settlers away from a gold mine.

Compiled from episodes of the syndicated television series *Ramar of the Jungle*.

Running time: 73 minutes. Release date: April 8, 1955.

542. The Glass Tomb (mystery) Directed by Montgomery Tully. Produced by Anthony Hinds. Screenplay by Richard Landau. Based on "The Outsiders" by A. E. Martin.

Cast: John Ireland, Honor Blackman, Geoffrey Keen, Eric Pohlmann, Sidney James, Liam Redmond, Sidney Tafler, Valerie Vernon, Arnold Marle, Nora Gordon, Sam Kydd, Ferdy Mayne, Tonia Bern, Arthur Howard, Stanley Little.

A carnival performer (Eric Pohlmann), enclosed in a glass cage for a publicity stunt, holds the key to solving the murder of a blackmailing young woman.

Running time: 59 minutes. Release date: April 15, 1955.

A Hammer Film Production for Exclusive Films Ltd.; produced and released in Great Britain as *The Glass Cage*; released in the U. S. by Lippert.

543. Air Strike (drama) Produced and directed by Cy Roth. Screenplay by Cy Roth.

Cast: Richard Denning, Gloria Jean, Don Haggerty, Bill Hudson, Alan Wells, John Kirby, William (Billy) Halop, James Courtney, Stanley Clements.

A Navy commander (Richard Denning) attempts to mold a jet attack squadron into an efficient fighting unit.

Running time: 67 minutes. Release date: May 6, 1955.

544. Phantom of the Jungle (adventure) Directed by Spencer Gordon Bennet. Produced by Rudolph C. Flothow. Screenplay by William Lively and Sherman L. Lowe.

Cast: Jon Hall, Ray Montgomery, Anne Gwynne, Kenneth MacDonald, Carleton Young, James Griffith, Nick Stewart, Milton Wood, James Fairfax, M'Liss McClure.

Tom Reynolds (Jon Hall), an American doctor in Africa, saves the lives of scientists who have incurred the wrath of a native tribe by refusing to return a sacred golden tablet.

Compiled from episodes of the syndicated television series *Ramar of the Jungle*.

Running time: 75 minutes. Release date: May 20, 1955.

Four intrepid space explorers are terrorized by a photographically enlarged lizard in *King Dinosaur* (1955).

545. King Dinosaur (science fiction) Directed by Bert I. Gordon. Produced by Bert I. Gordon and Al Zimbalist. Screenplay by Tom Gries. Story by Bert I. Gordon and Al Zimbalist. A Zigmore Production.

Cast: Bill Bryant, Wanda Curtis, Douglas Henderson, Patricia (Patti) Gallagher. Narrated by Marvin Miller.

Four scientists are sent on an expedition to a new planet; when they arrive, they discover it is inhabited by prehistoric beasts.

Running time: 59 minutes. Release date: June 17, 1955.

Uses footage from *One Million B. C.* (United Artists, 1940).

546. The Lonesome Trail (western) Directed by Richard Bartlett. Produced by Earle Lyon. Screenplay by Richard Bartlett and Ian MacDonald. Based on the story "Silent Reckoning" by Gordon D. Shirreffs.

Cast: John Agar, Wayne Morris, Edgar Buchanan, Adele Jergens, Margia Dean, Earle Lyon, Ian MacDonald, Douglas Fowley, Richard Bartlett, Betty Blythe.

A half-breed frontiersman (John Agar) returns home to battle landgrabbers.

Running time: 73 minutes. Release date: July 1, 1955.

547. Simba (drama) Directed by Brian Desmond Hurst. Produced by Peter de Sarigny. Screenplay by John Baines and Robin Estridge. Original story by Anthony Perry. In Eastman Color.

Cast: Dirk Bogarde, Virginia McKenna, Donald Sinden, Earl Cameron, Basil Sidney, Marie Ney, Joseph Tomelty, Orlando Martins, Ben Johnson, Huntley Campbell.

An Englishman (Dirk Bogarde) arrives in Kenya, Africa, where he learns that his brother was a victim of Mau Mau terrorism.

Running time: 99 minutes. Release date: September 9, 1955.

Produced and released in Great Britain by the J. Arthur Rank Organization; released in the U. S. by Lippert.

Short Subjects Released by Lippert Pictures

A complete listing of Lippert short subjects was unavailable. In 1949 the company announced they would be distributing six one-reel "Western Kid Komedies in Kolor": *The White Phantom, Showdown at Sun-Up, Hal's Half-Acre, Last of the Good Guys, Hurry-Along Harrigan, Bar-Bar-Black Sheep*. Release dates for these titles could not be found (assuming that they *were* made and *were* released).

Known Lippert short subject releases are *The Return of Gilbert and Sullivan* (1952), running 35 minutes and filmed in Ansco Color, and two 3-D shorts filmed in Ansco Color, *A Day in the Country* (1953) and *Bandit Island* (1953). *A Day in the Country*, released March 13, 1953, ran 15 minutes and was produced by Jack Rieger and narrated by comedian Joe Besser. *Bandit Island*, produced and directed by Robert L. Lippert, Jr., from a screenplay by Orville Hampton, ran 25 minutes and starred Glenn Langan, Lon Chaney, Jim Davis and Jay Lawrence; reportedly, it used footage from the Lippert feature *The Big Chase* (1954).

Bibliography

Books

Adams, Les, and Rainey, Buck. *Shoot-Em-Ups*. New Rochelle, N. Y.: Arlington House, 1978.
Bojarski, Richard. *The Films of Bela Lugosi*. Secaucus, N. J.: Citadel, 1980.
Everson, William K. *Classics of the Horror Film*. Secaucus, N. J.: Citadel, 1974.
Eyles, Allen; Adkinson, Robert; and Fry, Nicholas. *The House of Horror: The Story of Hammer Films*. N. Y.: The Third Press, 1973.
Fernett, Gene. *Poverty Row*. Satellite Beach, Fla.: Coral Reef Publications, 1973.
Gifford, Denis. *The British Film Catalogue 1895-1970*. Great Britain: David & Charles Holdings, 1973.
―――――. *Karloff: The Man, The Monster, The Movies*. N. Y.: Curtis, 1973.
Grossman, Gary. *Superman: Serial to Cereal*. N. Y.: Popular Library, 1976.
Hardy, Phil. *The Western*. N. Y.: William Morrow, 1983.
Hirschhorn, Clive. *The Hollywood Musical*. N. Y.: Crown, 1981.
Lennig, Arthur. *The Count: The Life and Films of Bela "Dracula" Lugosi*. N. Y.: G.P. Putnam's, 1974.
McCarthy, Todd, and Flynn, Charles. *Kings of the Bs*. N. Y.: E. P. Dutton, 1975.
Maltin, Leonard, editor. *TV Movies*. N. Y.: New American Library, 1982.
Miller, Don. *"B" Movies*. N. Y.: Curtis Books, 1973.
―――――. *Hollywood Corral*. N. Y.: Popular Library, 1976.
Parish, James Robert, editor. *The Great Movie Series*. Cranbury, N. J.: A. S. Barnes, 1971.
Peary, Danny. *Cult Movies*. N. Y.: Dell, 1981.
Pohle, Jr., Robert W., and Hart, Douglas C. *The Films of Christopher Lee*. Metuchen, N. J.: Scarecrow, 1983.
Quinlan, David. *The Illustrated Directory of Film Stars*. N. Y.: Hippocrene Books, 1981.
Rothel, David. *The Singing Cowboys*. Cranbury, N. J.: A. S. Barnes, 1978.
Sampson, Henry T. *Blacks in Black and White: A Source Book on Films*. Metuchen, N. J.: Scarecrow, 1977.
Schelly, William. *Harry Langdon*. Metuchen, N. J.: Scarecrow, 1982.
Warren, Bill. *Keep Watching the Skies! Vol. 1*. Jefferson, N. C.: McFarland, 1982.

Published articles

Dixon, Wheeler. "PRC: The Unknown Studio." *Films in Review*, September 1984, pp. 405-410.

Robison, Robert J. "PRC, a Filmography (parts one and two)." *The Films of Yesteryear*, #3, pp. 5–84, and #4, pp. 5–69.
———. "A Short History of Producers Releasing Corporation." *The Films of Yesteryear*, #2, pp. 27–84.

Name Index

The number after each name refers to the film entry number, not the page number. The spelling of some names varied from film to film; these have been noted wherever possible.

Abbott, Anthony 147
Abbott, W.J. 388
Abbott, Walter 459
Abraham, David 489
Abrahams, Derwin 375
Ace the dog 295, 376
Ackerman, Hildegard 351
Ackland, Josh 505
Acquanetta 469
Acuff, Eddie 285, 298
Adair, Alan 488
Adair, Phyllis 105
Adair, Robert 75, 510
Adam, Gordon 389
Adam, Ronald 477
Adams, Abigail 310
Adams, Betty (Julie) 426, 437, 439, 440, 442, 444, 446
Adams, Elayne 271
Adams, Ernie 56, 68, 82, 383
Adams, Eustace L. 112
Adams, Gerald D. 125, 132
Adams, Jane 322
Adams, Joey 422
Adams, Julie *see* Adams, Betty
Adams, Kathryn 317
Adams, Peter 509
Adams, Richard 6
Adams, Ted 68, 70, 87, 89, 90, 94, 97, 100, 116, 117, 136, 144, 145, 157, 163, 168, 170, 172, 177, 200, 325, 336, 365, 387, 414, 427
Adams, Victor 41
Adamson, Ewart 66, 143

Adamson, James 158
Adamson, Victor *see* Dixon, Denver
Adler, Luther 497
Adrian, Iris 122, 197, 217, 227, 244, 248, 251, 353, 430, 447, 459, 466, 468
Afrique 76
Agar, John 546
Ahern, Patrick 443
Ahn, Philip 38, 42
Ainsley, Norman 36
Ajay, Irene 482
Akkerman, Willem 273
Alberni, Luis 39, 186, 197, 213, 220, 241, 246
Albert, John A. 111
Albertson, Frank 165, 277, 292, 393
Albiin, Elsy 516
Alda, Robert 433
Aldana, Vida 384
Alden, Betty 215
Alderson, Erville 33
Aldon, Mari 537
Aldridge, Kay 263, 268
Alexander, Arthur 36, 41, 50, 51, 52, 151, 166, 173, 174, 181, 187, 190, 194, 198, 205, 210, 216, 219, 225, 232, 233, 236, 245, 250, 256, 259, 269, 274, 276, 277, 282, 288, 296, 297, 303, 313, 315, 347, 348, 371a, 371b, 371c, 371d, 371e, 371f
Alexander, Ben 110
Alexander, K.C. 78
Alexander, Max 36, 41, 50, 51, 52, 122,

126, 133, 141, 209, 299, 371a, 371b,
371c, 371d, 371e, 371f
Alexander, Richard (Dick) 52, 58, 210,
216, 232, 257, 282, 379, 381, 417
Allan, Drew 385
Allan, Michael 490
Allen, Bob 329
Allen, Ethan 67, 68, 74
Allen, Eugene 193
Allen, Glen 395
Allen, Harry 4
Allen, Irving 309
Allen, Joseph (Joe), Jr. 186, 399
Allen, Judith 15, 449, 451
Allwyn, Astrid 37, 50
Alper, Murray 16, 469
Alzep, Fedor 23
Amann, Betty 199
Ambler, Eric 472
Ambler, Joss 273, 505
Amendt, Rudolph 10
Ames, Adrienne 72
Ames, Leon 63, 72
Ames, Ramsay 353
Amsterdam, Morey 187
Anders, Bill 540
Anders, Lynn 36
Anders, Rudolph 320
Anderson, George 209
Anderson, James 507
Anderson, Kyle 491
Anderson, Les 429, 438, 463
Anderson, Margaret 530
Anderson, Robert 448
Andre, Gwili 35
Andre, Lona 32, 392
Andre, Marvelle 115, 463
Andre, Olga 391
Andren, Jean 350
Andrews, Andy 16
Andrews, Carol 270, 302
Andrews, Lloyd "Arkansas Slim" 131
Andrews, Slim 463
Andrews, Stanley 376, 388, 393, 404,
413, 430, 475
Andrieux, Paulette 488
Anglim, Sally 467
Angold, Edith 430
Angus, Bernadine 261
Ankers, Evelyn 313, 378
Ankrum, Morris 443, 540
Appleby, Dorothy 33
Apus and Estrellita 396
Archer, John 109

Arden, Mary 271
Argyle, John 188
Arlen, Richard 321, 387, 404, 424
Arliss, Leslie 188
Armetta, Henry 99
Armida 208, 241, 403
Armondo and Lita 468
Arms, Russell 359, 362, 366
Armstrong, Joanna 441
Armstrong, Margaret 132
Armstrong, Robert 35, 160, 277, 378
Arness, James 491
Arno, Sig 115
Arnold, George, and His "Rhythm on
Ice" Show 453
Arnold, Joan 507
Arnold, Phil 351, 387, 390, 463, 466,
467, 528
Arnt, Charles 264, 278
Artaine, Wong 494
Arthur, Johnny 38
Arthur, Robert 335
Ashe, Martin 147
Ashley, Carol 215
Ashley, Iris 13
Ashley, June 496
Aslan, Gregoire 477
Astell, Bettey 71
Asther, Nils 251
Astor, Gertrude 9, 96
Ates, Roscoe 118, 310, 314, 323, 325,
327, 329, 332, 341, 360, 363, 365,
366, 367, 368, 369, 370, 410
Atkinson, Frank 23
Atwill, Lionel 57, 222, 261, 265
Aubert, Lenore 306, 402
Aubrey, Jimmy 119, 126, 134, 136, 161,
163, 170, 179, 181, 189, 198, 202, 203,
204, 205, 207, 219, 234, 254, 303,
308
Auer, Mischa 501
Austin, Lois 126
Austin, Terry 331, 340, 352, 353
Austin, William 34
Avelier, Don 445
Averill, Anthony 80
Avery, Ted 464
Avonde, Richard 486
Ayers, Robert 503
Aylmer, Felix 20, 30, 260
Ayres, Robert 530

Name Index

Babcock, Dwight V. 322, 476
Bachmann, John G. 111
Bacon, David 171
Bacon, Gwen 511
Bacon, Max 495
Bacon, Shelby 498
Baddeley, Hermione 501, 503, 511
Baer, John 475
Baerwitz, Sam 356, 358
Bailey, Richard (Dick) 165, 395, 399
Bailey, Sherwood 17
Bailey, William Norton 419, 448, 455
Baines, John V. 496, 547
Baker, Benny 485
Baker, Robert S. 518
Baker, Roy 472
Bakewell, William 141
Balderston, John L. 13
Baldwin, Alan 95
Baldwin, Robert 99, 115
Baldwin, Walter 248, 280
Balenda, Carla 486
Balfour, Michael 510, 530
Ball, Vincent 531
Ballew, Smith 263
Balzamo, Ignazio 512
Bamby, George 360, 363, 365, 367, 368, 370
Banbury, Jack 475
Bane, Holly 387, 404, 407, 424, 432, 434
Banks, Howard 122, 156, 169, 206
Banks, Leslie 78
Bannon, Jim 412, 474, 507
Bara, Nina 360
Baratoff, Paul 153
Barber, Bobby 9
Barclay, Don 4, 15, 26
Barclay, Joan 51, 70, 100, 127, 145, 400
Barcroft, Roy 140
Bardette, Trevor 376, 420, 428
Baring, Aubrey 477
Barlow, Reginald 148
Barnard, Ivor 55, 242, 273
Barnett, Griff 318, 352
Barnett, Vince 5, 7, 10, 27, 29, 32, 67, 69, 73, 74, 109, 121, 129, 138, 150, 160, 182, 201, 356, 386, 410, 427, 463
Baron, Lita 465; see also Isabelita
Barr, Anthony 409

Barr, Byron (Gig Young) 96
Barrat, Robert 61, 293, 435
Barrett, Anne 196
Barrett, Paul 74
Barrie, Mona 38, 133
Barrie, Wendy 196
Barrier, Edgar 506
Barrier, Ernestine 509
Barringer, Barry 54
Barris, Harry 38
Barron, Robert 190, 210, 216, 225, 232, 287, 305
Barry, Don 72, 422, 426, 429, 430, 432, 448, 449, 451, 452
Barry, Phyllis 46
Barsky, Bud 40
Bartell, Eddie 39, 213
Bartell, Richard 249, 540
Barthelmess, Richard 2
Bartholomew, Freddie 255
Bartlett, Bennie 356, 358
Bartlett, Hall 481
Bartlett, Richard 532, 546
Bartok, Eva 508, 510
Barton, Gregg 341
Barton, Joan 300
Barton, Larry 425
Barton, Otis 62
Barvis, Tony 475
Basquette, Lina 180
Bass, Alfie 523
Batcheller, George R. 143
Bates, Amie 466
Bates, Barbara 318
Bates, Charles 295
Bates, Jeanne 299
Bathurst, Peter 531
Bauer, Dodie 423
Bautista, Aurora 536
Baxley, Jack 50, 123, 150, 165
Baxter, Alan 155, 183, 197, 402
Baxter, George 418
Baxter, Jane 30
Beach, Guy 381
Beach, Richard 111
Beadon, Steve 22
Beatty, Clyde 498
Beatty, Robert 214, 483
Beaudine, William 96, 104, 107, 112, 123, 125, 129, 132, 134, 147, 149, 150, 350, 351, 353, 356, 430
Beaudine, William, Jr. 132
Beaumont, Diane 487
Beaumont, Hugh 106, 270, 279, 302,

311, 317, 339, 350, 460, 461, 462, 465, 469
Beavers, Louise 240
Beck, John 153
Beckles, Gordon 142
Beddoe, Don 265
Bedell, Charles 401
Bedoya, Alfonso 482, 538
Beebe, Ford 382, 411, 426, 432, 449
Beebe, William 62
Beeby, Bruce 517
Beecher, Elizabeth 140
Beery, Noah, Jr. 443
Beich, Albert 192
Belasco, Leon 267, 353
Belden, Barbara 246
Bell, Hank 136, 200, 204, 275, 364, 366, 432
Bell, James 337
Bellamy, Madge 375
Belmont, Steve 455
Belmore, Bertha 76
Benedict, Brooks 37, 86, 339, 351
Benedict, Richard 420
Benedict, William (Billy) 267
Benge, Wilson 27, 36, 40, 44, 384
Bennet, Spencer Gordon 153, 544
Bennett, Bruce 248
Bennett, Edward 101, 110
Bennett, Harriet 56
Bennett, Lee 305, 310, 311, 323, 327, 329, 369, 370, 388, 447, 455
Bennett, Raphael 85
Bennett, Ray 155, 189, 200, 202, 234, 250, 281, 412, 417, 426
Benson, Martin 495
Benson, Robert 260
Bent, Buena 13
Bentley, John 530
Bentley, Nicholas 535
Benton, Bob 377
Benton, Dean 53
Beresford, Harry 1, 66
Berg, Karen 522
Bergh, Jerry 18
Berhle, Fred 69
Berke, William 280, 380, 383, 386, 415, 421, 423, 425, 427, 441, 448, 449, 451, 452, 454, 460, 461, 462, 465, 476, 489
Berkeley, Bollard 518
Berkeley, Martin 487
Berman, Monty 518
Bernard, Barry 147

Bernard, Sam 133, 160
Berne, Josef 314
Berne, Tonia 542
Bert, Flo 248
Berti, Marina 521
Besser, Joe 514
Bevan, Billy 61
Bevans, Clem 415, 427
The Beverly Hillbillies 56
Bianco, Peggy Lou 280
Biberman, Abner 72, 461
Bice, Robert 187, 198, 478, 485
Bill, Buffalo, Jr. see Wilsey, Jan
Billinger, Richard 409
Billquist, Trillot 484
Binyon, Conrad 209
Birdwell, Russell 262
Birell, Tala 4, 199, 226, 337, 340
Birt, Daniel 535
Bishop, Julie 427; see also Wells, Jacqueline
Bishop, Norman 478
Bissell, Whit 469, 478
Black, Dorothy 188
Blackburn, Tom 351
Blackley, Douglas 386
Blackman, Honor 542
Blackmer, Sidney 147, 150
Blair, Anthony 196
Blair, Barbara 75
Blair, George 498
Blair, Joan 186
Blair, Lionel 517
Blake, Bobby 333
Blake, Gladys 217
Blake, Guy 246
Blake, Marie 476
Blake, Pamela (Adele Pearce) 59, 280, 380, 388, 391, 392, 415, 423, 452, 460
Blake, Rubie 396, 398
Blakely, Douglas 397
Blakely, James 33, 36
Blanchard, Jerri 196
Blanchard, Phyllis 354, 367
Blanco, Eumonio 241
Bland, Joyce 2
Blandick, Clara 1, 33, 353
Bleifer, John 233
Bletcher, Billy 212
Bliss, Lela 356
Blitz, Peter 484
Block, Irving 474
Blore, Eric 197

Name Index

Blue, Monte 6, 128, 385, 455
Bluhm, Carl 409
Blystone, John G. 9, 16
Blystone, Stanley 68, 80, 288, 296, 351, 386, 427
Blythe, Betty 96, 104, 125, 143, 192, 546
Blythe, John 518
The Bobby Harrison Trio 468
Bodalo, Jose 536
Boddey, Martin 477, 484, 510, 520
Bogarde, Dirk 547
Bogge, Niels 180
Bohn, Walter 63
Boles, Buddy 118
Bond, Raymond 395
Bond, Tommy 356, 358
Bond, Ward 16, 491
Bondi, Beulah 435
Bonn, Walter 50, 76
Boon, Eric 495
Boon, Robert 425
Booth, Ernest 149
Bordeaux, Jeannette 532
Borden, Eddie 438
Borg, Sven-Hugo 128, 153
Borg, Veda Ann 86, 132, 199, 208, 261, 278, 309, 321
Borneman, Ernest 520
Bosworth, Hobart 56, 65
Bottrill, Charles 517
Bouchier, Chili 71
Boucicault, Nina 21
Bovard, Mary 239
Boya, Bill 155
Boyce, Helen 390
Boyce and Evans 467
Boyce, Evans and Betty Jane 468
Boyd, Beverley 192, 215
Boyd, Bill "Cowboy Rambler" 130, 135, 144, 154, 159, 163
Boyett, Bill 494
Boyle, Walden 395, 399
Bradbury, Robert N. 8, 14, 18, 25, 28
Bradford, David 318
Bradford, Lane 87, 108, 307, 316, 355, 357, 360, 361, 363, 365, 366, 368, 405
Bradford, Marshall 491
Bradley, Grace 82
Bradley, Harry 176
Brady, Scott 518, 539
Braislin, John 463
Bramhall, Dorothy 487

Branch, Houston 40
Brand, Christianna 490
Brande, Ruth 270
Branden, Michael 271, 321
Brandes, Alaine 108
Brandt, Ivan 24
Brash, Henry 320
Braxton, Steve *see* Robins, Sam
Brazeal, Hal 128
Brazzi, Rossano 512
Breakston, George 53, 149
Brecher, Egon 284
Brechignac, H. Vincent 488
Breed, John 494
Breinholm, Ruth 522
Brendel, El 241, 248
Brennan, Jay 196
Brennan, Marguerite 502
Brent, Evelyn 107, 119, 176
Brent, George 476, 480
Brent, Linda 217
Brent, Lynton 9, 31, 42, 45, 56, 59, 135, 140, 161, 164, 174, 230
Brent, Roy 200, 207, 216, 234, 257, 294, 296, 319
Bressart, Felix 320
Bretherton, Howard 400, 401
Brian, Mary 13, 201, 397
Bricker, Clarence 54
Bricker, Elsie 324
Bricker, George 81, 86, 88, 91, 322, 324, 342, 354
Bricker, Jack 95
Bridge, Al 98
Bridge, Lori 139
Bridges, John 329
Bridges, Lloyd 443, 464, 497, 517, 535
Brien, Edwin 168
Brieux, Eugene 46
Briggs, John 503
Bris, Virginia 280
Briskin, Jerry 352
Bristow, Frank 390
Britton, Barbara 416, 454
Brock, Lou 138, 291
Brodel, Betty 244
Brodie, Don 73
Brodie, Steve 425, 430, 456
Brodney, Oscar 160
Bromberg, J. Edward 271, 384, 416
Bromfield, John 407
Bromley, Sheila 80
Bronson, Lillian 267
Bronsten, Nat A. 484

Brook, Clive 11
Brooke, Hillary 98, 116, 469, 525
Brooke, Ralph 494
Brooks, Clarence 48
Brooks, Edwy, Searles *see* Gray, Berkley
Brooks, Jean 171
Brooks, Jess 158
Brooks, Paul 461
The Broome Brothers 429, 463
Brophy, Edward 9, 35, 383, 421, 460, 461, 462
Brother Bones 467
Brown, Alan 537
Brown, C. Carleton 494
Brown, Charles D. 231, 279
Brown, Harry 386
Brown, Helen 295
Brown, Hennie 96
Brown, James 342
Brown, John 455
Brown, Karl 1, 4, 17
Brown, Melville 47
Brown, Tom 176, 422, 441
Brown, Vernon 139
Browne, Laidman 505
Browning, Jill 246, 255
Brownley, Frank 150
Bruce, David 447, 462
Bruce, Earle 244
Bruce, Rodman 338
Brune, Gabrielle 518
Bryan, Arthur Q. 95
Bryan, Dore 502
Bryant, Bill 545
Bryant, Jan 358
Bryant, Joyce 84
Bryant, Nana 342
Bryar, Paul 88, 91, 112, 125, 132, 158, 173, 182, 311, 317, 324, 328, 339, 470, 473
Bryon, Allan 192
Buchanan, Edgar 540, 546
Buchanan, Jack 224
Buck, Frank 206
Buck the dog 524
Buckley, Jack 134
Bucko, Buck 163, 211
Bucko, Roy 163, 195, 211
Budd, Norman 81
Buell, Jed 107, 134
Bull, John 487
Bupp, Tommy 12, 18, 42
Burbridge, Elizabeth (Betty) 400, 401, 404

Burden, Hugh 505
Burgess, Dorothy 175, 192
Burke, Caroline 168, 345
Burke, Denny 256
Burke, James 9, 292, 340, 358
Burke, Marie 500
Burkett, James S. 326, 385
Burnell, Janey 487
Burns, Bill, and His birds 453
Burns, Bob 6, 159
Burns, David 75, 224
Burns, Fred 32
Burns, Paul 475
Burr, Ann 335
Burr, Raymond 476, 533, 539
Burt, Ben 66
Burton, Devera 420
Burton, Frederick 255
Burtwell, Frederick 273
Busch, Mae 148
Buschell, Brian 2
Bush, James 77
Bush, Nora 230
Bushman, Francis X. 123
Bushnell, Anthony 30
Buster, Budd 6, 8, 12, 25, 51, 60, 86, 89, 91, 101, 105, 108, 114, 113, 116, 120, 136, 145, 157, 170, 172, 185, 195, 200, 205, 219, 221, 223, 225, 228, 230, 236, 247, 250, 254, 276, 279, 281, 283, 288, 296, 297, 298, 301, 307, 312, 363, 364, 365, 367
Butler, Roy 190, 423, 427, 454, 457
Butterworth, Charles 240
Byrd, Ralph 96, 112, 132, 134, 403, 410, 434
Byrne, Bobby, and His Band 196
Byrne, Paula 520
Byrnes, Gene 118
Byron, Allan 201
Byron, Kathleen 273, 495
Byron, Richard 258
Byron, Walter 44, 60

Cabanne, Christy 240, 263, 388
Cabot, Bruce 37, 309
Caesar, Arthur 249, 421
Cagney, James 9, 38
Cahn, Edward L. 331, 358
Caithness, Wilfrid 2
Call, Inez 150
Callahan, Bob 323

Callahan, Danna 118
Callahan, Foxy 14
Callahan, George 66
Callam, Alex 82, 109, 125
Callard, Kay 534
Calo, Carla 512
Cameron, Earl 547
Cameron, Rod 489
Campana, Nina 4
Campbell, Alice 21
Campbell, Colin 40, 306
Campbell, Huntley 547
Campbell, Judy 142
Campbell, Sterling 389
Campeau, Frank 65
Campion, Cyril 21, 76
Campo, Del 3
Camron, Rocky 287, 300, 374
Canale, Gianna Maria 515
Candido, Candy 38
Cannon, Raymond 43
Cansino, Rita (Rita Hayworth) 14
Canutt, Yakima 14, 28
Canzoneri, Tony 422
Card, Ken 31
Card, Virginia 116
Cardwell, James 335, 407
Carey, Timothy 491
Carle, Richard 53
Carleton, Claire 350
Carlin, Jean 296, 305, 308, 329, 369
Carlin, Roberta 246
Carlisle, Mary 160, 178
Carlson, June 239, 368
Carlton, George 104
The Carlyle Dancers 433
Carnavale, John 36
Carney, Bob 463
Carney, Marion 323
Carnovsky, Morris 436
Carol, Joan 505
Carole, Joseph 248, 292
Caron, Doris 262
Carpenter, Elliott 467
Carpenter, Horace B. 32, 56, 59, 116, 127, 136, 144, 152
Carpenter, Ike, and His Orchestra 453
Carpenter, John (Josh) 287, 375
Carpenter, Paul 520, 525, 529, 534
Carpenter, Virginia 103
Carr, Jane 516
Carr, Joe 389
Carr, June 418, 433

Carr, Stephen 437, 439, 440, 442, 444, 446, 475
Carr, Thomas 437, 439, 440, 442, 444, 446
Carradine, John 199, 233, 251, 314, 533
Carreras, Michael 508, 520, 523, 524, 535
Carrillo, Leo 265
Carroll, Jack 403
Carroll, Jean 468
Carroll, Vance 5
Carroll, Virginia 135, 485
Carson, Charles 24, 55, 224
Carson, Renee 187
Carson, Robert 121, 434, 479
Carter, Ben, and His Choir 240
Carter, Jack 396, 398
Carter, Lavada 398
Caruso, Anthony 187, 208
Casey, Claude 429, 463
Cason, John (Bob) 135, 232, 247, 257, 266, 272, 275, 283, 294, 297, 308, 312, 316, 319, 405, 408, 417, 419, 430, 432, 437, 439, 440, 442, 444, 446
Cass, Maurice 137
The Cass County Boys 453
Cassell, Wally 464
Cassidy, Edward 6, 12, 18, 29, 32, 42, 45, 56, 59, 85, 148, 195, 200, 207, 211, 212, 221, 228, 232, 235, 236, 243, 252, 256, 259, 269, 272, 274, 275, 277, 288, 297, 304, 312, 349, 365, 387, 451
Castle, Dolores (Delores) 341, 403
Castle, Don 330, 331, 445
Castle, Mary 518
Castle, Ruth 407
Caswell, (Captain) Wallace, Jr. 22
Catlett, "Big" Sid, and His Band 394
Catlett, Walter 73, 263
Catto, Max 500
Cavanaugh, Paul 289, 447, 478
Caven, Taylor 295, 338
Cavin, Jess 198
Cawdron, Robert 513
Cawthorne, Peter 13, 23
Cecil, Nora 44
Cederlund, Gosta 484
Celano, Guido 515
Cellier, Antoniette 75
Cervi, Gino 521
Chaliapin, Feodor, Jr. 73
Chalton, Syd 213
Chamberlain, Cyril 477

Chambers, Wheaton 279, 298, 427, 435
Champion, John C. 491
Chance, Naomi 483, 495, 531
Chandler, Chick 160, 238, 469
Chandler, Eddy 9, 187
Chandler, George 33, 299
Chandler, Helen 44
Chandler, Lane 179, 183, 203, 220, 243, 252
Chandos, John 516
Chaney, Lon 528, 538, 540
Chang, Bobby 453
Chapin, Ann Morrison 37
Chapin, Robert 154
Chaplin, Charles, Jr. 524
Chapman, Helen 219, 382
Chapman, Marguerite 480
The Charles Weidman Dancers 196
Charters, Spencer 17, 44, 73
Chase, Alden (Stephen) 60, 81, 90, 100, 102, 108, 109
Chase, James Hadley 480
Chatburn, Jean 3
Chatterton, Tom 415
Cheatham, Jack 134, 149, 351
Cheirel, Micheline 378
Chernus, Sonia 342
Chesebro, George 87, 89, 90, 94, 100, 103, 105, 108, 117, 136, 140, 144, 154, 189, 202, 204, 207, 211, 212, 223, 234, 272, 275, 301, 305, 307, 316, 359, 360, 361, 362, 363, 364, 365, 366, 412, 437, 439, 440, 442, 444, 446, 463
Cheshire, Harry 386
Chester, Alfred 398
Chevreau, Cecile 508, 529
Chief, Denmore 66
Chief Many Treaties 387
Chief Thunder Cloud 34, 300, 383, 402, 431
Chief Yowlachie 329, 402
Christian, John 239
Christine, Virginia 302, 306
Christy, Grace 300
Chryst, Kenny 160
Chrystall, Belle 242
Chun, William 456
Churchill, Diana 242
Churchill, Robert B. 330, 331, 341, 362
Churchill, Savannah 398
Cianelli, Eduardo 306, 512
Cianelli, Lewis E. 512

Cilento, Diane 483
Cirillo, Charles 429, 433
Cirino, Natale 512
Claire and Arene 196
Clare, Mary 188
Clark, Bobby (13-year-old World's Champion Junior Cowboy) 84
Clark, Bobby 463
Clark, Cliff 340
Clark, Dane 472, 495, 523, 529, 533
Clark, Davidson 253
Clark, Edward 460, 465
Clark, Gordon 313, 385
Clark, Janet 519
Clark, Jean 423
Clark, Jimmy 264
Clark, John 25
Clark, Judy 237, 258
Clark, Mamo 40
Clark, Roger 192, 290
Clark, Steve 89, 98, 100, 108, 117, 152, 154, 163, 170, 175, 200, 230, 275, 287, 296, 303, 307, 312, 332, 336, 357, 359, 362, 364, 366, 368
Clark, Wallis 9
Clarke, Mae 9, 39, 173
Clarke, Richard 112, 150, 165, 192
Clarke, Robert 478, 538
Clarke, Walter D., Jr. 9
Clavering, Eric 214
Claxton, William 524
Clement, Dora 137
Clement, Lyle 91
Clements, Marjorie 250
Clements, Stanley 543
Cleveland, George 246, 417
Clifford, Molly Hamley 513
Clifton, Elmer 122, 126, 174, 181, 210, 212, 216, 219, 225, 228, 232, 236, 238, 245, 250, 256, 259, 274, 276, 294, 297, 319, 341, 348
Cline, Brenda 101
Cline, Rusty 181
Clute, Chester 263, 277, 314, 429, 459, 463
Clyde, June 238, 267
Coates, Phyllis 475, 498
Cobb, Edmund 383, 387
Cobb, Lee J. 497
Cochran, Dorcas 306
Cody, Bill, Jr. 135
Cody, Frank 385
Cody, Harry 408
Cody, J.W. 400

Name Index 195

Coe, Peter 491
Coffin, Tristram 400, 434, 435
Cogan, Dick 474
Cohen, Bennett 40
Cohen, Nat 513
Cohen, Octavius Roy 150
Cohen, Sammy 132
Coits, Joe 81
Colby, Fred 326, 402, 403
Colby, Marian 199, 418
Cole, Mary 47
Cole, Sidney 490
Coleman, Charles 271
Coleman, Jean 466
Coleman, Nancy 320
Coleman, Pat 491
Coleman, Ruth 40
Coleridge, Ethel 11
Colin, James 380
Colin, Jean 47
Collier, Lois 186
Collins, Charles 244
Collins, Jack 284
Collins, Joan 503
Collins, Lewis D. 393, 403
Collins, Monte (Monty) 255, 354
Collins, Paul 504
Colmes, Walter J. 213, 321, 395, 399
Colombo, E. 512
Colonna, Jerry 463
Comandini, Adele 264
Combs, Pat 390
Companeez, Jacques 539
Compson, Betty 201
Compton, Joyce 33, 86, 137, 388, 424
Compton, Viola 20
Conklin, Charles "Heine" 111
Conklin, Chester 25
Conlan, Frank 293
Conley, Onest 403
Conlin, Jimmy (James) 255, 441
Conn, Maurice H. 60, 397
Conrad, Bill 527
Conrad, Eugene 340, 356
Conrad, Jack 399
Conrad, Mike 454
Conrad, Mikel 338, 349, 365
Conte, Richard 537
Conti, Steve 448
Conway, Bert 397
Conway, Tom 510
Conwell, Mary 338
Coogan, Jackie 468, 486
Cook, Elisha, Jr. 280

Cook, Tommy 318
Cooley, Spade 429, 438
Cooper, Clancy 192, 291, 306
Cooper, Dee 355, 357, 359, 361, 364, 365, 414
Cooper, Inez 328, 378, 379, 381
Cooper, Jack 139
Cooper, James Fenimore 402
Cooper, John 537
Cooper, Tex 116, 127, 172, 200, 286, 300, 429
Cooper, Tom 14
Copas, Cowboy 429
Copeland, James 537
Coppel, Alec 75
Copper the horse 366, 367
Corbett, Ben 52, 92, 269
Corbett, Louis J. 370
Corda, June 142
Cordet, Helene 517
Cording, Harry 383, 401
Cordova, Fred 29, 69
Corey, Jeff 475
Corio, Ann 126, 158
Corman, Roger 526
Cornell, Ann, and the International Jitterbugs 394
Cornish, Dr. Robert E. 53
Corrigan, Ray 383
Cortesa, Valentina 490
Cortez, Lita 92
Cortez, Ricardo 162
Corthell, Herbert 34, 132
Cosgriff, Robert 99
Costello, Maurice 141
Costello, Pat 176
Costello, William 147
Coticchia, Enzo 500
Cotton, Carolina 248
Coulouris, George 537
Counts, Eleanor 194
Court, Hazel 505, 511
Courtney, James 543
Cowan, Jerome 73, 237, 261, 378
Cox, George Harmon 41
Cox, Morgan 112
Coy, Walter 476
Coyle, Ellen 308, 316
Coyle, John T. 112, 125, 132
Crabbe, Buster 120, 121, 127, 136, 145, 157, 158, 164, 168, 177, 182, 185, 191, 200, 202, 204, 211, 218, 221, 223, 230, 231, 234, 235, 243, 247, 254, 257, 266, 272, 275, 281, 283, 286, 294,

301, 307, 308, 312, 316, 319, 343, 344, 345, 346
Craig, Alec 217
Craig, Davina 30
Cramer, Richard (Dick) 127, 134, 136, 287, 332, 334, 349
Crandall, Suzi 408
Crane, Mrs. Gardener 192
Crane, Jocelyn 62
Crane, Steve 360
Cravat, Noel 339
Craven, Eddie 314
Craven, Frank 246
Craven, James 133, 509
Craven, John 378
Crawford, Caritz 34
Crawford, Howard Marion 529
Crawford, John 268
Crawford, Sarah 484
Crehan, Joseph 41, 246, 340, 422, 432
Criner, Lawrence 398
Cripps, Kernan 9
Crocker, Harry 180
Crocker, Lou 267
Cromer, Tex 438
Cromien, Larry 389
Cromley, Ed 265
Cromwell, Richard 160
Crosby, Bob 14
Crosby, Wade 478
Cross, Jimmie 466
Crothers, Scatman 467
Croy, Homer 416
Cruz, Angel 240
Curcy, Elvira 186
Currie, Finlay 535
Currie, Louise 89, 97, 329, 339, 369
Curt Barrett's Trailsmen 458
Curtis, Alan 337, 340, 378, 383, 428, 512
Curtis, Billy 475
Curtis, Dick (Richard) 149, 165, 232, 383, 426
Curtis, Donald 101, 110
Curtis, Dorothy 387
Curtis, Ken 431
Curtis, Wanda 545
Curwood, James Oliver 128, 375, 379, 381, 400, 401
Curzon, George 71
Cutler, Lester 147, 150, 167, 175, 180
Cutting, Richard 507

Daily, Pete, and His Chicagoans 467
Dairoli, Charlie, and Paul 490
D'Albrook, Sid 27, 29
Dale, Esther 46
Dale, Virginia 397, 460
Daley, Amy 188
Daley, Jack 485
Daly, Jack 528
Dalya, Jacqueline 183, 197, 313
Damita, Lili 3
Danagger, Theo 409
Danch, William 526
The Danches Brothers 407
Dandridge, Ruby 150, 180, 184
Danforth, William 35
Daniels, Billy 396
Daniels, Hank 395
Daniels, Leslie 515
Daniels, Robin 129
D'Antonio, Carmen 514
Darcel, Denise 410
Darcey, Sheila 121
D'Arcy, Roy 7
Dare, Dorothy 167
Darien, Frank 66, 72
Darling, W. Scott 65, 331, 350
Darling Sisters 468
Darmour, Roy 262, 299
Darnborough, Antony 472
Darnell, Steve 294
Darrell, Steve 301, 307
Darrin, Theila (Diana) 519
Darville, Jeanne 522
Davenport, Devvy 433
Davenport, Gail 244
Davenport, Harry 66, 73, 291
David, Richard 421
David, William B. 374, 375, 376, 377, 378, 379, 381, 382, 388
Davidson, John 95
Davidson, Max 34
Davidson, William 38, 263
Davies, Betty Ann 503, 523
Davies, Glyn 76
Davis, Art 70, 114, 130, 135, 144, 154, 159, 163
Davis, Chess 467
Davis, Dix 74
Davis, Eddie M. 137, 143
Davis, Frederick C. 222
Davis, George 137, 425
Davis, Jim 447, 455, 464, 528
Davis, Karl 457, 458
Davis, Lynn 453

Davis, Redd 76
Davis, Sally 407
Davis, Tim 42
Davis, Wee Willie 374
Daw, Evelyn 38
Dawson, Anthony 484
Dawson, Hal K. 160, 475
Dawson, Jon 239
Dax, Donna 266
Day, Doris 104, 123
Day, Regina 453
de Alba, Felipe 482
Dean, Basil 11
Dean, Dinky 441
Dean, Eddie 131, 135, 287, 300, 305, 310, 314, 323, 325, 327, 329, 332, 341, 360, 363, 365, 366, 367, 368, 369, 370, 374
Dean, Margia 239, 411, 417, 422, 424, 425, 432, 435, 436, 445, 447, 450, 454, 457, 462, 463, 465, 470, 473, 475, 476, 478, 485, 494, 514, 524, 546
Deane, Richard 126
Dearing, Edgar 238, 471
de Brulier, Nigel 4
de Castro, Eduardo 49
Deckers, Eugene 472
de Cordoba, Fernando Fernandez 536
de Cordoba, Pedro 17, 46, 289, 420
de Cordova, Arturo 482
De Cordova, Leander 80, 430
Deep, Harry 134
de Grunwald, Anatole 76, 502
Dehner, John 527
Dein, Edward 160, 171, 176
De La Cruz, Juan 169, 227
Delamar, Mickey 537
De LaMotte, Marguerite 118
Delany, Charles 19, 27
De Latour, Charles 517
DeLay, Melville 203
Delevante, Cyril 268
Delgardo, Roger 535
de Liguoro, Eugenio 459
Dell, Claudia 5, 10, 29
Dell, Myrna 207, 215, 434
Delmonte, David 76
Del Rio, Diana 166
Deltgen, Rene 409, 493
de Lyle, Monti 525
DeMain, Gordon 148
Demarest, Drew 149
de Marney, Terence 75

Demetria/Demetrio, Anna 169, 197, 454
Dempsey, Janet 118
Dempster, Hugh 525
Denison, Leslie 151, 153, 292
Denning, Glenn 459
Denning, Richard 543
Denny, Reginald 10
DeNormand, George 361
Dent, Vernon 79, 143
De Orduna, Juan 536
Depina Troupe 433
DeRobertis, F. 406
Derr, E.B. 101, 110
Derwin, Hal 438
de Saint-Colombe, Paul 55
de Sarigny, Peter 547
DeSarro, Raoul 521
Desmond, Cleo 48
Desmond, William 6, 8, 12, 135
Dessy, Angelo 515
Deven, Carrive 251
Devi, Chitra 489
DeVillard, Joseph 180
Devine, Andy 533
Devlin, Joe 222, 240, 386
Dewey, Earl 253
Dewhurst, Dorothy 71
DeWit, Jacqueline 261
DeWitt, Jack 326, 333, 385
DeWolf, Karen 352
Dexter, Anthony 538
Dexter, Aubrey 242
Dexter, John 387
The Diacoffs 468
Diamond, David 43
di Ciccio, Pat 309
Dickerson, Dudley 110
Dickinson, Thorold 57, 490
Diege, Samuel 65, 67, 69, 74
Diffring, Anton 510
Dillard, Art 105, 154, 159, 163
Dillard, Bert 136, 145, 211, 288, 308, 455
Dilson, John 9, 88, 91, 182
Dinehart, Alan 237
Dineley, Peter 535
Dingle, Charles 306
Dix, Billy 412
Dix, Kenny 51
Dixon, Denver (Victor Adamson) 93
Dixon, Eileen 418
Dixon, Larry 295
Dobkin, Larry 485, 527
Dobson, James 479

Dodd, Jimmy 380, 466
Dolciame, Ray 356
Dominguez, Joe 103, 454
Donath, Louis 173
Donath, Ludwig 514
Doniger, Walter 215
Donovan, King 464
Doran, Ann 110, 399
Doret, Nica 189
Dorian, Ernest 155
Doro, Mino 515
Dorr, Lester 9, 69, 106
Dors, Diana 480
D'Orsay, Fifi 197, 218, 239, 240
Doten, Jay 231
Doucette, John 395, 399, 478, 498
Douglas, Don 289
Douglas, Earl 68
Douglas, George 88
Douglas, Rita 121
Douglas, Sharon 261
Dover, Nita 521
Dowling, Joan 502
Downing, Rex 324
Downs, Johnny 148, 213, 429
Doyle, Jack 15
Drake, Chris 462, 471
Drake, Claudia 270, 280, 290, 333, 383
Drake, Oliver 89, 97, 117, 122, 133, 135, 136, 140, 190, 194, 198, 205, 347
Drake, Steve 355, 360, 367
Drake, Tom 476
Draper, Billy 481
Dreifuss, Arthur 69, 118, 160, 171, 176
Dreon, Edna 463
Dreon, Gracia 463
Dresden, Curley 92, 93, 98, 105, 108, 113, 116, 120, 127, 131, 135, 136, 144, 152, 154, 159, 161, 163, 164, 177, 198, 203
Dresser, David *see* Halliday, Brett
Drew, Ellen 435
Drew, Paula 460
Drew, Roland 79, 82, 231
Dubov, Paul 138, 171, 318
DuBrey, Claire 326, 385
Dudan, Pierre 488
Dudley, Robert 187
Duff, Howard 508
Dugan, Tom 258, 263, 321
Dumas, Alexander 306
Dumbrille, Douglass 397, 413
Dump and Tony 76
Duna, Steffi 79

Dunbar, Robert 535
Duncan, Archie 511
Duncan, Arlene 46
Duncan, Bob 282, 305, 310, 325, 329, 336, 349, 367, 375, 414, 418
Duncan, Danny 146
Duncan, Johnny 215, 239
Duncan, Julie 112, 130, 163, 172
Duncan, Kenne 60, 84, 85, 87, 89, 92, 97, 103, 113, 127, 130, 131, 135, 136, 140, 157, 170, 177, 194, 195, 205, 427, 434
Duncan, Renault *see* Renaldo, Duncan
Dunham, Phil 15, 27, 32
Dunhill, Steve 408, 414
Dunn, Eddie 416
Dunn, James 61, 83, 88, 187
Dunn, Pat 139
Dunn, Ralph 302, 311, 324, 328, 339, 350, 397
Dunn, Tay 295
Duprez, June 153, 206
Dupuis, Claudine 512
Durlam, Arthur 87, 126, 371a, 371b, 371c, 371d, 371e, 371f
Duryea, Dan 516
Dutko, Eddy 538
Dutra, John 443
Duval, Juan 58
Dvorak, Ann 450
Dwire, Earl 6, 8, 12, 14, 18, 28, 31, 52
Dwyer, Marlo 137
Dyall, Valentine 273
Dykes, Hubert 22
Dyne, Michael 284

Earle, Edward 81, 249, 321
Earnshaw, Fenton 351, 465, 476
Eason, B. Reeves 379, 381, 417
Easton, Bob 465
Eaton, Evelynne 280
Ebe, Earle 128
Eben, Al 284
Eburne, Maude 73, 248, 255, 421
Eddy, Buck 463
Eddy, Chickie 463
Edmonds, William 199, 422
Edwards, Alan 220
Edwards, Blake 293
Edwards, Bruce 384
Edwards, Henry 21, 142
Edwards, James 456, 541

Edwards, Joaquin 107, 147
Edwards, Meredith 480, 495, 537
Edwards, Robert 410
Edwards, Thornton 102, 103, 112, 125
Edwards, Weston *see* Fraser, Harry
Edwards, Wilson 114
Efenberg, Jorgen 522
Egan, Beresford 273, 531
Eggers, Fred 533
Eilers, Sally 264
Einstein, Harry *see* Parkyarkarkus
Elder, Ray 287
The Elder Lovelies 429
Eldredge, George 447, 457, 485
Eldredge, John 262, 429
Elliott, Dick 263, 436
Elliott, Edythe 252, 268
Elliott, Gerald 78
Elliott, Gordon ("Wild Bill") 37
Elliott, John 45, 90, 114, 116, 127, 135, 144, 148, 161, 172, 189, 200, 203, 235, 247, 267, 334, 362
Elliott, Ross 484
Ellis, Frank 69, 70, 87, 92, 98, 102, 103, 108, 113, 114, 116, 120, 124, 130, 135, 145, 152, 159, 161, 163, 168, 170, 179, 189, 191, 200, 203, 204, 205, 207, 211, 219, 221, 247, 254, 266, 269, 274, 276, 297, 301, 307, 312, 316, 325, 349, 359, 361, 367, 374
Ellis, John 79, 95, 198
Ellison, James (Jimmie or Jimmy) 16, 267, 413, 437, 438, 439, 440, 442, 444, 446, 463
Elman, Irving 321
Elmes, Guy 500, 511
Elson, Lee 407
Elvey, Maurice 2, 20, 78
Emden, Margaret 273
Emery, John 443
Emmett, Fern 178
Emmett, Robert *see* Tansey, Robert Emmett
Emory, Richard 457, 458, 464, 491
England, Sue 335
English, Jack 12
English, Richard 44
Enright, Ray H. 515
Eraine 504
Erbe, Berit 522
Erickson, Paul 518
Erlenborn, Ray 110
Erskine, Laurie York 34, 58
Erway, Ben 411

Erwin, Stuart 33, 44, 252, 393
Erwin, Ted 91
Escane, Stanley 503
Escrina, Vicente 536
Espantaleon, Juan 536
Essex, Harry 397
Estrella, Esther 159
Estridge, Robin 547
Evans, Charles 351, 402
Evans, Clifford 214, 242, 496
Evans, Douglas 397, 470, 473
Evans, Edward 503
Evans, Gene 456
Evans, Helena P. 278
Evans, Herbert 423
Evans, Jack 412
Evans, Nancy 149
Evanson, Edith 540
Everest, Barbara 76
Evers, Ann 45
Everton, Paul 183
Eybner, Richard 409

Fabian, Olga 233
Fadden, Tom 397
Fain, Matty 9, 83
Fairfax, James 499, 506, 541, 544
Fajardo, Eduardo 536
Fallman, Gil 448
Farmer, Richard 453
Farmer, Virginia 293
Farnum, William 133, 374, 376, 382
Farr, Derek 260
Farrar, David 214
Farrar, Stanley 498
Farrell, Charles 11, 13
Farrell, Glenda 180
Farrell, Kenneth 337, 349, 354
Farrell, Tommy 448
Faversham, William 12
Fawcett, William 323, 325, 327, 332, 355, 357, 360, 365, 370
Fay, Dorothy 60, 66, 68
Fay, W.G. 260
Faylen, Frank 471
Feher, Frederick 215
Feld, Fritz 306, 320, 463, 473
Felix, Art 70
Fellows, Edith 138
Felton, Felix 495
Fennel, Albert 510
Fenton, Frank 199, 337, 506

Ferguson, Al 97, 203, 211, 243, 294, 307, 316, 329, 374, 375, 376
Ferguson, Frank 165, 171, 315, 317, 328, 351
Ferguson, Myrtle 246
Ferguson, Ron 111
Fernald, John 188
Ferraday, Lisa 423
Ferrari, Mario 521
Fetchit, Stepin 398
Fetherstone, Eddie 88, 91
Field, Ben 55
Field, John 490
Field, Margaret 479
Fielding, Richard see Maxwell, Robert
Fields, Benny 237
Fields, Eddy 399
Fields, Stanley 53, 73
Filauri, Antonio 299
Finley, Evelyn 230, 286
Finn, Arthur 47
Finney, Edward 6, 8, 14, 18, 25, 28, 31, 42, 45, 56, 59, 184, 318, 384, 402, 431
Firth, Anne 214
Fisher, Elliot 37
Fisher, Leck 522
Fisher, Robert C. 153
Fisher, Steve 516
Fisher, Terence 480, 483, 487, 508, 520, 523, 534, 537
Fiske, Robert 6, 81, 133
Flame the dog 411
Flash the horse 323, 325, 327, 329, 332, 336, 369, 370
Fleming, Alice 313
Fleming, Ian 510
Fleming-Roberts, R.T. 328
Fletcher, Tex 70
Flick, Pat C. 196
Flint, Sam 86, 178, 226, 231, 285, 450, 470, 473
Flood, James 11, 342, 352
Flothow, Rudolph C. 499, 506, 541, 544
Flowers, Bess 215, 423
Flowers, Morgan 159
Fluellen, Joel 284, 395, 498, 499
The Flying Taylors 438
Flynn, Joseph (Joe) 528
Fodor, Ladislas 515
Fontaine, Jacqueline 486
Foote, Fred 532
Foran, Dick 427
Ford, Daisy 111, 118
Ford, Francis 192, 321, 374
Ford, Jan (Terry Moore) 335
Ford, Ross 509
Ford, Toby 433
Ford, Wallace 43, 47, 146, 241, 507
Forester, Cay 384
Forman, Carol 409
Forrest, Don 98, 108, 112
Forrest, William 335, 421
Forwood, Anthony 495, 529
Foster, Edward (Eddie) 54, 115, 187, 386
Foster, Maxwell 511
Foster, Norman 481
Foster, Preston 416, 455
Fostini, John 395
Fouldes, Angela 490
Foulger, Byron 73, 147, 193, 277, 350, 385, 416, 421, 426, 432, 450, 475, 476
The Four Dandies 433
The Four Moroccans 453
Fowler, Art 190
Fowler, Harry 480
Fowley, Douglas 119, 222, 227, 311, 332, 339, 358, 379, 381, 388, 421, 546
Fox, Fred 387
Fox, Jimmie 111
Fox, Paul Harvey 30
Fox, Sunna 213
Fox, Wallace 208, 217, 220, 252, 499
France, Alexis 487
Francis, Wilma 27
Francisci, Mario 521
Francisci, Pietro 521
Frank, Charles 504
Frank, Joane 340
Frank, John 139
Franklin, Irwin R. 233, 237, 270
Franklin, Louise 541
Franklin, Paul 64
Franz, Eduard 514
Fraser, Harry 48, 52, 121, 216, 219, 236, 249, 250, 256, 269, 274, 276, 282, 288, 296, 297, 303
Fraser, Richard 284, 285, 317
Fraser, Robert 141
Frawley, William 38
Frazee, Jane 413
Frazer, Robert 10, 58, 70, 110, 180
Fredericks, Charles 533
Freeland, Thornton 224
Freeman, Dusty 396
Freeman, Kenneth 398
Freiberger, Fred 528, 538

French, Charles K. 8
French, Harold 242
French, Ted 334, 336, 341, 368
Frenke, Eugene 23, 53, 73
Freshman, William 229
Freuchen, Ib 522
Frey, Arno 92, 130, 158, 206
Friedgen, Ray 22
Friedman, Alan 393
Friedman, Monk 265
Friedman, Seymour 485, 496
Frische, Grethe 522
Frisco, David 313
Frome, Milton 69
Fromkess, Leon 186, 215, 237, 246, 251, 252, 261, 263, 264, 267, 289, 290, 293
Frost, Terry 208, 226, 233, 243, 298, 305, 329, 355, 357, 359, 360, 365, 366, 368, 369, 370, 401, 405, 418, 435
Frye, Dwight 38, 155, 178
Frye, Gilbert 155
Fuller, Jimmy 396
Fuller, Lt. Lou 445
Fuller, Samuel 39, 416, 435, 456
Fuller, Walter 396
Fulton, Lou 87, 90, 92
Fung, Harold 456
Fung, Paul 151
Furst, Werner H. 251
Fyffe, Will 71

Gabor, Eva 306
Gadd, Renee 20
Gaffney, Liam 513
Gaffney, Marjorie 71
Gage, Russell 192
Gahan, Oscar 25, 31, 56, 59, 136
Gailbraith, Archie 76
Galbin, Roc 482
Gale, Allan 213
Gallagher, Jack 95
Gallagher, Patricia (Patti) 545
Gallagher, Skeets 39
Gallagher, Thomas 495
Galvan, Gilbert 385
Gamble, Warburton 11
Gamboa, Elias 454
Gan, Chester 61
Gardner, Arthur 122
Gardner, Joan 24
Gardner, Shayle 76

Gargan, Ed 9
Garland, Maria 522
Garner, Don 460, 476
Garner, Stewart 277
Garr, Eddie 468
Garralaga, Martin 6, 28, 29, 326, 411, 454
Garrett, Diane 459
Garrett, Gary 407
Garrett, Otis 73
Garrett, William 20
Garrick, John 23
Garrison, Patricia 407
Garvie, Parker 302
Gasnier, Louis 19, 27, 64
Gates, Harvey 375
Gates, Nancy 364, 365
Gault, Slim 429
Gavin, Grace 487
Gay, Frank 65
Gaye, Gregory 238
Geary, Bud 9, 303
Geddes, Jack 430, 436, 439
Gee, Parker 239
Gendron, Pierre 226, 237, 251, 261
George, Gladys 237
George, Isabel 530
George, Jack 215, 270, 384, 407, 470
Geray, Steve 57, 423, 465
Gerber, David 402
Germaine, Mary 502
Gerry, Toni 538
Gest, Inna (Ina Guest) 90, 122
Gibson, Dana 429
Gibson, Helen 440, 446
Gibson, Hoot 378
Gibson, John 361
Gibson, Judith 151
Gibson, Julie 231, 239
Gibson, Kathleen 57
Gibson, Walter B. *see* Grant, Maxwell
Gibson, Wynne 111
Giermann, Frederick 79
Gifford, Frances 83, 88
Gigli, Benjamino 24
Gilbert, Fran 387
Gilbert, Franklin 330
Gilbert, Helen 376, 377
Gilbert, Lewis 503
Gill, Tom 517
Gillern, Grace 277, 285
Gilling, John 483, 518
Gingold, Hermione 503
Ginsberg, Donald 517

Name Index

Girard, Joseph 31, 51, 54, 60, 69
Girardot, Etienne 73
Gladstone, Marilyn 281
Gladwin, Frances 190, 195, 200, 213, 221, 223, 275, 347
Gleason, James 519
Gleason, Pat 16, 27, 137, 165, 253, 295
Glecker, Robert 9
Glenn, Roy E. 498
Glesch, Pat 125
Glorie, Gertrude 288
Goddard, Paulette 514, 534
Godfrey, Renee 314
Gofe, Richard 24
Goldberg, Jack 394, 396, 398
Golden, Michael 516, 523
Golden, Nora 523
Golder, Lew 48
Goldsmith, Al 134
Goldsmith, I. 75
Goldsmith, Martin 290
Goldstone, Phil 46
Gombell, Minna 255
Gomez, Augie 56, 84, 108, 136, 154, 163
Gonzalez, Gilberto 482
Good, John 309
Goodrich, John F. 53
Goodwin, Harold 471
Goodwins, Leslie 397
Gordon, Bert 292
Gordon, Bert I. 545
Gordon, C. Henry 66
Gordon, Dorothy 273, 502
Gordon, Edward 69, 74
Gordon, Fred 396
Gordon, G. Swayne 196
Gordon, Gavin 109, 123, 339, 340
Gordon, Hal 13, 30
Gordon, Jack 265
Gordon, Mary 9, 86, 111, 171, 415, 427
Gordon, Nova 542
Gordon, Paul 433, 468
Gordon, Robert 208
Gordon, Roy 428
Goring, Marius 472
Gost, Derek 71
Got, Archie 173
Gotcher, Les 429
Gottlieb, Buck 351
Gottschalk, Ferdinand 4
Gould, William 34, 165
Goya, Mona 21
Graff, Wilton 329, 409
Graham, Carroll 17, 26

Graham, Fred 387
Graham, Garrett 26
Graham, Tim 540
Granass, Gardy 493
Garnby, Joseph 295
Granger, Dorothy 393
Granstedt, Greta 79, 119
Grant, Cary 13
Grant, Helena 403
Grant, Jack 285
Grant, James Edward 9
Grant, John 184, 458
Grant, Maxwell (Walter B. Gibson) 36, 50
Grant, Neil 30
Grant, Wylie/Wiley 305, 323
Grasiosi, Georgio 521
Grasso, Giovanni 512
Gray, Berkley (Edwy. Searles Brooks) 510
Gray, Billy 175
Gray, Gloria 436
Gray, Hugh 24
Gray, Larry 123
Gray, Linda 61
Gray, Nadia 484
Gray, Sally 496
Grayler, Sidney 82
Great Velardi 438
Greaves, William 398
Green, Anne 320
Green, Billy 467
Green, George D. 208, 420, 428
Green, Gertrude 9
Green, Guy 530
Green, Joseph 435
Green, Seymour 535
Green, William E. 447, 469
Greene, Clarence 255
Greene, Harold 91
Greene, Joe 445
Greenleaf, Raymond 462, 476
Greenway, Tom 427
Gregg, Evereley 487
Gregory, Thea 529
Greig, Robert 267
Greville, Edmond T. 55
Grey, Claire 175
Grey, Gloria 453
Grey, Joe 125
Grey, Virginia 455
Gribbon, Eddie 58
Gries, Tom 545
Griffin, Bob 507

Griffith, Bill 51, 95
Griffith, James 544
Griffith, Kenneth 516
Griffiths, Jane 495
Gross, Milt 187
Grove, Venise 215
Gruber, Frank 321
Guage, Alexander 511
Guard, Kit 60, 70, 447
Gudrin, Ann 516
Guest, Ina *see* Gest, Inna
Guhl, George 183
Guihan, Frances 60
Guilbert, Nina 68, 84
Guilfoyle, Paul 271, 280
Guillermin, John 501
Guinle, Armand 531
Guiol, Fred L. 471, 494
Gunn, Earl 85, 126
Guthrie, Jack 390
Guyse, Sheila 394, 396, 398
Gwynne, Anne 262, 393, 421, 544

Haade, William 61, 413, 455, 470
Haas, Dolly 2
Hack, Herman 25, 59, 87, 93, 116, 136, 163, 191, 211, 286
Hackel, A.W. 318
Hacker, Slim 70
Hackett, Dotti 390
Hackett, Karl 19, 25, 42, 45, 56, 59, 87, 97, 98, 100, 103, 108, 113, 114, 116, 130, 140, 144, 145, 152, 154, 159, 163, 170, 177, 179, 185, 189, 191, 195, 202, 223, 228, 236, 254, 257, 266, 269, 272, 276, 286, 294, 301, 307, 308, 319, 343, 344, 345
Haddon, Pauline 92, 94
Hadley, Reed 64, 404, 413, 416, 417, 424, 435, 445, 450, 464
Hagen, Julius 1, 20, 21, 30
Haggerty, Don 543
Hagney, Frank 96, 98, 102, 108, 117, 123, 124, 130, 134, 137, 154, 162, 184, 202, 203, 204, 350, 400, 407
Haimson, Abrasha 409, 459
Hajos, Karl 263
Hale, Alan, Jr. 494
Hale, Jane 162
Hale, Jonathan 380
Hale, Michael 304
Hall, Alfred 115, 123, 134

Hall, Archie 84, 108, 116, 152, 257, 279, 281
Hall, Cameron 142, 260
Hall, Cliff 196
Hall, Eddie 184
Hall, Ellen 236, 303
Hall, Henry 148, 182, 192, 210, 213, 250, 256, 259, 269, 279, 288, 298, 307, 311, 332, 355, 357
Hall, Jon 427, 499, 506, 541, 544
Hall, Sherry 321
Hall, Thurston 429, 454
Hall, William 88
Halliday, Brett (Davis Dresser) 302, 311, 317, 339, 350
Halligan, William (Bill) 107, 109, 111, 123, 129, 134, 215, 252
Halop, Billy (William) 324, 543
Halperin, Victor 80, 81, 138
Halton, Charles 255
Hamel, William R. 491
Hamill, Eva 220
Hamilton, John 248, 264, 350, 375
Hamilton, Neil 55, 104, 119, 137
Hammond, Bill (Billy) 336, 341
Hammond, Peter 477
Hampton, Louise 242
Hampton, Orville 445, 447, 449, 451, 455, 457, 458, 470, 473, 486, 492, 524
Hanburg, Victor 530
Handl, Irene 260
Handley, Tom 474
Hankinson, Michael 30
Hanley, Tom 431
Hanneford, Gracie 375
Hanneford, Poodles 375
Hannon, Chick 14, 25, 31, 59, 93
Hanray, Lawrence 11
Hansen, Earle 532, 540
Hanslip, Ann 520
Harbin, Robert 517
Harcourt, James 242
Hardin, Eileen 367
Harding, John F. 47
Harding, Lyn 2
Hardtmuth, Paul 472, 513
Hardy, Arthur 13
Hare, Doris 76
Hare, Madilyn 190, 347
Harlan, Kenneth 34, 36, 54, 101, 109, 112, 119, 141, 209
Harlan, Otis 53
Harlan, Richard 83

Harlen, Hubert 229
Harlow, John 260
Harmon, Julian 460, 461, 462
Harmon, Marie 311, 315
Harolde, Ralf 160
Harper, Patricia 159, 189, 191, 204, 234, 344, 349, 357
Harr, Silver 179, 308
Harrigan, William 196
Harrington, Buck 227
Harris, Alan 453
Harris, Edna 180
Harris, Edna Mae 48
Harris, Mildred 9
Harris, Vernon 503
Harrison, Kathleen 75, 76
Harrison, Lottie 300, 323
Harrison, Stephen 435
Harron, Red 390
Hart, Dorothy 485
Hart, Maria 486
Hart, Vivian 35
Hartl, Carl 409
Hartley, Doc 139
Hartnell, Billy 214
Hartnell, Robert 263
Harvey, Don 397, 417, 419
Harvey, Harry 41, 52, 54, 65, 83, 85, 111, 174, 210, 232, 245, 248
Harvey, Harry, Jr. 65, 98
Harvey, Jack 268, 413, 424
Harvey, Laurence 502
Harvey, Paul 16
Harwin, Dixon R. 146, 153, 165, 184
Haskell, Al 191
Haskin, Louise 229
Hastings, Henry 150
Hatcher, Mary 478
Hatton, Raymond 375, 380, 437, 439, 440, 441, 442, 444, 446, 463, 533
Hatton, Rondo 322
Hauff, Angelika 493
Haverly, Ned 467
Havier, J. Alex 206
Hawk, Jeremy 534, 537
Hawkins, Jack 477
Hawley, Monte 398
Haworth, Joe 331
Hayden, Harry 462
Hayden, Helene 507
Hayden, Russell 379, 380, 381, 400, 401, 427, 428, 437, 438, 439, 440, 442, 444, 446
Hayden, Sterling 491

Hayes, Bernadene 9, 17, 26
Hayes, George 71, 142
Hayes, Gordon 184
Hayes, "Spot" 22
Haynes, Manning 229
Haynes, Marjorie 137
Hayward, Lydia 229
Hayworth, Rita *see* Cansino, Rita
Hazard, Jayne 264
Heade, William 328
Healey, Myron 447, 541
Healy, Mary 122, 167
Hearn, Lew 196
Hearn, Lou 50
The Heat Waves 196
Heath, Ariel 217, 241
Heatherton, Ray, and His Band 196
Hecht, Ted 173, 184, 386, 428
Hector and His Pals 433
Hedloe, John 509
Heinlein, Robert A. 509
Heller, Little Jackie 167
Helm, Fay 278
Helsengreen, Betty 522
Hemingway, Frank 402
Henderson, Betty 502
Henderson, Douglas 545
Henderson, "Evolution" 22
Henderson, Ray 87, 105, 136
Hendricks, Ben, Jr. 9
Hendricks, Jack 276, 366, 408, 412, 439
Henning, Pat 69
Henreid, Paul 479, 487
Henry, Bill 445
Henry, Carol 455
Henry, Kenneth 531
Henry, Robert "Buzzy" 123, 252, 295, 329, 369
Henry, Robert Dee 380
Henson, Gladys 472
Hepburn, Audrey 490
Hepburn, Barton 146, 165
Herbert, Holmes 35, 41
Herbert, Tom 134, 137
Herman, Albert 34, 58, 59, 141, 156, 169, 174, 181, 227, 239, 253, 268, 271, 348
Herman the Hermit 429
Hern, Pepe 454
Hernandez, Joe 66
Herrick, Samuel R. 497
Herring, Moree 405, 408
Hersholt, Alan 423

Hervey, Irene 35
Hetzer, Evilyn 433
Hewitt, Enid 260
Hewitt, Henry 57
Heyburn, Weldon 72, 110, 121
Hibbert, Geoffrey 490
Hickman, Darryl 335
Hicks, Lou 10
Hicks, Russell 16, 279, 463, 471, 494
Hickson, Joan 525
Highland Dale the horse 404
Hill, Bob (Robert) 51, 192, 195, 205, 212, 235
Hill, Morgan 16
Hill, Paul 387
Hill, Riley 434
Hill, Ronald 47
Hilliard, Stafford 2, 20, 260
Hillyer, Lambert 391, 392
Hilton, Arthur D. 450, 528
Hilton, Paul 318
Hinds, Anthony 480, 483, 487, 492, 495, 500, 516, 525, 529, 542
Hinton, Edgar 407
Hirliman, George 3, 5, 7, 10, 15, 19, 27, 37, 64, 65, 69, 74
Hittleman, Carl K. 391, 392, 400, 401, 404, 413, 416, 424, 430, 435, 450, 464
Hoag, Robert 181
Hobart, Rose 150
The Hobnobbers 467
Hobo the dog 209
Hobson, Valerie 53
Hodgins, Earle 66, 84, 146, 314, 321, 333, 390, 507
Hoerbiger, Paul 409
Hoerl, Arthur 48, 63, 64, 67, 69, 72, 74, 110, 118, 171, 208
Hoffman, Joseph 46, 61, 165
Hoffman, M.H. 29, 32
Hoffman, Max, Jr. 43
Hoffman, Otto 17
Hogan, James 53
Hogan, Michael 71
Hohl, Arthur 176
Holcombe, Herb 52
Holcombe, Jean 519
Holden, Eddie 80, 148
Holden, Gloria 318
Holland, Edna 402, 411, 419
Holland, John 119, 143
Hollister, Gloria 62
Holloway, Sterling 374, 377
Hollywood, Jimmy 39, 213

Holman, Harry 137, 146, 244
Holmes, J. Merrill 144, 159
Holmes, Jack 140, 163, 195
Holmes, Maynard 41
Holmes, Salty 12
Holst, Ernie, and His Band 196
Holt, Andrew 309
Holt, David 423
Holt, Hans 409
Holt, Jack 378, 383, 432
Holt, Jennifer 287, 355, 357, 359, 362, 363, 366, 368, 370, 387, 400, 401
Holt, Patrick 534
Holtz, Tennen 50, 63
Homans, Robert 86, 111, 253
Hoo, Hayward Soo 151
Hoo, Walter Soo 173
Hooker, Bud 446
Hooker, Hugh 454
Hoosier Hot Shots 433
Hope, James 246
Hope, Vida 502
Hopper, Victoria 11
Hopton, Russell 80
Hordern, Michael 472
Horen, Adrian 493
Horman, Arthur T. 53
Horne, David 508
Horney, Brigitte 55
Horsbrugh, Walter 477
Horton, Edward Everett 20, 224, 255
Hoshelle, Marjorie 317
Hough, E. Morton 29
House, Billy 486
Houser, Lionel O. 37
Houser, Mervin 37
Houston, George 7, 40, 60, 98, 102, 108, 116, 117, 124, 131, 140, 152, 161, 170
Houston, Glyn 530
Howard, Arthur 542
Howard, Edward 270, 274, 288, 303
Howard, Esther 290
Howard, F. Ruth 278
Howard, John 434, 463
Howard, Joyce 188
Howard, William K. 246
Howell, Kenneth 138
Howes, Reed 70, 87, 89, 108, 135, 154, 163, 194, 203, 207, 219, 236, 250
Howland (Howlin), Olin 255, 413, 424
Hoyt, Arthur 9, 37, 86
Hoyt, Frank 10
Hoyt, Harry O. 222, 271

Hoyt, John 469, 485, 514
Hoyt, Russell 166
Hubbard, Tom 533
Huber, Harold 173
Huckelmann, Charles 427
Hudson, Bill 543
Hudson, Rochelle 182, 388, 423
Hugh, Helene 320
Hughes, Adrian 70
Hughes, Ann Ruth 118
Hughes, Carol 34, 107, 112, 125, 186
Hughes, Charles 431
Hughes, Diana 129
Hughes, J. Anthony 149
Hughes, Kathleen 479
Hughes, Kay 269, 283
Hughes, Ken 525
Hughes, Mary Beth 220, 249, 270, 404, 413, 417, 424, 429, 453
Hughes, Roddy 496
Hughes, Rupert 457, 476
Hugo, Mauritz 299, 315, 317
Hull, Henry 450
Hull, Mary 126
Hull, Warren 91
Humbert, George 128
Hume, Marjory 517
Hunt, Eleanor 5, 10, 15, 19, 27
Hunt, Marsha 66
Hunt, Martita 142
Hunter, Alastair 492
Hunter, Shirley 393
Huntington, Laurence (Lawrence) 75, 214
Huntley, Harvey 80
Huntley, Raymond 480
Hurst, Brian Desmond 547
Hurst, David 530
Hurst, Pat 379
Hurst, Paul 33, 377
Hutchinson, Charles 137
Huth, Harold 142
Hutton, Malcolm 118
Hutton, Robert 456
Hyans, Eddie 309
Hyatt, Bobby 438
Hyde-White, Wilfrid 472
Hyland, Dick Irving 262
Hymer, Warren 138, 160, 201
Hytten, Olaf 498

Igou, Joan 62
Illing, Peter 525, 537

Image, Jean 504
Imhof, Roger 1, 17, 26
Imhoff, Fred 409
Ince, John 100, 119, 123, 125, 134, 147, 149, 150, 175
Indrisano, Johnny 462
Ingraham, Lloyd 7, 67, 74, 171, 305
Ingram, Jack 60, 106, 108, 117, 131, 136, 140, 144, 162, 163, 168, 181, 185, 190, 194, 195, 201, 205, 211, 212, 216, 219, 221, 223, 225, 228, 230, 234, 254, 259, 269, 276, 346, 348, 355, 357, 419, 454
Ireland, Anthony 21, 495, 508
Ireland, John 416, 450, 464, 542
Iris and Pierre 289
Irving, George 39, 222
Irving, Margaret 7
Irving, Stanley 24
Irwin, Boyd 82, 101, 110
Isabelita 289, 326; *see also* Baron, Lita
Isham, Gyles 55
Ivan, John 5
Ivo, Tommy 352, 441

Jackson, Al 394
Jackson, Donny 248
Jackson, Fred S. 289
Jackson, Freda 502
Jackson, Gary 467
Jackson, Ginny 429, 438
Jackson, Selmer 109, 352
Jackson, Thomas 50, 280, 292
Jackson, Warren 106, 125
Jacobs, Herb 509
Jacquard, Ciela 56
Jacquard, Jacques 56
Jacques, Ted 436
Jacquet, Frank 96, 165, 184, 445
Jaeger, Ernst 304
Jaffe, Carl 510
James, Clare 502
James, John 304
James, Lyle 491
James, Rosemond 315
James, Sidney 500, 510, 525, 542
James, Walter 147
Jansson, Walther 409
January, Lois 53
Jarlbak, Else 522
Jarrett, Arthur 68, 196
Jarrett, Curtis 425

Jason, Will 438
Jay, Griffin 19, 27, 299, 304
Jean, Gloria 543
Jeans, Ursula 20
Jeayes, Allan 24, 57
Jeffreys, Anne 136
Jeffries, Jan 466
Jeffries, Jim 123
Jenkins, Allen 391, 392
Jenkins, Megs 490
Jenkins, Patrick 495
Jenks, Frank 184, 221, 240, 253, 258, 268, 271, 337, 340, 411, 445, 494
Jenks, Si 376, 463
Jennings, Al 6
Jergens, Adele 425, 434, 438, 528, 546
Jerome, Jerry 277, 300
Jerrold, Mary 229
Jester Hairston Singers 467
Jewell, Isabel 43, 91, 201
Jielson, Williard 246
Jillson, Willard 407
Jim the crow 291
Jimmez, Yadiro 482
Jimmy LeFieur's Saddle Pals 45
Joby, Hans 79
Jochim, Anthony 436, 455
Joe the raven 309
Johns, Larry 509
Johnson, Adrian 22
Johnson, Ben 547
Johnson, Brad 486
Johnson, Duke 468
Johnson, Erskine 175, 180
Johnson, Florence 249
Johnson, Fred 520
Johnson, Harry 137, 468
Johnson, Henry 9
Johnson, Katie 30
Johnson, Linda 179, 403
Johnson, Marilyn 315
Johnson, Robert Lee 263, 291
Johnson, Russell 479, 485
Johnson Brothers 433
Jolley, I. Stanford 107, 110, 112, 159, 161, 170, 174, 177, 181, 184, 189, 193, 195, 204, 205, 210, 219, 227, 236, 245, 256, 272, 275, 276, 282, 283, 286, 294, 296, 297, 307, 332, 365, 379, 381, 417, 418, 435, 437, 442, 446
Jones, Arthur V. 378, 379, 381
Jones, Darby 499
Jones, Dickie 34
Jones, Gordon 66, 86
Jones, Jay 437
Jones, Johnny 418
Jones, Lu Anne 423
Jones, Marcia Mae 166, 222, 421, 447
Jones, Ray 59, 152, 200, 296, 366, 446
Jordan, Charles 165, 184, 267, 271, 332, 399
Jordan, Paul 448, 452
Jordan, Robert (Bobby) 425
Joseph, Edmund 39
Joyce, Brenda 291, 352
Joyce, Harold 64
Juanita Hall Choir 398
Judell, Ben 79, 80, 81, 82, 83, 96
Judels, Charles 160, 217
Judge, Arline 192, 231
Juergens, Curt 409
Juergens, Philip 129
Junior, Don 425

Kaaren, Suzanne 4, 41, 95
Kalmar, Bert, Jr. 9
Kane, Eddie 33, 237, 292, 304, 392
Kane, Sugar 64
Karloff, Boris 21
Karnes, Robert (Bob) 509, 540
Karns, Roscoe 186, 237, 262, 309
Kaufman, Millard 474
Kaufman, Willie 79
Kaus, Gina 320
Kavanaugh, Frances 287, 300, 305, 310, 323, 325, 327, 329, 369, 374
Kax, Holger 484
Kay, Arthur 34
Kay, Bernice 138
Kay, Joel 115
Kaye, Donna 463
Kaye, Edward E. 167
Kaye, Mary Ellen 533
Kayne, Jan 476
Kayyam, Hassam 384
Keane, Charles 338, 509
Keane, Edward 61, 111, 253, 391, 435
Keane, Robert Emmett 280
Keating, Fred 3
Keaton, Buster 376
Keats, Viola 23
Keays, Vernon 278
Keckly, Jane 52
Keefe, James 66
Keen, Geoffrey 492, 520, 542
Keen, Malcolm 11

Keene, Richard 302
Keigh, Helene 302
Keith, Ian 176, 184, 261, 287, 349, 375
Kelland, Clarence Budington 44
Kelley, Albert 111, 197
Kellogg, Bruce 474
Kellogg, Gayle 430
Kellogg, William (Bill) 36, 153, 165
Kelly, Jeanne 82
Kelly, John 16
Kelly, John King 505
Kelly, Patsy 106, 201
Kelsey, Fred 292, 438
Kelso, Edmond 31, 42, 45, 56, 59
Kemp, Jack 398
Kemp, Matty 41
Kendal, Cy 36, 222, 285, 317
Kendall, Henry 13
Kendall, Kay 483, 513
Kendall, Victor 169
Kennedy, Bill 392, 449, 452
Kennedy, Douglas 479, 528
Kennedy, Edgar 208
Kennedy, Florence 389
Kennedy, Jack 209
Kennedy, Tom 43, 66, 392, 395, 410, 429, 452
Kenney, James 503
Kennington, Alan 188
Kenny, Joan 501
Kent, Crauford 15
Kent, Keneth 242
Kent, Robert 129
Kent, Robert E. 165, 353, 356, 358, 434
Kent, William C. 118
Kenyon, Gwen 252
Kenyon, Mary 310, 315
Kerner, Hazel 351
Kerr, Adele 137
Kerr, Donald 95, 267, 302
Kerr, Gene 138
Kester, Karen 435
Keymas, George 452
Keys, Stephen 405
Kibbee, Guy 240
Kibbee, Milton 100, 131, 135, 136, 140, 145, 158, 182, 191, 204, 231, 253, 284, 298, 311, 318, 455
Kiely, Helen 238
Kilgore, Judy 115
Kilian, Victor 416, 417, 450, 454, 474
Kimball, Anne 526
Kimbley, Billy 411

Kincaid, Lisa 420
King, Charles 8, 14, 18, 25, 28, 31, 42, 45, 56, 58, 59, 68, 93, 97, 100, 102, 103, 105, 108, 113, 114, 117, 120, 124, 127, 133, 135, 154, 157, 159, 161, 163, 164, 170, 172, 174, 177, 181, 191, 194, 198, 200, 201, 207, 210, 211, 212, 219, 221, 223, 228, 230, 232, 235, 236, 243, 245, 250, 252, 254, 257, 259, 266, 269, 272, 274, 276, 281, 282, 283, 288, 297, 303, 305, 308, 310, 312, 313, 319, 334, 339, 348, 351, 368
King, Diana 260
King, Hal 429
King, Henry, and His Orchestra 64, 167
King, John 383
King, Max M. 149, 318, 375, 393
King, Walter Woolf 156
King Brothers *see* Kozinsky, Maurice and Frank
Kinney, Jack 136, 159
Kinney, Ray 465
Kinsky, Leonid 73
Kipling, Richard 169, 183, 295
Kippen, Manart 158
Kirby, Fred 463
Kirby, George 227
Kirby, John 396, 543
Kirk, Jack 6, 164, 307
Kirk, Michael 201
Kirk, Phyllis 530
Kirke, Donald 1
Klauber, Marcy 196, 248
Klein, Harold 401
Kleinert, E.H. 248
Knaggs, Skelton 80
Knapp, Charles 540
Knapp, Robert 532
Knight, Charles 393
Knight, Esmond 273
Knight, Fuzzy 6, 19, 417, 428, 439, 440, 442, 444, 446
Knight, Harry 14
Knight, Red 132
Knight, Rod 129
Knott, Frederick 480
Knowles, Bernard 510
Knox, Mickey 436
Knox, Patricia 161, 166, 192, 205, 249, 282, 301, 312
Knuth, Gustav 493
Kohler, Fred 280
Kohler, Fred, Jr. 430, 435

Kolker, Henry 1, 9, 251
Komroff, Manuel 33
Korda, Alexander 24
Kortman, Bob (Robert) 98, 212, 225, 228, 256, 259, 275, 281
Kortner, Fritz 306
Kosleck, Martin 306, 318
Kosloff, Maurice 519
Kozinsky, Frank 109
Kozinsky, Maurice 109
Krafft, John 41, 50
Krah, Mark 473
Kramer, Hope 298
Krasne, Phil 68
Krueger, Lorraine 217
Kruger, Otto 166, 184, 224
Kruger, Stubby 132, 134
Krushat, Olive 466
Kundi, Anne 390
Kuznetzof, Adir 80
Kydd, Sam 542

LaBlanche, Ethel 73
Lacedo, Rita 482
Lacey, Catherine 242
Lack, Simon 78
Lackteen, Frank 151, 401, 419
Ladd, Alan (Allan) 79, 109
Ladd, Tom 453
Laffan, Patricia 496
Laidlaw, Betty 35
Laidlaw, Ethan 6, 194
Laird, London 139
Lake, Arthur 16
Lake, Veronica 482
LaMal, Elizabeth 92
LaMal, Isabel 98, 166, 182, 186, 220
Lamare, Nappy, and His Dixieland Band 453
Lamb, Ande 213, 392
Lambert, Michael 57, 389
Lamble, Lloyd 518
Lamont, Charles 40, 50, 61, 63, 66, 72
Lamont, Marten 233
Lamont, Molly 237, 304, 388
Lancaster, Richard 54
Landau, Richard H. 469, 476, 487, 500, 507, 508, 514, 523, 537, 542
Landers, Lew 248, 265, 277, 285, 291, 299, 377
Landi, Elissa 184
Landin, Hope 299, 324

Landres, Paul 424, 429, 433, 506
Landry, Gerard 488
Lane, Arthur 483, 520
Lane, Dick (Richard) 438, 449
Lane, Lola 169, 280
Lane, Nora 85
Lane, Rosemary 213
Lang, David 313
Lang, Harold 483, 516, 523
Lang, Howard 15, 41, 511
Lang, June 137, 165, 330
Lang, Karin 267
Langan, Glenn 425, 528
Langdon, Harry 47, 96, 143
Langford, Frances 217, 240, 427
Lansing, Joy (Joi) 462, 476
Lanza, Rocco 324
LaPlanche, Rosemary 293, 304
LaRocque, Rod 36, 50
LaRose, Rose 313
Larson, Bobby 209
LaRue, Frank 60, 68, 87, 93, 94, 211
LaRue, Jack 5, 109, 122, 126, 176, 208, 224, 241, 389
LaRue, Lash (Al) 287, 305, 329, 334, 349, 354, 355, 357, 359, 361, 362, 364, 369, 405, 408, 412, 414, 418, 419
Latell, Lyle 104, 220
Latimer, Hugh 505, 511
Latimer, Ross 455
Laurenz, Nancy 454
Laurin, Odessa 215
Lauritzen, Lau 522
Lawrence, Babe 45
Lawrence, Fanya Foss 280
Lawrence, Jay 528
Lawrence, Mady 228, 232, 254, 294
Lawrence, Marc 289, 430
Lawson, Wilfrid 188, 229
Lazare and Castellanos 196
Lazarus, Milton 246
Leary, Nolan 293, 304, 313
Lease, Rex 43, 94, 97, 100, 103, 113, 135, 162
Leaver, Philip 508
LeBaron, Eddie, and His Orchestra 213
Leber, John 291
LeBorg, Reginald 337, 466, 500, 507, 514
Lee, Belinda 523
Lee, Bernard 477
Lee, Billy 118
Lee, Bryant 22
Lee, Christopher 484

Name Index

Lee, Eddie 458
Lee, George 197
Lee, Ruth 255, 263, 471
Lee, Vera 453
Lee, Wendy 449
The Lee Sisters 468
Leewood, Jack 453
LeFerre, Michael 511
Leffingwell, Tom 387
LeFieur's Saddle Pals *see* Jimmy LeFieur's Saddle Pals
Leftwich, Alexander 43
LeGron, Jennie 186, 416
Leicester, William 423
Leister, Frederick 260
Lenard, David 385
Lenoiv, Leon 515
Leon, Connie 151
Leonard, Arthur 394, 396
Leonard, David 326, 337
Leonard, Leon 420
Leonard, Murray 313
Leonard, Sheldon 213, 265, 280, 285, 411
Leonardo and Zola 396
Leong, James B. 173, 494
Leopold, Ethelreda 9
Lerdorff-Rye, Preben 522
Lerner, Murray 466
LeRoy, Rita 88
LeSaint, Edward 19
Lescoulie, Jack 107
Leslie, Joan 491
Leslie, Kay 114
Leslie, Maxine 99, 117, 164, 185, 186, 346
Leslie, Nan 451
Leslie, R. Murray 260
Lesser, Budd 454
Lester, Bruce 478
Lester, Vicki 125, 131
Letuli, Freddie 453
Leurini, Gino 521
Leutzkendorf, Felix 539
Levine, Jules 352
Levinson, Selwyn 399
Levis, Carroll 76
Levis, Cyril 76
Levy, David S. 19, 27
Levy, Stuart 513
Lewis, Alyce 407, 506
Lewis, George 7, 156, 426, 437, 439, 440, 442, 444, 446
Lewis, Joseph H. 110, 151, 166, 237

Lewis, Ralph 295, 298
Lewis, Sybil 394, 398
Lewis, Vera 267
Lexy, Edward 224
L'Herminier, Commandant 488
Liberman, Don 67
Lightning the dog 34
Linaker, Kay 220
Lincoln, Elmo 246
Lindell, Jack 65
Linden, Eric 1, 17, 26, 41, 110
Lindgren, Sten 484
Lindsay, Margaret 289, 320
Lindsay, Vera 260
Ling, Eugene 485, 515
Link, John F. 431
Lion, Leon M. 13
Lippert, Robert L. 403, 413, 416, 424
Lippert, Robert L., Jr. 507, 524, 528, 538
Lisa, Anna 88
Lister, Moira 517
Liszt, Margie 471
Litel, John 171, 197, 291, 330, 375
Lithman, Ben 209
Little, Stanley 542
Littlefield, Lucien 246
Littlewood, Frank 531
Lively, Robert 35
Lively, William 83, 84, 87, 100, 102, 108, 114, 130, 366, 544
Livingston, Bob 172, 179, 189, 193, 195, 203, 207
Lloyd, Dorothy 438
Lloyd, Frederick 55
Lloyd, George 249, 261, 284
Lloyd, Jimmie 466
Lloyd, Rollo 4, 17
Lockhart, Gene 38
Lockwood, Alyn 452
Lockwood, Margaret 472
Loder, John 306
Lodge, Jean 531
Loft, Arthur 277
Logan, Sidney 272
Logue, Charles 34
London, Jack 80
London, Tom 52, 98, 116, 181, 190, 202, 218, 408, 432
Long, Johnny, and His Band 196
Long, Reginald 517
Long, Walter 52
Longden, John 273
Loo, Richard 61, 151, 456

Name Index

Lopez, Paul 28
Lord, Marjorie 459, 541
Loring, Teala 239, 251, 324
Loschiavo, G.G. 512
Louis, Joe 248
Love, Lenita 335
Lovell, Raymond 55
Lovett, Bill 287
Lowe, Edmund 291
Lowe, Sherman L. 12, 156, 167, 169, 180, 499, 506, 541, 544
Lowell, Robert 249
Lowery, Robert 9, 324, 328, 351, 376, 377, 384, 411, 415, 421, 426, 431, 436, 448, 449, 451, 452
Luana, Lew 118
Luban, Milton 424, 430
Luber, Bernard 485, 496, 515, 521
Lufkin, Sam 125
Lugosi, Bela 95, 388
Luke, Keye 292
Lunai, Manuel 536
Lundigan, William 531
Lunge, Romilly 23, 71
Lyden, Pierce 153, 160, 405
Lydon, James 246, 255, 264
Lynch, Don 402
Lynch, Sean 503
Lynd, Helen 39
Lynn, Emmett 162, 165, 182, 192, 210, 221, 244, 246, 251, 255, 267, 272, 285, 287, 300, 305, 401
Lynn, George 351
Lynn, Mara 466, 470, 473
Lynn, Peter 63, 81
Lynn Proctor Trio 398
Lynne, Sharon 118
Lyon, Ben 47, 75
Lyon, Earle 532, 540, 546
Lyon, Priscilla 318
Lyon, Theresa 293
Lytton, Bert 162

Maben, Alvis (Alvys) 523, 534
McArthur, Hugh 72
McAvoy, Charles 318
MacBride, Donald 322, 453
McCallum, John 54, 484
McCarroll, Frank 159, 191, 200, 219, 225, 235, 243, 247, 257, 266, 387
McCarthy, Henry 9, 16
McCarthy, John P. 6

McCarthy, Leo J. 139, 293
McCarthy, Patti 198, 199, 211, 216, 235, 243, 245, 251, 307, 316, 319
McClary, Clyde 28
McCloud, Helen 138
McClure, Greg 410, 423, 426, 459, 461
McClure, M'Liss 441, 499, 506, 541, 544
McConnell, Fred 126
McConnell, Marilyn 259
McCormack (McCormick), Merrill 10, 67, 69, 74, 93, 124, 152, 207, 506
McCoy, Horace 9
McCoy, Tim 85, 87, 90, 92, 94, 103, 114
McCullough, Philo 58
McCullough, Rusty 182
McCully, Johnston 326
McDaniel, Etta 26
McDaniel, Sam 106, 187
MacDonald, David 477
MacDonald, Edmund 270, 290, 386
McDonald, Francis 419, 428
McDonald, Frank 422, 428, 533
MacDonald, Ian 126, 540, 546
MacDonald, J. Farrell 86, 128, 206, 382, 411, 426, 437, 475
MacDonald, Kenneth 285, 544
Macdonald, Nesta 504
MacDonald, Philip 278
McDowall, Roddy 438
McDowell, Buddy 429
McDowell, Claire 220
MacFadden, Hamilton 146
MacFarlane, Louella 459
McGee, Roger 471
McGill, Ormond, and His East Indian Miracle Show 468
McGinnis, Joel 262
MacGinnis, Niall 142
McGlynn, Frank, Sr. 239, 253, 390
McGovern, Johnny 325
MacGowan, Robert A. 356
McGown, Billy 125
McGrail, Walter 36, 54, 58, 89, 136
McGrath, Larry 125
McGrath, Pat 505
McGraw, Charles 342
MacGregor, Casey 238, 277, 341, 349
McGuiggan, Peggy 463
McGuinn, Joe 85, 89
McGuire, John 423
McGuire, Marion 196
McGuire, Michael 295

McGuire, Tucker 188
McHugh, Jack 70
McHugh, Kitty 101
McHugh, Matt 137, 292, 421
McIntyre, Christine 194
Mack, Betty 44
Mack, Cactus 426
Mack, Frederick A. 482
Mack, Helen 319
MacKay, Norman 338
McKay, Wanda 144, 152, 157, 184, 193, 201, 226, 267, 403, 461
McKeag, Michael 503
McKean, Donald C. 227, 239, 253
McKee, John 434
McKee, Lafayette 146
McKee, Lafe 31, 52
McKee, Pat 150
McKenna, Kate 137
McKenna, Siobhan 477
McKenna, Virginia 547
Mackenzie, Mary 487, 492
McKenzie, Robert 25, 54, 81, 215, 300, 310
Mackinnon, Alex 501
Macklin, James 519
MacLane, Barton 175, 209, 218, 454, 540
McLaren, Mary 96, 198
McLaughlin, Gibb 21, 260
MacLean, Douglas 9, 16
McLeod, Gordon 525
McLeod, Mary 264
McLeod, Victor 138
McMillan, Julia 302, 311
McMinn, Frazer 418
McNamara, Edward J. 9
McNamara, James H. 81
McNamara, Richard 515
McNaughton, Gus 75
MacOwen, Norman 484
MacPherson, Quinton 13
MacPherson, Virginia 438
The McQuaig Twins 463
McQuarrie, Murdock 6, 9, 53
Macrae, Arthur 30
McTaggart, Malcolm "Bud" 70, 136
McTaggart, Ward 101, 119
McVey, Paul 72, 81
Maddern, Victor 513
Madison, Julian 80
Madison, Noel 151, 169, 193
Maggnetti, Kathleen 448
Maher, Wally (Wallie) 16, 318

Mahoney, Jeanne 466
Makeham, Eliot 214
Malandrinos, Andrea 13, 47
Malatesta, Fred 19
Malcolm, Robert 299, 305
Mallalieu, Aubrey 75
Malleson, Miles 260
Mallinson, Rory 399, 413, 455, 457, 491, 507
Mallory, Boots 41
Mallott, Yolande 95
Malloy, Doris 184, 186
Malone, Joel 342
Mamakos, Peter 462
Mango, Alec 537
Manners, Marjorie 154, 170, 180, 191, 204, 213, 321, 344, 345
Mannheim, Lucie 57
Mansfield, Duncan 17, 26
Mansfield, John 465
Mapes, Ted 189, 235, 250
Mapes, Virginia 374
Marburgh, Bertram 137
March, Eve 295
Marchand, Johnny 488
Marden, Adrienne 475
Mardo, Al 468
Margetson, Arthur 21
Margolis, Herbert 460, 461, 462, 479
Mari, Ricci 453
Marin, Guillermo 536
Marion, Beth 60
Marion, Don 45
Marion, Paul 465
Marion, Sidney 292
Mark, Michael 149
Marks, Clarence 43
Marks, Garnett 340
Markus, Winnie 409
Marle, Arnold 542
Marlen, Gloria 349
Marlow, Aileen 433
Marlowe, Jo Anne 278, 380
Marlowe, Katherine 443
Marmont, Percy 495
Marnen, Richard 537
Marr, Leslie 537
Marrerro, A.F. 536
Mars, Marjorie 2
Mars, Monica 304
Marsh, Caren 288, 315
Marsh, Garry 13, 20
Marsh, Marian 143
Marshal, Alan 73, 183

Marshall, E.G. 338
Marshall, Gregory 352
Marshall, Pete 453, 476
Marshall, Red 313
Marshall, Trudy 350
Marshall, Tully 183
Marshall, William 162
Marshe, Vera 268, 436
Marston, Joel 476
Martel, Alphonse 208
Martell, Donna 509
Martell, Eva 453
Martell, Gregg 470
Martell, Neva 453
Martin, A.E. 542
Martin, Al 36, 99
Martin, Carla 436, 445, 458
Martin, Chris-Pin 404, 417
Martin, Don 330, 391
Martin, Dorothea Knox 39
Martin, Helen 270
Martin, Irene 445, 475
Martin, Jimmie (James) 228, 296, 341, 379, 383, 407, 408, 412, 437, 439, 440, 442, 444, 446
Martin, Marion 252, 313, 330, 410
Martin, Paul 454
Martin, Scoop 440
Martino, Marie 328
Martins, Orlando 547
Marty, Syra 457
Marud, Henry 449
Marvin, Jerry 475
Marvin, Ronn 356
Mason, A.E.W. 242
Mason, Basil 55
Mason, James 188
Mason, James (not the noted actor) 8, 57, 127, 136
Massen, Osa 443
Masters, Howard 100, 101, 102, 120, 163
Mastrocinque, Camillo 412
Mather, Aubrey 20
Mathess, Gisella 512
Mathews, Carl 29, 52, 56, 58, 60, 70, 84, 87, 90, 92, 94, 117, 136, 159, 174, 198, 327, 334, 341, 359, 360, 361, 362, 363, 364, 367, 368, 387, 439, 440
Matthews, Forrest 332, 412
Matthews, Joyce 478
Matz, Johanna 539
Maurstad, Alfred 484
Mavi, Neila 453

Max, Ed 318
Maxey, Paul 337, 450
Maxwell, Edwin 37, 183, 233
Maxwell, John 171, 176, 222, 421
Maxwell, Lois 492, 502
Maxwell, Robert 475
Mayberry, Lynn 69
Mayer, Edwin Justus 72
Mayer, Ray 43
Maynard, Ken 29, 32, 51, 52
Maynard, Kermit 157, 159, 163, 164, 168, 185, 189, 191, 194, 204, 207, 211, 216, 221, 223, 234, 236, 247, 254, 259, 269, 272, 275, 282, 283, 286, 297, 307, 312, 325, 327, 346, 361, 379, 412, 455
Maynard, Mary 361
Mayne, Ferdy 518, 535, 542
Mayo, Donald 182, 230, 231
Mayo, Maren 118
Mays, Betti 394
Mazurki, Mike 393, 462
Meade, Cynthia 27
Meade, Laurence 27
Meade, Walter 57
Meader, George 350, 438
Means, Grant 407
Meaton, George 76
Medbury, John P. 22
Medwin, Michael 508
Meehan, John, Jr. 47
Meehan, Lew 51
Meeker, George 66, 238, 249, 265, 302, 320, 375, 392, 420, 423
Meglin Glee Club 118
Mehaffey, Blanche 54
Meinke, Donna Lee 139
Melford, Jill 523
Melton, Frank 46
Melton, Sid 192, 425, 430, 434, 436, 438, 445, 447, 449, 450, 453, 455, 456, 457, 458, 459, 465, 469, 470, 473
Melville, Herman 420
Mendoza, Victor Manuel 538
Meredith, Charles 485
Meredith, Frank 88
Meredith, Iris 31, 99, 174, 177
Meredith, John 308
Meredith, Robert (Bob) 247, 252
Merrick, Fred V. 2
Merrick, George M. 122, 126, 133, 141, 156, 169, 197
Merritt, George 2

Merritt, Sybil 295
Merton, John 87, 89, 93, 145, 157, 159, 163, 164, 168, 177, 198, 211, 230, 235, 345, 364, 414, 449, 452, 454
Merton, Roger 384
Mesnier, Paul 488
Messinger, Gertrude 115
Metaxa, George 197
Metcalf, James 295, 298
Michael, Gertrude 155, 183, 289
Michael, Johnny 215
Middlemass, Robert 39, 176, 193, 222
Middleton, Charles 121, 149, 193, 255, 292, 293, 375
Middleton, Guy 23
Milan, Frank 19, 27
Miles, Art 91
Miles, Betty 203, 245
Miles, Vera 479
Miljan, John 111, 171, 249, 374, 384
Millan, Victor 506
Miller, Charles 99, 115
Miller, Edwin 83, 88
Miller, Emmett 467
Miller, Eve 462
Miller, F.E. 467
Miller, Lorraine 274, 276, 281, 283, 297
Miller, Marvin 545
Miller, Ray 162
Miller, Robert Alan 367
Miller, Shorty 14
Miller, Sidney 72
Miller, Skins 149
Millican, James 352, 404, 413, 417, 424, 426, 438
Millott, Gayle 122
Mills, Frank 9
Mills, Hugh 20
Mills, Warren 239, 246
The Milo Twins 248, 259
Milton, George (George Wallace Sayre and Milton Raison) 144, 145, 202, 247, 281, 307, 343
Miner, Allen H. 538
Mr. Moto 458
Mitchell, Billy 96, 147
Mitchell, Bruce 9
Mitchell, Charles 340, 342, 350, 354
Mitchell, Grant 246, 265
Mitchell, Howard 351
Mitchell, John 481
Mitchell, Spring 485
Mitchum, Jack 402

Mitchum, Julie 393
Mix, Art 172
Moana 453
Modupe, Prince 218
Moehring, Kansas 179
Mohr, Barbara 433
Molina, Carlos, and His Music of the Americas 289
Monahan, Richard 456, 460, 462, 466, 470, 476
Monroe, Tom 452
Montgomery, Doreen 242
Montgomery, Jack 154
Montgomery, Ray 499, 506, 541, 544
Montoya, Alex 341, 429
Moody, Ralph 429
Mooney, Martin 104, 107, 109, 123, 129, 134, 147, 149, 201, 213, 227, 233, 237, 252, 262, 265, 268, 271, 278, 290
Moore, Dennis 113, 124, 127, 130, 131, 140, 144, 151, 152, 161, 170, 172, 310, 323, 370, 437, 439, 440, 442, 444, 446
Moore, Dickie 215
Moore, George 54
Moore, Ida 470
Moore, Monette 467
Moore, Pauline 111
Moore, Ray C. 396
Moore, Robin 507
Moore, Terry *see* Ford, Jan
Moore, Tim 394
Moore, William 37, 50
Moran, Frank 104, 111
Moran, Patsy 137
Morante, Milburn 14, 52, 128
Mordant, Edwin 17, 61
Moreland, Mantan 48, 60
Moreland, Sherry 443
Morell, Andre 487
Morey, Elaine 247
Morgan, Charles 360
Morgan, Harry Hays 309
Morgan, John 342
Morgan, Lee 359, 360, 361, 362, 363, 364, 367, 412
Morgan, Ralph 61, 226, 267
Morgan, Verne 517
Morheim, Louis 460, 461, 462, 479
Morison, Patricia 384, 404
Morrell, George 14, 29, 56, 59, 154, 200, 207, 256, 257, 286, 301, 308, 402
Morris, Amarillo 156

Name Index

Morris, Dorothy 289
Morris, Edna 502
Morris, Rolland 471
Morris, Wayne 546
Morrison, Barbara 509
Morrow, Neyle 456
Morse, Ella Mae 292
Morse, Gloria 139
Morse, Terry (Terrell) O. 261, 295, 326, 385, 474
Mortimer, Edward 95
Morton, Danny 265
Moss, Stirling 537
Moulan, Frank 34
Moustafa, Amira 384
Movita 7
Mowbray, Alan 268
Mowery, Helen 309, 336
Moxey, Hugh 508
Moyer, Charles 10
Mozelle, Maurice B. 350
Mudge, Betty 390
Mudie, Leonard 498
Muir, Esther 96
Mulcay, Jimmie 468
Mulcay, Mildred 468
Mulhall, Jack 54, 104, 112, 119, 122, 141, 182, 263, 268, 379, 381, 423
Mullen, Virginia 479
Munier, Ferdinand 4, 46
Mura, Corinna 155
Murdock, Tim 353
Murphy, Arthur 338
Murphy, Bill 315, 402
Murphy, Don 323
Murphy, Earl 360, 363, 365, 367, 368, 370
Murphy, Horace 12, 14, 25, 28, 31, 42, 43, 45, 56, 59, 287
Murphy, Ralph 255, 292
Murray, Don 419
Murray, Forbes 83, 300, 457
Murray, John T. 17
Murray, Zon 308, 341, 391, 401, 424, 457
Murray-Hill, Peter 242
Muse, Clarence 48
Muzquiz, Carlos 482
Mycroft, Walter C. 142, 224, 242
Myers, Art 88
Myers, Zion 33, 38
Mynell, Laurence 513
Myton, Fred 70, 116, 120, 148, 154, 177, 178, 193, 203, 218, 223, 254, 258, 266, 275, 279, 286, 301, 302, 312, 317, 328, 339, 350, 436, 447

Nader, George 514
Nagel, Anne 141, 148
Nagel, Conrad 5, 15, 19, 27, 37
Naish, J. Carrol 226, 233
Naismith, Laurence 503
Namblar, M.N. 489
Napier, Russell 487, 534
Nash, Marilyn 474
Nash, Noreen 335, 342
Nash, Patsy 175
Natchenaro, Pete 287
Natheaux, Louis 7
Natteford, Jack 50, 119, 128, 146, 153, 450
Nazarro, Cliff 244, 248, 379
Neal, Ella 140
Neal, Tom 125, 265, 289, 290, 322, 382, 391, 392, 428, 432, 434, 449, 451, 457, 459, 460, 466, 468, 507
Nebenzal, Seymour 155, 162
Nebley, Howard 342
Neill, Noel 419
Neise, George 153
Nelson, Billy 233, 246
Neufeld, Sigmund 84, 85, 86, 87, 88, 89, 90, 91, 92, 93, 94, 97, 98, 100, 102, 103, 105, 108, 113, 114, 116, 117, 120, 124, 127, 130, 131, 135, 136, 140, 144, 145, 148, 152, 154, 157, 158, 159, 161, 163, 164, 168, 170, 172, 177, 178, 179, 182, 185, 189, 191, 193, 195, 200, 201, 202, 203, 204, 207, 211, 218, 221, 223, 226, 230, 231, 234, 235, 243, 244, 247, 249, 254, 257, 258, 266, 272, 275, 279, 281, 283, 284, 286, 294, 298, 301, 302, 307, 308, 311, 312, 316, 317, 319, 324, 328, 339, 343, 344, 345, 346, 436, 447, 455, 457, 458, 469, 470, 473, 514
Neuman, Sam 217, 240, 241, 291, 314
Neumann, Kurt 443, 539
Neumeyer, Fred 139
Neville, John Thomas 95, 104, 227, 253, 298
Newell, William 82, 88, 99
Newfield, Jackie 218
Newfield, Joe 120
Newfield, Joel 145, 231, 455
Newfield, Sam 60, 68, 70, 79, 82, 84,

85, 86, 87, 88, 89, 90, 91, 92, 93, 94, 97, 98, 100, 102, 103, 105, 108, 113, 114, 116, 117, 120, 124, 127, 130, 131, 135, 136, 140, 144, 145, 148, 152, 154, 157, 158, 159, 161, 163, 164, 168, 170, 172, 177, 178, 179, 182, 185, 189, 191, 193, 195, 200, 201, 202, 204, 206, 207, 211, 213, 218, 221, 223, 226, 230, 231, 234, 235, 243, 244, 247, 249, 254, 257, 258, 266, 270, 272, 275, 279, 281, 283, 284, 286, 294, 298, 301, 302, 307, 308, 311, 312, 313, 316, 317, 319, 324, 328, 339, 343, 344, 345, 346, 434, 436, 445, 447, 455, 457, 458, 469, 470, 473, 486, 492, 495, 541
Newill, James 34, 38, 58, 174, 181, 190, 194, 198, 205, 210, 212, 216, 219, 225, 228, 232, 236, 347, 348
Newlan, Paul 248, 385, 397
Newson, J.D. 10
Newton, Paul 326
Ney, Marie 547
Ng, William 494
Nicol, Alex 520, 525
Nielsen, Helen 523
Nigh, Jane 441, 445
Nigh, William 101, 165, 173, 184, 187, 209
Nilson, Hazel 429
Nilsson, Anna Q. 138
Nixon, Allan 397, 486
Nixon, Marion 7
Nocowitz, Eric 409
Nogueras, Fernando 536
Nolan, Doris 196
Nolan, Virginia 433
Nolte, William L. 334, 429
Noonan, Pat 23
Noonan, Tom (Tommy) 342, 416, 453, 476
Norcross, Van 183
Norden, Eric 452
Norman, Mady 395
Norris, Edward 217, 220, 354
North, Ted 220
Norton, Barry 7
Norton, Harold 396
Nosseck, Max 115, 333
Novak, Eva 279
Novak, Jane 167, 175
Novak, Jeritza 425
Novak, Peggy 47
Novarese, Nino 521

Novello, Jay 126
Nugent, J.C. 196
Nunes, A. Robert 533
Nunes, Maury 391, 392, 438

Oakie, Joe 215
Oakland, Vivian 263
Oakman, Wheeler 27, 46, 80, 81, 208
Oboler, Arch 318
O'Brian, Hugh 443, 450, 464
O'Brien, Bill 9
O'Brien, Chris 540
O'Brien, Dave 34, 51, 59, 60, 67, 74, 88, 90, 95, 113, 114, 120, 145, 155, 157, 164, 167, 174, 181, 190, 194, 198, 205, 210, 212, 216, 219, 225, 228, 232, 236, 245, 250, 256, 259, 263, 268, 269, 274, 276, 282, 347, 348
O'Brien, Florence 147, 180
O'Brien, Jimmy 467
O'Casey, Ronan 518
O'Connor, Frank 9, 386, 387
O'Connor, Gwen 445
O'Connor, Patsy 17
O'Day, Nell 210, 212, 226
O'Dea, John 393
O'Dell, Doyle 419
O'Dell, Janette 48
O'Doherty, Mignon 505
O'Donnell, Joseph 82, 85, 90, 92, 93, 94, 95, 98, 113, 124, 125, 189, 195, 200, 202, 207, 211, 221, 230, 243, 343, 349, 361, 365
O'Donnell, Spec 150
O'Driscoll, Martha 314
O'Farrell, Bernadette 492
Offley, Hilda 396, 398
O'Flynn, Damian 335, 353
O'Fredericks, Alice 522
Ogg, Sammy 481
O'Hara, Brian 153, 425
O'Hara, Shirley 385
O'Keefe, Dennis 9
Oldfield, Barney 129
Oliver, David 82
Oliver, Gordon 196
Oliver, James 303
O'Malley, Pat 118
O'Neal, Anne 271
O'Neil, Robert 435
O'Neill, Jimmy 425
Oppenheim, Edward Phillips 13

Orczy, Baroness 2
Ordung, Wyott 526
O'Reagan, Terence 487
O'Regan, Kathleen 229
Orlean, Will 393
Orloff, Arthur E. 331, 364
Ormond, Ron 405, 408, 411, 412, 414, 417, 418, 419, 422, 426, 429, 432, 437, 439, 440, 442, 444, 446, 463, 467, 468, 486
Ornelas, Adolfo 435
Ortego, Artie 181, 185, 191, 205, 211, 381, 400
Orth, Frank 331, 354
Ortiz, Peter 494
Osborn, Andrew 508, 523
Osborne, Bud 8, 52, 59, 174, 181, 194, 207, 211, 219, 225, 230, 243, 250, 257, 274, 281, 282, 283, 286, 288, 296, 303, 305, 307, 310, 316, 319, 329, 349, 360, 361, 375, 412, 418, 437, 439, 440, 442, 444, 446, 452
Osborne, Ted 81
Osborne, Vivienne 249
Oscar, Henry 2
O'Shea, Jack 70, 124, 300, 305, 316, 319, 325, 327, 334, 414, 463
O'Shea, Oscar 50
Osmond, Hal 495
Ostrer, Bertram 510
Ostrow, Lou 53
Owen, Garry 328
Owen, Michael 272
Owen, Tudor 498
Owens, Pat 534

Pack, Charles Lloyd 530
Packer, Netta 118
Padden, Sarah 118, 148, 157, 287, 329, 369, 374, 382, 412
Pagano, Joseph 403, 410
Page, Adrian 354
Page, Dorothy 67, 69, 74
Page, Katherine 502
Palange, Inez 99, 526
Palmer, Dick 14
Palmer, Tex 8, 12, 25, 28, 31, 32, 93, 100, 116, 127, 144, 163, 235, 368, 370
Paltz, Robert 509
Pamplona, Clements 536
Pandolfini, Turi 512
Pangborn, Franklin 39, 267

Papas, Irene 515
Pape, Lionel 4
Paquin, Robert 519
Parker, Andy 363, 365, 367, 368, 370
Parker, Austin 38
Parker, Carol 234
Parker, Cecil 78
Parker, Cecilia 1, 17, 26, 115
Parker, Dolores 433
Parker, Eddie 363, 368, 370
Parker, Fred 14
Parker, Jean 162, 222, 251, 380
Parker, Mary 535
Parker, Willard 454, 507
Parkinson, Cliff 70
Parks, Eddie 309, 351
Parkyarkarkus (Harry Einstein) 156, 167
Parnell, Effie 293
Parnell, Emory 313, 356
Parnell, Reg 537
Parrish, Claire 96
Parrish, John 471
Parry, Gordon 502
Parsons, Lindsley 8, 12, 28, 42, 56, 59
Pastell, George 495
Patch, Wally 57, 71
Paton, Charles 477
Patrick, Dorothy 533
Patrick, Gil 148, 379, 387
Patrick, Millicent 499
Patterson, Hank 262
Patterson, Shirley (Shawn Smith) 323, 325, 327, 360
Patterson, Walter 29, 69, 394
Patton, Bill 159
Patton, Virginia 395
Pavia, Nestor 386, 533
Pawley, William 50, 83
Paxton, Richard 464, 491
Payne, Bunty 142
Payne, John 39
Payton, Barbara 500, 507
Pazen, Joe 70
Peach, L. DuGarde 30
Pearce, Adele *see* Blake, Pamela
Pearman, Philip 47
Peclet, Georges 488
Peil, Edward 4, 52, 74, 86, 94, 97, 105, 108, 114, 116, 152, 161, 177, 266
Peisley, Frederick 11
Pelufo, Manuel 10
Pembroke, George 81, 109, 141, 251
Pendleton, Gaylord (Steve) 333, 338, 415, 421, 423, 448, 507

Pendleton, Nat 377, 388
Penn, Leonard 351, 391, 448, 486, 506
Pennick, Jack 9
Penrose, John 511, 513
Pepper, Barbara 192
Perceval, Hugh 55
Percy, Esme 23
Perkins, Gil 528
Perrin, Jack 134, 454
Perrins, Leslie 55, 57, 75, 214, 224
Perrott, William 418
Perry, Anthony 547
Perry, Frank 389
Perry, Pasquel (Pascale) 93, 303
Peters, House, Jr. 414, 418, 447, 455, 541
Peters, John 79
Peters, Ralph 70, 94, 100, 103, 117, 423
Peterson, Dorothy 17, 246
Peterson, Teddy 160
Petrie, Hay 24, 55, 260
Petroff, Boris 39
Petroff, Gloria 237
Peyser, Julian I. 354
Pharr, Frank 329
Phelps, Buster 17, 31
Phelps, Lee 66, 436, 447
The Phelps Brothers 18
Philharmonic Trio 390
Phillips, Arnold 115, 251
Phillips, Eddie 128, 130, 136
Phillips, Joe 440
Phillips, Leo 508
Phillips, Leslie 517
Phillips, Minna 451, 454
Philpotts, Ambrosino 487
Phipps, Charles 101
Phipps, Nicholas 496
Phipps, William 485
Picel, Irving 73, 80
Pickard, John (Jack) 464, 491
Picker, George S. 420
Picker, Leonard S. 425, 428
The Pied Pipers 248
Pierce, William 88
Pierlot, Francis 292, 340, 465
Pierre, Lora 396
Pierson, Arthur 196
Pilot, Bernice 110
Pinner, Dick 526
Piper, Frederick 142, 496
Pitti, Carl 454
Pivar, Ben 44, 322
Pizor, William M. 521

The Plainsmen 360, 363, 365, 367, 368, 370
Plank, Tom 463
Plant, Mark 422
Plummer, Rose 146, 200, 205
Plympton, George H. 51, 68, 103, 105, 257, 272, 379
Pohlmann, Eric 472, 495, 516, 542
Pola, Isa 521
Poland, Joseph F. 359, 360
Pollack, Lee 167
Pollack, Lew 167, 175
Pollard, Alexander 226
Pollard, Snub 4, 8, 12, 18, 25, 28, 42, 45, 56, 59, 177, 429
Pollexfen, Jack 425
Pollock, Ellen 78
Polonsky, David 230
Pooley, Olaf 472
Pope, Alexander 395, 476
Porter, Jean 463, 466
Potel, Victor 33, 264
Poule, Ezelle 423, 452
Pounds, Toots 535
Powell, Lee 68, 98, 130, 135, 144, 154, 159, 163
Powell, Lester 492
Powell, Michael 273
Power, Paul 268
Powers, Richard 278
Prather, Lee 85
Pressburger, Emeric 273
Prest, Patricia 171
Price, Dennis 477, 501
Price, Hal 14, 85, 87, 89, 95, 105, 113, 117, 121, 124, 131, 135, 157, 163, 164, 178, 185, 186, 191, 235, 243, 247, 374
Price, Kate 9
Price, Stanley 67, 74, 107, 179, 198, 268, 300, 377, 388, 417, 426, 430, 437, 439, 440, 442, 444, 446, 461, 491
Price, Vincent 435
Prival, Lucien 79, 106, 197, 499
Prouty, Jed 33, 73
Pryor, Roger 106, 115, 258
Pughe, George 142
Purcell, Charles 167
Pyle, Denver 400

Quigley, Charles 101, 311, 339
Quigley, Rita 199
Quillan, Eddie 240

Name Index

Quine, Richard 53
Quinn, Tom 215

Rabin, Jack 474
Rackin, Martin 485
Radamsky, Serjei 196
Radio Rascals 76
The Radio Rogues 39, 213
Raffetto, Michael 133, 238
Raft, George 485, 496, 515
Raines, Steve 412, 419
Rains, Claude 318
Rairdon, Wally 95
Raison, Milton 111, 144, 145, 151, 158, 164, 173, 202, 247, 268, 281, 307, 343, 436, 438
Raitt, John 237
Raker, Lorin 478
Ralston, Esther 10
Ramage, Cecil 11
Ramakrishna 489
Rand, Sally 64
Randall, Chris 463
Randall, Frankie 463
Randall, Gene 455
Randall, Rebel 238, 250, 392, 461
Randall, Robert *see* Livingston, Bob
Randell, Ron 420
Randolph, Isabel 263, 271
Randy, Julius 22
Ransom, Lois 202, 343
Ransome, Jean 271
Rauh, Stanley 217
Rawlinson, Herbert 134, 147, 218, 227, 321
Ray, Alan 466
Ray, Bernard B. 119, 128, 137, 143, 387, 390, 519
Ray, Joey 99, 129, 410
Ray, Lois 433
Ray, Phillip 477
Ray, Rene 502
Ray Knapp Rough Riders 139
Raymond, Cyril 47
Raymond, Dick 263
Raymond, Felice 401
Raymond, Jack 71, 227, 263, 267, 420
Raymond, Robin 192, 253
Rayner, Minnie 23
Read, Barbara 137
Reagen, Charles 425
Redman, Joyce 260

Redmond, Liam 542
Redpath, Patricia 139
Redwing, Rodd 464, 491
Redwing, Roderic 428
Reed, Barbara 377
Reed, David 302, 324
Reed, Donald 34
Reed, George H. 264
Reed, Larry 390
Reed, Marshall 245, 359, 362, 364, 366, 368, 405, 408, 426, 429, 434
Reed, Phillip 320, 454
Reed, Walter 475
Rees, Lanny 382
Reeves, George 403, 410, 475
Reeves, Kynaston 78
Regan, Michael 485
Regas, Pedro 206, 401
Reggiani, Serge 490
Reicher, Frank 53, 475
Reichow, Otto 92
Reinhardt, John 7
Reisner, Dean 441, 448
Reitzen, Jack 453, 458, 460, 463, 466
Remey, Dot 429
Renaldo, Duncan 106, 156, 206, 326, 385
Rense, Dan 438
Repp, Ed Earl 370
Rettas, Rosa Alback 409
Rex the horse 65
Rey, Fernando 536
Reyes, Chuy, and His Mambo Orchestra 438, 453
Reyes, Juan 376
Reynolds, Craig 86, 313, 382
Reynolds, Don Kay 300
Reynolds, Harrington 69
Reynolds, Marjorie 42, 52, 101, 128
Reynolds, Peter 480
Rhodes, Grandon (Grandin) 267, 350
Riano, Renie 289
Rice, Florence 171, 187
Rice, Marie 88
Rich, Dick 134, 351, 395
Richards, Addison 73, 166, 315
Richards, Cully 26, 38, 41, 43
Richards, Frank 430, 436, 541
Richards, Gordon 284, 311, 378
Richards, Jill 540
Richards, Joseph 442
Richards, Keith 384, 392, 399, 400, 478
Richardson, Emory 396

Richardson, Jack 90, 123, 300
Richardson, Ralph 273
Richfield, Edwin 510, 537
Richman, Charles 1, 73
Richman, M.H. 323, 325, 327, 332, 336, 341
Richmond, Felice 362
Richmond, Kane 111, 122
Richmond, Ted H. 68, 99, 106, 115, 121, 129
Richmond, Warner 1, 4, 8, 19, 40, 52, 67, 74, 310
Richter, Georg 493
Ricks, Archie 18
Ridgeley, John 471
Ridgeway, Freddy 524
Ridley, Arnold 487
Rienits, Rex 530
Rietti, Victor 21
Riggio, Jerry 300, 418
Rilla, Walter 224
Rin-Tin-Tin III 333
Rinehart, Mary Roberts 16
Ring, Cy 267, 390
Rio Brothers see 3 Rio Brothers
Riordan, Robert 386
Rios, Lalo 454
Ripley, Arthur 155, 183
Ritchie, Alice 423
Ritter, Tex 6, 8, 12, 14, 18, 25, 28, 31, 42, 45, 56, 59, 245, 250, 256, 259, 269, 274, 276, 282, 453
Rivero, Julian 92, 94, 97, 100, 102, 105, 152, 172, 241
Roach, Bert 34
Roach, Hal, Jr. 471, 478, 494
Roadman, Betty 395
Robards, Jason, Sr. 4, 26, 63, 417, 436
Robeling, Albin 390
Rober, Richard 486
Roberts, Beatrice 37
Roberts, Ben 106, 115
Roberts, Beverly 81
Roberts, Ewan 530
Roberts, J.H. 21
Roberts, Lee 300, 305, 323, 325, 327, 329, 332, 334, 357, 407, 408, 414, 417, 426, 429
Roberts, Nancy 503
Roberts, Ned 439
Roberts, Rachel 517
Roberts, Thayer 473
Roberts, William 167
Robertson, Chuck 454

Robertson, Lou 528
Robins, Sam 131, 152, 156, 168, 170, 172, 173, 179, 345
Robinson, Charles 196
Robinson, Dewey 267, 270, 430
Robinson, James 66
Robinson, John 505
Robinson, Lewis 57
Robinson, Nancy June 263
Robinson, Ruth 258, 352
Robles, Rudy 403, 420
Roc, Patricia 214
Rocco, Eddie 252, 278
Roche, Aurora 433
Rochelle, Claire 150, 152, 166, 213, 220, 227, 233, 317
Rockwell Jack 28, 154, 190, 202, 216
Rodgers, Gene 386
Rodgers, Red 265
Rodgers, Sondra 471
Roeca, Samuel 497
Rogan, Gerta 147
Rogers, Allan 34
Rogers, Charles 143, 153
Rogers, John 278
Rogers, Mildred 34
Rojo, Gustavo 482
Rolfe, Charles 229
Romantini, Joe 63
Rome, Tina 435
Romero, Cesar 469, 476, 489, 492, 513
Romney, Edana 142
Roosevelt, Buddy 98, 100
Root, Jerome 270
Root, Wells 482
Roper, Jack 88, 134, 144, 459
Ropes, Bradford 280
Roquemore, Henry 9, 27, 37, 73
Rorke, Hayden 509
Rose, Blanche 182
Rose, George 342
Rose, Harry 468
Rosen, Anita 409
Rosen, Phil 109
Rosenbloom, "Slapsie" Maxie 167, 186
Rosener, George 79
Rosewald, Franz 306
Rosing, Basil 79
Ross, Stanley 393
Ross, Vera 34
Rossi, Rex 288
Rossitto, Angelo 388, 435
Rosson, Arthur 29, 32
Roth, A.J. 461

Roth, Bernard R. 255
Roth, Cy 543
Roth, Gene (Gene Stutenroth) 227, 262, 435, 442, 444, 446
Roth, Martha 538
Rotter, Fritz 264
Roubert, Matty 300, 325, 327, 329, 334
Rouse, Russell 255
Rousseau, Louise 235, 244, 283
Rowan, Don 81
Rowland, Steve 540
Rowland, William 47, 196, 378
Royce, Lionel 106, 284
Royle, William 34
Rubin, Jack 160
Ruby, Herman 175
Ruddock, John 490
Ruffo, Leonora 521
Ruskin, Harry 9, 16
Ruskin, Simen 299
The Russ Sanders Troupe 468
Russell, Ed 507
Russell, Loretta 112
Rutherford, Ann 441
Rutherford, Jack 92, 94, 184, 338
Rutherford, Margaret 30
Ryan, Arthur 248
Ryan, Eddie 433
Ryan, Peggy 138
Ryan, Sheila 337, 342, 354, 422, 436, 457, 458
Ryan, Tim 290

Sabin, Cea 96
Sabin, Olga 183
Sabu 465
Sachs, Beryl 434
St. Claire, Arthur 141, 150, 156, 163, 167, 169, 175, 180, 197, 206, 239, 277, 285, 299, 313, 315, 319, 340, 402, 417
St. John, Al "Fuzzy" 25, 60, 68, 89, 91, 93, 97, 98, 100, 102, 105, 108, 113, 116, 117, 120, 124, 127, 131, 136, 140, 145, 152, 157, 159, 161, 163, 164, 168, 170, 172, 177, 179, 185, 186, 191, 195, 200, 202, 203, 204, 207, 211, 221, 223, 230, 234, 235, 243, 247, 248, 254, 257, 266, 272, 275, 281, 283, 286, 294, 301, 307, 308, 312, 316, 334, 343, 344, 346, 349, 355, 357, 359, 361, 362, 364, 405, 408, 412, 414, 418, 419

St. Leo, Leonard 137
St. Polis, John 36, 50
Saintenoy, Jane-Edith 488
Sais, Marin 32, 113, 221, 254, 281, 286, 294, 307, 507
Sale, Richard B. 61
Sale, Virginia 391, 392
Salew, John 214, 520
Salvatori, Albert 512
Sanders, George 534
Sanders, George (not the Academy Award–winning actor) 463
Sanders, Sandy 412, 414, 419
Sands, Johnny 331
Sandy and His Seals 433
Sanford, Ralph 180, 447, 460, 463
Sarecky, Barney A. 387, 434, 445, 475
Sargent, Tony 335
Sauber, Harry 292
Saunders, Gertrude 396
Saunders, Nancy 414
Saunders, Vicki 263
Savage, Ann 279, 290, 328, 383
Savage, Paul 338
Sawyer, Joe 9, 427, 441, 471, 494
Sax, Sam 280
Saylor, Syd 8, 12, 40, 213, 288, 296, 297, 303, 309, 497
Sayre, George Wallace 80, 144, 145, 157, 164, 166, 182, 185, 202, 231, 247, 281, 307, 315, 343, 346
Sayre, Jeffrey 9, 149
Scardon, Paul 133, 314
Schaeffer, Rube 425
Schallert, Edwin 180
Scheff, Fritzi 196
Schertzinger, Victor 38
Schiller, Fanny 482
Schillor, Frederick 510
Scholl, Jack 453
Schonberg, Ib 522
Schrecker, Frederick 511
Schreibman, Paul 433
Schrock, Raymond L. 88, 199, 220, 231, 237, 252, 262, 265, 271, 284, 289, 295, 311, 324, 447
Schroeder, Doris 377
Schumm, Hans 79
Schuster, Joe 475
Schwabacher, Leslie J. 375, 400
Schwarz, Jack 138, 160, 171, 176, 197, 201, 206, 208, 217, 222, 240, 241, 291, 387, 390

Scott, Anthony 48
Scott, Dick 377
Scott, Ewing 338, 407
Scott, Fred 139
Scott, Lizabeth 487
Scott, Mary 334, 353
Scott, Paul 107, 121
Scott, Sherman *see* Newfield, Sam
Scott, Zachary 482, 483
Seabrook, Edward E. 471
Seabrook, Gay 66
Seabrook, Ned 494
Seaman, Jack 509
Seay, James 123, 354
Seddon, Margaret 455
Seidel, Tommy 155
Sekely, Steve 183, 222, 233, 482
Selten, Morton 21
Seman, Maxine 397
Sepulveda, Carl 131, 135, 185, 202
Serato, Massimo 515
Serrano, Manuel 453
Sessions, Almira 240
Severn, Billy 291
Severn, Winston 320
Sewell, Vernon 273, 505, 511, 531
Seyler, Athene 490
Seymour, Dan 151, 206, 340
Shaff, Monroe 63
Shakleforth, Floyd 121
Shannon, Frank 104
Shannon, Harry 246, 262, 265
Sharp, Alex 407
Sharpe, John 525
Sharpe, David 310
Shattuck, Edward 240
Shattuck, Ethel 240
Shaw, Annabel 351
Shaw, C. Montague 122, 399
Shaw, Janet 115, 181, 348
Shaw, Peter 78
Shaw, Richard 495
Shaw, Sebastian 142
Shaw and Lee 433
Shay, Jack 149
Shay, John 271
Shayne, Robert 262, 494, 506
Sheehan, John 37, 176
Sheff, Monroe 72
Sheik the horse 65
Sheldon, Charles M. 1
Sheldon, Kathryn 169
Sheldon, Lorell 271
Sheldon, Sidney 106, 115, 119

Shelton, John 342, 356, 399, 514
Shelton, Joy 510
Shepherd, Norma 398
Shepley, Michael 490
Sherill, Martha 431
Sherman, Arthur 363
Sherman, Fred 137
Sherman, Robert 479
Sherman, Shavd 433
Sherman, Tex 14
Sherwood, Choti 120
Sherwood, Dale 135, 161
Sherwood, George 107, 279, 387
Sherwood, Robert 464
Shimada, Teru 4
Shiner, Ronald 71, 75, 76, 224
Shipman, Barry 506
Shires, Alan 47
Shirreffs, Gordon D. 546
Sholem, Lee 475
Shooting Star 387
Shores, Lynn 36, 41
Short, Dorothy 74, 87, 124
Short, Robin 416, 435, 450
Shrum, Cal, and His Rhythm Rangers 174, 181
Shumate, Harold 464
Shumway, Lee 9, 387
Shumway, Walter 51, 70, 111
Shute, Nevil 11
Shutta, Jack 395
Sidney, Basil 547
Siebert, John 409
Siegel, Jerry 475
Siletti, Mario 459
Silva, Franco 515, 521
Silva, Simone 513, 535
Silver King the dog 58
Silverheels, Jay 208, 356, 402
Silverstein, Dave 217
Sim, Alistair 20
Simpson, Harold 2, 229
Simpson, Hugh 430
Simpson, Mickey 392, 399, 463
Simpson, Russell 377, 382
Sinclair, Eric 271, 289
Sinclair, Upton 46
Sinden, Donald 547
Singer, Campbell 492
Singer, Ray 458
Slate, Henry 485
Slater, Barbara 162, 270
Slater, John 500
Slaughter, Anna May 423, 424

Name Index

Slavin, Brad 334, 336, 349, 359, 361, 364, 366
Sloan, James B. 229
Sloane, Olive 47
Slocum, George 432, 478
Smart, John 72
Smiley and Kitty 429
Smith, A.L. 323, 325, 327, 332, 336, 341
Smith, Adele 137
Smith, Albert J. 19
Smith, Cyril 487, 502
Smith, Elwood 394
Smith, George 368
Smith, Gerald Oliver 104
Smith, Girard 407
Smith, Hal 327
Smith, Hinton 1, 17
Smith, J.O. 323, 325, 327, 332, 336, 341
Smith, Jack C. 8, 14, 18, 25, 31, 45, 60, 118
Smith, Paul 360, 363, 365, 367, 368, 370
Smith, Paul Gerard 338
Smith, Raylene 139
Smith, Robert 278
Smith, Robert T. 498
Smith, Roberta 115, 255
Smith, Tom 205
Smith, Vernon 96
Snow, Heber 18, 25, 28, 31, 42; see also Worden, Hank
Snowey the horse 69
Soderling, Walter 295
Sokoloff, Vladimir 435
Solon, Ewen 484
Somers, Julian 495, 518
Sondergaard, Gale 199
The Song Spinners 196
Sons of the Pioneers 438
Sooter, Rudy 14, 56, 59
Sorel, George 278
Sorel, Jean 423
Sorel, Sonia 251, 264, 289, 317
Sowards, George 437, 440
Sparrow, Anitra 227
Spellman, Martin 88
Spence, Ralph 224
Spencer, Marian 260
Spreckles, Geraldine 166
Squire, Ronald 30
Stahl, Marvin D. 331, 342, 354
Stahl, Walter 79

Stallmaster, Lynn 456
Stanhope, Ted 395
Stanley, Barbara 451
Stanley, Louise 25, 28
Stanlow, Frank 532
Stanton, Ernie 39
Stanton, Val 39, 132
Starr, Irving 46
Starr, Jimmy 180
Starr, Lynn 147, 150, 167, 180
Staunton, Ann 155, 351, 353, 354
Steadman, Vera 9
Stebbins, Bobbie 318
Steele, Bob 89, 93, 97, 100, 105, 113, 288, 296, 297, 303, 374, 375
Steele, Marjorie 430
Steers, Larry 284
Stein, Sammy 377, 386
Sten, Anna 23, 73
Stenn, Ingrid 539
Stephen, Susan 487, 525
Stephens, William 333, 410, 415, 421, 423, 427
Stephenson, Henry 320
Sterling, Anne 251
Stern, Alfred 133, 151, 166, 173, 174, 181, 187, 190, 194, 198, 205, 212, 219, 220, 228, 238, 270, 299, 313, 315, 347, 348
Stern, Tony 167
Sternbach, Bert 182
Stevens, Charles 387, 506
Stevens, Clarke 245, 387, 418, 429
Stevens, Janice 515
Stevens, Onslow 53, 445, 524
Stevens, Phillip 515
Stevens, Roseanne 162
Stevenson, Robert 524
Stewart, Al 246
Stewart, Athole 30, 75
Stewart, Eleanor 8, 12, 149
Stewart, Larry 464
Stewart, Nick 186, 541, 544
Stewart, Paul 485
Stewart, Peggy 192, 405, 412, 433
Stewart, Peter see Newfield, Sam
Stewart, Richard 531
Stewart, Slam 394
Stillwell, Bruce 22
Stobart, John 47
Stock, Nigel 78
Stockdale, Carl 119
Stockman, Boyd 379
Stoloff, Ben 335, 354, 356

Stone, Andrew L. 35
Stone, George E. 66
Stone, Marianne 508, 516
Stone, Milburn 44, 393
Stone, Paula 35
Storey, June 119, 138
Storm, Gale 115
Storm, Lesly 142
Storm, Rafael 197
Story, Glen 463
Stossell, Ludwig 251, 499
Stowe, Tiny 478
Stowell, Don 118
Strange, Glenn 6, 12, 14, 51, 52, 120, 127, 131, 135, 136, 144, 148, 172, 177, 191, 193, 210, 226, 230, 231, 417
Strange, Harry 215
Strange, Henry 5
Strange, Robert 109, 148, 178
Straub, John 509
Strauss, Jay 26
Strayer, Frank R. 262
Strede, W. Chetham 23
Street, David 453
Strong, Jeri 466
Stroud, Claude 448, 449, 451, 452
Strueby, Katharine 57
Stuart, Ian 517
Stuart, Jeanne 24
Sturdevant, Carlin 126
Sucher, Harry 125
Sullivan, Francis L. 2, 23
Sully, Frank 146
Sulochana 489
Summerfield, Eleanor 480, 520, 523
Summerville, Slim 248
The Sunshine Boys 323, 325, 327, 332, 336, 341
The Sunshine Girls 248
Sutherland, John 350
Sutton, Ellen 467
Sutton, Grady 37, 340, 413, 424
Sutton, Paul 61
Swaffer, Hannen 260
Swanson, Maureen 535
Swanstrom, Carl 532
Swickard, Josef 34
Swinburne, Nora 11
Switzer, Carl "Alfalfa" 118, 252, 324, 356, 358
Sylvester, William 534

Tabori, Paul 484, 508, 529
Tafler, Sidney 490, 542
Taggart, Ben 122, 125
Taggart, Hal 267
Tait and Harris 49
Talbot, Lyle 80, 153, 175, 180, 240, 302, 381, 410, 411, 415, 422, 438, 452, 457, 458, 468, 486
Talbott, Lori 390
Talmadge, Richard 509
Tannen, William 461, 485, 506
Tanney, Arno 410
Tansey, Robert Emmett (Robert Emmett) 6, 8, 14, 18, 25, 28, 287, 300, 305, 310, 323, 325, 327, 329, 369, 374, 376
Tansey, Sherry 8, 59, 70, 87, 93, 103
Tapley, Colin 483, 518
Tarzan the horse 29, 32, 51, 52
Tate, Reginald 490, 496
Tatum, Dee 457, 458
Taussig, Frank Hart 498
Taute, Gus 332
Taylor, Al 159, 163
Taylor, Beth 402
Taylor, Cliff 405, 408, 412, 418, 426, 429, 433, 437, 439, 440, 446, 463, 467
Taylor, Eric 499
Taylor, Forrest 6, 8, 12, 31, 42, 45, 84, 87, 92, 97, 98, 105, 167, 174, 175, 176, 180, 184, 222, 227, 255, 278, 300, 305, 310, 323, 363, 427
Taylor, Geoffrey 537
Taylor, Henry 39
Taylor, Kent 436
Taylor, Lawrence Edmund 209, 240, 337, 340
Taylor, Ray 31, 42, 45, 332, 334, 336, 341, 349, 355, 357, 359, 360, 361, 362, 363, 364, 365, 366, 367, 368, 370, 404, 405, 408, 412, 414, 418, 419
Taylor, Rex 36
Tead, Phil 524
Teaford, John K. 321
Teixeira, Virgilio 536
Tell, Olive 1
Teller, Eloise 481
Teller, Francis Kee 481
Teller, Linda 481
Teller, Mrs. 481
Temple, Brooke 296
Tenbrook, Harry 9
Terhune, Max 429

Terrane, Alain 488
Terrell, Ken 271
Terry, Bill 519
Terry, Bob (Robert) 34, 52, 58
Terry, Dick 99
Terry, Ethelind 12
The Texas Tornadoes 14, 18, 28
Thane, Dirk 94, 152
Thayer, Tiffany 3
Thayer, Tina 166, 176, 215
Thiele, Lawrence 39
Thomas, Gretchen 46
Thomas, Jameson 17
Thomas, Jerry 332, 334, 336, 341, 349, 355, 357, 359, 360, 361, 362, 363, 364, 365, 366, 367, 368, 370
Thomas, Lowell 22, 62
Thompson, Craig 398
Thompson, Hal 196
Thompson, J. Lee 142
Thompson, Larry 246
Thompson, Nick 40, 161, 383
Thordahl, Grethe 522
Thorne, William L. 19, 27, 37
Three Ginx 76
3 Rio Brothers 433
Thurber, Kent 155
Thurn-Taxis, Alexis 167, 175, 180, 267
Thurston, Carol 428
Tilton, Martha 244, 265
Tinling, James 478
Tobin, Genevieve 20
Todd, Mabel 187, 314
Todd, Toni 337, 340
Toler, Sidney 199
Tombragel, Maurice 410, 415, 421, 423, 437, 439, 440, 442, 444, 445, 446, 463
Tomecko, John 509
Tomelty, Joseph 547
Tondelayo 396
Toney, Jim 187
Toomey, Regis 246, 264, 320, 342
Toones, Fred "Snowflake" 135, 182
Tor, Sigfrid 153
Tordesillas, Jesus 536
Torena, Juan 7, 40
Totter, Audrey 476
Towne, Lester 132
Tracy, Emerson 66
Tracy, Lee 176
Tracy, William 471, 494
Train, Dean 497
Trainer, Leonard 67

Traube, Shepard 79
Travers, Bill 511, 513
Travis, Richard (Dick) 423, 441, 445, 457, 458, 460, 461, 462
Treadway, Charlotte 96
Treen, Mary 43
Trent, Phillip 109
Trent, Russell 433
Trenton, Cecil 308
Trevor, Austin 30
Trevor, Elleston 483
Triana, Luisa 385
Trowbridge, Charles 386
Truex, Ernest 289
Tryon, Glenn 33
Tubb, Ernest 390
Tucker, Forest 107
Tucker, Richard 34, 38, 58
Tully, Montgomery 516, 529, 542
Tully, Tom 255
The Tumbleweed Tumblers 429
Turich, Felipe 385, 418, 454
Turich, Phillip 102, 103
Turich, Rosa 418
Turnbull, George 453
Turnbull, John 13
Turner, George 231, 336
Turner, Mae 48
Turner, Maidel 53
Turner, Tim 537
Turrell, Jac 246
Tuttle, Gene 139
Tuttle, W.C. 374
Twirl, Whirl and a Girl 433
Twitchell, Archie 449, 463, 467
Tyler, Harry 34, 37, 44, 262
Tyler, Lclah 421
Tyler, Leon 252
Tyler, Tom 416, 429, 437, 439, 440, 442, 446
Tyne, George 380

Ullman, Daniel B. 422, 429, 432
Ullman, William A., Jr. 81, 86, 183
Ulmer, Edgar G. 155, 162, 184, 186, 192, 199, 201, 215, 251, 264, 289, 290, 306, 320
Underdown, Edward 513
Unger, Bertil 453
Unger, Gustav 453
Urecal, Minerva 60, 84, 258, 459
Usher, Guy 86, 88, 95

Vadet, Michel 488
Vale, Virginia 106, 129, 134, 265
Valentine, Bobby 295
Valentine, Elizabeth 209, 279
Valentine, Val 57
Valentini, Vincent 394, 396, 398
Valerie, Joan 77, 461
Valin, Jimmy 184
Valk, Frederick 500
Vallin, Michael 141
Vallin, Rick 147, 166, 173, 180, 184, 199, 315
Vallon, Michael 181, 194, 216
Vallon, Nanette 324
Van, John Tee 62
Van Beers, Stanley 531
Van Dine, S.S. (Willard Huntington Wright) 337, 340, 353
Van Duinen, Peter R. 192, 199
Van Gyseghem, Andre 517
Van Horn, Jimmy (James) 437, 439, 446
Van Marter, George 533
Van Sloan, Edward 299
Van Zandt, Phil 244, 309
Vance, Byron 84, 108, 114
Vance, Lucille 181, 212
Vanel, Charles 512
Vanni, Renato 459
Varconi, Victor 104, 153
Varela, Trina 454
Varelli, Alfredo 515
Varga, Bill 462
Varno, Roland 378, 388
Van Dias, Selma 500
Vaughan, Tony 76
Vaughn, Dorothy 41, 101, 255
Vaughn, Ray 429
Vaughn, William 156, 169
Veddes, Edward 409
Vedey, Julien 76
Vejar, Harry 341
Velez, Lupe 47
Venters, Pearl 76
Vernac, Denise 299
Verney, Anthony 517
Vernon, Anne 501
Vernon, Dorothy 286, 429
Vernon, Glenn 433
Vernon, Richard 513
Vernon, Valerie 542
Vernon, Wally 429, 448, 449, 451, 452, 453
Verria, Raquell 102

Vershel, Irving 248
Verwayen, Percy 396
Victor, Charles 142, 273
Vidon, Henry 515
Vidor, Charles 445
The Vigilantes 213
Vigran, Herbert 118, 166
Vilar, Jean 488
Vilmont, Jean 488
Vincent, Russ 402
Visaroff, Michael 326, 378
Vischer, Blanca 97
Vitale, Milly 512
Vivian, James 511
Vlahos, John 175
Vogan, Emmett 104, 107, 110, 119, 270, 315, 421
Vohs, Joan 471
Voight, Jon 79
von Brincken, William 40, 50, 72
von Meyendorf, Irene 409
von Morhart, Hans 79, 141
von Seyffertitz, Gustav 63
von Stroheim, Erich 299
Von Twardowski, Hans 79, 141
Von Zell, Harry 292
von Zynda, Henry 79
Vorhaus, Bernard 30
Vosper, Frank 2
Vosper, John 169, 478

Wade, Russell 383, 386
Wade, Stuart 526
Wagenheim, Charles 330, 445, 462
Wagner, Frederick H. 22
Wagner, Jack 215
Wahl, Evelyn 158
Wainer, Lee 453
Wakefield, Hugh 24
Wakely, Jimmy 248, 540
Wald, Marvin 209, 215
Waldis, Otto 474
Walker, Bruce 503
Walker, Cheryl 292, 302, 311, 339
Walker, Gertrude 201, 382
Walker, Norman 229
Walker, Ray 143, 253, 315, 475
Walker, Syd 75, 224
Walker, Terry 16, 58, 93, 119
Walker, Tom 507
Walker, Wade 70
Wall, Geraldine 331

Wallace, Bryan 71
Wallace, Edgar 71
Wallace, Edward F. 323, 325, 327, 332, 336, 341
Wallace, Irving 215
Wallace, Milton 238
Wallace, Regina 183, 309
Waller, Eddy 271, 309
Walsh, Dermot 505, 511
Walsh, Kay 71, 78
Walters, Luana 96, 146
Walters, Susan 386
Walton, Douglas 40, 46
Ward, Al C. 538
Ward, Julian 531
Ward, Mackenzie 78
Ward, Ronald 47
Ward, Warwick 214
Warde, Anthony 187, 240, 241, 315, 326, 381, 385, 393, 400, 461
Warde, Harlan 485
Ware, Linda 109
Ware, Mary 315
Waring, Leslie 71
Warner, Franklyn 60, 61, 63, 66, 72
Warner, H.B. 156, 171, 253, 465
Warner, Hansel 200
Warner, Jack 484
Warner, Molly 484
Warren, Anne 464
Warren, Bruce 54
Warren, C. Denier 2
Warren, Charles Marquis 464, 491
Warren, Gloria 385
Warwick, John 71, 531
Warwick, Robert 1, 4
Washbourne, Mona 495
Washburn, Beverly 475
Washburn, Bryant 109, 208, 218
Watkin, Pierre 252, 262, 264, 279, 302, 315, 434
Watkins, Edith 267
Watson, Deek, and His Brown Dots 394, 396
Watson, Robert (Bobby) 466
Wattis, Richard 487, 510
Watts, Chick 467
Watts, Cotton 467
Way, Eileen 513
Wayne, Carter 82
Wayne, Naunton 472
Webb, Ira 405, 408, 414, 418, 419
Webb, Packham 483
Webster, Judith 437, 444

Webster, M. Coates 322
Weidman, Charles *see* The Charles Weidman Dancers
Weigel, Paul 19, 169
Weiser, Grethe 493
Weiss, Helmut 493
Weiss, Thea 409
Weissner, Hilde 493
Welden, Ben 271, 350, 393, 430, 478
Wellesley, Alfred 13
Wellesley, Gordon Wong 57, 273
Wells, Alan 428, 543
Wells, Ingeborg 502
Wells, Jacqueline (Julie Bishop) 80
Welsch, Gloria 405, 408
Welsch, Howard 337, 340, 353
Wenster-Brough, Jean 508
Wenzel, Art 181
West, Victor 451, 452, 454, 461, 462
West, Wally 29, 84, 98, 105, 116, 120, 127, 136, 202, 207, 272, 316, 355, 359, 365, 439
Westcott, Helen 485
Westerby, Robert 477
Weston, Cecile 134, 454
Weston, Don 181
Westrate, Edwin V. 380, 383, 386
Westwood, Patrick 535
Wetjen, Albert Richard 40
Whalen, Michael 141, 358, 410, 411, 415, 419, 420, 423, 425, 430, 438, 457, 458, 463, 466, 540
Whateley, Roger 10
Wheatley, Alan 508, 517, 525
Whelan, Albert 47
Whipper, Leigh 338
Whitaker, Charles "Slim" 6, 60, 93, 120, 127, 131, 135, 145, 148, 152, 168, 177, 189, 195, 207, 234, 316, 319, 334, 355, 361, 367
White, Alice 138
White, Bob 101
White, Dan 116, 154, 189, 198, 202, 205, 212, 282, 414
White, Johnstone 112
White, Jon Manchip 537
White, Lee "Lasses" 237
White, Leonard 530
White, Leslie T. 119
White, Meadows 505
White, Philip Graham 32
White, Renee 208, 217
White, Walter, Jr. 318, 498
White Cloud the horse 360, 363, 365

Name Index

White Flash the horse 6, 8, 12, 14, 18, 28, 31, 42, 45, 56, 59
Whitehead, Joe 149
Whitehead, O.Z. 476, 479
Whitfield, Robert "Smoki" 403
Whitley, Crane 392
Whitley, Ray, and his Range Ramblers 18, 31, 267
Whitlock, Lloyd 50
Whitman, Gayne 96
Whitmore, Dorothy 296
Whitney, Crane 150, 153, 192
Whitney, John 261
Whitney, Peter 322
Whittaker, Ian 503
Whyne, Key 433
Wilbur, Crane 3, 5, 7, 10, 15, 330, 335
Wilcox, Frank 353
Wilcox, Robert 81
Wilcoxon, Henry 23, 397
Wilenchick, Clem 79, 81
Wiles, Gordon 44
Wiley, Jan 165, 209, 215, 262, 322
Wilhelm, George 519
Wilhelm, Wolfgang 490
Wilkerson, Billy 428
Wilkerson, Guy 126, 168, 174, 181, 190, 194, 198, 205, 210, 212, 216, 219, 225, 228, 232, 236, 245, 250, 256, 259, 269, 274, 276, 282, 347, 348
Wilkie, Robert 491
William, Warren 264
Williams, Ben 502
Williams, Bill 441
Williams, Charles 91, 138, 208, 217, 263, 267, 328, 424, 463
Williams, Chili 354, 356
Williams, Don 300
Williams, Duke 394
Williams, Elmo 497, 527
Williams, Frances 320
Williams, George 396
Williams, Guinn "Big Boy" 263, 399
Williams, Lawrence 226
Williams, Lorraine 527
Williams, Milton 398
Williams, Robert 485, 499
Williams, Roger 32, 51, 52, 60
Williams, Slim 467
Williams, William H. 511, 513, 531
Williams, Zack 132, 403
Willis, Austin 389
Willis, F. McGrew 20
Willis, Matt 183, 395, 411

Willis, Norman 279
Willow Bird 400
Wills, Chill 354
Wills, Si 63
Willumsen, Orlander Dam 522
Wilmot, Robert 267
Wilsey, Jan (Buffalo Bill, Jr.) 102, 108
Wilson, Bill 213
Wilson, Charles 104, 262, 311, 317, 324
Wilson, Clarence 33, 39, 46
Wilson, Jerry 118
Wilson, Lois 53
Wilson, Robb 224
Wilste, John 415
Wilton, Eric 153
Wilton, Myron 295
Wimperis, Arthur 24
Windheim, Mavek 38
Windsor, Claire 292
Windsor, Marie 464, 486, 489, 497, 540
Wing, Toby 44
Winkler, Robert 90
Winters, Isabelle 183
Wisbar, Frank 293, 304, 315, 330, 402, 409, 417
Wisberg, Aubrey 342, 395, 399, 425
Wissler, Ruby 356, 358
Withers, Googie 224, 273
Withers, Grant 54
Withers, Isabel 271
Witherspoon, Cora 196
Wiwstrand, Njama 484
Wolf the dog 91
Wolfe, Sammy 433
Woller, Edward 33
Wong, Anna May 151, 173
Wong, Beal 155
Wong, Victor 61
Wood, Britt 401, 405, 408, 429, 433
Wood, Craig 217
Wood, David King 534
Wood, Douglas 9, 248
Wood, John 487
Wood, Mary Laura 484
Wood, Milton 544
Woodbridge, George 535
Woodbury, Joan 6, 63, 109, 156, 375
Woodell, Barbara 416, 435, 438, 449, 450, 464, 507
Woods, Bill 8
Woods, Donald 184, 333, 352, 385
Woods, Edward 61
Woods, Grace 32

Woods, Harry 133
Woods, T. Frank 497
Woodward, Bob 60, 93, 355, 359, 361, 364, 367, 370, 405
Woodward, Horace 372, 373
Woodward, Stacy 372, 373
Wooley, Sheb 464, 491
Woolf, William 78
Worden, Hank 45, 56; *see also* Snow, Heber
Worth, Barbara 397
Worth, Brian 501
Worth, Constance 110, 141, 258, 280
Worth, Harry 82
Worth, Irene 490
Worth, Stephen 161
Wrangell, Basil 340, 354
Wray, Ted 111
Wright, Cobina, Jr. 201
Wright, Florence 96
Wright, Leslie 535
Wright, Marie 13
Wright, Tony 500
Wright, Wen 256, 259
Wright, Willard Huntington *see* Van Dine, S.S.
Wright, William 299, 314, 353, 356
Wrixon, Maris 233, 284, 415, 471
Wyndham, Dennis 11
Wyndham, Joan 21
Wynn, Mason 357, 365
Wynn, Zoe 76
Wynne, Peggy 258, 332
Wynters, Charlotte 63, 72, 175, 209, 213

Yaconelli, Frank 175
Yaconelli, Zachary 435
Yarbrough, Jean 95, 99, 106, 322
Y-Knot Twirlers 463
York, Duke 83, 231
Young, Al 396
Young, Arthur 529
Young, Carleton 89, 90, 93, 97, 100, 105, 127, 313, 450, 544
Young, Carroll 469, 489
Young, Clara Kimball 123
Young, Gerra 215
Young, Gig *see* Barr, Byron
Young, Gordon 7
Young, Harold 241
Young, Nedrick 151, 178
Young, Terence 484
Younger, Eric 295
Yung, Victor Sen 61

Zaner, Jimmy 239
Zanett, Guy 208
Zanetti, C. 406
Zarco, Estelle 376
Zeidman, B.F. 1, 4, 17, 26
Zeisler, Alfred 13
Zelnick, Fred 75
Zero the dog 128
Zimbalist, Al 545
Zimmerman, Elisabeth 493
Zoadman, Betty 128
Zucco, George 148, 178, 193, 261, 298, 388
Zumalt, Oral 14

Film Title Index

The number after each film title and year of release refers to the entry number, not the page number.

Accent on Horror *see* Scared to Death (Screen Guild, 1947) 388
Accomplice (PRC, 1946) 321
Adventure in Rio *see* They Were So Young (Lippert, 1955) 539
The Adventurers *see* The Great Adventure (Lippert, 1951) 477
Air Strike (Lippert, 1955) 543
Alive in the Deep (PRC, 1941) 373
Along the Sundown Trail (PRC, 1942) 163
The Amazing Adventure *see* Romance and Riches (Grand National, 1937) 13
The Amazing Mr. Forrest (PRC, 1944) 224
The Amazing Quest of Ernest Bliss *see* Romance and Riches (Grand National, 1937) 13
Ambush Trail (PRC, 1946) 297
Another Chance *see* Twilight Women (Lippert, 1953) 502
Apache Chief (Lippert, 1949) 428
Apology for Murder (PRC, 1945) 279
Arizona Days (Grand National, 1937) 12
Arizona Gangbusters (PRC, 1940) 92
Arson - Inc. (Lippert, 1949) 421
Arson Squad (PRC, 1945) 277
As You Were! (Lippert, 1951) 471
The Autopsy *see* Scared to Death (Screen Guild, 1947) 388
Avalanche (PRC, 1946) 309

Baby Face Morgan (PRC, 1942) 160
Bachelor in Paris (Lippert, 1953) 501

Bad Blonde (Lippert, 1953) 500
Bad Men of Thunder Gap (PRC, 1943) 181
Bandit Queen (Lippert, 1950) 454
Bank Alarm (Grand National, 1937) 27
Barber of Red Gap *see* Shadows of Death (PRC, 1945) 266
The Baron of Arizona (Lippert, 1950) 435
Battling Hoofer *see* Something to Sing About (Grand National, 1937) 38
Beasts of Berlin *see* Hitler, Beast of Berlin (PRC, 1939) 79
Behind Prison Walls (PRC, 1943) 183
Bells of San Fernando (Screen Guild, 1947) 385
The Big Chase (Lippert, 1954) 528
Big Deadly Game *see* The Deadly Game (Lippert, 1954) 535
The Big Fix (PRC, 1947) 342
Billy the Kid in Blazing Frontier *see* Blazing Frontier (PRC, 1943) 204
Billy the Kid in Cattle Stampede *see* Cattle Stampede (PRC, 1943) 200
Billy the Kid in Fugitive of the Plains (PRC, 1943) 185
Billy the Kid in Law and Order *see* Law and Order (PRC, 1942) 157
Billy the Kid in Santa Fe (PRC, 1941) 113
Billy the Kid in Texas (PRC, 1940) 93
Billy the Kid in the Mysterious Rider *see* The Mysterious Rider (PRC, 1942) 168
Billy the Kid in the Renegade *see* The Renegade (PRC, 1943) 202

Billy the Kid in Western Cyclone *see* Western Cyclone (PRC, 1943) 191
Billy the Kid Outlawed (PRC, 1940) 89
Billy the Kid Rides Again *see* The Kid Rides Again (PRC, 1943) 177
Billy the Kid, Sheriff of Sage Valley *see* Sheriff of Sage Valley (PRC, 1942) 164
Billy the Kid Trails West *see* Billy the Kid's Fighting Pals (PRC, 1941) 105
Billy the Kid Trapped (PRC, 1942) 136
Billy the Kid Wanted (PRC, 1941) 120
Billy the Kid's Fighting Pals (PRC, 1941) 105
Billy the Kid's Gun Justice (PRC, 1940) 97
Billy the Kid's Range War (PRC, 1941) 100
Billy the Kid's Roundup (PRC, 1941) 127
Billy the Kid's Smoking Guns (PRC, 1942) 145
The Black Glove (Lippert, 1954) 520
Black Hills (PRC, 1947) 360
The Black Pirates (Lippert, 1954) 538
The Black Raven (PRC, 1943) 193
The Black Stallion *see* The Return of Wildfire (Screen Guild, 1948) 404
Blackout (Lippert, 1954) 523
Blazing Frontier (PRC, 1943) 204
Blazing Guns *see* Marshal of Heldorado (Lippert, 1950) 439
The Blonde Comet (PRC, 1941) 129
Blonde for a Day (PRC, 1946) 317
Bluebeard (PRC, 1944) 251
Bombs Over Burma (PRC, 1942) 151
Boots of Destiny (Grand National, 1937) 29
Border Badmen (PRC, 1945) 281
Border Buckeroos (PRC, 1943) 194
Border Feud (PRC, 1947) 349
Border Rangers (Lippert, 1950) 452
Border Roundup (PRC, 1942) 161
Born to Speed (PRC, 1947) 331
Boss of Big Town (PRC, 1942) 171
Boss of Rawhide (PRC, 1943) 212
Boy! What a Girl! (Screen Guild, 1947) 394
Brand of the Devil (PRC, 1944) 236
Broadway Big Shot (PRC, 1942) 134
The Brute Man (PRC, 1946) 332
Buffalo Bill Rides Again (Screen Guild, 1947) 387
Buried Alive (PRC, 1939) 81

The Burning Cross (Screen Guild, 1947) 395
Bush Pilot (Screen Guild, 1947) 389

Call of the Forest (Lippert, 1949) 431
Captain Calamity (Grand National, 1936) 7
Captain Hurricane *see* Captain Calamity (Grand National, 1936) 7
The Caravan Trail (PRC, 1946) 305
Career Girl (PRC, 1944) 217
The Case of the Baby Sitter (Screen Guild, 1947) 392
Castle of Crimes (PRC, 1944) 242
Cattle Stampede (PRC, 1943) 200
Caught in the Act (PRC, 1941) 99
Check Your Guns (PRC, 1948) 365
Checkmate *see* Shadow of Terror (PRC, 1945) 285
Cheyenne Takes Over (PRC, 1947) 364
Children of the Wild (Grand National, 1939) 77
Cipher Bureau (Grand National, 1938) 63
City of Silent Men (PRC, 1942) 165
Club Havana (PRC, 1945) 289
Code of the Plains (PRC, 1947) 343
Colorado Ranger (Lippert, 1950) 442
Colorado Serenade (PRC, 1946) 310
Congo Pongo *see* White Pongo (PRC, 1945) 284
The Contender (PRC, 1944) 231
Corregidor (PRC, 1943) 184
Cosh Boy *see* The Slasher (Lippert, 1953) 503
Counterspy *see* Undercover Agent (Lippert, 1953) 511
The Cowboy (Lippert, 1954) 527
Crime, Inc. *see* Paper Bullets (PRC, 1941) 109
Crime, Inc. (PRC, 1945) 265
Crime Squad *see* The Man from Cairo (Lippert, 1953) 515
Criminals Within (PRC, 1941) 110
Crooked River (Lippert, 1950) 440

Daisy Goes to Hollywood *see* Hollywood and Vine (PRC, 1945) 267
The Dalton Gang (Lippert, 1949) 426

Film Title Index 233

Damaged Goods (Grand National, 1938) 46
Danger! Women at Work (PRC, 1943) 201
Danger Zone (Lippert, 1951) 460
Dangerous Intruder (PRC, 1945) 278
Dangerous Lady (PRC, 1941) 119
Dangerous Voyage see Terror Ship (Lippert, 1954) 531
Danny Boy (PRC, 1946) 295
Dawn Express (PRC, 1942) 141
Dead Man's Gold (Screen Guild, 1948) 405
Dead Men Walk (PRC, 1943) 178
Dead or Alive (PRC, 1944) 250
The Deadly Game (Lippert, 1954) 535
Death Rides the Plains (PRC, 1943) 189
Death Valley (Screen Guild, 1946) 377
Delinquent Daughters (PRC, 1944) 239
The Demon Doctor see Juggernaut (Grand National, 1937) 21
Deputy Marshal (Lippert, 1949) 427
Desperate Cargo (PRC, 1941) 112
Destination Danger see Eyes of the Jungle (Lippert, 1953) 506
Detour (PRC, 1945) 290
The Devil Bat (PRC, 1940) 95
Devil Bat's Daughter (PRC, 1946) 304
Devil on Horseback (Grand National, 1936) 3
The Devil on Wheels (PRC, 1947) 335
Devil Riders (PRC, 1943) 211
Discoveries (Grand National, 1939) 76
Dixie Jamboree (PRC, 1944) 240
Don Ricardo Returns (PRC, 1946) 326
Double Alibi see Law and Order (PRC, 1942) 157
Double Cross (PRC, 1941) 111
Down Missouri Way (PRC, 1946) 314
The Dragnet (Screen Guild, 1947) 397
The Drifter (PRC, 1944) 234
Driftin' River (PRC, 1946) 323
Duke of the Navy (PRC, 1942) 132
Dummy Trouble see Misbehaving Husbands (PRC, 1940) 96
Dusty Ermine see Hideout in the Alps (Grand National, 1937) 30

East of Piccadilly see The Strangler (PRC, 1942) 142
East Side Rascals see Gas House Kids (PRC, 1946) 324
Emergency Landing (PRC, 1941) 107

The Enchanted Forest (PRC, 1945) 291
Enemy of the Law (PRC, 1945) 269
Escape Route see I'll Get You (Lippert, 1953) 496
Everybody's Dancin' (Lippert, 1950) 438
The Executioner see Lady in the Death House (PRC, 1944) 222
Exile Express (Grand National, 1939) 73
Eyes of the Jungle (Lippert, 1953) 506

Face the Facts see Mr. Boggs Steps Out (Grand National, 1938) 44
Face the Music (Lippert, 1954) 520
Fangs of the Wild (Lippert, 1954) 524
Fast on the Draw (Lippert, 1950) 446
F.B.I. Girl (Lippert, 1951) 476
Federal Fugitives (PRC, 1941) 104
Fighting Bill Carson (PRC, 1945) 283
The Fighting Men (Lippert, 1953) 512
The Fighting 7th see Little Big Horn (Lippert, 1951) 464
Fighting Valley (PRC, 1943) 198
The Fighting Vigilantes (PRC, 1947) 362
Fingerprints Don't Lie (Lippert, 1951) 457
Five Days see Paid to Kill (Lippert, 1954) 529
Flaming Bullets (PRC, 1945) 282
The Flanagan Boy see Bad Blonde (Lippert, 1953) 500
Flight to Nowhere (Screen Guild, 1946) 378
The Flying Serpent (PRC, 1946) 298
Fog Island (PRC, 1945) 261
Follies Girl (PRC, 1943) 196
Follow the Leader see Fangs of the Wild (Lippert, 1954) 524
For Men Only (Lippert, 1952) 479
Forever Yours (Grand National, 1937) 24
Fortune in Diamonds see The Great Adventure (Lippert, 1951) 477
Frontier Crusader (PRC, 1940) 87
Frontier Fighters (PRC, 1947) 344
Frontier Fugitives (PRC, 1945) 276
Frontier Outlaws (PRC, 1944) 221
Frontier Revenge (Screen Guild, 1948) 412
Frontier Scout (Grand National, 1938) 60

234   Film Title Index

Frontier Town (Grand National, 1938) 45
Fugitive of the Plains (PRC, 1943) 185
Fuzzy Settles Down (PRC, 1944) 235

Gallant Lady (PRC, 1942) 150
The Gambler and the Lady (Lippert, 1952) 495
Gambling Daughters (PRC, 1941) 115
The Gang's All Here see The Amazing Mr. Forrest (PRC, 1944) 224
Gangs, Inc. see Paper Bullets (PRC, 1941) 109
Gangster's Den (PRC, 1945) 272
Gangsters of the Frontier (PRC, 1944) 245
Gas House Kids (PRC, 1946) 324
Gas House Kids Go West (PRC, 1947) 356
Gas House Kids in Hollywood (PRC, 1947) 358
Gentlemen with Guns (PRC, 1946) 301
The Ghost and the Guest (PRC, 1943) 187
Ghost of Hidden Valley (PRC, 1946) 308
Ghost Ship (Lippert, 1953) 505
Ghost Town Renegades (PRC, 1947) 357
G. I. Jane (Lippert, 1951) 466
The Girl and the Gorilla see Nabonga (PRC, 1944) 218
The Girl from Monterey (PRC, 1943) 208
Girl Loves Boy (Grand National, 1937) 17
The Girl Said No (Grand National, 1937) 35
Girl Trouble see Too Many Women (PRC, 1942) 137
Girls in Chains (PRC, 1942) 192
Girls Town (PRC, 1942) 138
The Glass Cage see The Glass Tomb (Lippert, 1955) 542
The Glass Tomb (Lippert, 1955) 542
Gli Inesorabili see The Fighting Men (Lippert, 1953) 512
God's Country (Screen Guild, 1946) 376
The Gold Racket (Grand National, 1937) 19
Goose Step see Hitler, Beast of Berlin

(PRC, 1939) 79
Gorilla see Nabonga (PRC, 1944) 218
Grand Canyon (Lippert, 1949) 424
The Great Adventure (Lippert, 1949) 477
Great Guy (Grand National, 1937) 9
The Great Jesse James Raid (Lippert, 1953) 507
The Great Mike (PRC, 1944) 252
Gun Code (PRC, 1940) 90
Gun Shy see House of Errors (PRC, 1942) 143
Gunfire (Lippert, 1950) 448
Guns of Justice see Colorado Ranger (Lippert, 1950) 442
Guns of the Law (PRC, 1944) 225
Gunsmoke Mesa (PRC, 1944) 216

Hard Guy (PRC, 1941) 122
Harpoon (Screen Guild, 1948) 407
Harvest Melody (PRC, 1943) 213
The Hat Box Mystery (Screen Guild, 1947) 391
Hats Off (Grand National, 1937) 39
The Hawk of Powder River (PRC, 1948) 368
He Loved an Actress (Grand National, 1938) 47
He Wanted to Marry see Swing It, Sailor (Grand National, 1938) 43
Headin' for the Rio Grande (Grand National, 1936) 8
Heartaches (PRC, 1947) 354
Heat Wave (Lippert, 1954) 525
Held for Ransom (Grand National, 1938) 54
Hellgate (Lippert, 1952) 491
Hell's Devils see Hitler, Beast of Berlin (PRC, 1939) 79
Her Last Mile see Lady in the Death House (PRC, 1944) 222
Her Sister's Secret (PRC, 1946) 320
Here's Flash Casey (Grand National, 1938) 41
Hideout in the Alps (Grand National, 1937) 30
The High Command (Grand National, 1938) 57
Highly Dangerous (Lippert, 1951) 472
Highway Patrol see Motor Patrol (Lippert, 1950) 445
Highway 13 (Screen Guild, 1949) 415

Film Title Index   235

Hi-Jacked (Lippert, 1950) 447
His Brother's Ghost (PRC, 1945) 257
Hitler, Beast of Berlin (PRC, 1939) 79
Hittin' the Trail (Grand National, 1937) 18
Hold That Woman! (PRC, 1940) 88
Holiday Rhythm (Lippert, 1950) 453
Hollywood and Vine (PRC, 1945) 267
Hollywood Barn Dance (Screen Guild, 1947) 390
Hollywood Thrill-Makers (Lippert, 1954) 519
Hollywood Varieties (Lippert, 1950) 433
Hostile Country (Lippert, 1950) 437
The House Across the Lake *see* Heat Wave (Lippert, 1954) 525
House of Errors (PRC, 1942) 143
The House of the Arrow *see* Castle of Crimes (PRC, 1944) 242
How Doooo You Do? (PRC, 1945) 292

I Accuse My Parents (PRC, 1944) 249
I Killed the Count (Grand National, 1939) 75
I Married a Spy (Grand National, 1938) 55
I Ring Doorbells (PRC, 1945) 262
I Shot Billy the Kid (Lippert, 1950) 449
I Shot Jesse James (Screen Guild, 1949) 416
I Take This Oath (PRC, 1940) 86
I'll Get You (Lippert, 1953) 496
I'm from Arkansas (PRC, 1944) 248
In His Steps (Grand National, 1936) 1
In Old Wyoming *see* Song of Old Wyoming (PRC, 1945) 287
Inside the Law (PRC, 1942) 146
International Crime (Grand National, 1938) 50
Intrigue in Paris *see* Miss V from Moscow (PRC, 1942) 169
The Invisible Killer (PRC, 1939) 82
Isle of Forgotten Sins (PRC, 1943) 199
It Stalked the Ocean Floor *see* Monster from the Ocean Floor (Lippert, 1954) 526

Jive Junction (PRC, 1943) 215
Johnny the Giant Killer (Lippert, 1953) 504
Juggernaut (Grand National, 1937) 21
The Jungle (Lippert, 1952) 489
Jungle Goddess (Screen Guild, 1948) 403
Jungle Man (PRC, 1941) 121
Jungle Siren (PRC, 1942) 158
The Jungle Woman *see* Nabonga (PRC, 1944) 218

Kentucky Jubilee (Lippert, 1951) 463
The Kid Rides Again (PRC, 1943) 177
The Kid Sister (PRC, 1945) 258
Killer at Large (PRC, 1947) 351
Killer Bats *see* The Devil Bat (PRC, 1940) 95
Killer Dill (Screen Guild, 1947) 393
Killers of the Sea (Grand National, 1937) 22
King Dinosaur (Lippert, 1955) 545
King of the Sierras (Grand National, 1938) 65

Ladies of the Chorus *see* Queen of Burlesque (PRC, 1946) 313
Lady Chaser (PRC, 1946) 328
The Lady Confesses (PRC, 1945) 270
Lady from Chungking (PRC, 1942) 173
Lady in the Death House (PRC, 1942) 222
Lady in the Fog *see* Scotland Yard Inspector (Lippert, 1952) 492
Larceny in Her Heart (PRC, 1946) 311
The Last Bullet *see* Crooked River (Lippert, 1950) 440
Last of the Wild Horses (Screen Guild, 1948) 413
The Last Page *see* Man Bait (Lippert, 1952) 480
Law and Order (PRC, 1942) 157
Law of the Lash (PRC, 1947) 334
Law of the Saddle (PRC, 1943) 203
Law of the Timber (PRC, 1941) 128
Leave It to the Marines (Lippert, 1951) 470
Life Returns (Grand National, 1938) 53
Lighthouse (PRC, 1947) 330
Lightning Raiders (PRC, 1946) 294
The Limping Man (Lippert, 1953) 517
Little Big Horn (Lippert, 1951) 464

Loan Shark (Lippert, 1952) 485
The Lone Rider Ambushed (PRC, 1941) 117
The Lone Rider and the Bandit (PRC, 1942) 131
The Lone Rider Crosses the Rio (PRC, 1941) 102
The Lone Rider Fights Back (PRC, 1941) 124
The Lone Rider in Border Roundup see Border Roundup (PRC, 1942) 161
The Lone Rider in Cheyenne (PRC, 1942) 140
The Lone Rider in Death Rides the Plains see Death Rides the Plains (PRC, 1943) 189
The Lone Rider in Frontier Fury (PRC, 1941) 116
The Lone Rider in Ghost Town (PRC, 1941) 108
The Lone Rider in Law of the Saddle see Law of the Saddle (PRC, 1943) 203
The Lone Rider in Outlaws of Boulder Pass see Outlaws of Boulder Pass (PRC, 1942) 170
The Lone Rider in Overland Stagecoach see Overland Stagecoach (PRC, 1942) 172
The Lone Rider in Texas Justice see Texas Justice (PRC, 1942) 152
The Lone Rider in Wild Horse Rustlers see Wild Horse Rustlers (PRC, 1943) 179
The Lone Rider Rides On (PRC, 1941) 98
The Lonely Road see Scotland Yard Commands (Grand National, 1937) 11
The Lonesome Trail (Lippert, 1955) 546
The Long Shot (Grand National, 1939) 66
The Lost Continent (Lippert, 1951) 469
Love Takes Flight (Grand National, 1937) 37

Machine Gun Mama (PRC, 1944) 241
Mad About Money see He Loved an Actress (Grand National, 1938) 47
The Mad Monster (PRC, 1942) 148
The Man at the Gate see Men of the Sea (PRC, 1944) 229
Man Bait (Lippert, 1952) 480

The Man from Cairo (Lippert, 1953) 515
The Man in the Mirror (Grand National, 1937) 20
Man of Courage (PRC, 1943) 175
Man, the Enigma (PRC, 1941) 372
The Man Who Walked Alone (PRC, 1945) 263
Mark of the Lash (Screen Guild, 1948) 408
Marked for Murder (PRC, 1945) 259
Marked Men (PRC, 1940) 91
Marshal of Heldorado (Lippert, 1950) 439
The Mask of Diijon (PRC, 1946) 299
Mask of Dust see Race for Life (Lippert, 1954) 537
Mask of the Dragon (Lippert, 1951) 458
Melody Roundup see Wild West (PRC, 1946) 329
Men of San Quentin (PRC, 1942) 149
Men of the Sea (PRC, 1944) 229
Men on Her Mind (PRC, 1944) 220
Mercy Plane (PRC, 1939) 83
Mexican Fiesta see Machine Gun Mama (PRC, 1944) 241
The Mind of Mr. Reeder (Grand National, 1939) 71
Minstrel Man (PRC, 1944) 237
Miracle in Harlem (Screen Guild, 1947) 398
The Miracle Kid (PRC, 1941) 125
Misbehaving Husbands (PRC, 1940) 96
Miss V from Moscow (PRC, 1942) 169
The Missing Corpse (PRC, 1945) 271
Missouri Hayride see Down Missouri Way (PRC, 1946) 314
Mr. Boggs Buys a Barrel see Mr. Boggs Steps Out (Grand National, 1938) 44
Mr. Boggs Steps Out (Grand National, 1938) 44
Mr. Celebrity (PRC, 1941) 123
Mr. Walkie Talkie (Lippert, 1952) 494
Monsoon see Isle of Forgotten Sins (PRC, 1943) 199
Monster from the Ocean Floor (Lippert, 1954) 526
The Monster Maker (PRC, 1944) 226
Monster Maker see Monster from the Ocean Floor (Lippert, 1954) 526
Motor Patrol (Lippert, 1950) 445
Motorcycle Squad see Double Cross (PRC, 1941) 111
The Mozart Story (Screen Guild, 1948) 409

Film Title Index   237

Murder by Proxy *see* Blackout (Lippert, 1954) 523
Murder Is My Business (PRC, 1946) 302
My Dog Shep (Screen Guild, 1946) 382
My Son, the Hero (PRC, 1943) 186
The Mysterious Mr. Reeder *see* The Mind of Mr. Reeder (Grand National, 1939) 71
The Mysterious Rider (PRC, 1942) 168
Mystery of the Hooded Horseman (Grand National, 1937) 31

Nabonga (PRC, 1944) 218
Navajo (Lippert, 1952) 481
The Navajo Kid (PRC, 1945) 288
Navy Spy (Grand National, 1937) 15
The Nazi Spy Ring *see* Dawn Express (PRC, 1942) 141
'Neath Canadian Skies (Screen Guild, 1946) 379
A Night for Crime (PRC, 1943) 180
The Night Has Eyes *see* Terror House (PRC, 1943) 188
Night Without Stars *see* Unknown World (Lippert, 1951) 474
Norman Conquest (Lippert, 1953) 510
North of the Border (Screen Guild, 1946) 381
Northwest Trail (Screen Guild, 1945) 375

Oath of Vengeance (PRC, 1944) 254
Omoo, Omoo *see* Omoo, Omoo, the Shark God (Lippert, 1949) 420
Omoo, Omoo, the Shark God (Lippert, 1949) 420
On the Great White Trail *see* Renfrew on the Great White Trail (Grand National, 1938) 58
Operation Haylift (Lippert, 1950) 441
Our Bill of Rights (PRC, 1941) 371a
Our Constitution (PRC, 1941) 371b
Our Declaration of Independence (PRC, 1941) 371c
Our Freedom of the Seas (PRC, 1941) 371f
Our Louisiana Purchase (PRC, 1941) 371e
Our Monroe Doctrine (PRC, 1941) 371d

Out of the Night *see* Strange Illusion (PRC, 1945) 264
Outlaw Country (Screen Guild, 1949) 414
Outlaw Fury *see* Hostile Country (Lippert, 1950) 437
Outlaw Gang *see* The Dalton Gang (Lippert, 1949) 426
Outlaw of the Plains (PRC, 1946) 319
Outlaw Women (Lippert, 1952) 486
Outlaws of Boulder Pass (PRC, 1942) 170
Outlaws of the Rio Grande (PRC, 1941) 103
Outlaw's Roundup (PRC, 1944) 219
Overland Riders (PRC, 1946) 316
Overland Stagecoach (PRC, 1942) 172

Paid to Kill (Lippert, 1954) 529
Panama Patrol (Grand National, 1939) 72
Panhandle Trail (PRC, 1947) 345
The Panther's Claw (PRC, 1942) 147
Paper Bullets (PRC, 1941) 109
Park Plaza 605 *see* Norman Conquest (Lippert, 1953) 510
The Park Road *see* Road to the Big House (Screen Guild, 1947) 399
The Payoff (PRC, 1943) 176
Perils of the Jungle (Lippert, 1953) 498
The Phantom of 42nd Street (PRC, 1945) 268
Phantom of the Jungle (Lippert, 1955) 544
Philo Vance Returns (PRC, 1947) 353
Philo Vance's Gamble (PRC, 1947) 340
Philo Vance's Secret Mission (PRC, 1947) 337
Pier 23 (Lippert, 1951) 462
The Pinto Bandit (PRC, 1944) 228
Pioneer Justice (PRC, 1947) 355
Pirate Submarine (Lippert, 1952) 488
Pluck of the Irish *see* Great Guy (Grand National, 1937) 9
The Prairie (Screen Guild, 1947) 402
Prairie Badmen (PRC, 1946) 312
Prairie Outlaws (PRC, 1948) 369
Prairie Pals (PRC, 1942) 159
Prairie Rustlers (PRC, 1945) 286
Prison Girls *see* Gallant Lady (PRC, 1942) 150

Prisoner of Japan (PRC, 1942) 155
Professional Bride see Hard Guy (PRC, 1941) 122
Project Moonbase (Lippert, 1953) 509

Queen of Broadway (PRC, 1943) 182
Queen of Burlesque (PRC, 1946) 313
Queen of Sheba (Lippert, 1954) 521
Queen of the Amazons (Screen Guild, 1947) 384

Race for Life (Lippert, 1954) 537
Radar Secret Service (Lippert, 1950) 434
Raiders of Red Gap (PRC, 1943) 207
Raiders of Red Rock (PRC, 1947) 346
Raiders of the West (PRC, 1942) 135
Ramar of the Jungle see The White Goddess (Lippert, 1953) 499
Range Beyond the Blue (PRC, 1947) 336
Rangeland Empire see West of the Brazos (Lippert, 1950) 444
The Rangers Take Over (PRC, 1942) 174
Ranson of the Mounted see North of the Border (Screen Guild, 1946) 381
Red Desert (Lippert, 1949) 432
Reg'lar Fellers (PRC, 1941) 118
Rendezvous in the Alps see Hideout in the Alps (Grand National, 1937) 30
The Renegade (PRC, 1943) 202
Renegade Girl (Screen Guild, 1946) 383
Renfrew of the Royal Mounted (Grand National, 1937) 34
Renfrew on the Great White Trail (Grand National, 1938) 58
Rest Cure see We're in the Legion Now (Grand National, 1937) 10
The Return of Jesse James (Lippert, 1950) 450
The Return of Rin Tin Tin (PRC, 1947) 333
Return of the James Boys see The Return of Jesse James (Lippert, 1950) 450
Return of the Lash (PRC, 1947) 361
Return of the Rangers (PRC, 1943) 210
The Return of Wildfire (Screen Guild, 1948) 404
Ride 'Em, Cowgirl (Grand National, 1939) 69
Riders of Black Mountain (PRC, 1940) 94
Riders of the Rockies (Grand National, 1937) 28
Rimfire (Screen Guild, 1949) 417
Ringside (Lippert, 1949) 422
River Beat (Lippert, 1954) 530
Road to the Big House (Screen Guild, 1947) 399
Roaring City (Lippert, 1951) 461
Rocketship Expedition Moon see Rocketship X-M (Lippert, 1950) 443
Rocketship X-M (Lippert, 1950) 443
Rodeo Rhythm (PRC, 1942) 139
Rogues' Gallery (PRC, 1944) 253
Rollin' Plains (Grand National, 1938) 56
Rolling Down the Great Divide (PRC, 1942) 144
Rolling Home (Screen Guild, 1946) 380
Romance and Riches (Grand National, 1937) 13
Romance of the West (PRC, 1946) 300
Rustlers' Hideout (PRC, 1944) 243

The Sagebrush Family Trails West (PRC, 1940) 84
Savage Drums (Lippert, 1951) 465
Scared to Death (Screen Guild, 1947) 388
Scotland Yard Commands (Grand National, 1937) 11
Scotland Yard Inspector (Lippert, 1952) 492
Secret Evidence (PRC, 1941) 101
Secret Lives see I Married a Spy (Grand National, 1938) 55
The Secret People (Lippert, 1952) 490
Secrets of a Co-Ed (PRC, 1942) 166
Secrets of a Sorority Girl (PRC, 1946) 315
Sepia Cinderella (Screen Guild, 1947) 396
Seven Doors to Death (PRC, 1944) 238
The Shadow see The Shadow Strikes (Grand National, 1937) 36
Shadow Man (Lippert, 1953) 513
Shadow of Terror (PRC, 1945) 285
The Shadow Strikes (Grand National, 1937) 36

Shadow Valley (PRC, 1947) 363
Shadows of Death (PRC, 1945) 266
Shadows Over Shanghai (Grand National, 1938) 61
Shake Hands with Murder (PRC, 1944) 227
Shep Comes Home (Screen Guild, 1948) 411
Sheriff of Sage Valley (PRC, 1942) 164
Shoot to Kill (Screen Guild, 1947) 386
Shootin' Irons (PRC, 1947) 347
The Siege (Lippert, 1954) 536
Silent Raiders (Lippert, 1954) 532
Silent Witness see Secrets of a Co-Ed (PRC, 1942) 166
The Silver Fleet (PRC, 1945) 273
The Silver Star (Lippert, 1955) 540
Simba (Lippert, 1955) 547
Sing, Cowboy, Sing (Grand National, 1937) 25
The Singing Cowgirl (Grand National, 1939) 74
Sins of Jezebel (Lippert, 1953) 514
Sins of the Children see In His Steps (Grand National, 1936) 1
Six Gun for Hire see Six Gun Man (PRC, 1946) 296
Six Gun Man (PRC, 1946) 296
Six-Gun Rhythm (Grand National, 1939) 70
Six-Shootin' Sheriff (Grand National, 1938) 52
Sky High (Lippert, 1951) 473
Sky Liner (Lippert, 1949) 423
The Slasher (Lippert, 1953) 503
Small Town Boy (Grand National, 1937) 33
Smoking Guns see Billy the Kid's Smoking Guns (PRC, 1942) 145
Something to Sing About (Grand National, 1937) 38
Son of a Bad Man (Screen Guild, 1949) 419
Son of Billy the Kid (Screen Guild, 1949) 418
Song of Old Wyoming (PRC, 1945) 287
Song of Paris see Bachelor in Paris (Lippert, 1953) 501
Song of the Gringo (Grand National, 1936) 6
Sons of the Finest see I Take This Oath (PRC, 1940) 86
Sons of the Sea (Grand National, 1939) 78

S.O.S. Submarine (Screen Guild, 1948) 406
South of Panama (PRC, 1941) 106
Spaceways (Lippert, 1953) 508
The Spell of Amy Nugent (PRC, 1945) 260
Spellbound see The Spell of Amy Nugent (PRC, 1945) 260
Spirit of Youth (Grand National, 1938) 48
Spook Town (PRC, 1944) 232
Spy of Napoleon (Grand National, 1936) 2
Square Dance Jubilee (Lippert, 1949) 429
Stage to Mesa City (PRC, 1947) 359
Stagecoach Outlaws (PRC, 1945) 275
Stardust see He Loved an Actress (Grand National, 1938) 47
Stars Over Texas (PRC, 1946) 327
The Steel Helmet (Lippert, 1951) 456
Stepchild (PRC, 1947) 352
A Stolen Face (Lippert, 1952) 487
Stop That Cab (Lippert, 1951) 459
Strange Holiday (PRC, 1946) 318
Strange Illusion (PRC, 1945) 264
A Stranger Came Home (Lippert, 1954) 534
Stranger in the Family see The Missing Corpse (PRC, 1945) 271
The Strangler (PRC, 1942) 142
Strangler of the Swamp (PRC, 1946) 293
Street of Shadows see Shadow Man (Lippert, 1953) 513
Stronghold (Lippert, 1952) 482
Submarine Base (PRC, 1943) 197
Sudden Death see Fast on the Draw (Lippert, 1950) 446
The Sunset Murder Case (Grand National, 1938) 64
The Sunset Strip Case see The Sunset Murder Case (Grand National, 1938) 64
Superman and the Mole Men (Lippert, 1951) 475
Suspected Person (PRC, 1943) 214
Swamp Lady see Swamp Woman (PRC, 1941) 126
Swamp Woman (PRC, 1941) 126
Sweetheart of the Navy (Grand National, 1937) 26
Swift Justice see Texas Renegades (PRC, 1940) 85

Swing Hostess (PRC, 1944) 244
Swing It, Sailor (Grand National, 1938) 43

Tales of Robin Hood (Lippert, 1951) 478
The Tall Lie *see* For Men Only (Lippert, 1952) 479
The Tall Texan (Lippert, 1953) 497
Terror House (PRC, 1943) 188
Terror Ship (Lippert, 1954) 531
Terror Street (Lippert, 1953) 516
Terrors on Horseback (PRC, 1946) 307
Tex Rides with the Boy Scouts (Grand National, 1938) 42
Texas Justice (PRC, 1942) 152
Texas Man Hunt (PRC, 1942) 130
The Texas Marshal (PRC, 1941) 114
Texas Renegades (PRC, 1940) 85
They Raid by Night (PRC, 1942) 153
They Were So Young (Lippert, 1955) 539
They Were So Young and So in Danger *see* They Were So Young (Lippert, 1955) 539
Third Party Risk *see* The Deadly Game (Lippert, 1954) 535
36 Hours *see* Terror Street (Lippert, 1953) 516
This Woman Is Trouble *see* Bad Blonde (Lippert, 1953) 500
The Thousand Dollar Bill *see* Small Town Boy (Grand National, 1937) 33
Three Desperate Men (Lippert, 1951) 455
Three in the Saddle (PRC, 1945) 274
Three on a Ticket (PRC, 1947) 339
Thunder in the Pines (Screen Guild, 1948) 410
Thunder Over Sangoland (Lippert, 1955) 541
Thunder Pass (Lippert, 1954) 533
Thunder Town (PRC, 1946) 303
Thundergap Outlaws (PRC, 1947) 348
Thundering Gun Slingers (PRC, 1944) 223
Tiger Fangs (PRC, 1943) 206
The Tioga Kid (PRC, 1948) 370
Titans of the Deep (Grand National, 1938) 62
Today I Hang (PRC, 1942) 133
Tomorrow We Live (PRC, 1942) 162

Too Many Winners (PRC, 1947) 350
Too Many Women (PRC, 1942) 137
Tornado Range (PRC, 1948) 366
Torture Ship (PRC, 1939) 80
Tough Assignment (Lippert, 1949) 430
Tough Guy *see* The Slasher (Lippert, 1953) 503
The Town Went Wild (PRC, 1944) 255
Trail of Terror (PRC, 1943) 205
Trail of the Mounties (PRC, 1947) 401
Trailing Trouble (Grand National, 1937) 32
Train to Tombstone (Lippert, 1950) 451
Treasure of Monte Carlo (Lippert, 1949) 425
Trigger Pals (Grand National, 1939) 68
Trigger Pals *see* Billy the Kid's Fighting Pals (PRC, 1941) 105
Tromba *see* Tromba, the Tiger Man (Lippert, 1952) 493
Tromba, the Tiger Man (Lippert, 1952) 493
Tropical Fury *see* Machine Gun Mama (PRC, 1941) 241
Trouble in Texas (Grand National, 1937) 14
Tumbleweed Trail (PRC, 1942) 154
Tumbleweed Trail (PRC, 1946) 325
23½ Hours Leave (Grand National, 1937) 16
Twilight Women (Lippert, 1953) 502
Two Who Dared (Grand National, 1937) 23

Undercover Agent (Lippert, 1953) 511
The Underdog (PRC, 1943) 209
The Unholy Four (Lippert, 1954) 534
Unknown World (Lippert, 1951) 474
Untamed Fury (PRC, 1947) 338
Utah Trail (Grand National, 1938) 59

Valley of the Eagles (Lippert, 1952) 484
Valley of Vengeance (PRC, 1944) 230
Varieties on Parade (Lippert, 1951) 468

Wallaby Jim of the Islands (Grand National, 1937) 40
Wanted for Murder *see* The Invisible Killer (PRC, 1939) 82

Film Title Index

Water Rustlers (Grand National, 1939) 67
Waterfront (PRC, 1944) 233
We Want a Child (Lippert, 1954) 522
We're in the Legion Now (Grand National, 1937) 10
West of Texas (PRC, 1943) 190
West of the Brazos (Lippert, 1950) 444
West to Glory (PRC, 1947) 341
Western Cyclone (PRC, 1943) 191
Western Pacific Agent (Lippert, 1950) 436
The Westward Trail (PRC, 1948) 367
When the Lights Go On Again (PRC, 1944) 246
Where the North Begins (Screen Guild, 1947) 400
Whirlwind Horseman (Grand National, 1938) 51
The Whispering Skull (PRC, 1944) 256
White Fire (Lippert, 1954) 518
The White Goddess (Lippert, 1953) 499
The White Legion (Grand National, 1936) 4
White Pongo (PRC, 1945) 284
Who Is Guilty? *see* I Killed the Count (Grand National, 1939) 75
Why Girls Leave Home (PRC, 1945) 280

The Wife of Monte Cristo (PRC, 1946) 306
Wild Country (PRC, 1947) 332
Wild Horse Phantom (PRC, 1944) 247
Wild Horse Rustlers (PRC, 1943) 179
Wild West (PRC, 1946) 329
Wildfire (Screen Guild, 1945) 374
Wings of Danger (Lippert, 1952) 483
Wolves of the Range (PRC, 1943) 195
A Woman Alone *see* Two Who Dared (Grand National, 1937) 23
Womantrap *see* The Shadow Strikes (Grand National, 1937) 36
Women of Twilight *see* Twilight Women (Lippert, 1953) 502
Wonder Plane *see* Mercy Plane (PRC, 1939) 83

A Yank in Lybia (PRC, 1942) 156
The Yanks Are Coming (PRC, 1942) 167
Yellow Cargo (Grand National, 1936) 5
Yes Sir, Mr. Bones (Lippert, 1951) 467
You Betcha My Life *see* Caught in the Act (PRC, 1941) 99

Zamboanga (Grand National, 1938) 49

www.ingramcontent.com/pod-product-compliance
Ingram Content Group UK Ltd.
Pitfield, Milton Keynes, MK11 3LW, UK
UKHW041937140426
5217IPUK00014B/533